TRUTH AND DUTY

TRUTH AND DUTY

The Press, the President,
and the Privilege of Power

MARY MAPES

ST. MARTIN'S PRESS ❧ NEW YORK

www.stmartins.com

Library of Congress Cataloging-in-Publication Data available upon request.

ISBN 0-312-35195-X
EAN 978-0-312-35195-3

First Edition: November 2005

10 9 8 7 6 5 4 3 2 1

To Mark, who made me believe in myself

To Robert, who made me believe in God

To Mom, who made me

CONTENTS

Chapter 1	1
Chapter 2	18
Chapter 3	23
Chapter 4	42
Chapter 5	55
Chapter 6	70
Chapter 7	87
Chapter 8	103
Chapter 9	131
Chapter 10	148
Chapter 11	175
Chapter 12	192
Chapter 13	216
Chapter 14	232
Chapter 15	249
Chapter 16	263
Chapter 17	281
Chapter 18	294
Chapter 19	313
Afterword	333
Appendix 1: A Killian Memo	339
Appendix 2: Meshing Document	343
Acknowledgments	355
Index	359

TRUTH AND DUTY

CHAPTER 1

I woke up smiling on September 9, 2004.

My story on George W. Bush's Guard service had run on *60 Minutes* the night before and I felt it had been a solid piece. We had worked under tremendous pressure because of the short time frame and the explosive content, but we'd made our deadline and, most important, we'd made news.

I was confident in my work and marveled once again at the teamwork and devotion of so many people at *60 Minutes*. They really knew how to pull together to get a story on the air. I was also deeply proud of CBS News for having the guts to air a provocative story on a controversial part of the president's past.

By the end of the day, all of that would change. By the end of the month, I would be barred from doing my job and under investigation. By the end of the year, my long career at CBS News would essentially be over, after a long, excruciating, and very public beating.

But this morning, all that was unimaginable. I was just eager to get into the office and get the reaction to the story. I raced to the hotel room door and pulled *The New York Times* and *USA Today* off the floor, curled up on the sofa, and read the front-page coverage of our story. Online, I checked *The Washington Post* and saw that there, too, it was front-page material.

It deserved to be, for a number of reasons.

Dan Rather and I had aired the first-ever interview with former

Texas lieutenant governor Ben Barnes on his role in helping Bush get into the Texas Air National Guard. Getting Barnes to say yes had taken five years and I thought his interview was a home run. Finally, there were on-the-record, honest, straight-ahead answers from a man who intimately knew the ins and outs of the way Texas politics and privilege worked in the state National Guard units during the Vietnam War. Ben Barnes's version of events was crucial to understanding a significant chapter in President Bush's life from thirty years ago, an important key to unlocking the questions many Americans had about the man in the White House.

What had George W. Bush done during the volatile Vietnam years? Who was he back then, really? Was he a young man who volunteered to pilot fighter jets off the country's coastline, a brave young flier ready and willing to risk his life in the skies over Vietnam?

Or was George W. Bush—like so many well-connected young men in the Vietnam era—simply doing whatever he could to avoid fighting or flying anywhere near the jungles of Southeast Asia? Did he complete his service in the National Guard or walk away without looking back simply because his family's status meant that he could?

Did he do his duty? Did he tell the truth about his time in the National Guard?

Our story on September 8, 2004, also presented never-before-seen documents purportedly written in 1972 and 1973 by Bush's then-commander, Lt. Col. Jerry B. Killian. Killian died in 1984 and his important testimony on Bush's service had not been part of the years of debate that raged over whether the president had fulfilled his Guard duties.

These documents appeared to show that Killian had not approved of Bush's departure from the Guard in 1972 to work on a U.S. Senate campaign for Republican Winton Blount in Alabama. They showed that Killian had ordered Bush to take a physical that was never completed and that Killian had been pressured from higher up to write better reports on Bush than were merited by the future president's performance. The Killian memos, as they came to be called, turned on its head the version of George W. Bush's Guard career that the White House had presented. These new memos made Bush look like a slacker, not an ace pilot.

I had spent weeks trying to get these pieces of paper and every waking hour since I had received them vetting each document for factual errors or red flags.

I worked to compare the new memos with Bush's official records, which I had received since 1999. They meshed in ways large and small.

Furthermore, the content, the essential truth of the story contained in the memos, had been corroborated by Killian's commander Gen. Bobby Hodges in a phone conversation two days before the story aired. On September 6, he had said the memos reflected Killian's feelings at the time and this was what he remembered about how Killian had handled Bush's departure from the Guard.

We had a senior document analyst named Marcel Matley fly to New York to look at all the documents we had, the official documents that had been previously released by the White House as well as the "new" ones. After examining them for hours, blowing up signatures and comparing curves, strokes, and dots, he gave his best opinion on their authenticity. Since the documents were copies, not originals, he could not offer the 100 percent assurance that came by testing the ink or the paper.

But he said he saw nothing in the typeface or format to indicate the memos had been doctored or had not been produced in the early 1970s. The analyst also vouched for the Killian signatures after comparing them with a number of other Killian signatures on the photocopied official documents. A second analyst, Jim Pierce, agreed with Matley after examining two of the new documents, one of which had a signature. Pierce came to this judgment after comparing our memos to the official records and signatures.

I felt that I was in the clear, that I had done my job, and that the story met the high standards demanded by 60 Minutes.

I called my husband and son to say good morning, just as I had done every morning in all the years past when I was out of town. As always, my husband told me my work had looked great and my seven-year-old boy told me to come home as fast as I could and to bring him a surprise. It was our ritual.

I was staying at my favorite home away from home, The Pierre, a grand old New York hotel. Without my CBS discount, I never would have seen the inside of the place.

The Pierre is also quiet, close to the office, and sweetly old-fashioned. Old-fashioned enough that Kitty Carlisle apparently still goes there often for "highballs," according to the staff, along with a male friend and their respective nurses. I once ran into her in the ladies' room, looking like she had just stepped off the set of *To Tell the Truth*, mink capelet and all.

The elevator operators and doormen were older, too, and they were kind, always looking out for me. They knew me because of my regular visits and irregular hours, and comfortingly clucked over how hard I was working when I stayed there.

On this trip, they had seen me leaving very early and coming in very late for the past few days. I had been staggering out to catch a cab to work by 9:00 A.M. and arriving back exhausted at about 3:00 A.M. after the bar had closed and the hotel was buttoning up for the night. By the time I arrived, there was often no one in the lobby except a bellman, me, and perhaps a gaudily dressed female guest or two.

I often wondered what those women thought I did for a living. Disheveled and limping, straggling along with a heavy briefcase full of files, I entered the hotel lobby each night looking like a failing hooker for that small subset of customers who preferred exhausted, unkempt professional women.

On this morning, though, my energy was back. I was exhilarated by another success.

When I got to work, my mood was reinforced. I made rounds to thank the video editors who had worked so hard to get the story put together in time for air. Their jobs are not for the faint of heart or for people who panic when time is short or the workload is overwhelming.

I ran into other producers and correspondents and collected hugs and kisses and congratulations. There were jokes about what we would do as a follow-up. Dan and I had broken the Abu Ghraib prison abuse story in late April. Now this. My team, the people at *60 Minutes*, and Dan all felt like we were on a roll.

The new executive producer of the Wednesday edition of *60 Minutes*, Josh Howard, gave me a hug and congratulations, following up on a flattering e-mail he had sent me around midnight the night before: "I was just sitting here thinking about how amazing you are. I'm buckled in, ready to see where you'll take us next. Let's go!"

There was no hint of what was to come, no whiff of doubt about the work we had done on the story.

I saw CBS vice president Betsy West standing in the building's eighth-floor lobby, waiting for the slow, unreliable elevators, and we laughed at how awful the previous night had been, how hurried and harried we were, trying to get the story on. There had been shouting and impatience and flashes of anger. She laughed and said, "That's as close to the sausage making as I ever want to get." I told her that we'd gotten sausage all over us and that was as close as I ever wanted to come to missing my deadline. We both felt good about the story and agreed that it had looked polished on the air, in contrast to the carnage left behind in the editing rooms and the offices where we had done our scripting.

This behind-the-scenes chaos was not particularly unusual in television news. For fifteen years at CBS I had pushed back against deadlines to perfect a script, to change a shot, to make a story better. I had never missed a deadline, never put on a story that I did not feel comfortable with.

There was nothing more important to me, or to any of us at *60 Minutes*, than getting the story right, no matter how limited the time or how tough the topic. I had a well-earned reputation for being able to "crash," to get a story on quickly and competently.

For whatever reason—probably because I grew up in a large, loud, distracting family—I was able to focus when others couldn't. I could keep writing when the room was full of people yelling at the top of their lungs. I was able to think clearly when the clock seemed to be ticking too fast.

The previous year, I had "crashed" an entire hour overnight for the Wednesday edition of *60 Minutes*. Dan Rather had done interviews with Ron Young and David Williams, the two Apache helicopter pilots who had been shot down and captured in Iraq. Rescued by U.S. Marines, the two men had been pursued by countless reporters and producers for an interview. My wonderful friend and associate producer, Dana Roberson, helped me talk the two pilots into trusting us to tell their story.

Steve Glauber, a veteran *60 Minutes* producer, had worked round the clock, flying to the other side of the world and then back from Kuwait in forty-eight hours, carrying precious videotape. He had done touching and important interviews with the rest of the pilots' unit, men and women who had mourned the two lost airmen after their crash. The unit members had vowed to find their comrades and had flown out on mission after mission wearing headbands with the two pilots' names on them.

We did the interviews with the pilots at two o'clock on Tuesday afternoon. They were great. But I only had a few hours to write the script and organize the editing of the broadcast, in order to make it to air the following night. And all of it had to be overseen and approved by Jeff Fager, then the broadcast's executive producer, and his right hand, senior producer Patti Hassler.

With their help and guidance, I was able to get the script done. The editors were phenomenal and put together a beautiful, heart-wrenching, and illuminating hour.

But there had been more than a few furrowed brows. Editor David Rubin had been doing his trademark shrieking down the hall from our office as he cut in pieces of digitized tape. Everyone was dead tired and on a brutal deadline. By airtime, we were all staggering around like the undead. But we had done it. And the next day, we'd had the same kind of tired but happy conversations we were having on September 9.

This was another day of exhausted exultation. I got congratulatory e-mails, phone calls, and pats on the back. Other reporters called repeatedly as they worked to catch up to my story. I was thrilled.

Things began to change at about 11:00 A.M., when I first started hearing rumbles from some producers at CBS News that a handful of far right Web sites were saying that the documents had been forged.

I was incredulous. That couldn't be possible. Even on the morning the story aired, when we showed the president's people the memos, the White House hadn't attempted to deny the truth of the documents. In fact, the president's spokesman, Dan Bartlett, had claimed that the documents supported their version of events: that then-lieutenant Bush had asked for permission to leave the unit.

Within a few minutes, I was online visiting Web sites I had never heard of before: Free Republic, Little Green Footballs, Powerline. They were hard-core, politically angry, hyperconservative sites loaded with vitriol about Dan Rather and CBS. Our work was being compared to that of Jayson Blair, the discredited New York Times reporter who had fabricated and plagiarized stories.

These Web sites had extensive write-ups on the documents: on typeface, font style, and proportional spacing, questions that seemed to come out of nowhere. It was phenomenal. It had taken our analysts hours of careful work to make comparisons. It seemed that these analysts or commentators—or whatever they were—were coming up with long treatises in minutes. They were all linking to one another, creating an echo chamber of outraged agreement.

I was told that the first posting claiming the documents were fakes had gone up on Free Republic before our broadcast was even off the air! How had the Web site even gotten copies of the documents? We hadn't put them online until later. That first error-filled and overblown entry, posted by a longtime Republican activist lawyer who used the name "Buckhead," set the tone for what was to come.

There was no analysis of what the documents actually said, no work done to look at the content, no comparison with the official record, no phone calls made to check the facts of the story, nothing beyond a cursory and politically motivated examination of the typeface. That was all they had to attack, but that was enough.

People from around the country, especially those with an angry far right political bent, began chiming in on the sites with accounts of their own experience with typewriters in the 1970s. Some incorrectly claimed to remember that electric typewriters at the time did not do "superscripts," small "th" or "st" or some such abbreviations following a number and lifted higher on the line than the other letters. This was important because, in the Killian memos, "111th" was sometimes typed as "111th," something that drove the bloggers wild. Other bloggers claimed there was no proportional spacing on old typewriters—using different widths for different characters—even though some of the old official documents had proportional spacing. The claims snowballed.

I remember staring, disheartened and angry, at one posting. "60 Minutes is going down," the writer crowed.

My heart started to pound. There is nothing more frightening for a reporter than the possibility of being wrong, seriously wrong. That is the reason why we checked and rechecked, argued about wording, took care to be certain that the video that accompanied the words didn't create a new and unintended nuance. Being right, being *sure*, was everything. And right now, on the Internet, it appeared everything was falling apart.

I had a real physical reaction as I read the angry online accounts. It was something between a panic attack, a heart attack, and a nervous breakdown. My palms were sweaty; I gulped and tried to breathe. My chest was pounding like I had become a cartoon character whose heart outline pushes out the front of her shirt with each beat. The little girl in me wanted to crouch and hide behind the door and cry my eyes out.

The longtime reporter in me was pissed off . . . and I hung on to her strength and certainty for dear life. I had never been fundamentally wrong, never been fooled, never been under this kind of attack. I resolved to fight back.

I talked to our document analyst Marcel Matley, now back in San Francisco, who said he had seen some of the comments and dismissed them out of hand. "They aren't even looking at the quality of copies I did," Matley said. He disdained the anonymity of the postings, saying that any real analysts would use their name and credentials. And he pointed out something that would be a huge problem for us in the days ahead: that in the process of downloading, scanning, faxing, and photocopying, some computers, copiers, and faxes changed spacing and altered the appearance and detail of fonts. He thought that this basic misunderstanding of how documents changed through electronic transmittal was behind the unfounded certainty and ferocity of the attack on the documents.

In retrospect, Matley was right and our story never recovered from this basic misunderstanding. Faxing changes a document in so many ways, large and small, that analyzing a memo that had been faxed—in some cases not once, but twice—was virtually impossible. The faxing destroyed the subtle arcs and lines in the letters. The characters bled into each other. The details of how the typed characters failed to line up perfectly inside each word were lost.

And these faxed, scanned, and downloaded documents were the only versions of the memos ever made public. A comparison of one of the documents before faxing and after faxing is in Appendix 1.

But I thought Matley's belief that a technical misunderstanding was all that was behind the ferocious attack was too good to be true.

I was afraid that this time Matley, who was an experienced document analyst and longtime expert witness, was out of his element. He knew a great deal about documents and signatures. But I knew attack politics.

I knew what we were seeing was not a simple mistake made because of technical differences in the way the documents looked. This was something else, something new and fundamentally frightening. I had never seen this kind of response to any story. This was like rounding a corner in the woods and spotting a new creature, all venom and claws and teeth. You didn't know what it was, but you knew it was out to get you.

As I watched the postings pile up and saw the words quickly become more hateful, it dawned on me that I was watching the birth of a political jihad, a movement conceived in radical conservative back rooms, given life in cyberspace, and growing by the minute. It fed on political anger and the deep-seated belief that CBS News was a longtime liberal stronghold out to get the president.

This bias on the part of some viewers had been around for decades. These were people who hadn't forgiven Edward R. Murrow for taking on Joseph McCarthy, people who still referred to CBS as the "Communist Broadcasting System."

That was something a man in rural Texas actually said to me not long after I started at CBS in 1989, when I approached him and asked if he would do a quick interview on a new boom in oil drilling.

"CBS?" he sneered. "Don't you mean the Communist Broadcasting System?" I was dumbfounded.

To these people, there was no such thing as unbiased mainstream reporting, certainly not when it came to criticism of the president, no matter how tepid. To them, there was FOX News commentary and everything else — and everything else was liberal and unfair.

All the producers and researchers who'd worked on our story were hunched over computers, reading everything they could find. It was not good. We marveled at what we believed to be just-plain-wrong assertions about superscript or proportional spacing and the overwhelming certainty the bloggers brought to their analysis.

One element of the attack was not a bit surprising: the savaging of former Texas lieutenant governor Ben Barnes. He had predicted an assault on his reputation and he had been right, in spades.

While Barnes had never answered questions about his assistance in getting the president into the Texas Air National Guard, over the years he had often hinted that he'd had a hand in it. He would drop into conversation that a Bush family friend had asked him to help out "young George." Barnes had told people in countless private settings that he remembered being asked to make a phone call on Bush's behalf. But while Barnes would confirm everything off the record and had even testified to it under oath in a convoluted lawsuit involving the Texas state lottery, he had never before sat down, answered questions, and told the story in front of God and everybody. Now, he had.

I could see that conservative Web sites were linking to a dossier on Barnes compiled by Republican operatives. It was a devastatingly one-sided account of Barnes's past financial troubles and long-ago political scrapes, along with ancient accusations about Barnes when he had been a Democratic leader in Texas.

Barnes had remained an active Democrat and now was working as a fund-raiser for John Kerry as well as a full-time lobbyist in Washington. He'd told Dan Rather and me that if he did the interview with us he could essentially lose his lobbying business. In Washington, D.C., where influence is measured in access, having doors slammed in your face would be the death knell for a lobbyist.

In fact, the fear of a brass-knuckle Republican backlash that demolished people emotionally and financially was what kept Barnes and many others in Texas from speaking out about Bush's military service for years. I had always dismissed that kind of fear, in Barnes and the many others who were reluctant to speak out. I thought their worries were overdramatic. I mean, how bad could it be? Sure, there'd be criticism, but having the truth finally out in the open would be worth it.

I was beginning to find out how wrong I was.

Political operatives were having a field day turning Ben Barnes into their latest piñata, and his larger-than-life history was making it easy. He had been a boy wonder in Texas politics until a financial scandal in the early seventies had tainted him—unfairly, as it turned out. He was investigated, along with a number of other state politicians, for taking bribes in the Sharpstown payola scandal. Sharpstown was a Texas-sized bribery and development scandal that muddied the reputations of a number of once powerful state politicians, who were accused of handing out political favors in exchange for cash. There were never any charges filed against Barnes, never any case brought against him.

He and former Texas governor John Connally had lost their fortunes together rather spectacularly during the savings and loan bust in the eighties. Furthermore, Barnes had a well-deserved reputation as the life of the party, a glib, funny, overwhelmingly charming man who turned heads, slapped backs, and twisted arms to get what he wanted.

He has always been louder than life, a living, breathing caricature of a Texas politician. Now the Republicans were turning over every aspect of his personality, every past action, and recycling them into mud to throw at him and defuse his story.

I felt terrible for him and for his family. He had told us that he worried most about the impact doing the interview would have on his wife and two young daughters.

I knew Barnes was pretty tough. He had been on the scene of countless political and financial implosions. It was his political good fortune to always be the one person who would come staggering out of the building when it blew up. He might be covered with smoke and ash, his clothes ripped and ragged, but he would be alive and he would begin rebuilding his career.

I knew he would be able to make it through again. I didn't know that *I* would not.

By that afternoon, I had taken dozens of increasingly nervous phone calls from Betsy West and Josh Howard. Both of them were reading the blogs and growing more worried by the moment.

I remember looking at the Drudge Report at about 3:00 P.M. and seeing that the lead was a huge picture of Dan with the headline saying something like "Shaken and Stunned, Rather Hiding in Office." The story went on to link to the other raging and derisive far right Web sites running critiques of the documents.

The phone rang and it was Dan. "Mary, someone has just handed me something from the Drudge Report saying that I am all shook up and hiding in my office. I just want you to know that's not true. I'm not worried and I'm not even in my goddamned office."

I knew I could count on Dan. In tough situations, he became "fightin' Dan," someone who told us "never back up, never back down, never give up, never give in." I was glad to hear from him and reassured by his reaction. Dan told me he was confident in the story and that he was lucky to work with me. He signed off by saying something that had become a shorthand for us over the years: "F-E-A." That was code for "F— 'Em All," a sentiment that needed to be expressed from time to time in any newsroom. Dan was too much of a gentleman to say the real thing—at least most of the time. But he knew that under deadline or work pressure I often felt that sentences could be improved by some form of the "f" word. At this point, I deeply appreciated the sentiment.

The day continued to deteriorate. I got a stream of tag team phone calls from Josh Howard and Betsy West. They each began with the same ominous words: "Mary, have you seen [fill in the blank]?" It could be the Drudge Report, Powerline, something on FOX News, or a new posting on Little Green Footballs. Or worse yet, "Mary, we've gotten a call from [fill in the blank]." It could be *The Washington Post*, *The New York Times*, the *New York Post*, the *Los Angeles Times*. It felt as though the whole world were reading these obscure blogs and repeating their talking points without questioning them.

When I walked down the hall, I saw groups of people clumped together talking animatedly, then watched as they grew silent when I approached. They'd squeak out a "Hi, Mary," as I trudged dejectedly past. It was sort of the journalistic equivalent of having toilet paper stuck to your shoe. I can't say that I blamed them or that I would have behaved any differently in their positions. Nothing like this had ever happened before to me or to anyone I knew of. What is journalistic etiquette for watching someone's story and career go up in flames? Everyone knew what was going on. Everyone knew it was going very badly. No one knew what to say.

Some people pitched in and tried to bail the water out of our sinking ship. I was touched by producer David Gelber's ideas and energy in trying to help. Steve Glauber lent moral support. People would appear in the office door and commiserate. Assistant producers offered to open up Andy Rooney's office and let us look at his collection of old typewriters. Everyone was desperate or depressed—or both.

Dan came over after the *CBS Evening News* and we talked about the need to do a story rebutting the attacks the following night. My team of researchers, associate producers, and assistants and I gathered information on IBM typewriters, on font styles, on peripheral spacing. We got lists of new document and computer analysts together. We arranged to do an on-camera interview with Marcel Matley, our original document examiner.

I left the building late with Roger Charles, the tenderhearted military consultant who had worked with me for years. Also on hand: Mike Smith, a dogged young researcher from Austin, Texas, who had long followed the Bush-Guard story.

If our demeanor the night before had been triumphant, on September 9 we were downright tragic. The three of us dragged our sad selves into the hotel and plopped down in the bar like limp hankies. I was too tense for small talk, but that has never actually stopped me from talking. So I continued to bray at Mike and Roger like a wounded wildebeest.

I was *incredulous* that the mainstream press—a group I'd been a part of for nearly twenty-five years and thought I knew—was falling for the blogs' critiques. I was shocked at the ferocity of the attack. I was terrified at CBS's lack of preparedness in defending us. I was furious at the unrelenting attacks on Dan. And I was helpless to do anything about any of it.

We vowed to work ourselves into a frenzy doing a great report on the *Evening News* the next night . . . and we did. We put on a strong and reasoned defense. Maybe that was the problem. The people who had begun the attack on us were not interested in reason, other than the reason behind the whole assault—partisan politics.

Dan ended the report by asking that the president answer the long-time questions about his service in the National Guard. No one listened. No one wanted to ask the president anything other than what he thought about the CBS report. Everyone in the media wanted to cover CBS, not the National Guard story.

Our Friday *Evening News* report didn't make a whit of difference. Nothing we did mattered. We were shouting into a wind tunnel.

The points we made rebutting the bloggers' critiques were ignored. And each new blogging attack was picked up by other bloggers and the mainstream press and taken at face value.

Friday night, September 10, we suddenly found we had a new problem. The phone in the office rang at 7:30 P.M. When I picked it up, I recognized the voice of Gen. Bobby Hodges, the man who had corroborated the content of the documents before we aired our story.

I had been trying wildly to reach Hodges for three days, but with no luck. He said he had been out of town for a few days but had seen all the coverage and was just calling to tell me that he, too, thought the documents were forgeries.

I was stunned. I had never had a source change his or her story on me before. In part, because key sources in our stories are usually video-taped. Once someone has appeared in an on-camera interview saying something, it's awfully hard for them to deny their actions. This was something much different for me. With horror, I realized I had no recording of what he had told me, no way to prove what he had said to me earlier. I felt sick. I read him the notes I had taken from our previous conversation on Labor Day, September 6. He admitted he had indeed said all those things but insisted that now he didn't think the memos were real. He said he had thought when he talked to me that they were hand-written and, besides, since the family of Jerry Killian, the purported author of the memos, had come out publicly to say they didn't think the memos were real, he was supporting the family.

Hodges said he didn't know that what he said to me was going to make such a difference, and he said he was angry that his corroboration would have been considered a key element in deciding whether to report the story. He was especially angry that in a *Washington Post* article an unnamed CBS executive had referred to Hodges's comments as a "trump card" in determining the truth of the memos.

After the *Evening News*, Dan came to my office and we talked together on the phone to Hodges. Dan was losing his voice. He had fought for and defended our story nonstop for two days. He was beat. And now we felt we had been terribly betrayed.

Hodges was a longtime Bush supporter, something that I felt made his corroboration all the more important when I got it on Monday night. Now, his support for the president made me doubt his recanting was anything more than the result of political pressure. But it was devastating to us. He had already spoken with other news outlets, telling them that he believed the documents were forged.

I begged him to do an on-camera interview with us as I had the first time we spoke. Hodges repeatedly said no. I believed if I could get him to sit down and talk, it would become clear that he *did* believe the memos were real. I think Hodges felt the same way, and he was unmovable in his refusal to meet with us or consider speaking on-camera.

Late that night, CBS News president Andrew Heyward showed up at the *60 Minutes* building, something that I didn't see happen very often. I was summoned, along with Josh Howard, to join him in Betsy West's office. Betsy was on the phone, as she had been for thirty-six hours. Her shoes were off, her clothes were disheveled, and she was fighting to get someone on the other end of the line to listen to her. I believe she was talking with someone at ABC News, someone who was telling her that they were working hard on a series of stories on our catastrophe. She hung up defeated.

Andrew asked how many document analysts we could get together over the weekend to look at the documents with the idea of holding a news conference on Monday. He visualized a sea of analysts who would literally "stand behind the documents." I repeated the tired mantra that I had gone through with Andrew and every other CBS News executive time and time again. I told him that no decent analyst could say with 100 percent certainty that the documents were real. They were photocopies, not original documents. There was no ink or paper to test. We had come to confidence about the documents through analysts *and* our vetting of the documents *and* our meshing of the memos with the official record *and* the corroboration of the former commander of the unit. I told Andrew that no reputable analyst would give a complete assurance of authenticity *or* of fabrication, a point I had made clear from the beginning.

Andrew was frustrated. "But *they* have people who are doing that, Mary," he spit out. "And it's killing us. If the blogs are using people that are lousy analysts to make their case," Andrew said, "then let's get some lousy analysts of our own."

I couldn't believe it. That's not what reporting is supposed to be.

I dragged myself back to the hotel. In my room, the phone rang. It was Dan. "Have you eaten anything today?" he rasped. I hadn't. Of course I hadn't. In fact, I didn't remember the last time I had eaten. I was shaky and trembling and weak and too tired to sleep. He told me if I didn't order some soup that instant, he was going to call and ask someone to come up and force-feed me.

I ordered some broth and sipped it begrudgingly, sobbed through a phone call to my husband, and then spent the night leaping on and off the bed, checking the computer repeatedly to see what was online.

What was *The Washington Post* running? How about the *Los Angeles Times*? What did *The New York Times* have in the morning?

Once again, it was bad. Now they were all including Hodges's recanting in their stories.

By the next morning, I felt used up and hurt. We had a conference call at 9:00 A.M. with our public relations people and Josh, Betsy, and Andrew. We agreed we were in deep trouble and tried to brainstorm ways to begin digging out of the mess.

Near the end of the call, Andrew yelled into the phone that "if someone fucked this up, they'll be phoning in from Alcatraz."

That was helpful, Andrew, a real rallying of the troops. Nothing like a vote of no confidence to help build your stamina for a long campaign.

I hung up and called Josh and told him I was worn out and worn down and angry at Andrew's outburst. I didn't need to hear that. None of us did.

I told Josh I wanted to go home for the weekend and he agreed. I called the hotel's front desk to tell them I was checking out. I needed to go home. I needed to be with someone who loved me. I missed Robert, my little boy. I needed my husband's good advice and strong support.

I sat glumly on the plane but eventually began to enjoy my first few hours of peace in what seemed like weeks. There were no ringing phones, no knocks on the door, no frantic faces, no messages that needed to be returned ASAP. I began to wish I could just keep flying, just keep going and going and not land for weeks or months until this whole thing had blown over.

I thought darkly about what former Clinton adviser Vince Foster had said in his suicide note, that in Washington "ruining people is considered sport." I could understand how being the subject of overwhelming attacks would make some people give up.

I knew that was not going to happen to me. But I had no idea what was ahead and I was terrified.

When the plane finally did touch down that night, Robert and Mark picked me up at the airport, hurrying to meet me and nearly holding me up as we walked back to our car. I lay down with my head in my little boy's lap as my husband drove us home. Robert stroked my hair and babbled on about exciting events at school and about his plans to ace his next spelling test. I fell asleep before we got home, so grateful to be back, so relieved to be out of the storm, so happy to hear my son's little voice. It would be my last real sleep for weeks.

CHAPTER 2

There was a great deal I didn't know back in September 2004.

I didn't know that the attack on CBS News and the story we aired was just another part of Bush camp's aggressive pattern of sliming anyone and everyone who raised questions about the president.

In the months before the 2004 election, the White House certainly didn't want the country talking about the choices young Lieutenant Bush made during the Vietnam war. I thought it was a good time to talk about it. But then, I didn't see our story as an attack on the president. We were simply reporting what we had found. To the defenders of George W. Bush, our story was a declaration of war. I didn't know the debilitating, swarming attack on us would turn out to be the first and the most successful, but definitely not the last, visited on any journalist—any American, really—who dared to raise the wrong kinds of questions in the age of Karl Rove.

I didn't know that the attack on our story was going to be as effective as a brilliantly run national political campaign, because that is what it was: a political campaign. I didn't know that we were being bombarded by an army of Bush backers with different divisions, different weapons, and different techniques, but always the same agenda: kill the messenger. They were ready to do anything that would distract from, detract from, and destroy the message.

I didn't know back then that a political flotilla would join the fight against CBS: from right wing radio ranters to the far-out far right anonymous Internet name callers, from the constantly conservative FOX "news" network to the Republican-friendly Talon News operation, which, of course, used a fake reporter to deliver skewed news. Who can ever forget the nakedly ambitious Jeff Gannon?

I didn't know that when it came to CBS News, Les Moonves was telling friends sometimes half-jokingly that he wanted to "bomb the whole building," according to *The New York Times Magazine*. It turned out that Moonves wasn't happy simply remaking prime-time television; he wanted to re-create CBS News, making it more entertaining, more upbeat, more fun. I didn't know that Moonves would seize on the memo imbroglio as an excuse to storm CBS News and begin rebuilding it in his image.

I didn't know that you could get slimed or "swift-boated," as *New York Times* columnist Frank Rich would later call the coordinated attack on Gold Star mother Cindy Sheehan.

Sheehan, who lost a son in Iraq, would be tarred-and-feathered by the Bush Leaguers. Her offense was unforgivable. She asked for a second chance to speak with the president about why her boy died. For her steadfast insistence on a meeting with the president, something that might have been readily obliged by a less rigid commander in chief who felt less vulnerable about his own military service, Sheehan quickly found herself cast as a "crackpot," a grandstander, and, of course, that old all-purpose epithet, a *liberal*.

I should have realized our story would be savaged after seeing what happened to Senator John Kerry during his campaign for president. Kerry's very real war service prompted an unprecedented and unbelievably ugly attempt by Bush backers to question whether the Democratic contender "earned" the medals given him when he served in Vietnam, patrolling the backwaters and fighting for his life. Four years earlier, the Bush campaign team had viciously attacked Vietnam war hero Senator John McCain as well. In an irony beyond imagining, the closest Bush had come to battle during Vietnam was serving in Houston, flying his F-102 on weekends, patrolling the bars, and fighting to get a drink faster than anyone else. The president has even joked about it. But that didn't matter. Reality didn't matter. Right and wrong didn't matter. Winning was the only thing that mattered to any of the people masterminding the slash-and-burn campaigns that benefited George W. Bush.

I can't speak for the two senators who served in Vietnam. I can't speak for Cindy Sheehan, who has suffered an unspeakable loss. I can't even speak for Dan Rather, my friend and colleague who has been the target of far more radical-right slime than any one person deserves.

I can only speak for myself. As a journalist who has never stepped outside the box to reveal publicly who I am or what I believe, I do so now with some trepidation. Caught between political and corporate interests, I ended up fired—cast out of the news clubhouse, tagged by many as a person whose politics drove her journalism. Journalists should do their best to set aside personal views when doing their jobs, and that's what I've always done in trying to meet the highest standards of fairness and accuracy. We are living in extraordinary times, and I can no longer stay silent. I must answer the bloggers, the babblers and blabbers, and the true believers who have called me everything from a "feminazi" to an "elitist" liberal to an "idiot"!

If I was an idiot, it was for believing in a free press that is able to do its job without fear or favor.

If I am an elitist liberal, I have to blame it on my privileged background. I grew up in an elitist liberal hothouse, a tiny farm in Washington state, where for generations my family worked from daylight to darkness, feeding cattle, raising crops, and watching the skies obsessively, hoping for good weather. Like most elitist liberals, I learned to drive a tractor, disc fields, rake hay, and harrow pastures long before I sat behind the wheel of a car.

When I stepped in shit—literally, on some days—nobody bailed me out. In my family, we learned quickly we had to clean up after ourselves. I did not have wealthy parents or influential family friends to step in and help me out. I still know manure when I see it. And I know the people who attacked my story are more gifted at working with fertilizer than facts.

I am the kind of elitist liberal who drives a nine-year-old car. So does my husband. I am the kind of elitist liberal whose son says the Pledge of Allegiance in school every morning and prays every night. My family and I believe in God. After eighteen years of marriage, I am the kind of elitist liberal who has proved I believe in old-fashioned love and loyalty.

I am the kind of elitist liberal whose best friend's son just graduated from Marine boot camp first in his class of five hundred. This is a young man my husband and I have known and loved since he was just a little boy. I will pray for his safety every day if he is sent to Iraq. I am praying already that he won't have to go.

I am the kind of elitist liberal who cooks for her family, knits gifts for friends, paints her own house, and has been known to sew her own clothes. All right, the clothes didn't look that great, but I was young and very poor. So poor that in my twelve years of public schooling, I yearned to be wealthy enough to someday be able to join the elite students eating hot lunch. It never happened. I was always a packed-lunch, peanut-butter-sandwich kind of kid.

In college, I was the kind of elitist liberal who had to pay her own way by waiting tables and taking advantage of governmental financial aid, something I hope I'm able to do again when I reach retirement age. I believe in Social Security for those who need it. And with the way my career is going, I am going to be one of the Americans who needs it. I got every job I ever had on my own, with nothing to recommend me other than a résumé of low-paying jobs and the promise that I would work harder and longer than anyone else they could find.

I am the kind of elitist liberal who had no family pull to help me get a job, unless I wanted to continue the hard work of farming. I think I could have commanded a rather high-level hired hand gig at a neighbor's farm if I had pushed my parents to help me out. But like George W. Bush, I wanted to do things on my own. He decided to be the owner of a baseball team and then president of the United States. I decided to be a journalist and a mom. I believed my job at 60 *Minutes* was the best job a journalist in this country could have.

I am the kind of elitist liberal who doesn't come from old money or new money. I come from no money. And I believe that is a very valuable and instructive way to grow up. My husband and I work every day, trying not to give our son too much, too soon. We want him to value hard work, have his priorities straight, and believe in something other than material wealth.

No one in this country can help where they are born or to whom. But all of us are shaped by our backgrounds. George Bush was. I was, too. The story that brought us together is a tale of those two different Americas, one for the well-connected and another for the working class. My perspective on the Bush-Guard story does not come from politics so much as my sense that this tale touches on some old truths about class in America, whether we're talking about this month or thirty years ago.

We saw what happened when the poor were left in New Orleans to face Hurricane Katrina while the better-off headed for high ground. During Vietnam, the poor were pushed to the front of the line, forced to face a war that the well connected were often able to avoid. That is a fact, not a political opinion.

For too long, the media have been behaving like intimidated referees in a big football game, one-time valuable mediators who have been badgered for so long about being unfair to one team that they have become gun-shy. These referees have become afraid to do their jobs for fear they may be seen as unfair.

It has gotten so bad that it has become unclear why the refs are even there. They are consistently looking the other way when they should be throwing flags, talking about something else when they should be citing players for unnecessary roughness, and watching the cheerleaders when they should be throwing someone off the field for tackling after the whistle. This is what has happened to too many news organizations. They are so afraid of being dinged by one side that they have become paralyzed. If we are afraid to report hard truths, afraid to piss people off, afraid of being singled out for criticism, then we are no longer relevant.

Not every referee who makes a tough call is being unfair. Not every reporter who files a story saying that President Bush didn't do his duty during Vietnam hates the president, or God, or freedom. I don't care what the rabid right says.

I have a right to vote and I have exercised that right, ever since I have been old enough to pull a lever, pencil in a circle, or push an electronic prompt. I am the kind of voter, the kind of American that politicians should be fighting for, not tearing apart.

If I am an elitist liberal, then most of this country is made up of the same kind of hard-working, God-fearing, child-rearing, penny-pinching, self-starting, freedom-loving, troop-supporting elitist liberals.

One more thing: Next time a smarty-pants radical pack of mean-spirited politicos and bloggers decides to attack a former farm girl's carefully researched report, destroy her career, beat up her friends, and trash her reputation, they might want to think twice. Elitist liberals like me aren't afraid to fight back.

CHAPTER 3

It had been less than a month since the Bush-Guard story had aired, but my career was in shambles and my future was shaky. Rather than stand its journalistic ground, CBS had formally apologized for the story. I felt Dan had been pushed by CBS News and Viacom to announce publicly his own doubts about the documents. He had issued a brief statement, saying in effect that if he had known then what he knew now, he wouldn't have aired the story at that time, in that way. I was heartsick about what was happening.

When CBS announced that it had hired an investigative panel to look into "what went wrong," I knew I was in even more trouble. Dan, along with a number of longtime CBS staffers, advised me to get some legal counsel.

I was desperate for some kind of help when I walked into a Washington, D.C., law office and waited to meet the man who would become my attorney.

On the table in the reception area was a graphic reminder of why I was there, that day's *Washington Post* opened to the Style section, October 4, 2004. A photo of me taken in Afghanistan beamed incongruously under the headline MARY MAPES' DARKEST HOUR. Ugh.

The receptionist had a sweet smile and a thick southern accent and she came out from behind her desk. Even though we had never met, she put her arm around my shoulders. She said she was worried about me and how I was doing, because she'd had a similar experience a few years earlier and she knew how awful I must be feeling. She had been peripherally caught up in one of the endless rounds of Clinton scandals and had to testify before a special prosecutor. For a time, her house and her life were under siege by reporters and cameras.

She said she just wanted me to know that I "need to drink lots of liquids, cut back on alcohol, and really should be on medication. You should also be sure to take time to shop for new shoes," she added helpfully, "try to find a little joy." I nodded numbly.

God, it had come to this. I was eagerly and gratefully taking medical and psychological advice from complete—if very kind—strangers.

Luckily, my attorney, Dick Hibey, proved to be an antidote for some of what ailed me. Dick is a large, gruff guy with a deep, booming voice who has a charming and sweetly ridiculous tendency to speak in the most formal way possible. He doesn't mail something; he "transmits material through the usual modalities." He actually used that phrase with a straight face when speaking to me.

Dick also, endearingly, looks like a six-year-old boy when he smiles. He wears well-tailored pin-striped suits, seems to need a haircut most of the time, and talks about his family constantly and with great love. He is loudest and happiest when he is either eating or in a high-stakes legal battle. Dick constantly uses his speakerphones, both in his office and in his car. He drives, dictates letters, writes, works, and talks all at the same time, a maniacal out-of-control maestro, carrying on several high-decibel conversations at once.

I probably should have had doubts about driving with someone who continually uses his dashboard as a desk. Instead, I was whisked around Washington, a passive passenger who put all my trust in Dick's driving as well as his legal wisdom.

Dick is a brilliant litigator who has represented people as diverse as Imelda Marcos and Jonathan Pollard. He spent a great deal of time with me, even taking me to his wife's birthday party, sharing his family with someone who felt awfully lost and alone.

I think he felt sorry for this wan little character, abandoned by her bosses, battered by bloggers, and beaten up by Rush Limbaugh. I was preparing to be grilled by a panel I believed was put together and paid for by corporate whizzes who didn't give a damn about anything except that their company and its executives be publicly vindicated and provided an escape route.

It's worth noting that Dick is a rooting-tooting Establishment type. When he met me, I believed he was probably diligently preparing to vote for George W. Bush in the November election. I didn't care if he was going to vote for Lyndon LaRouche. I clung to Dick like a grateful barnacle that had found a friendly whale. I had been cast about alone in rough seas long enough.

By the time Dick and I got together, CBS had appointed former attorney general Dick Thornburgh and former Associated Press chief executive Lou Boccardi to head the "independent" investigative panel.

Like my friend Dan Rather, I was deeply uncomfortable with the naming of lifelong Republican Thornburgh and the hiring of his equally staid corporate law firm to oversee the process. We would have much preferred—and we deserved—a panel made up of journalists or at least with a significant journalistic representation. We would have gotten a much fairer shake from someone who actually understood news gathering and what we did for a living, someone who, in fact, had done it.

In fact, all I knew about Thornburgh, except for his lifelong Republican ties, was that he was the first attorney general to drape the nude statues at the Justice Department, just as John Ashcroft would do years later. I did not consider this a strong indication of Thornburgh's ability to be open-minded in my case.

In retrospect, the panel's makeup should have been a huge warning flag that the review was not a journalistic endeavor at all. This was a corporate, political, and public relations operation, designed to take the heat off and allow Viacom to walk away unscathed, unencumbered by lingering anger from the White House or the various Republican-dominated committees that the corporation lobbied constantly.

Lobbying was a year-round endeavor for Viacom, the leviathan owner of a bouquet of cable channels and a nationwide chain of theaters, along with billboards, extensive radio holdings, publishing company Simon & Schuster, and motion picture studio Paramount. The company's representatives regularly appeared in Washington, pushing hard for favorable action on media ownership rules, debt structure, a variety of cable issues, and leniency in television (particularly cable) decency standards. Billions of dollars were at stake and an angry administration could have upset the whole applecart, costing Viacom untold sums of money.

This was driven home to me at the height of the *60 Minutes* crisis in September when a CBS executive told me, "You don't have any idea how many millions of dollars Viacom is spending on lobbying in Washington, and *nothing* you've done in the past year has helped." That could only have meant that my Abu Ghraib story also had caused heartburn at the highest levels of CBS.

I considered breaking the story of Abu Ghraib, the prison in Iraq that had been a sickening ground zero for abuse of Iraqi detainees by American soldiers, to be the finest work I had done journalistically, the story of which I was most proud. If that story, which later won a prestigious Peabody Award for excellence in investigative journalism, had not pleased my corporate leaders, then I wasn't the only one in deep trouble. Journalism, by any measure, was in deep trouble at CBS News.

When I first talked with Dick Hibey, he seemed certain that this whole trauma over the Bush-Guard story would turn out well. Before Dick agreed to represent me, he asked me a series of questions about my background to see whether there were any red flags. I remember he asked me whether I had a "substance abuse problem." I joked weakly that I was still working on developing one.

He asked if I was, as had been reported by the conservative press, radio, and blogs, someone with a "radical feminist agenda." I pulled my knitting out of my briefcase and told him that there was no such thing as a "radical" knitter. I certainly believed women should be paid as much as men and I hadn't changed my name when I got married. So what? On reflection, what exactly is a "radical feminist"? To me, advocating rights for women is about as radical as being in favor of civil rights or human rights or the American right to life, liberty, and the pursuit of happiness. I disliked being asked about such basic beliefs, even by my advocate. But the radical right's attacks against my work and my name had made even the most mundane and moderate aspects of my life look suspect.

I didn't want any of my wild beliefs about women being the equal of men to offend some fragile soul sitting in judgment of my work.

I was on the defensive like never before. I felt heavy pressure to self-censor and I hated it.

I told Dick that I was most radical about being a mother, that I loved the unconditional love of mothering, and that I was never happier than when I was walking downstairs after putting my little boy to bed and hearing him call out, "I love you more than words you can say," the little chant he recited to me every night.

There is nothing like losing everything you have worked for professionally—and, in my case, very publicly—to suddenly strip your life down to its most basic components. I began to travel very lightly. It didn't take an elaborate structure of career success, prosperity, and public approval to sustain me anymore. I just needed the fundamentals, and I reminded myself constantly that I was lucky enough to have them: "My husband loves me; my son loves me; my sisters love me. I have friends who love me. My dogs love me. That's enough."

I guess I passed muster with Dick Hibey, because he agreed to help me. In the end, his gentle questioning was just a precursor to what was to come. His questions about my personal life marked the beginning of months of McCarthyesque speculation on who I was and what I believed. It had started with the hyperactive conservative bloggers who used every element of my life and work to paint an unrecognizable portrait of me as a politically motivated, personally obsessive shrew. According to the bloggers, I was a liberal, lesbian, ugly, angry woman. Some were demented enough to pull out that faded old bogeyman from the fifties: "She's a communist." Good God, cue the scary music. Does a communist have a Neiman Marcus credit card? I don't think so.

It was both surprising and absolutely predictable that the grilling over my core beliefs continued with a panel that questioned my politics, along with my professional and personal relationships. The suspicion, panic, and sense of isolation spread to CBS, where my fifteen years of work seemed forgotten in a heartbeat, replaced by raw fear over the possibility of continued outside political attacks that were judged too risky and potentially too costly for Viacom to bear.

The people I had worked with on the story for 60 Minutes were, like me, terrified. But some of them were scared enough to begin blaming others in the group for what had gone wrong. CBS's decision to name a panel and begin Star Chamber hearings turned the 60 Minutes weekday offices into *Survivor*, the kind of show Viacom executives preferred anyway. Employees were pitted against one another, everyone trying to outlast, outwit, outplay, and outmaneuver everyone else. In the end, most of us were voted off the island, an outcome that I think was in the works all along.

Despite my railing on and on about the unfairness of the panel and despite the fact that he agreed with me, Dick Hibey wanted to approach the review panel as he would any other internal investigation. But we soon realized that wouldn't work, because journalism is a business like no other. And these were times like no other for journalists: Reporters now had to tread lightly around certain stories and certain people for fear of riling the conservative attack machine. People—including myself—had chuckled a bit when Hillary Clinton referred to the "vast right-wing conspiracy," but seeing is believing. There *is* a well-coordinated attack machine out there in the media world, a monster that waits in the woods for an opening and then overpowers its victim.

The onset of Internet blogging and wildly political Web sites have done nothing but strengthen this machine, which includes everything from media outlets such as FOX News and all of its programs with hosts like Sean Hannity and John Gibson, radio broadcasts like those of Rush Limbaugh and all of his local imitators, columnists like William Safire and Peggy Noonan, and magazines like *The Weekly Standard*.

Internet blogging actually did more than make this machine stronger—it has had the insidious effect of weakening the victims of any conservative attack. It very quickly feels as though the whole world is against you when you are inundated with a swarm of angry e-mails, when your employer is bombarded with pissed-off Web postings, and when your friends can see you being berated very personally and very publicly on the Internet.

CBS, Dan Rather, and I had gotten on the wrong side of that political attack machine, and what happened to us served as a graphic warning to other reporters who thought about looking into forbidden territory. In the end, we were the heads on the posts that told everyone else to beware. And they did. Other media outlets, like *The Washington Post* and *The New York Times*, turned on us and reported on our perceived errors, ignoring the basic and indisputable story we had covered or the fact that we had verified and confirmed its details in large and small ways before we had gone to air. They didn't investigate the facts of the story—they critiqued our coverage.

In many ways, I can't blame them, because of what has become the superficial nature of daily news reporting. Journalism, particularly television, no longer does complex, complicated, or subtle very well. It rarely does real investigation. And God knows, journalism today has devolved into *repeating* more than reporting. If it's online, it will soon be on the air. And the anchors and reporters broadcasting it are not checking out the facts in each case. They can't. There is just no time in a world of twenty-four-hour-a-day news cycles, where a story erupts, gets beaten like a dead horse, and then gets dragged off-screen to make way for something new.

Rarely are journalists as careful or as thoughtful as they could be. My complaints are aimed at myself as well. But nothing clears your mind like being on the other side of the television set, watching yourself and your story turned into a toss to break, a quip, or a news flash running along the bottom of CNN's screen.

Newspapers weren't much better, taking elements of the story out of context, scrambling quotes, accepting claims at face value, and refusing to investigate anything on their own. Basically, reporters used faulty techniques in determining that I was guilty of using faulty techniques. I wish for all of them the insight of seeing themselves covered by others. They won't believe how breathtakingly bad we can be.

Watching the digital lynch mob at work was confusing, terrifying, and demoralizing. Seeing Dan Rather under attack reminded me of watching a dignified old lion trying to defend himself all alone as he was pulled apart by a pack of shrieking hyenas. I know Dan will hate that analogy, but that's what I felt I was watching. And it hurt terribly.

When once-powerful CBS News bowed to the bloggers, everyone became a potential victim, everyone in mainstream news became more vulnerable. With political blogging, there is very little gatekeeping, very little vetting of information before it goes out into the ether. For many of the more amateurish sites, the operators don't seem to want any fact-checking, any making sure, any of the editorial oversight that has always been the hallmark of all the old, imperfect mainstream media outlets.

With the bullying crowd of far right bloggers, there was no pretense at fairness, no attempt to focus on the other side of any story or belief system. There was just this almost murderous rage that pursued its version of the truth blindly, destroying anyone and everyone who got in the way, disagreed, or paused to think.

When we were attacked and taken out, suddenly there was blood in the water. And the conservative blogging community was looking to draw more. It wouldn't be long before CNN's Eason Jordan would lose his job to a conservative attack after an international conference at which he made comments that some people found inappropriate. Then the plugged-in, angry bloggers went into action. Jordan had the temerity to express concern about the number of journalists killed in Iraq, some of them in actions by American soldiers. The details of what he actually said were unavailable on videotape or audio recording, so there was no formal record to rely on, only the reporting of people who were there. Jordan tried to defend himself, but the bloggers acted as a lynch mob, reconstructing whatever was said through a harsh political filter. For conservative bloggers, even launching this line of conversation was unforgivable. It was a death penalty offense, and they were the "thought police" on the job to make sure the sentence was handed out. It worked.

Dick Hibey initially expected to find that I had made terrible errors in reporting the Guard story and that I wanted to make a case that I had been wrong, but I shouldn't be fired. Like many Americans, he believed what he read in the papers. When he learned that I was not apologetic but ready to fight for my work, he was surprised. When he saw my reasons for believing in my story, he became convinced that I had a powerful case to make. Something had gone wrong, but it was not my work. It was that the old journalistic axiom of standing by a story had been overwhelmed by new technology, new partisanship, and new financial imperatives for the bottom-line-obsessed corporations that now owned news operations.

It wasn't that long ago that journalism was considered different from any other kind of business. It was something people went into almost as an act of public service. This point of view is probably a reflection of the fact that I came of age watching Watergate unfold, seeing the moral difference that reporters could make in the world.

The companies that owned news entities, whether it was *The Washington Post* or CBS News, treated their newsrooms as almost sacred places, where decisions were made based solely on what was right journalistically. Ratings and circulation figures didn't drive what went on the front page or led the broadcast. Reality did. Journalists reported what the public *needed* to know, not what might be the most fun to watch.

That has all changed now. Money—how it is made, how it is spent, and how important it is—dominates the discussion in virtually every newsroom.

"We can't cover that story, it costs too much."

"We can't go to Darfur, no one cares and no one will watch."

"Why don't we drop that story on Iraq and do something on Chris Rock?"

These are the kinds of conversations that dominate too often today. And at CBS, I believe it was concern about potential financial fallout that dictated how our little disaster would be handled.

Dick Hibey was surprised and disturbed by CBS's self-interest and the corporate strategy to cut its losses. Clearly, I had unwittingly become a living, breathing loss leader.

Dick also believed that we would be in the clear if we showed the panel that what I had done, the checks I had made, the precautions I had taken, the background evidence I had, and the way the story was presented were all in line with the journalistic code of ethics. He assumed that there had to be some kind of independent oversight board that put out standards and regulations for reporters to adhere to, some group that punished reporters when they got things wrong and praised them when their work was exceptional.

Now, Dick wanted to know what association had jurisdiction of that code. He said he needed a reporters' group comparable to the American Bar Association, with the oversight it provided lawyers.

I told him there was no such thing. No balanced appellate group. No keeper of a sacred code.

"My God, you guys have absolutely no rules," he roared. "It's incredible!" He shook his head in disbelief. I told him I thought it was hilarious for a lawyer to be pointing fingers about ethical behavior. He laughed but refused to entirely concede the point. He just started thinking about a different way to proceed.

Our exchange stayed with me, though. That perceived lack of adult supervision, the lack of a central authority, is one of the vulnerabilities of journalism, a huge opening for critics to attack us—whether it's over alleged personal bias, conflicts of interest, or what outsiders see as a lack of clear standards. There is no unbiased hiring and firing body that disciplines all of journalism. There is no Better Business Bureau or Plumbers Board to complain to. On occasion, there is an ombudsman for a specific publication or broadcast operation. In most cases, there is no one to go to, no one to talk with, no sleek and simple way to seek redress, correction, or reexamination of a flawed story. I've certainly found this to be true in the just plain dippy reporting done on me.

Still, Dick's question and my whole dilemma were powerful reminders of what it is we do in journalism and how we are supposed to do it.

It's terribly old-fashioned to say this, but while reporters get paychecks from various companies, all of us are always supposed to be working for the same group of clients: the American people—black and white, rich and poor, red state and blue state. A reporter's obligation is to represent those people and the public interest as well as he or she can. That is a standard that I have strived to live up to.

Critics, far right bloggers in particular, like to make fun of reporters' highfalutin' ideas about the supposedly sacred nature of their work. These critics are just plain wrong. Journalism has a rich and proud history in this country. People who just appear on television to regurgitate their own political opinion, the spin doctors, the hangers-on, the bloggers who don't bother with the facts, the people who sing to the hallelujah chorus in hate-talk radio, haven't done one damn thing to keep America strong. Good reporting has.

Journalism, particularly investigative journalism, is a sometimes wildly flawed but absolutely crucial endeavor. The field is full to bursting with imperfect people like me, people who can, despite our best efforts, make mistakes, who often seem obsessive, who have only the rules of those who've gone before to guide us.

But journalism—aggressive journalism—is the most important tool we have in this country to keep government honest, to keep people informed, and to keep democracy intact. Sometimes journalism is practiced in ways that make us proud, sometimes in ways that cause us profound embarrassment. But at its core, news gathering is a noble profession.

That's why—like us or not, agree with us or not—journalists are singled out for special mention in the U.S. Constitution: "Congress shall make no law . . . abridging the freedom . . . of the press." The First Amendment provides protection and encouragement for every person who holds a press card. We are part of this country's inherent strength, not a symptom of its weakness.

The founding fathers were not talking about the new pseudojournalism that particularly dominates television, offering endless interviews with movie stars and previews of upcoming films. They were talking about real journalism, the kind of reporting that gets people in power, no matter their political stripe, to answer difficult questions. The kind that holds leaders in politics and business accountable and sometimes makes them mad. The kind of journalism the Constitution talks about is the kind that makes us a better country.

The Americans, Iraqis, Afghans, and others who have died in the past few years "fighting for freedom," to quote President Bush, did not lose their lives for the right to talk to Angelina Jolie. They died protecting their right to know what their government is doing, who is in charge, and how those in charge are using their precious power.

The least we can do as journalists is honor their memory with hard work, tough questions, and true independence.

Right now, especially in television, that independence has become awfully rare. News outlets are a piece of the profit picture like never before. They're owned by conglomerates that are invested in churning out little except timid and innocuous reporting, because they care more about money than they do about their public mandate. That doesn't mean they are bad people; they're just people in the wrong business.

Les Moonves, the head of CBS, is a powerful case in point. For some time, those of us at CBS News had joked about his longtime relationship with Julie Chen, a news anchor on the decidedly less-than-filling CBS *Early Show*. I used to say that everything Les knows about journalism had been sexually transmitted. Now I know even that hasn't taught him much.

While Moonves and Chen publicly denied the relationship, the years-long romance was one of the network's worst-kept secrets.

Moonves had been married for decades when he and Chen began seeing each other, and newspeople, terrible gossips that they are, delighted
in trading dishy tidbits on "sightings" of the couple.

Seeing the two out of the office in some kind of compromising position became the CBS employee equivalent of catching a glimpse of
that rare ivory-billed woodpecker recently found alive in the Arkansas
swamps after having been considered extinct for decades.

I had my own sighting experience. A few years before the National
Guard fiasco, long before Moonves would divorce his wife and marry
Julie Chen, Dan Rather, my associate producer Dana Roberson, and I
had just entered a small private plane terminal in Washington, D.C.,
after a day of shooting interviews in the capital. We were stricken when
we looked out the window toward the tarmac and saw Moonves and
Chen walking dreamily hand in hand off a Viacom-owned plane that
had just taxied in and landed. The couple, oblivious to the staring,
stammering "little people" gazing at them from the airport lobby,
tripped in gaily and stopped short when they saw Dan standing there.

Dan introduced us and we engaged in an awkward conversation
about the bar mitzvah the couple had flown in to attend. I remember
that Les was wearing a brown zip-front leather jacket and his hair was
heavily moussed into that kind of randomly tousled look that can only
be created with lots of careful mirror time. He has very striking eyes
that look almost as though he is wearing eyeliner. I can see how he got
a part years ago as a villain on *The Six Million Dollar Man*. I mean that
as a compliment.

Julie Chen looked almost unbearably glamorous, cuddled in a soft
mohair wrap and wearing the kind of glittering, large-stoned jewelry
that I would reject as too gaudy, because if it were mine, it wouldn't be
real. I strongly suspect she, however, was sporting the real thing. Dana
and I silently counted carats while we pretended to listen and laugh in
all of the right places. I drank in the details of this rare viewing.

Our little working group was not looking as well turned out as Les
and Julie. We were tired from a long round of interviews, disheveled
and bedraggled from the rush to get to the airfield and fly back to New
York so Dan could do the *Evening News*. In the car on the way to the
plane, Dan had, as always, unceremoniously wiped all of his makeup

off, like a little boy tearing off his tight and uncomfortable Sunday clothes the moment church ended. He had done, as always, a half-assed job and was sporting some telltale streaks of man-tan on his shirt collar. His hair was messed up and his clothes were rumpled. But then he always had to be forced to look in a mirror. And Dan was the camera-ready member of our group. You can imagine how stunning the behind-the-camera crowd at CBS tended to be. Dana and I were dressed like regular working stiffs. We looked like barn swallows next to a peacock like Julie Chen.

I remember sensing that this situation was a rarity as I watched them talk, and not just because we were seeing the company's illicit power couple out in the wild. It was interesting to watch as Dan communicated with someone from work whose professional power and personal fortune eclipsed his own and left Dan in the same category of hapless "employee" as the rest of us.

Dan was unfailingly polite to Moonves, as he was to every bag handler, busboy, and cabdriver we came in contact with. But there was something different in the relationship between him and the head of CBS, an almost tangible sense that Les could snap his fingers and make us all, Dan included, disappear.

Mercifully, it was soon time for us to board our plane. We walked onto the tarmac with Dan walking stiffly beside us, instructing us under his breath to "just act normal. Don't look back. Don't laugh. Behave yourselves."

At first, I thought Dan believed Moonves and Chen might be looking out the window at us, waiting to see a smirk or some subtle signal that would get us in trouble. In retrospect, I think Dan was just so polite that he didn't want us acting up and embarrassing anyone.

Dana and I were incorrigible beyond repair, barely making it to the plane before beginning to whoop. We lay down on the seats and roared with laughter at our world-class sighting as the plane took off.

In a way, some of us at CBS News found it oddly comforting that Moonves was close to someone who had at least some experience with news. Or at least we did until he made it clear that he had some innovative ideas about how best to use a newsperson's precious credibility. Moonves found it perfectly acceptable for Chen to host *Big Brother*, a

prime-time reality show. He felt her night job fronting for a bit of entertainment fluff in no way reflected on what should have been her more
serious work from 7:00 to 9:00 A.M. weekdays. He didn't see any difference between CBS paying her to announce the winner of a reality
game show and paying her to announce the death of a real-life Marine
in Iraq. Moonves thought using a newsperson's credibility to boost an
ailing prime-time show was just fine. He hadn't considered the possibility that the arrangement could cut the other way, lending an unreal-
ity to her work for CBS News. But then, I think that whole *Big Brother*
move actually signaled some of Moonves's constantly evolving notions
of what a good news broadcast could be. In Moonves's fantasized marriage between news and entertainment, perhaps Dan Rather could be
locked in a modular home filled with cameras rolling twenty-four
hours a day while he and other reporters ate bugs, performed complex
tasks, and competed for tidbits of breaking news. Hey, it could work.

Moonves is coming closer to choosing this sort of path for CBS
News. In September 2005, he told *The New York Times Magazine* that
he believed viewers wanted news to be more like his entertainment
shows. He discussed with envy the British cable program, *The Naked
News*, where a female anchor recounts the day's events as she undresses
on camera. That's something people would watch and, apparently,
that's all that matters. As Moonves says, "News is commerce, too."

I think Moonves believes this kind of complaining is nothing but
uppity bitching by a bunch of people who work in television but are
trying to pretend they're investigative reporters for some obscure publication that is so elitist no one reads it. The truth for me and many other
journalists at CBS News is that we never saw ourselves as working in
television; we worked in *news*.

Les Moonves lives an opposite life. He is a television mogul, not a
newsman. He can make brilliant programming choices and seems to
be a whiz at building a prime-time schedule. It was under Moonves's
guidance that the reality show *Survivor* became a monster hit. It was
Moonves who nurtured and guided the creation of a bouquet of *C.S.I.*
broadcasts, in the process turning Americans into a nation of people
obsessed with the science of solving crimes.

He has turned around the geriatric CBS prime-time demographics,
taking the operation from being must-see TV for the retirement set to

the network of choice for advertisers seeking young and moneyed audiences. But Moonves has about as much business making journalistic choices as I do determining what will go up against *American Idol*.

Andrew Heyward, the president of CBS News, is a different case. For years I had enjoyed his sense of humor and his habit of talking so rapidly that I had to put my slow Texas-paced ears on fast-forward to keep up when listening to him. For years I thought he was a good man, a good newsman.

After what happened during the Bush National Guard debacle, I am left wishing that Andrew had fulfilled the mandate he was given when he became the news department president. He did not protect and defend his department or his employees. Instead, when the going got tough, this captain of the vessel got tough, too. He made sure *he* survived.

I'm afraid if Andrew Heyward had been on the *Titanic*, he would have been among the handful of men said to have slipped on long gowns and elaborate veiled hats and shoved their way to the lifeboats. As one of the people unable to make it safely aboard a rescue craft, I resent that. But I resent more deeply the fact that Heyward, knowing better, turned his back on a proud history and let down many, many wonderful people. He let the country down. And he allowed decades of invaluable tradition to slip under the icy waves.

I was never a big shot at CBS. I was a worker bee, but that is exactly the way I liked it. There was no pressure to take myself seriously, only my work. That is still the way I see myself. For me, that is the ultimate rule of news gathering. I am not important. The story is.

For many reporters, those kinds of unwritten rules of journalism are internalized. They are with us every day at work, with us at home, with us wherever we go. There are things my husband and I have never done because we both work in news. We have never been to a political fund-raiser unless we were covering it. We've never had a political yard sign, added our name to a petition, or given money to any organization that smacks of politics. It is not that we don't care; it's that we want to scrupulously avoid the bias that comes with investing financially or personally with one side or another.

These internal rules tell good reporters what to do in very tough situations as well. Sometimes that means making choices that are personally difficult. Good reporters don't reveal sources, even though that may mean facing jail, a lesson I learned firsthand.

Good reporters go where the story is, even though it may be frightening and dangerous. Someone has to bring the American people on-the-scene accounts of war, natural disaster, and revolution. I have always been proud to be part of that. I count myself as profoundly blessed to have seen American soldiers in action, seen our system of justice at work, and seen my country share its wealth and its hope with others less fortunate. But there are places where America could do better, and I have been equally blessed in having had the opportunity to report those stories, too.

Good reporters are not put off by controversy. They believe that "news is what someone else doesn't want you to know," and they seek that information as ferociously as a terrier chasing a squirrel.

Good reporters are not afraid of criticism. They are not afraid of questions. They are not afraid of politicians or political attack machines.

And they shouldn't have to be afraid of losing their jobs for reporting a story that makes powerful people uncomfortable. In fact, that is what we are *supposed* to do. We are supposed to afflict the comfortable and comfort the afflicted.

All that has changed in the past several years. We now seem pushed to cater to the comfortable and ignore the afflicted. I don't know if that is due to corporate ownership, the rise of the conservative attack apparatus, the ferocious patriotism we all felt after September 11, or the change in the kind of people working in news. Maybe it's the lack of time and money invested in investigative reporting. Maybe it is a cultural shift that deepened the public's interest in escapist entertainment or raised the level of interest in celebrity culture. Maybe it is some combination of the above.

Whatever it is, it has changed the equation for reporters and editors, along with their readers, listeners, and viewers. I don't agree with the choices that have been made recently by many newspapers and news divisions. Broadcast networks are no longer doing documentaries with any regularity at all. Foreign coverage is something reporters and producers at all the networks have to fight for. Newspapers and networks have encouraged jingoistic coverage of the war in Iraq, rather than a realistic look at what this kind of violent clash means on the ground, what it really costs in terms of lost lives, what this amount of death looks like, whether it is visited on American soldiers, Iraqi citizens, or the insurgents who seem hell-bent on taking any and every life they can. By not covering these things, I am afraid we have let people down terribly in the past few years.

I know that many people believe I made terrible mistakes in my coverage of the Bush-Guard story or, in the ringing words of Barbara Bush as she and her husband did one of their "catch up with a former first family" interviews with Larry King last May, "Didn't the girl take most of the blame?"

Well, the "girl" was the only one who got fired. Spectacularly, publicly, embarrassingly fired.

On January 10, the day I was let go, I told my son after he came home from school that I had quit my job. He said "hooray," that made him happy. He said I would be home more and we could make more cookies. I agreed heartily because I was already planning to start eating compulsively, so that worked right in with my schedule.

The next day, little Robert came home from school, sat me down, and said in a concerned voice, "Mama, a girl at school says you got fired and you really got screwed." My God, even his fellow second graders knew about my professional humiliation. There was truly no place to hide. Of course, being a good mother, I told Robert, "We don't use the word *screwed*." To comfort him, I told him his little friend had gotten mixed up.

But I realized in that moment that I had no real choice but to embrace what had happened, explain it, and try to turn it all on its head. That's what this book is about.

Much of the conventional wisdom about the Bush-Guard story is just plain wrong. I want people to know what I know: that there has always been more smoke, more smoldering embers, and more flare-ups in this story than they ever realized.

The president's military service record is strewn with unexplained gaps, his full record has still not been released, and very serious questions about his service still exist. That is not an opinion. That is fact.

And it would be true if he were not a Republican but a Democrat or a Green Party candidate or a Communist.

I strongly disagree with those who say his thirty-year-old military service record doesn't matter anymore. It *has* been a long time. But if President Bush's service doesn't matter, then the suffering John McCain endured doesn't matter. The service of Chuck Hagel, John Kerry, Bob Kerrey, Sam Johnson, Daniel Inouye, Bob Dole, George H. W. Bush, and hundreds of thousands of others doesn't matter, either. The lost lives honored on the Vietnam War Memorial don't matter. The ongoing loss suffered by Max Cleland—the former senator from Georgia who lost three limbs in Vietnam—doesn't matter.

If military service doesn't matter, then the brave men and women who lost their lives in Iraq and Afghanistan don't matter.

I am old-fashioned enough to believe it all matters. The way individuals conduct themselves when serving their nation is an insight into their character, their commitment to the country, and their courage. Sometimes that means having the courage to refuse to fight; sometimes it means fighting a war against the war. Sometimes it means just showing up. All those choices are reflections of what's inside people, what they think is important, who they are at their core. And I can't imagine that there is anything more important for us to know about the person we elect as president.

And if George W. Bush did not serve out his time according to the agreements that he signed, did not offer this country the service intended by the training that he took advantage of, then he has been dissembling, covering up, and just plain lying throughout his public life. And that matters.

Bush's critics might even say that his success in skewing the public perception of his military service was a prelude to his success in shaping public opinion around the reasons for the war in Iraq, the treatment of detainees, the need for a tax cut, and every other political battle he has fought and won in his White House years.

The facts behind the president's abortive service record got no hearing in the CBS-handled public relations disaster that followed the disputed Bush-Guard story. By adhering to CBS dictums, I was forced to sell short my work, my research, and the reasons behind it. By doing things their way, I was done in. I'm hoping what follows will bridge that gap.

For twenty-five years I've continually asked people to share their stories with me, to share their emotions, their secrets, their souls. Now the tables have been turned and I can do no less. I want to be as honest, as open, and as straightforward about who I am and what I believe as the generous people who shared their stories with me.

My old journalism professors used to tell students that their real education begins when they leave school, start work, and begin collecting a career's worth of stories behind the stories, the tales of news gathering, competition, run-ins with executives, and journalistic triumphs in spite of the odds.

This book is a chronicle of my education in the real world of journalism, culminating with the story that cost me my job and taught me more than anything else in a quarter century of reporting.

I am not without flaws, but I've done my best. I am battered but still a true believer in the importance and the imperative of getting the story and getting it to the public. I think reporting is not just a profession, it is an act of patriotism.

Journalism is not medicine, but it can heal. It is not law, but it can bring about justice. It is not the military, but it can help keep us safe. That's how our founding fathers saw it. That is what history has taught us. That is what I, with great imperfection and profound humility, have tried to do.

CHAPTER 4

George W. Bush's lackluster National Guard performance had to be one of the Vietnam War's worst-kept secrets, at least in Texas.

At the CBS News bureau office near Dallas, phone calls regularly came in from a variety of people, anonymous and otherwise, claiming that Bush had run out on his commitment, that he had "frozen up" as a pilot, or at least that he had received special treatment in getting into the Guard in the first place. A lawsuit brought by a fired former lottery director was bubbling up, and it included allegations that Ben Barnes had helped then-governor Bush get into the Texas Air National Guard during the Vietnam War.

Throughout George W. Bush's first race for governor, in 1994, there were whispers about his incomplete Guard duty. During his second race four years later, the whispers became louder; the rumors became rumbles. The Texas media covered the story and there was some national reporting on it. I didn't chase the story at the time, because I was busy with other projects, and whether a Texas gubernatorial candidate served out his full commitment to the National Guard didn't seem an issue of nationwide import.

When it became clear that the governor of Texas would probably make a run for the presidency, however, I began to take a hard look at his career in the military.

I wasn't gunning for then-governor Bush at all. Proximity, not politics, determined that I look at the story.

As for my personal feelings about Gov. George W. Bush, I certainly didn't agree with all of his policies, but as chief executive of Texas, he struck me as pretty middle-of-the-road. He had the support of longtime Texas Democratic leader Bob Bullock, and I thought their across-the-aisle cooperation and affection could be a sign of how Bush might behave in Washington, D.C. Bullock died in 1999 and never saw his Republican friend become president. The rest of us certainly haven't seen much of the bipartisan camaraderie that Bush displayed in Texas make its way to the Potomac.

If I saw one red flag about the governor back then, it was his handling of the death penalty. While the governor of Texas could not reverse or commute a death sentence, he could call for a thirty-day execution delay or ask for a review of the case. He always had the option of signaling to his handpicked pardon and parole board that he felt leniency or compassion was in order in a specific case. Bush did not seek those delays or reviews. During his years in office, Bush's pardon and parole board turned down case after case, regardless of the facts. During his tenure as governor, Bush approved some 150 executions, more than any other American governor in modern history.

Governor Bush and his lieutenants seemed consistently and completely cavalier in the way they signed off on death sentences without any true review. According to his chief legal counsel at the time, now U.S. attorney general Alberto Gonzales, Governor Bush at one point actually restricted his reviews of death penalty cases to only fifteen minutes before giving the go-ahead for an execution. At the same time, his schedule allotted at least a full hour to work out each day. He seemed to have unusual physical discipline but a dangerous lack of curiosity about the cases where he had been handed, literally, the power of life and death.

Over the years, I covered a number of death row issues around the country, and I knew that many Texas cases deserved more time and attention than they were getting. In other states, governors would agonize for days over an individual case, while Texas's death chamber operated like an execution conveyor belt.

The cases Bush had before him often were complicated, involving issues and circumstances that were far from cut-and-dried. Many of the individuals who faced execution were minorities who had been tried and sentenced years earlier by all-white juries, inmates who suffered from mental retardation or mental illness, and those sentenced to death for crimes they committed as juveniles. In some of the cases, defense attorneys had fallen asleep in court or arrived before the judge as drunk as skunks.

Because some of the convictions were decades old, the guilty verdicts had been reached without any DNA testing, which was transforming criminal forensics in the 1990s. Sometimes inmates' requests for the latest testing techniques were denied before execution.

There was one category in which all the death penalty cases were alike, though. The inmates were invariably poor. Rich, white folks simply do not end up on death row in Texas, no matter what they do.

One of those cases affected me greatly. The inmate was Karla Faye Tucker, who would become the first woman put to death in Texas in some sixty years.

I met Karla Faye in 1994 when I visited the state's death row for women, a forbidding one-story brick building surrounded by razor wire and armed guards that stands on the state prison grounds in Gatesville, Texas. It was a tragic place where girlish penmanship formed a lacy filigree of grafitti on the interior walls and was carefully scrolled onto the long letters the inmates wrote in their cells, day in and day out. I peeked at some of the letters they were working on and received others over the years. Many of the women made little hearts over the letter "i," more like high school girls writing home than members of a dark and violent sorority.

The facility has changed drastically since then, but back in 1994, during my first visit, women's death row was brightly painted, with comfortable seating. Each individual cell was painted a different pastel color. The fewer than ten women housed there had colorful pillows, afghans, and lacy touches on their cots. The cells could have been dorm rooms in a particularly austere college. Curlers and hair spray sat beside the women's sinks.

In most of the small cells, the walls were covered with pictures of movie stars and models, family and friends. Sometimes, the pictures were of people the women had killed.

Women's death row was designed for a unique prisoner, a Texas inmate who would be treated, even by a notoriously harsh prison system, as a "girl." I was surprised to see that the women on death row were all carefully made up and had their hair cut and curled. I found out that in Texas the paternalistic prison system ensured even the doomed ready access to a hairdresser. They may have been women with big problems, but by God, maintaining big hair was not going to be one of them.

Unlike the men on death row, these inmates lived as a group, free to move around within limits. They had a small exercise area about the size of a dog run outside their building, and one by one they would pace around and around the fenced cage, beating a path into the tough grass.

The quarters consisted of one big room with cells along the wall and a communal area for watching television in the center. Off to the side was a crafting center, where the women worked to make smiling stuffed dolls for critically ill children in nearby hospitals. The sight of these women, some of whom had killed their own children, cramming tiny figures full of batting, sewing up faces, and snipping at flopping bodies with sharp scissors was gasp inducing. The women said they loved it. Making dolls beat the heck out of watching television.

On my first visit there, one of the inmates was moaning loudly in her cell. A small woman standing in the shadows inside the cell next door motioned me over. She pressed against the bars and I saw that she was in her thirties and had long, curly dark hair and bright eyes. I was stunned. She was so pretty, she looked more like a former homecoming queen than a killer. Karla Faye Tucker introduced herself and perkily told me not to worry about the moaning from the nearby cell. She said it was just a new arrival having trouble adjusting.

Karla showed me a small photo of a nice-looking man and whispered with a giggle, "This is my new husband." Karla had met a young pastor named Dana Brown through a prison ministry. They married not long before my visit.

I was reeling from Karla's story and strongly considering the possibility that she was completely nuts. It wasn't possible that a minister had married a death row inmate, was it? I didn't question her or ask what she had done to end up there. I listened and drank in the contradictions of seeing someone who looked and sounded and acted so normal—abnormally nice, actually—in a place like this.

Karla, like so many other inmates, felt she had found Jesus during her years in prison. She was incredibly animated in talking about how she finally discovered peace and security. She said that going to prison had saved her life and that God had helped her rid herself of drugs once she got there. She was a big fan of religious television programs and was regularly razzed by her "roommates" for wanting to watch *The 700 Club* when something racier and more interesting was on. Often, Karla won out and the whole group of convicted killers had to sit and watch religious programs while Karla sang along and made sweeping motions with her arms and hands, "signing" the evangelical songs in American Sign Language, a skill she had learned behind bars.

The female guards there clearly liked Karla and teased her relentlessly about how much she wanted to be alone with her husband to consummate the marriage, something that wasn't possible under prison rules.

When we left, I asked David Nunnellee, the prison's public information person, whether Karla's tale was true. "Oh yeah, they're married," he replied, laughing. "Karla's a good-looking woman." When I asked what she was in for, he moved close to me. "She hacked a man and a woman to death with a pickax and left the ax embedded in the man's chest," he told me. Good Lord. Beautiful ax murderer marries minister. Only in Texas does a story line like this make sense.

I began to look into the background of Karla's case and found it was as complicated as her current life. She had committed the crime with a male friend, who died while being held on the men's death row. She was a heavy drug user when she was arrested, but she cleaned up and testified for the prosecution in the man's trial. She referred to him, in the lingo of a longtime inmate, as her "fall partner."

I was fascinated by whether Karla Faye Tucker had changed as completely as she seemed to. How could such a seemingly pleasant woman do something so awful? She politely refused to talk about it, turning down all my requests for interviews, until 1997, when her execution date was drawing close.

Since 1989 I had worked for the *CBS Evening News*, often with my great friend correspondent Bob McNamara, who went with me to women's death row that first day. In the fall of 1997, I was asked to do a story for *60 Minutes*. Lesley Stahl was shopping for a new producer and someone had recommended that she try me. Since I had to come up with a story proposal, I thought I would try again with Karla.

This time, Karla said yes. Her execution date was fast approaching. She wanted to live and she knew she needed to make her case to the public, asking that her sentence be commuted to life, something that would need the governor's support.

In doing her story nationally for the first time, I felt a great responsibility, not only to Karla but also to the victims of the horrible crime that had sent her to prison. I have always thought it was terribly important to understand how and why capital crimes happened. How can we prevent them if we don't understand them?

Some people will find that an incredibly liberal-sounding argument. That is because they have probably never met death row inmates or victims' families. They have never seen crime scenes or execution chambers or the toll executions take on prison employees. They have never really been concerned with stopping crime as much as exploiting it for political argument.

I knew firsthand that these prisoners' lives, their lies, their failings and their weaknesses, their tragic tales, teach us more about murder and how it can be prevented than any number of statistical studies.

I wanted to examine what should be done and what had been done with Karla's life as a result of her crime. After all these years, after she had built a productive life in prison, would the state of Texas even be executing the same person who had wielded the ax?

In her *60 Minutes* interview, Karla talked about her mother, a drug-addicted prostitute who injected Karla with heroin from the time she was about ten years old. She said her mother sold her sexually to make money for drugs. In other states, that kind of abusive history might be a mitigating factor in sentencing, but that was not the case in Texas.

Still, I thought old-fashioned politics might accomplish what mercy couldn't. If he was going to run for president, George W. Bush had to be concerned about public sentiment. The religious right, in particular, viewed Karla Faye Tucker as a truly born-again soul. She had done short interviews on faith for the Christian Broadcasting Network and was one of their favorite examples of how God can turn a life around.

Lesley and I interviewed CBN's Pat Robertson at his *700 Club* head-quarters in Virginia Beach. It was an odd experience, in part because Robertson has an unusual habit of smiling broadly and speaking in a boyish, aw-shucks manner when he is making outrageous, cruel, and intolerant claims. There's a strange disconnect between this man's soft eyes and gentle, smiling manner and the angry, judgmental words that come out of his mouth.

In fact, the whole *700 Club* operation has a surreal quality to it, like a Mormon college campus run by a private army. The women are lovely, the men clean-cut. The buildings are sturdy brick and the grounds expansive, spotless, and well-groomed. But if your car stops for more than a minute, you'll find yourself surrounded by armed guards. Don't even *think* about taking a picture.

The 700 Club did its own news broadcasts, and as a journalist I found them strangely fascinating. Long before FOX News became a player, these programs were co-opting the look and cadence of news-casts and adding heavy Christian conservative commentary.

As in local television newscasts, carefully coiffed and heavily made-up anchors sat behind a gleaming desk reading from the teleprompters. Computer graphics popped and whizzed in the background. The pro-grams were interspersed with breaks. The difference here was not visual but verbal. Every now and then, you'd hear a word like "Armageddon" sneak into the copy or catch a quick reference to the "Antichrist," all spoken matter-of-factly and offered along with appropriate Bible refer-ences. The newscasts often focused on what the anchors called Christ-ian persecution, such as reports of kids who got in trouble for praying at school or Nativity scenes that had to be removed from public property.

Invariably, the attractive female anchor would fawn before Pat Robertson, her voice full of wonderment as she asked for explanations on politics or wifely submissions or maybe just the weather. Robertson played the role of an all-knowing, evangelical Wizard of Oz, a beaming figure with an oversize head that appeared via satellite and delivered what would sound to many Americans like horrifying news—the world was reaching the "end-times." Whatever the story or political develop-ment, it always came back to the same thing: We were about to be goners, and sooner rather than later.

In his interview with us, however, Robertson sounded more reasoned than many of the Texas judges and prosecutors who had been involved in Karla Faye Tucker's case. He said he supported commutation of her sentence to life and, in our story, he personally asked Governor Bush to consider making an example of her by showing mercy and compassion and sparing her life.

I have to admit that I was hoping pressure from the Christian right would prevail. But it wasn't looking good at all. Governor Bush refused to speak with us, his top adviser, Karen Hughes, refused to speak with us, and in fact the entire governor's office closed us out, saying they would let justice take its course. To me, that was Bush-code for death.

To Lesley Stahl, the story represented a chance to explore a different question: Was Bush man enough to kill a woman? I think Lesley believed that he would draw the line at executing a singing, praying, good-looking Christian girl. I had lived in Texas long enough to know that no matter the case, it was nearly impossible to stop the Texas execution machine once it geared up. I also believed that Governor Bush might be eager to show that he wasn't going to be controlled by Christian conservatives, even if it meant taking a life to prove a political point. Even as governor, George W. Bush felt comfortable applying Old West and Old Testament absolutes, at least to other people's lives. You kill, you die. No exceptions, no excuses.

In the end, that's the way it went down. On February 3, 1998, Governor Bush announced that he would not intervene. He made a statement asking for God's blessings on the souls of Karla Faye Tucker and her victims.

I had been with Karla a few days before she was moved to a cell near the execution chamber, where she would await her death. She was as perky as ever and began the conversation by asking whether I thought she was going to get a reprieve. Her team of excellent and devoted lawyers was working frantically around the clock, filing appeal after appeal, speaking to the press, trying desperately to make something happen. I told her I didn't know what was ahead and tried to be encouraging. She knew I was lying, but still she was buoyant.

As always when we met, Karla was wearing her white jumpsuit. This time, because of the winter cold, she was bundled up in a green quilted barn coat to keep her warm in the frigid visitors' room.

Karla leaned close to the glass that separated us and told me, "It doesn't matter to me now. I'm ready for whatever comes, because Jesus gave me a dream last night and now it doesn't matter what happens." She seemed unreasonably happy and gushed about what had taken place the night before. The camera wasn't rolling, but I remember her words. Mostly, I remember the way she looked, clearly delighted at her great good fortune. She was already on her way out of this world, transported by a dream, convinced that God had singled her out and given her a great blessing.

"I prayed for a pardon, the way I do every night, and then I went to bed and had the most wonderful dream. I dreamed that I could hear shouting all through the prison. It got closer and closer and I could hear them yelling, 'She got it; she got it.' I got my reprieve. And everyone was laughing and clapping and jumping in the air and we all hugged and it was wonderful and I was so happy. And then I woke up and realized it hadn't really happened at all. But you know what? It doesn't matter, because Jesus let me have those feelings and let me know what it would be like and so now I don't need to have it happen for real. I am just so grateful to Jesus that he gave me that gift." Karla was teary-eyed and triumphant.

God, I felt so sad. I knew she was going to die. It is hard to look in people's faces, no matter who they are or what they've done, and know that even though they are healthy and strong, they are just a few days away from dying.

I stood there, sad and sorry for what had happened in Karla's life and what she had done in her life. I wished that Governor Bush had visited death row just once. I wished he had witnessed one execution, talked to one inmate, or taken some kind of personal responsibility for his choices. But I knew it was easier for everyone, especially the governor, who seemed to keep his distance from real-life inmates, to avoid these kinds of contacts, these kind of moments. I didn't like being there, either.

I knew that someday soon the Texas love affair with execution would end and that for these villains, just like their victims, the difference between life and death was a mundane matter of timing. They all died at the whim of flawed, often selfish human judgments.

I believed that another death was not going to ease the pain of her victims' families or honor the lives that Karla Faye had taken. We touched hands through the glass that separated visitors from inmates and Karla told me she was so excited because she was going to be in heaven soon. I told her that if she got there to "save me a seat." I wished her luck and I meant it. I walked out the door envying her for her unwavering faith, her profound confidence in God, and her certainty that something wonderful awaited her on the other side of the death chamber.

A few days later, on the night she died, I was in New York, helping the *Evening News* broadcast cover the story. Lesley Stahl called me as I was working in an editing room, just to talk about what was happening. We were both saddened and talked for a long time, marveling that Karla Faye, the good, disciplined Christian girl to the end, had ordered diet salad dressing as part of her last meal. As women, we understood the tragically goofy significance of Karla's choice. Lesley and I both dreaded what would be happening in the next few hours. I think this may have been the first time Lesley would see someone she knew fairly well executed. It wasn't the first time for me, but it would be the worst.

That night, my friend Bob McNamara had pulled the unenviable duty of being posted outside the prison in Huntsville, reporting on the countdown to Karla's death amid the protests, the prayer vigils, and the drinking parties that accompany big executions in Texas.

I kept calling Karla's lawyers for updates every few minutes as they struggled to file final appeals and register new arguments. Whenever someone answered the cell phone at their headquarters, there was shouting and scurrying in the background and whoever picked up hurriedly filled me in on their latest legal moves.

Finally, late in the broadcast, I called one of Karla's attorney's cell phones again and this time I heard crying in the background. "It's over," he said of their legal maneuvers. "They're doing it. They're doing it right now. They're killing her right now."

I felt sick. I called the control booth and gave the latest information to Jeff Fager, then the executive producer of the *Evening News*. Dan announced there was an update and within seconds Bob McNamara was live on the air, reporting that the execution was under way. It may have been a reporting coup for CBS, but I felt numb and unspeakably sad.

I went into the ladies' room and slid down the wall, collapsed on the tile floor, and just cried for a while. Whenever someone would enter the bathroom, I'd leap up and hide in the stall, ashamed of my tears, ashamed that I had real feelings about a person I'd done a story on, ashamed that I actually had feelings. I had come of age professionally believing there wasn't room for that in journalism. Certainly not in death penalty cases.

Finally, as women in news have done for years, I got up, looked in the mirror, tried to undo the damage done by my tears and trauma, and went back to work.

Jeff Fager was just bounding back in from the control room and, God bless him, he was profoundly oblivious as always to the sensibilities and sensitivities of others. He was focused solely on how CBS had covered a big breaking news story. Not for a nanosecond did Jeff notice or acknowledge that my eyes were red and swollen, that I was slumped dejectedly in a chair, that I looked very much like someone who had spent the last half hour sobbing, crawling, and staggering around the ladies' room.

Instead, Fager gave me a massive smile and pumped his arm in the air with a thumbs-up. "Way to go, Mary!" he yelled, whooping giddily, thrilled that our coverage had gone so well and that we had gotten a small scoop.

All this came back to me a year and a half later, in September of 1999, when I read a profile of Governor Bush by Tucker Carlson in *Talk* magazine. In it, Carlson recounted an exchange with then–presidential candidate Bush about Karla Faye. Bush described an interview Karla had done with Larry King by claiming that when asked what she would say to Bush, she begged, "Please don't kill me." He mimicked her cruelly in a high-pitched voice. Later in the article, Carlson wrote that Karla and King had never had that exchange. Still, Bush's unkind portrayal of Karla Faye's plea for mercy spoke volumes about his lack of compassion for someone he saw as a bit player in what would later become his supposedly bedrock notion of the "culture of life."

By that time, in the fall of 1999, I had already spent a few months digging into the National Guard story. Along the way, I had gone to see the governor in action at a Dallas juvenile facility that specialized in a sort of boot camp approach to getting juveniles back on-track. He went through the facility slapping the backs of the mostly minority young men who were trotted out for a photo op. I couldn't help thinking that this was what many of the inmates now on death row had looked like and acted like just a few years before their murder convictions. I wasn't at all sure that a politician's slap on the back would help turn these young men's lives around.

Bush held a small news conference well attended by reporters from outside Texas, because by this time everyone knew the governor of Texas was a political comer. I remember standing next to E. J. Dionne from *The Washington Post*.

I even remember what E. J. was wearing, a gray pin-striped suit. I have to confess, ever since I was a little girl it has been an odd ability of mine to recall details of an event or an occasion, to store all kinds of meaningless information in my memory. My husband and four sisters tease me that no matter the occasion—an execution or a tea party—I always remember what someone was wearing. It's true. I'm embarrassed to admit that I even can recall what my second-grade teacher, Mrs. Marilyn Pomeroy, was wearing when she told us that President Kennedy had been shot: a white short-sleeved blouse and a straight navy blue skirt.

For me as a reporter, that kind of memory has been a blessing. For me as a human being, it has sometimes been a curse. But it allows me to recall a great deal of an individual moment, everything from what people were wearing to how I felt that fall as I watched the Washington reporters size up the future president.

I remember chuckling to myself because they all seemed so enamored of Governor Bush's twang and quirky retorts, something Texans had seen in large doses since he took office. Even back then, he was tossing around what sounded like endearing nicknames to reporters. Some of the reporters who had covered Bush for years even took a perverse pride in the nicknames he had bestowed on them. Outsiders didn't yet realize the joking and make-believe good humor masked a deep disrespect and disdain for the press in general, for our blunt questions, our lack of deference, our constant deadlines.

Sadly, I never got a nickname, as far as I know. If I ever did have one, I'm sure it couldn't be said in public. After Bush held his press conference, I was introduced to him as the producer of the Karla Faye Tucker story. He sized me up, shook my hand, nodded his head, and moved on, not saying a word. He worked his way through the crowd of reporters and supporters slapping backs, shaking hands, and cracking wise.

I had the strong feeling that I had probably just met the next president of the United States. Since he lived in my backyard, I knew that finding out who he was, where he came from, and what he was made of had become my job. I thought it would make for some interesting work. I didn't realize that five years later his life story would set the stage for the story of my lifetime.

CHAPTER 5

In the summer of 1999, I made my first round of phone calls on George W. Bush's military service. By then, Karla Faye was on the way to being forgotten, Bush was preparing to run for the presidency, and I was working full-time at *60 Minutes II*. The Wednesday night offshoot of the long-running Sunday program geared up in the summer of 1998 and went on the air in January 1999.

It quickly became clear there was a sharp split in how George W. Bush was regarded by the people with whom he served in the Guard. They seemed to either love him or loathe him. Those who loved him were eager to talk. Those who believed that he had received special treatment or hadn't done his job were scared to death to talk on the record and terrified of the fallout of speaking frankly. Sometimes, when I reached sources, they would say something cryptic, implying they knew more than they were willing to share, and hang up.

That sort of response is basically catnip to a reporter, or at least it was to me, so I kept digging and dialing. I took extensive notes, as I always do, and that is where the following recollections, comments, and quotes come from. None of the conversations were off-the-record. They were interviews that I did as I looked for people who would be willing to go on-camera.

Most of these people were too afraid to go on television with their stories, and their words or beliefs were never quoted in any story that I did. Many of them have never been quoted on the record before, but everything they told me was part of the background that eventually led me to do my first and only story in September 2004 on the president's National Guard service.

One of the first people I spoke with that initial summer of investigation was retired general Walter "Buck" Staudt, the big, loud, cigar-chomping commander of the squadron Bush had been assigned to some three decades earlier and a longtime supporter of his former pilot. Staudt was already into old age when we first talked, but he made an indelible impression. Even by Texas standards, this man was a world champion cusser. Within the first few minutes, his vulgarity kept escalating in what seemed like an attempt to shock me and dissuade me from looking into the story. After years in newsrooms, I was no stranger to foul language, so I just kept chatting and asking him questions. Within five minutes, Staudt had reached nuclear levels, calling me a four-letter "c" word because, like all of those other "goddamned" reporters who had been calling him, I was trying to get his young friend George W. Bush "in trouble."

I laughed off Staudt's terrible talk and told him his mother would be ashamed of him. He growled back at me that anything negative said by anyone about Bush's entry to the Guard was untrue. Staudt told me that Ben Barnes may have claimed to get Bush into the Texas Air National Guard, but that in actuality it was he who had plucked the future president from obscurity and elevated him to pilot training.

Staudt said Bush became one of the best pilots he had and he resented reporters nosing around and implying that something fishy had gone on. Staudt was crusty and crabby, conservative, and a constant source of unbelievably inappropriate language. I liked him. Still, I knew there was no way this guy would ever willingly examine the fairness of the National Guard system during Vietnam, its mission, or its open-door policy for the well connected. He would not even acknowledge that Bush, one of his handpicked pilots, appeared to have been extraordinarily blessed with good contacts and good timing.

Ben Barnes told me in the summer of 1999 that when he became Speaker of the Texas House of Representatives back in 1968, people regularly asked for his help in getting relatives, friends, or professional partners into the Texas National Guard. Barnes said that the favoritism he provided the privileged was something he was not proud of.

Barnes claimed that in 1968 Sid Adger, a Houston oilman and friend of the Bush family, came to Barnes's office and asked for assistance in getting young George W. Bush into the Guard as a pilot. Barnes admitted being an ambitious politician who believed he was at the beginning of a long and promising political career and wanted to win friends almost any way he could, even by passing out favors to the powerful and passing over the poorly connected. He particularly hoped to win the goodwill of George H. W. Bush, then a Texas congressman. Barnes claimed he called his close friend Gen. James Rose, then the head of the Texas Air National Guard, on young Bush's behalf. Bush was quickly accepted, Barnes said.

General Rose has been dead for years, but I contacted his son Mark Rose, who told me his father was unusually close to his two sons, one of whom was himself in the Guard. Rose said his father shared with him some of the politics and personalities behind Guard decisions at the state headquarters in Austin. "There's no politics like Guard politics," Mark Rose told me when I spoke with him in September 1999. He said his father would never have juggled the waiting list or broken federal law. But at the local level, he said, "everybody knows that slots were held open" for the kind of well-connected young men the Guard wanted to get into its squadrons as a way of maintaining the approval and funding of important people.

At the time we talked, Mark Rose was working at the Lower Colorado River Authority, a water supply and control program in Texas. He said his father "would enjoy this" dustup over then-governor Bush's Guard service. Rose said his father had been a personal and political ally of Ben Barnes, and if Barnes had asked that Bush's name be passed up and down the chain, his father would have done it. Rose said that if "Barnes says he talked to my dad, I can't dispute that."

In 1980, a series of scandals within the Guard exploded into Texas newspapers. Many former Guard members were discovered to be on the payroll when they hadn't been active for years.

The Texas National Guard relied on state and federal funding to survive. The more names that Guard officials listed on the rosters, the more federal money they could tap. The listing of so-called ghost soldiers, unknown names put on Guard rosters to boost manpower reports, was rampant. In fact, according to newspaper reports, a number of men were found to have been paid for Guard duty while they were in state prison.

A *Dallas Morning News* article in 1980 described the Guard as "embroiled in a war from within, its combat readiness undermined by corruption, fraud, waste, and serious manpower shortages." The investigation by the paper concluded that the Guard suffered "widespread corruption, including theft of military equipment, clothing and supplies, forged medical, payroll, supply and testing documents, and the diversion of National Guard funds and equipment to personal use."

In late 1980, then Texas governor Bill Clements called for a cleanup of the Guard and declared, "The Guard's very nature is such that it is conducive to problems."

The scandals rocked the Texas National Guard. I remember thinking, as I read all the old reports, that this had happened just seven years after Bush disappeared from the roster. Could the Guard have been a fair and inviolate military institution in 1973 and been run into the ground in such a short time? Could the Guard have gone downhill that fast? Or were the problems revealed in 1980 there during Bush's tenure as well?

Any agency that operates under an odd amalgam of federal and state requirements and funding is probably destined for trouble, particularly in a place such as Texas. The state had a huge and sprawling Guard operation and an old-boy political system that offered all kinds of opportunities for people looking to play the system or make a quick buck.

In theory, the state was supposed to run the National Guard while adhering to federal military rules and regulations. In exchange, the Guard received its federal money and was duty bound to turn out when the federal government called them into an emergency or combat situation.

But in Texas, state administrators either could not or would not control what was going on in individual units. Everything from equipment to actual soldiers went missing. The system reeked of corruption.

In 1980, an independent inspector general was brought in to investigate and assist in revamping the Texas National Guard.

Ultimately, thousands of undesirables, as they were called by *The Dallas Morning News* in its report on the Guard crisis, were purged from rosters for missing drills and other offenses.

The official inquiry into the Texas National Guard revealed that, far from being the crack military outfit described by Bush and his friends, the Guard appeared to be an organization with a split personality. There was the very real obligation of military service, but it was organized under the auspices of a hyperpolitical group with a long history of favoritism, cronyism, and corruption, certainly at the local levels in a number of units.

Some members of the Texas National Guard did go to Vietnam; they did fight and fly and die. But they were, far and away, the exceptions, volunteers who appeared to take their duty to a different level than many others in their units or in the Texas National Guard system itself.

Just looking at the roster of the 147th Fighter Group in Houston during the Vietnam years raises serious questions about who got in and why. Lloyd Bentsen's son, John Connally's son John Jr., billionaire H. L. Hunt's grandson, the heirs to the Sakowitz department store fortune, Bush family friend oilman Sid Adger's two sons, professional football players, and many other privileged young men were in the unit with Bush. You don't have to be a rocket scientist to see that there seemed to be a pattern to the admission policy. It consistently appeared that out of all the young men in Texas who wanted to get into the Guard, time after time, somehow the wealthy and well-connected appeared to have succeeded in winning slots. Coincidence? I don't think so.

More than two decades later, the man who would serve President George W. Bush as secretary of state was blunt about how the National Guard system worked throughout the United States during the Vietnam War. In his 1995 autobiography, *My American Journey,* Colin Powell wrote: "The policies . . . determining who would be drafted and who would be deferred, who would serve and who would escape, who would die and who would live . . . were an antidemocratic disgrace."

Colin Powell, like so many others born not to privilege but to something less, served in Vietnam. It appears he never forgot the unfairness of the system that sent so many poor men to fight a war that the wealthy were often able to avoid: "I am angry that so many of the sons of the powerful and well placed . . . managed to wangle slots in the reserves and National Guard units. Of the many tragedies of Vietnam, this raw class discrimination strikes me as most damaging to the ideal that all

Americans are created equal and owe equal allegiance to their country."

President Bush has always insisted that his entry into the Guard was fair and square. But early on, there were signs that Bush's entrance into the Guard was very different. Most young men who wanted to get into the National Guard had to sign up on state waiting lists, some of them hundreds of names long. They had to literally wait for someone to leave the Guard in order to get in.

Young George W. Bush didn't do that. In the spring of 1968, when he no longer had a legal student deferment available—after he met with leaders of the Texas Air National Guard—he was chosen outright to test for a pilot position. He passed—though not with flying colors—and was given a slot. No wait. No worry.

Bush's supporters have always said that happened because the Texas Air National Guard was looking hard for pilots. But the president's critics counter that with so many pilots cycling out of Vietnam, there was no shortage of fliers for state Guard units.

Whatever the circumstances, unlike most of the other wealthy young men entering the Guard, George W. Bush did become a pilot, a position that held no small degree of inherent danger.

In the National Guard, being a pilot meant being perched in a top spot, something akin to being the race car driver rather than a member of the pit crew. Many young men wanted to learn to fly. Very, very few in the National Guard were paid to do so.

The situation reminded me of a young man I met in Saudi Arabia while I was covering the first Gulf War. At the large hotel where the media and the military hung around, I'd became acquainted with a young Kuwaiti prince who said he flew for his country in the U.S.-led war against Iraq. He was smart and friendly and I asked him to do me a favor and take a small video camera along on his missions and record for me pictures of the Kuwaiti oil fields ablaze. Because of travel and flight restrictions in the area, no one had been able to get aerials of the huge fires, so any video at all would be a major coup.

The prince took the camera all right, but instead of bringing me back great shots of the hellish fields of fire outside Kuwait City, I got what looked like tapes from a teenage boy's airborne party. The Kuwaiti pilot and his friends were flying upside down, doing loops, and shrieking and laughing wildly. They were actual enlisted pilots in the

Kuwaiti Royal Air Force, but to them, the military was all fun and games. They acted like they were taking a joyride in their father's Maserati rather than flying a jet in their country's defense. They did not appear to have the sort of strict military regulations governing their flying or any part of their performance that others in the Kuwaiti service did. It appeared these lucky young men counted on those less privileged to do the dirty work of fighting and dying. Later, I thought about George W. Bush and wondered where he fit into this complicated continuum of military obligation, high-powered machines, and young men with connections.

In the summer of 1999, no one I knew had Bush's complete official records, so I began preparing a Freedom of Information request to ask for the material. As part of that process, I called the Air Force Personnel Records Center in Denver, the national clearinghouse for all air force records requests. In many cases, the records were actually kept there and accessible to the staff.

I reached a person working there who was extremely helpful and who convinced me there really was something unusual about Bush's service. He gave me tips on what information I would need to request in order to receive the full records. When I asked him if he could take a peek at Bush's file and call me back with a preview, I didn't know what he would find or what he would report to me.

I only knew him as a voice on the phone, but he seemed to be a straight-arrow, by-the-book air force man, first and foremost. I could tell by the way he talked, the way he looked at his job. When he called back and described what he saw in the records, he spoke as an objective and candid observer, not as a friend or a political enemy of George W. Bush.

His assessment of Bush's service record was devastating. "I look at this and I say the military didn't lose anything," he told me, referring to Bush's early withdrawal from the Guard.

He told me that Bush's National Guard service was "not a typical record, not by any stretch." He described his reaction to what he found in the official documents as a "smack yourself in the head kind of thing."

He found that Bush had been suspended from flying in August 1972 for simply not taking his physical, the most mundane obligation pilots need to meet. Then, it seemed, Lieutenant Bush just disappeared for more than a year.

My contact explained that he went to the files expecting to see a fairly uneventful but consistent level of performance . . . not a drop-off from good service as a pilot to Bush's disappearance into thin air. "How could you go from being a top-notch pilot to someone who didn't even take his physical?" he asked. "What the hell happened?"

He said there was nothing in the record that began to explain Bush's decision to stop flying. He did point out that then-lieutenant Bush wasn't promoted to captain after four years of service and that most fliers are. He added that the lack of promotion didn't clarify the rest of the details he gleaned from the record.

He was astounded that Bush had "resigned his commission. You're commissioned for life. And he resigned in 1974. *Very* unusual. I have never met a commissioned officer who would do that."

George W. Bush's records show that he stopped flying in March 1972. A form filled out by Lt. Col. Jerry Killian notes that Bush left his Houston base on May 15, 1972, for a civilian job. The form also states that the young pilot had been performing "equivalent duty in a non-flying status" with the 187th Tactical Recon Unit at Dannelly Air National Guard Base in Alabama.

Some of Bush's records spell out the civilian job he was so anxious to get to in Alabama—working on the campaign of Republican Winton Blount, who was running for Senate.

My source found the transfer downright shocking. "Man, what was going on?" he said. "He just didn't want to participate anymore. Just didn't feel like doing it anymore."

The records show that between May 1972 and at least May 1973 Bush did not register any points—like hours on a sort of National Guard time card—for performing his duty, flying or not. He just didn't participate, didn't do anything.

What was most inexplicable to my contact in Denver was the fact that any pilot would give up his time in the plane. He described flying as "the premier spot. To just give that away is just unreal.

"What I can tell you from looking at his record is that it makes me say this is not the kind of guy we would want to keep."

When I asked this air force man if he would go on-camera and talk about all this, he laughed. "An officer may not go on-camera for you at all," he said. "Because this is not a good military record and this guy could be our commander in chief in a few months." It was a sentiment I would hear repeated for the next five years. No one would talk publicly because George W. Bush was either climbing the ladder of power or sitting at its peak.

Over the years, Bush's file of official documents has been a relatively short but regularly evolving collection of fuzzy photocopies filled with National Guard and Air Force Codes. After a crash course in military codes and legal requirements, just about anybody can interpret them, if they put in the time.

Here are the basic facts.

In May 1968, at the height of the Vietnam War, with graduate school deferments no longer an option, Bush and thousands of other young American men faced a dilemma: How could they meet their service requirement stateside, find a deferment, or in some other way avoid being sent to Vietnam?

For some of these young men, the National Guard was the answer. But Guard units were often full. The question of what, if anything, was available in the Texas Air National Guard at that time has never been fully answered. It appears that Guard records and the reasons for accepting or rejecting people were peculiar to each individual unit. Most of the people who claim to know one way or the other are pushing one political view or another.

One retired high-ranking general in the Texas Air National Guard at the time did tell me flat-out that the Guard had no room at all in 1968—not for pilots, not for broom pushers, not for any personnel.

According to Gen. Belasario Flores, the onetime head of the Texas Air National Guard, who talked to me first in 1999, "There was a list for going in. Must have had one hundred and fifty to two hundred names on the list. The Guard was popular."

The consensus among many former officials seems to be that the Texas Air National Guard, like state Guard operations around the country, was technically full. But it seemed arrangements could be made in special cases.

However it happened, George W. Bush was admitted into the Guard in May 1968, ironically the bloodiest month of the Vietnam War. In that four-week period, more Americans died in the jungles of Vietnam than at any other time in the war. George W. Bush spent the month preparing to report for duty in his coveted new slot in the National Guard.

His initial pilot training took place at Moody Air Force Base in Georgia, a special privilege in and of itself. It was a tremendous rarity for a National Guard pilot to be trained from start to finish. Complete flight training cost close to $1 million for an individual, and most pilots were accepted into the Guard only after they had already been trained in another service branch. Often, Guard pilots were retired air force pilots who wanted to retain their flying status. Many of them had already served in Vietnam. George W. Bush was a fresh-faced kid just out of Yale. He was all promise, not a sure thing at all in the pilot's seat. But his father's political connections were certainly no secret.

Everyone knew that his father was an up-and-coming politician with strong Republican ties and a big future. Then-congressman George H. W. Bush wrote a letter to his son's commander at Moody, commending him and thanking him for the special care and attention being shown his son.

The well-connected young pilot was infamous for another incident at Moody Air Force Base, when then-president Richard Nixon summoned the young pilot for a date with his daughter Tricia. Bush was flown to Washington in an air force plane for this star-crossed rendezvous of Republican royalty. Nothing seems to have come of the date, but Bush's fellow pilots still laugh about the teasing they gave their colleague when he came back from his high-profile, high-flying date.

After his training at Moody, Bush was transferred to the 111th Fighter Interceptor Squadron in Houston, a unit that functioned under the auspices of the 147th Fighter Group.

As a pilot, George W. Bush appears to have acquitted himself well, excelling in training, performing his duties, and making lifelong friends in the process.

After completing training, Lieutenant Bush was a part-time flier, who showed up one weekend a month to pull "alert duty," basically standing by to scramble his F-102 over the Gulf of Mexico and ward off any possible attacks. Much has changed in the past thirty years, but with a hot war raging in Southeast Asia and the Cold War gripping the rest of the world, Cuba and the USSR were serious threats and the coast of Texas was seen as a vulnerable point of entry.

I talked with Maurice Udell, Bush's trainer in the 147th and a long-time friend: "I'm very much a disciplinarian. During the Vietnam War, he had his hair cut short and boots shined." Udell clearly liked his young trainee, describing him as "always good at coming up with a joke." As for discipline problems, Udell said that young Bush "responded very well. I thought he'd be a great American and fighter pilot."

Had Bush joined the Guard to avoid Vietnam? "That's bullshit, that he avoided the war," Udell told me in 1999. "They try to put George down . . . He performed very well. I'm not saying that because he's running."

Udell told me that Bush had wanted to go to Vietnam. Despite those claims, the only document in Bush's official record that deals with a possible transfer overseas shows that young George W. Bush decisively checked the "no" box. His old trainer says that must have been a mistake and claims he remembers Bush asking to go. According to Udell, when it came to flying "George did this all on his own. Tough little guy. Great kid. Can do a lot for us. I think he'll be president."

Even before Bush became president, politics played a huge role in what many people said about his days in the National Guard. Most everyone I talked with saw Bush's actions during Vietnam through a political prism; rarely could I find an unbiased, apolitical source on the story.

Jake Johnson, a longtime Democratic Texas state legislator, laughed when I asked whether George W. Bush had help getting into the Guard. "Does a big black bear shit in the woods?" Johnson asked.

Johnson was a sick man when I talked to him, confined to bed with a case of post-polio syndrome, a recurrence of the polio that had plagued him as a young man. His voice was sometimes weak, but his language was always strong enough to strip the bark off a tree. More than once he described someone as being "as full of shit as a Christmas turkey." He even said it to me, about me, using the phrase as both an insult and a compliment, depending on the conversation.

Johnson at one time had been head of the Military and Veterans Affairs Committee in the Texas House, where he worked closely with General Rose. He described Rose as "very bright and politically astute, an all-around good guy." Johnson recalled, "In my office one day, we were talking about other things and Rose just said it. Rose said he put Bush in the Guard."

According to Johnson, in the Texas Air National Guard, Bush's "chances of going to Vietnam were slim to none." The Democrat said he feared Bush's election as president, describing him as Icarus. "Too high, too fast," he said. "That's what's happening to him."

On occasion, some of the Republicans I spoke with would pull back the curtain and reveal something of what they knew about the advantages of having young men with connections serve in a Guard unit.

Earl Lively, a former Texas Air National Guard director of operations, began his conversation with me by announcing, "I'm a Republican." He went on to say, "The Air Guard is always political."

Lively himself had been involved in tussles within the Guard in what he described as an internal political coup. Like many Guard members, his career there was marked with intrigue and political infighting.

Lively, who owns a Dallas real estate firm with his wife, is active in Republican causes. He told me a story that he said took place prior to 1969, after George W. Bush entered the Guard but before he arrived at Ellington Air Force Base in Houston. "Staudt was commander in Houston," Lively said. "Congress was going to shut down Ellington. [General] Rose, Staudt, and I wanted it to be an Air Guard base. We went to visit Congressman Bush to try to convince him and [Staudt] mentioned his son in the unit." Lively said that as a result of their lobbying members of Congress, including Representative Bush, "the Air Guard is still there."

As for whether anyone received help getting into the Guard or getting promoted, Lively conceded that some well-connected Guardsmen were given "haloed" or sweetened performance reports. As to why there were so many wealthy white guys in the Guard, Lively recounted a decades-old defense of the system: "Some say it was racist, 'cause there were no blacks, but blacks didn't know about it."

Actually, some blacks did know about the Guard. Colin Powell knew it as a haven for the pale and politically connected. The few blacks in George W. Bush's unit tended to be either in low-level positions or pro football players who were somehow always able to spend their all-important Sundays off-duty.

Later that summer I had my first conversation with former Air National Guard commander Bobby Hodges, the source who would later speak out against my Bush-Guard story after it aired in 2004.

General Hodges told me in 1999 that getting into the Guard was a "legal and honest way" to serve your country and that no one got in unless "we had vacancies. We had a waiting list at one time." He said he didn't know Bush well, but that he was "like all second lieutenants, young and eager, bright eyed and bushy tailed." Hodges said Bush stayed with the unit as a pilot until he moved out of state and reiterated that there were "no strings pulled" in getting Bush into the Guard. Then Hodges recommended that I call some other members of the unit, men whose names and sentiments would become very familiar to me in the years ahead. Hodges suggested I talk with Dean Roome first. The other names on the list never changed through the years: Maury Udell, Tom Honeycutt, Albert Lloyd, Buck Staudt, and a few others. I talked with them all, but something bothered me about their comments.

This pattern of referencing the same group of men started in 1999. These guys were all well-acquainted, longtime supporters of the soon-to-be candidate for president. In fact, by 1999 Albert Lloyd was working for the Bush campaign and had the great fortune to discover some of the missing Bush records supposedly misfiled at Texas Air National Guard headquarters.

These men's comments about Bush's service invariably sounded like what we now call talking points, rather than spontaneous comments about a man they remembered from decades previous. They all emphasized how "no strings were pulled," what a "great guy" Bush had been to fly with, and the fact that going into the Guard was "legal and honorable"; then invariably, they suggested that I speak with another member of the clique and they always helpfully had phone numbers and locations where these other men could be found.

Reporting on anyone's life thirty years before usually wasn't this easy. And frankly, the constant references to the same people and the use of the same phrases made me suspicious, especially when there was a strong diametrically opposed interpretation of events. The Guard records clearly showed that Bush had missed more than a year of service.

Bush and his aides had told reporters for years that he had left the Guard in 1972 because his plane, the F-102, was being phased out. Gen. Belasario Flores, the head of the Texas Air Guard at the time, scoffed at that claim: "They trained pilots for new planes all the time. I'm just guessing, but it's possible that he probably had to have real good reasons for him to be excused." Flores thought that Bush's official departure from the Guard in 1973 to attend Harvard Business School was another red flag that this wasn't a normal record: "Anybody else would have had to join a reserve unit in Boston. I know people, poor working stiffs, who couldn't convince them [the National Guard] to let them out early."

Whenever I went outside the core group of Bush backers, I got comments like that, either openly hostile or not entirely helpful to then-governor Bush. Some other members of the unit fell into the muddled middle, not critics exactly, but they had clearly either not gotten or not quite understood their talking points. These men were all former Guardsmen and forever Texans, men who had lived out their lives in the Lone Star state, diverging in careers and lifestyles, but coming together in their politics and their connections to a man who might soon be president.

Bill Hollowell told me that he didn't "think Bush got any more help than anyone else" and that "even if he got help, it's a nonissue."

Bill Penny acknowledged that there had been a group of particularly well-connected members of the Guard and helpfully noted, "We called them blue-chippers." But he said there was "no need to dwell on it."

Robert McElroy told me he hadn't heard any scuttlebutt about Bush, but that "we [the Guard] were not recruiting. Everybody had some help." McElroy said there had been "so much politics in the Texas Air National Guard."

This had always been the case, according to what I was told by Robert Strong, a college professor who had worked in the Texas Air National Guard headquarters in Austin. But Strong said, "Vietnam further politicized the Guard, no question." He said "it was particularly obvious in state headquarters. There were only ten slots there and eight or nine of them went to the politically connected." He said "everyone knew Bentsen and Bush were in Buck Staudt's unit, because he bragged all the time." As to how that was worked out, Strong was adamant: "They held slots. Clearly waiting lists were supposed to be first come, first serve. But they were selective about who those slots went to. There's no other way to explain how this happened."

Dan Rather and I did an interview with Robert Strong that summer, just in case I could get the rest of the story together. We also talked on-camera with Bill Minutaglio, a friend of my husband's and former *Dallas Morning News* reporter, who had just finished a book on George W. Bush called *First Son: George W. Bush and the Bush Family Dynasty*. Bill's head researcher on the book was Mike Smith, who would later join me in working on the Bush-Guard story. *First Son* remains the definitive book on Bush's personal history and raises questions about his National Guard service, but despite Bill's and Mike's extensive work, they were never able to find a solid answer on how Bush got into the Guard or how he was allowed to walk away.

I passed all this information, in thumbnail form, on to my bosses, *60 Minutes II* executive producer Jeff Fager and senior producer Patti Hassler. One e-mail I sent in 1999 breezily summed up my latest conversations with former Bush colleagues and other sources and ended with the words: "Well, I'm off to make nice with a racist killer. Talk to you later."

I didn't know the racist killer I was going to speak with would prevent me from completing my story on George W. Bush that fall, or that it would land me in a court battle with a small-town Texas prosecutor, which ended up with me doing a brief stint in jail.

That's the best thing (and the worst thing) about working in news. You just never know what's going to happen.

CHAPTER 6

When the judge's name is Joe Bob, you could be in trouble.

That's what I learned the hard way in September 1999 when CBS and I went up against a small-town prosecutor who demanded all my notes, recordings, and videotapes following an interview that Dan Rather and I broadcast with an accused killer on *60 Minutes II.*

CBS spent tens of thousands of dollars fighting the prosecutor's subpoena. I spent weeks utterly exhausted from stress, fear, and worry over what I should do. It was a good dry run for all the angst that would come exactly five years later.

I didn't want to turn over my notes to *anyone* and, in the process, betray names, sources, and confidences I had promised to keep. I didn't want the prosecutor to have my unedited tapes to use in court any way he chose. I suspected he would not be as careful as we had to be at *60 Minutes,* where we were required to make sure that every response was preceded by the actual question asked, that no answer was taken out of context, that any paraphrase of a person's opinions could be backed up by direct quotes from our own interview.

On the surface, it might seem as though a journalist should have no trouble sharing information with the authorities, in effect promoting justice. But that's not how a free press promotes justice. We cover trials, engage the public in policy debates, and try to illuminate the details of a given case. That's it. We don't work for either side.

The overriding argument against turning anything over to authorities is as old as journalism itself—why would anyone ever do an interview with us again if it was clear that talking to CBS was the equivalent of talking to the prosecutors or police? We were not detectives for anyone or anything other than the public. And our obligation was to the public's right to know, not the prosecution or the defense.

Shortly after being subpoenaed, I was called into a hearing at the historic courthouse in Jasper, Texas, in early October. I remember standing beneath the gently twirling old ceiling fans in the courtroom and thinking how odd I felt to be standing in *front* of the bar instead of behind it where the other regular folks sit.

As a newsperson, you know something has gone wrong when the defendant whose murder case you have been covering is now sitting in the audience and you are standing before the judge. You know it's *really* bad when the defendant, who is facing the very real prospect of a death sentence, clearly feels sorry for *you*.

I tried hard to smile and look like a nice, normal woman instead of a media jackal when I was brought before Joe Bob Golden, the state district judge in charge of hearing my case.

Inside, I had been wilting since the moment I saw his nameplate. Someone with that small-town southern moniker was not going to overturn a prosecutor's request. In the colorful lottery of Texas legal names, you wanted to draw a judge with a last name like "Justice" and you wanted your attorney to be named "Racehorse."

Not only was the judge's name a bad omen, but a check of his work history showed that he had once shared a law practice with the prosecutor. The clincher was my attorney, a pleasant young man who had a broken leg and a cast that went up to his crotch. He would later be joined by other, more seasoned attorneys, but I certainly felt I was in trouble.

For reasons that now appear obvious, the judge, the court clerk, and most of the spectators at my stream of hearings seemed to find it amusing to have at their mercy a "real-live New York City producer" from the world of tay-vay, as "TV" is pronounced in East Texas.

It didn't matter to anyone there that I had grown up in a town smaller than Jasper, that I lived in *Texas*, for crying out loud, not Manhattan. They kept referring to my being from New York. And figuratively speaking, I *was* from New York. I was part of the media onslaught that had engulfed Jasper since June 7, 1998, when three young men and an act of unspeakable violence had rekindled the country's collective memory of lynchings, arrogant southern justice, and ignorant locals.

The nation and national media turned on Jasper, pouring into town to eat at the restaurants, complain about the food, bitch about the heat, and paw through the town's secrets. Reporters from all over the country held Jasper's citizens' lives up for inspection and judgment by outsiders. It seemed the media was seeking a kind of public retribution, not just for the horrific killing of one man but for all the deaths, all the unfairness, all the pain that generations of racism had represented. There was plenty to work with.

The murder itself was the stuff of southern nightmares.

After a night of drinking, three young white men had stopped to give a lift to James Byrd, a well-known local who was hitchhiking home in Jasper. The men drove their pickup into a wooded area, had a few more beers, and then turned on Byrd.

Byrd, an older, partially disabled black man, couldn't put up much of a fight. He was chained to the back of the pickup and dragged along a paved country road. His body was practically torn to pieces.

I was considering doing a story for 60 Minutes on the case, if I could come up with something that would advance the story beyond what we already knew.

Executive producer Jeff Fager was the driving force in deciding which stories we went with. The rest of us could argue or beg, but that usually had little effect. If Jeff didn't find it new or interesting, it probably wasn't going to see the light of day. And Jeff wanted us to find new angles or new interviews to push a story further than what was being offered by other news organizations.

I had been in court to listen to the testimony in the trials of the two men who had already been tried and convicted in the case. John William King and Lawrence Russell Brewer were both sent to death row for their roles in the horrible murder.

King and Brewer had met years earlier in a state prison. Both appeared to have spent much of their time behind bars getting their squat bodies virtually covered in racist tattoos.

I never talked with Brewer, who appeared to be intellectually challenged, to say the least. King, however, appeared to be lucid but was a rotten punk of the first order. Before the trial began, I spoke with his pitiable father, who obviously still loved Bill, as he called his son, very much. King's father was confined to a wheelchair and smelled of urine and desperation. When I talked with him, he was sweating in the oppressive heat, crying and inconsolable, completely lost over what his son had apparently done. He pleaded with me to please try to talk with his boy Bill. Like everyone else, he wanted to know why this crime had been committed. He told me Bill was really a good kid beneath that tough exterior. I had serious doubts, but thought I'd give it a try, at least for the old man's sake. Maybe just knowing that I had tried would give the elderly man some peace.

So during a break in the trial, I sent a note to King's attorney asking if his client would be interested in doing an interview with Dan Rather. I was standing near the front of the courtroom when King, sneering, was brought back into the chamber for resumption of the trial. He was wearing an electric shock belt in case he misbehaved, something I would soon wish I had the controls for.

As King asked his attorney something I saw the lawyer point to me. I perked up. Was it possible that King would indicate whether he was interested in an interview? Well, he did. I leaned forward expectantly and King looked directly at me and mouthed the words "Eat me." It seemed all traces of the "good boy" his father loved so much were long gone, driven away by misplaced egotism and the hopelessly tough persona that young men develop in prison. For King, hate, disrespect, and smoldering anger had become "cool."

Shawn Berry, the third defendant, seemed to be a different sort. He didn't have a prison record or a history of racial abuse and he had both black and white friends who were willing to vouch for him. Berry worked as the manager of the town's small theater and was planning to marry a local girl with whom he had a child. His brother was an outspoken advocate for Shawn. And Shawn had a good lawyer out of Beaumont with the quintessential Texas name of Lum Hawthorne.

Hawthorne told me that Berry might be interested in talking before his trial and that if he did an interview, he would be very forthcoming about the crime and his role in it. I agreed to meet with Berry in Jasper's small jail facility.

I stopped my work on the Bush-Guard story to drive the two hundred miles or so to Jasper, past the Dairy Queens and the plywood cutouts of women in bloomers bending over in people's front yards. Some people might not like this part of the country, but I loved it. I often took the back roads on drives like this, enjoying the chance to get off a plane, out of the city, and onto a rural road. I could eat something deep-fried and not feel guilty. I could listen to Paul Harvey and remember how that same voice used to fill our family garage when it boomed out of my father's radio when I was a little girl.

Out here, you can read a family's profile in every patch of front yard. Just by driving by, you know whether they are tidy, sloppy, or just too damn tired to plant flowers. You know who is poor and who is poor but proud. You knew whether they have kids. Maybe even how many, how old, and how well behaved.

I zipped through the town of Tyler, known as the rose capital of Texas, and vowed, as always, to buy flowers on the way back from one of the many people hawking gorgeous blossoms along the city's intersections. Then I turned south and drove deep into the piney woods, a dark, humid, and mosquito-laden corner of Texas culture, which had once been the slave-holding center of the state. Now East Texas was back in an unwanted spotlight. And, once again, it was for the way the area's racial divisions and demons still stalked its small towns and the people who lived there, whether they were black or white, poor or powerful.

Shawn Berry's attorney was waiting for me in the parking lot of the boxy little jail in downtown Jasper.

We walked in and were greeted by Sheriff Billy Rowles, who had become a media sensation through the constant coverage from Jasper that followed the crime. Rowles was lanky and laid-back and always in full sheriff costume, including his white hat. He liked to flirt with the women and joke with the men, and he did it all with a thi-yick East Texas twang.

Sheriff Rowles led us behind the entry area into the tiny cell block. Berry was waiting there, inside an empty cell that served as a visiting room. He was a small man, with coal black hair cut very short. He was dressed all in white and shuffled nervously as he sat uncomfortably at an old pine table.

Berry looked like such a kid. For me, as the mother of a little boy, it was heartbreaking to think that a young man could make such a terrible mistake at such an early age. I vowed to hug Robert, then only a toddler, even closer when I got home.

Berry and I were initially very guarded and suspicious of each other. He knew he was in a nearly hopeless situation. I knew he had played a role in an unimaginable crime. As he told his story, though, a good portion of it had the ring of truth.

He talked about how aimlessly the evening had begun, how he and the two others weren't really friends and hadn't planned to get together or do anything in particular that night. King was from Jasper and had come back after serving prison time. Brewer had only been in town a few weeks. The three had gotten together on a whim. It had all just happened, as much of life does in places like this.

I'd come of age in a small rural town and knew that on weekend nights an awful lot of young, undereducated, underemployed men tooled around in pickups with a case of beer on the seat, looking for trouble and finding it. Some of them seemed to be born and grow old without really growing up. Life was what happened in between birth and death. There was precious little planning for anything, beyond where the next paycheck or the next beer was coming from.

Berry said that they had all been very drunk that night. He said he thought nothing of it when Brewer and King had wanted to pick up Byrd and give him a ride or when they decided to take him back into the woods and continue drinking.

But Berry said that once they got there and had a few more beers, everything changed. He claimed Brewer and King had pulled Byrd out of the truck and started kicking and beating him. Berry told me how Byrd had clung to the door of the pickup trying to protect himself from the men's blows.

Berry told me he had protested and the two other men had threatened him, saying they would kill him as well. He said he last saw Byrd alive when the older, injured man was down on all fours and one of the men grabbed a can of black spray paint and painted Byrd's face. Berry said he turned away and sat on the running board of the truck. He spoke chillingly about hearing the chain being pulled out of the back of the pickup to attach to James Byrd. He graphically described how Byrd's body had bounced from one side of the road to the other as the pickup roared up the backcountry asphalt and how Bill King and Russell Brewer laughed and ridiculed Byrd.

Berry cried several times as he told his story. He confessed that he had gotten so scared that night that he'd wet his pants.

I thought the story, true or not, was profoundly disturbing. It was disgusting but important. People needed to hear how cruel, how unnecessary, how brutal, James Byrd's death had been.

And I thought that Berry's behavior and recollections, whether brought on by actual new insight or his impending trial, reflected real human regret. I thought that what had happened to this young man would be a good object lesson for all Americans in how quickly life can change when you find yourself in the wrong company on the wrong night doing the wrong things.

I left the jail convinced that we should do the interview. On the way out of town, I made a detour to the country road where the murder took place. It was late evening and I drove the road slowly in the golden light, recognizing the landmarks Berry had mentioned.

The woods were eerily quiet, but my head was full of the violent imagery I'd just heard described in excruciating detail. Each bend in the road took on a sickening new meaning. Each bump and curve made my heart ache for the man who had died here so horribly.

Most upsetting were the still-visible red and yellow Xs painted on the road by police on the day after the crime. They marked the spots where pieces of James Byrd's body had been found.

Our interview aired on September 28, 1999. It was a mesmerizing story, the first time anyone had heard about the crime from someone who was there. Dan Rather prodded Berry to tell the story in full, and time after time Dan asked difficult questions, some of them impossible to answer, that left Berry shaken and in tears, facing publicly the enormity of what he had done.

Berry said he had thought again and again about what he might have done differently. "When they jumped out of the truck and opened his door, I wished I'd have just punched that gas and left them out there, Mr. Byrd with me," he said. "If I'd a done that, nothing would have happened."

Berry said even though he didn't take part in the crime, he had done something just as bad. He failed to stop it. "I wish I wouldn't have chickened out," he said. "I think I let a lot of people down."

Police and prosecutors had already heard this story from Shawn Berry many times. So even though we were airing this prior to his trial, we didn't anticipate any legal problems. Why would they subpoena from us material they already essentially had?

Just days after the story aired, I got a call from Sheriff Rowles. He said he was going to be in Dallas in a few days and wanted to stop by my office for a cup of coffee. Ever the innocent, I told him that sounded great. I actually made a pot of coffee and, like a fool, washed out the coffee cups before the sheriff got there. I was trying to be nice.

It turned out the sheriff didn't want coffee at all. He wanted a face-to-face meeting so he could hand me a subpoena. I took it open-mouthed and asked him why on earth they were doing this. Rowles told me there was nothing in particular they were looking for, that the prosecutor was "just fishin'."

Subpoenas like this were delivered with great frequency in Texas at that time. It seemed that all over the state, prosecutors were flexing their muscles and enjoying their ability to make reporters turn over notes and tapes or just show up to testify in court. It was a blatant violation of the unique trust that reporters are supposed to offer their sources. Every time a reporter testifies or turns over confidential materials, it has a chilling effect on the next story, the next interview. Sources, identified or not, won't be encouraged to talk to us if they know we will blab out their identities or turn over their secrets the moment a subpoena pops up and the going gets tough. As a consequence, the public learns less, hears less, and knows less about what is going on in the world.

So far, forty-nine states have recognized the need to protect reporters in this kind of situation, instituting so-called shield laws that prevent prosecutors from doing what was done to me. Sadly, but not surprisingly, Texas is one of the states that offers the least protection to reporters. If a prosecutor wants what you have, you're on your own.

Luckily, CBS was wonderful about pressing our case. We had little chance of winning, considering that the holes in state law providing protection for reporters were big enough to drive a herd of longhorns through. At least by not giving in easily we all hoped to make prosecutors think twice before taking us on again.

But very quickly the showdown became so nasty that I was seriously worried about whether a search warrant would be served at my home. I didn't have the tapes, but I did have all my notes and the typed transcripts of the interview. I had been warned that the prosecutor wanted to launch a search and teach me a lesson. I spent many nights looking out the front window waiting for sheriff's deputies' cars to pull up. My husband and I kept a video camera at the ready to record anything that deputies did in searching our home.

I was particularly concerned about some of my notes. People who worked within the legal system, in law enforcement and in the prosecutor's office, had talked to me on background about what they saw as the prosecutor's stubborn refusal to acknowledge that Berry's role in the crime was different from that of the other defendants. They thought Berry should have been given some kind of deal so that the other prosecutions would be more certain. These people didn't feel Berry was nearly as culpable as the other two men.

Whether I agreed with them or not, I did not want those people's names and thoughts revealed, exposing them to a prosecutor who appeared to be both powerful and vindictive.

District Attorney Guy James Gray, the prosecutor behind this unfair "fishin'" expedition, was himself a big fish in this tiny Texas town. This caricature of a southern district attorney had been the law in Jasper for years, and he walked with the swagger of a small man who could make big differences in people's lives. He gleefully used the court and his sway with the judge to bully CBS and me personally, telling local radio and newspaper reporters that he was going to have me handcuffed and led into the courthouse, presumably shamed and shackled.

I was certainly no safety risk. I had good attorneys and big money backing me. I can only imagine how much clout I would have had if I had been a poor local kid standing before the prosecutor hoping for a bit of mercy when he decided whether or not a case would go forward or whether a maximum sentence would be pursued.

Dan Rather was subpoenaed as well, but he found a measure of protection in the New York courts, which would decide whether he had to respond to a Texas summons. He, of course, was eager to join the fight in Texas, but none of us wanted him to come down here. CBS executives and I agreed that he was very likely to be thrown in jail with lightning speed. And who could know when he would be released? Jasper would have wanted to hang on to their celebrity hostage as long as possible.

In fact, people in Jasper liked Dan. The *CBS Evening News* had broadcast from the city live on the night of King's conviction. I remember afterward how the prosecutor brought his wife over to get Dan's autograph. The sheriff and other town dignitaries wanted one, too. If they got Dan into jail, they would have had him signing books and jail admission slips until he had writer's cramp.

In my case, CBS had decided to fight the subpoena, and I wholeheartedly agreed, although I did feel a little like a sacrificial lamb. The case was hopeless, and a few weeks into our fight I was beginning to feel real fear that I would see more of the inside of the Jasper jail than I ever wanted to. By this time, Judge Golden had threatened me with a six-month minimum sentence for criminal contempt of court.

Every time Judge Golden ruled against us, we would go to a higher court and at the last minute get a reprieve. Then the process would start over. But the legal machinations meant every time I left home for court, left my husband and little boy for the three-hour drive to Jasper, I didn't know whether I'd be coming home. I knew that if this face-off continued, at some point Mama wouldn't be back for a while. It was unsettling and frustrating to feel so unfairly targeted for doing my job.

I remember visiting New York in the middle of all this and meeting with our executive producer, Jeff Fager, to talk about what was happening. Although he certainly saw and understood the free press issues being fought over in the case, he thought my entire dilemma was wildly hilarious. I think Jeff enjoyed watching some of the jams I got myself into. I remember confessing to him that I was really worried about going to jail. He erupted into laughter, saying, "My God, they're not going to put you in jail. Come on." He thought I was being silly.

The truth is, I wasn't just worried; I was scared shitless. In fact, I was so rattled by the tumultuous ups and downs of my case that I didn't even notice I was becoming terribly ill with a kind of respiratory infection. When I was called to the witness stand to be questioned by the prosecutor, I had lost my voice. I could only croak out my responses. I could just about clear a room with my tubercular appearance. I felt awful and looked worse.

When reporters asked me to comment on the case, I literally couldn't. That didn't stop anyone from shouting repeated questions outside the courthouse, of course. I wanted to tell them that they could find themselves in my position, that I was doing something they should be supportive of, but I didn't feel I could make some kind of stirring plea for freedom of the press when I sounded like the demon-possessed child in *The Exorcist*.

Besides, the CBS attorneys were telling me not to talk at all. They said I would just hurt my case. Because the law was so unhelpful, they were not pushing free press arguments as much as arguing that the court couldn't punish a corporate employee for a decision the corporation, based in another state, had made. That was the untested, undignified option we were trying to push, the only option that might work in Texas.

I hated being trailed in and out of the courthouse time and again during the weeks the fight went on, by a group of journalists and photographers who bellowed nonsensical "how does it feel?" kinds of questions. They waved notebooks in a bizarre ritual of reporting known as the "perp walk." I walked through the small clutches of jostling reporters, silently vowing I would never let this happen to me again.

I remember very clearly that finally, on the evening it was undeniable I was going to jail, a heavily made up local newswoman squawked at me, "What's it gonna feel like to sleep next to Shawn Berry tonight?"

Good Lord, lady, are you kidding me? I was newly sensitive to how awful it is to be in the center of that moving, squawking, shifting, and shuffling little gaggle that appears outside a courthouse whenever an interesting case is under way. It had been a long time since I'd had to do that kind of "reporting," and I swore anew I would never torment someone that way.

It was at this time that some thoughtful photographer took the world-class bad picture of me that was bandied about endlessly during the Bush National Guard fiasco. I was sicker than a dog, upset because I was going to jail, and madder than hell. No wonder I looked terrible. The picture captured a moment when I was being pursued by cameras and reporters just as I was about to be delivered by my attorneys to the jail where I had first met Shawn Berry. My eyes look small, my chin looks weak, my hair is a mess, and I look just plain scared. I was. My husband, Mark, a great mimic and relentless teaser, has tormented me for ages by doing a hilarious impression of it. We both stopped laughing when, years later, that bad photo became my public face because media outlets had it in their files. Still, it turned out to be a mixed blessing. That picture ensured that no one would recognize me on the street.

My legal battle in Jasper was resolved when CBS decided to make the entire interview public and put the written transcript up on its Web site. The prosecutor could download a copy and the whole world could see what we'd talked with Shawn Berry about. My notes and names of sources and the tape itself were preserved. That was the most I could have hoped for in this face-off.

I did end up spending several hours in jail, time I whiled away by chatting with the guards. It was humiliating to be fingerprinted, publicly answer questions about my personal health ("When *was* your last period?"), and watch as jail officials argued about whether I should have to change into an orange jumpsuit. In the end, I didn't have to, thank God. Very unflattering color for anyone.

My greatest discomfort that night was having to pose for a damned mug shot while I held up a slate of numbers underneath my face. I knew the photo would be in newspapers and on television. What kind of look was I supposed to have on my face? Should I smile? Frown? Look like I was making some kind of professional point? What if I blinked at the wrong time?

Mercifully, I didn't have time to think. The mug shot was taken with even less preparation and care than a driver's license photo. No wonder everyone in a mug shot looks like a nut.

My family was relieved when the whole ordeal was over. My husband was proud of me for refusing to cave in. My son had been thrilled to see me on television, though he had no idea what was going on. My mother was glad she could stop worrying herself sick. My four sisters had found the whole thing alternately frightening and amusing.

To commemorate my freedom, one sister had my official arrest photo printed on a coffee mug with the inscription "Mary's Mug" on the other side. What began as a date with a sheriff for coffee ended with a coffee cup. Perfect symmetry. My son likes us to use that one for special breakfasts in bed, like Mother's Day. He thinks it is particularly festive. What a typical journalists' kid.

At trial, Shawn Berry's life was spared. The jury gave him a forty-year sentence, apparently after seeing the same differences in his culpability that I did. The whole story offered a powerful lesson in the most fundamental question of character, knowing when to stand up and fight for someone else's life as though it were your own.

For me, the case offered difficult lessons on how fine the line is that separates reporters and the people we are reporting on. Never again would I assume I had the safe anonymity of a producer's job to protect me from having the cameras or the questions turn my way. Most reporters go their whole lives without having that kind of thing happen. I swore it would never happen to me again, but as it turns out, I haven't had much luck with that kind of resolution.

During his years in prison, Berry has met with relatives of Byrd's family and tried to make some kind of amends for the role he played in the horrible crime.

Then-governor Bush did not support a bill before the Texas legislature to crack down on hate crimes, citing the Jasper case as an example of how well the current system worked. All three defendants had been found guilty. Two of them were even going to be executed. What more could anyone want? Actually, the hang-up for Bush and Republican lawmakers reportedly was the bill's provision to establish gay Texans as being especially vulnerable to hate crimes.

There have been attempts to pass a shield law in Texas, none of them successful. This past year, such a bill was proposed, but it lost out to the state legislature's interest in other subjects, like banning overtly sexual cheerleading. I'm not kidding.

In the years since I fought to protect my notes in Jasper, reporters have continued to turn over notes, testify, and be forced to betray confidences. Most of the newspapers and broadcast entities in Texas know that when it comes to battling these kinds of cases, without new laws they are being forced to take a spoon to a knife fight. They're gonna lose.

After my ordeal, I was just worn out. I had already spent too much time in an uncomfortable limelight and I was not eager to go back to another high-stakes, controversial story. George Bush's bid for the presidency was months away and I decided to just let the Guard story go for a while.

I didn't pick up my work on the National Guard investigation again until the summer of 2000, when I started working full-time with Mike Smith, the young researcher in his early thirties I'd met the previous year. Mike had been the primary investigator on *First Son*, so he had a leg up on everyone else when it came to delving into Guard records. He'd been into the swamp already.

Mike is a unique guy, a visitor from the planet Austin, Texas. There his ponytail and his deceptively dazed and confused mannerisms fit right in. At first blush, Mike might seem like any other slacker to be found in Texas's capital city's political hip-hick circles. But he is much more than that. Mike knows the players on both sides of the aisle, and he knows the Lone Star political playbook as well as anyone I've met in Texas. He doesn't just know who's who in Democrat and Republican circles; he knows who used to be dating whom. He knows who has a drinking problem, who's been arrested, who's behind the latest round of rumors, and whether the rumors are likely true. He is a sort of Texas political Columbo, a disheveled low-key detective who won't stop until he gets the answer or gets the story.

Mike has a good sense of humor, an uncanny ability to tolerate outsize personalities and difficult egos, and he is a genuinely kind person with a solid moral compass. I decided to work with him anyway. Actually, I have always been lucky to work with Mike. He is as tenacious as I am.

In the summer of 2000, we began working together on a few stories, including a fascinating death penalty case in Georgia. But we also picked up my old notes and phone numbers from the National Guard story and began refocusing and retooling the work I'd done the previous year.

We would soon stumble across a new version of a formal Bush document I'd gotten my hands on previously. It raised a fascinating name in the then–presidential candidate's past.

In 1999, I'd gotten my first copy of Bush's formal suspension from flying issued by air force headquarters, dated September 1, 1972. I couldn't help but notice that another pilot, also from Bush's unit, had been suspended on the same day for the same reason: failure to have an annual physical. That seemed odd. The second pilot's name had been redacted or blacked out on the document. I was extremely curious about who this was. Perhaps there would turn out to be a connection between the two men.

So I employed a painstaking but effective old reporter trick for getting information out of the government. I kept filing repeated Freedom of Information requests in the hope that somewhere along the line, someone would forget to redact the second pilot's name.

That is exactly what eventually happened.

I received a number of new versions of the document, and one of them had the second pilot's name uncovered, there in black-and-white. He was James Reynolds Bath, a former air force pilot who joined the National Guard after completing his regular service. It wasn't Bath's military past that made him interesting, however. It was what happened after he left the Guard that raised all kinds of questions about his links with the Bush family and with big-money Middle Eastern oil interests.

In 1978, Bath, without much previous financial experience, became a shareholder and director of Houston's Main Bank. Fellow investors included former U.S. Treasury secretary John Connally and a Saudi banker by the name of Khalid bin Mahfouz, who would later become embroiled in a separate banking scandal.

Around the same time, Bath, again with no résumé to recommend him, became the Texas financial representative for the Bin Laden family. Yes, *that* Bin Laden family.

But in the summer of 2000, the Bin Laden family name was not yet synonymous with terrorism. Back then, it just meant money, big money.

I began trying to find links between Bush and Bath. It didn't take long to find that Bath had been one of the initial investors, offering up fifty thousand dollars to Arbusto, Bush's ill-fated start-up oil company.

I contacted Bill White, a former business partner of Bath's who had been engaged in a long-running court battle with his onetime friend. White and I only spoke briefly in 2000, but it was clear from court records, newspaper accounts, and word of mouth that if I wanted the goods on Bath, White was a good place to begin.

Mike and I began researching bank records and business arrangements that Bath had been involved in. There were already some written reports saying that Bath had CIA connections that traced back to the days when George H. W. Bush was running the agency. Bath adamantly denies any CIA connections. "I am not a member of the CIA or any other intelligence agency," he told *Time* magazine in 1991. The Bath connection was tangled and raised incredibly complicated questions about everything from Bath's dealings with offshore banks to his operation of a controversial airline leasing firm.

The Guard story itself was a simple and welcome relief from days spent trying to track down and unravel the ins and outs of Jim Bath's background.

I went back to my old phone friend Gen. Belasario Flores, who was even more outspoken than he had been the summer before. Flores had been nominated by the Texas governor to head the Air Guard in 1971.

Flores described his career to me as the first Hispanic head of the Air Guard as "stormy," saying he had to go "against the Establishment" time and again. He had been involved in a number of discrimination cases filed against the Guard by Hispanics.

That was only one of Flores's complaints about the organization. In a series of phone calls in that summer of 2000, he revealed his animosity toward the old-boy network that had dominated the Guard in the 1970s. And he went much further than he had before about George W. Bush's record.

It is important to remember that Flores was the man in charge of the Air Guard when Bush left for Alabama and didn't come back for more than a year. Flores had every reason to know what was going on with one of the most well-connected pilots in the 147th Fighter Squadron at Ellington, a man under his command.

I asked Flores what he thought the explanation was for Bush's failure to drill for so long. "In my opinion, it would be someone that just did not complete his obligation. I have no respect for someone who did not fulfill his obligation." Flores continued, "This is like buying medals and wearing 'em when you didn't earn them. This is fraud." Flores insisted there had to be more information and more records to dig up. "How the hell did he get an honorable discharge?"

Flores really got wound up talking about the supposed loss of Bush's records, saying that the explanation that part of Bush's record, the part explaining the gap in service, had vanished into thin air was just plain ridiculous. "I'm a military man. Have been since I was seventeen. It's incredible. There has got to be a paper trail somewhere. I've got pay records from thirty years ago."

On the subject of Bush's giving up his pilot's seat, Flores was adamant. Something had happened that wasn't noted in the records. He didn't buy the Bush campaign's explanation that the F-102 was being phased out: "A pilot is a pilot. They went from jets to tankers. Pilots have a very unique association. For a pilot to turn in his wings—unthinkable."

Flores told me he was about to remarry, wedding a close friend of his late wife, who had died several years before. He said he lived in a retirement home in San Antonio where the residents were "95 percent retired officers. I got some real good friends here. All pro-Bush." He said he would have to move if he did a 60 *Minutes* interview. Besides that, he joked, his new wife would kill him.

Flores was colorful and funny and smart. Maybe too smart to do an on-camera interview. Instead he invited my husband and me to his wedding. I've always wished I had been able to attend. We seriously talked about going.

One Saturday night in mid-September, I went to bed feeling confident about my work, happy with my family, and at peace with the world. My husband woke me up a few hours later and gave me the worst news I've ever heard. I had suffered a loss so grievous that I would spend the rest of the month, the rest of the year, and the rest of my life reliving and regretting that instant when everything changed.

Suddenly and unexpectedly, the center of my life gave way. Without warning, I lost my mother.

CHAPTER 7

A grown woman turned little girl again, I stood by my mother's casket. Just as I had when I was small, I adjusted Mom's necklace, stroked her soft hair, and smoothed her dress. I touched her skin, always so perfect, but this time so terribly cold.

She was gone. Irretrievably gone.

Her hands were clasped tightly and unnaturally on her lap. She never held her hands that way. I looked again. Nail polish? We had all given up so much so quickly in the last few days: to death, which gave no warning and showed no mercy, to the church that demanded from all of us countless internal compromises in her service, and now to the unstoppable train of small indignities that is the funeral industry. This felt like the last straw.

I told the professional griever running the funeral home that I hated the idea of someone painting my mother's nails as she lay helpless: "Take that stuff off. My mother never wore nail polish. She's not going out to dinner, for God's sake. She's going to heaven."

It occurred to me that my mother would have laughed out loud and approved of my outburst. She always approved of her daughters' laying out their feelings, speaking up, making their presence felt. She loved to chuckle at my lifetime of authority-challenging behavior. If she had been there, really been there, I could imagine her sitting up and telling the funeral home director, "Now, don't think badly of Mary. She really is a good girl." She spent my teenage years reciting this mantra time and again, until she believed it. Until I believed it.

My scolding of the man in charge was the kind of thing my mother reveled in and would have acted out herself if she hadn't been a minister's daughter raised in the Midwest, shaped in the depression, and shadowed by rigid ideas about how women were supposed to live their lives.

She might have had a life much like mine if she hadn't married and had five baby girls in ten years. If she'd had the chance to find herself through education and career. If the handsome young man she married hadn't disappeared into anger and alcoholism. Instead, her daughters got to be the women she might have been. And I was not going to waste her legacy.

I loved the way my mother loved my work. She was intensely interested in whatever I was doing, and I regaled her for years with stories of what happened behind the scenes, outside the script, and off-camera. When I went to cover the war against Iraq in 1991, she was as proud and as worried as any mother sending a soldier off to fight. She thought my job was just as important to the country.

She was pleased when my younger sister decided to work in television news, since Mom loved to talk about what was going on in the world. And she was happy that we both married men who worked in news. That meant two more knowledgeable people to add to our lively, irreverent, loud dinner table discussions.

Another one of my sisters is a writer, and the other two are as opinionated and passionate as the rest of us. My mother had always been eager to tell people she had five daughters. Five, just think. Appearing together when we were girls, we looked like a growth chart of the female body. When we grew up, we became a set of girlfriends for her, a staircase of younger women who could tease her, thrill her, make her laugh, and ultimately, I believe, make her proud.

She appreciated her daughters' lack of conformity, having decided long ago she didn't want to raise up women who were afraid to speak their minds, set the agenda, or push the envelope. Her only demand was that we be "good" people, that we do the right thing, that we care about something or someone other than ourselves, that we tell the truth, even when it was hard.

Above all else, she taught us to laugh at the hopeless and ridiculous circumstances life sometimes dealt. She gave us the priceless gift of teaching us to laugh at ourselves.

While others were put to sleep with bedtime stories, our mother recounted for us tales of brave little girls breaking the rules, people slipping on banana peels, and the lengthy dull church services of her childhood that seemed to have been regularly interrupted by snoring, fainting, or some other loud and hilarious human failing. She loved to laugh and so did her girls.

That day, as I stood beside her body, I missed her desperately, but I knew that she had died the way she lived, full steam ahead. On September 16, at the small farm where my mother was happiest, the home where she had raised her girls and welcomed her grandkids, she got up, cleaned the house, mowed the lawn, baked a pie . . . and died. Her heart had simply stopped.

For her daughters, the world stopped. The five of us, little girls going gray, most of us now with crow's-feet and kids, mortgages and marriages of our own, huddled together, all open wounds and raw nerves, to do the impossible: to say good-bye.

As hard as it was for us to accept, this was the ending she wrote for herself, the ending she wanted.

For me, my mother's death marked an abrupt end to my work on the George W. Bush National Guard story. My youngest sister, Peggy, five months into her first pregnancy when my mother died, lost the baby just days after the funeral. We'd all been so eager for our family to expand, eager to have a new life to celebrate. Now we were living tragedy upon tragedy and I felt pulled in many directions, everywhere except back to my job.

I wanted to be there for Peggy and for my other sisters. I wanted to be with my son and my husband. I wanted to make sure the family farm stayed in the family. In the meantime, there were other stories I could do that weren't so controversial or time-consuming as the Bush story. For the first time in my life, I felt fragile. I didn't think I could do it all or get through it all.

My mom had told me shortly before she died that when it came to my work, "Mary, you spend yourself so." I clung to that memory of her voice on the phone and for once, I took her advice without protest and without putting it off.

She and I had talked about the National Guard story at length, in part because my mother was a big fan of George W. Bush. She was a longtime Republican who thought the world of the elder Bushes, particularly Barbara Bush. My mom liked Mrs. Bush's sassiness and was eager to vote for a sassy woman's son. Mom liked his politics, which she viewed as fairly centrist, and his willingness to speak frankly about religion, which had been an important element in her own life.

As a child of World War II, however, she believed service to country was right behind service to God. As an adult who saw the inequities involving the draft during Vietnam, she understood how he might have been well-connected enough to ease his entry into the National Guard. She knew that his early and inadequately explained exit raised serious questions about the commitment he had shown his country. And her belief that he was the best man to be president didn't prevent her from asking questions or wanting answers. As a good Republican, my mom wanted the whole thing resolved, and if I was the one to help do that, so much the better.

It would be four years before I would once again give it a go, picking up where I left off, trying to finish the job. Seeing things through, no matter how difficult, was another one of my mother's strong points, one of the nuggets of advice she gave her girls about how to live life.

But for months I felt I was almost sleepwalking through work. Although I produced a number of good stories, nothing could divert me from my family obligations. I flew back and forth between Seattle and Dallas repeatedly, working at the farm and spending time with my sisters, then rushing home to be with Mark and Robert. My life was torn in two pieces, thousands of miles apart. Just keeping up with my family's needs was a full-time job on its own.

Then as we were bracing for the first anniversary of my mother's death, September 11 plunged the country into trauma. That day I was in Dallas, talking on the phone nonstop with my friends and colleagues in New York and Washington. I remember Dana Roberson calling me as she climbed into a car to go to the World Trade Center towers. As we talked, I updated her on what I was seeing on the air. Horrified, I saw the first tower come tumbling down. I passed this on to

Dana and begged her to be careful, sounding more like my mother than a news professional. Like all the other people at CBS in New York, the danger just made Dana drive faster to get there.

I was terrified for her and for all my colleagues who were working in a hellish and deadly atmosphere, trying to gather information as a great tragedy unfurled around them. It was a catastrophe that enveloped all Americans—no matter where we were physically—in a plume of smoke and dust and death.

I had to stay in Dallas for a few days, until flights were resumed, then caught the first plane out to New York. The three-and-a-half-hour flight, once so predictable and familiar, was now unforgettable. A woman seated next to me was going to be with her sister, who had lost her husband in the towers. There was raw fear among the passengers that something would go wrong on our flight as well, that in a heartbeat all of us and our airplane would be forced to reenact the gruesome scenes we'd been watching on television nonstop for days.

When we flew over the still-smoking Trade Center ruins, everyone crowded onto one side of the plane to see the great wound for themselves. It was awesome and terrifying, as though one of the city's limbs had been torn off. The place where the towers once stood was filled in our minds by the collective memory of what used to be. The black hole at Ground Zero was still flashing flames, still pouring dark smoke, still bleeding.

When the plane landed there was applause and the flight attendant's voice broke as she welcomed us to New York's LaGuardia Airport. People wept at the announcement. The mundane had become moving beyond words.

The city itself was haunting. Restaurants were empty, the streets were quiet, and a new and humbling concern for others permeated everyone's interactions. People at CBS were exhausted after days of nonstop work. Throughout it all, Dan had been the picture of calm for much of the country. Now he, too, was reaching the very limits of how long he could stay up, how much tragedy he could recount for the camera. The enormity of what had happened swept over all of us again . . . and then again. I recall feeling as though life would never be the same. In some ways, it never would.

The horrifically large attacks of September 11 were followed by the smaller-scale terror of the anthrax assaults. At CBS, we scrambled to understand and explain each new threat, taking crash courses in anthrax exposure, skin versus ingestion, plain powder versus weapons grade. When Tom Brokaw's NBC office was hit by anthrax, it came home to all of us as well. Dan Rather's lovely British assistant, Claire Fletcher, was diagnosed as having been exposed to anthrax, and we felt like the rest of the country, maybe a little more scared, more under siege, more vulnerable. Someone out there had tried to kill one of us.

My work focused on the war we all knew was coming. Dan wanted to be there, of course. And I wanted to go with him.

We made it to Kabul, Afghanistan, in November, before the United States had fully acknowledged the presence of large numbers of American troops there. Getting in was no small feat. We bounced around the Middle East and Central Asia for what felt like days, boarding plane after plane, hopping from one exotic place to another.

Finally, in Islamabad, Pakistan, we climbed aboard our last flight, to make the trek across the mountains to Baghram Air Base outside Kabul. I felt like it might be my last flight ever. The scruffy little UN plane seated only a handful. The windows frosted over on the inside as we crossed the great swath of saw-toothed mountains that fiercely guard Afghanistan. As we began being buffeted by high winds, I worried that we might end up crumpled on a snowy peak.

It was the kind of flight I hate and Dan loves. *CBS Evening News* executive producer Jim Murphy, another fearless flier, was with us. Jim is a good friend and a terrible teaser. He and Dan ribbed me mercilessly, reveling in my raw fear. They didn't get a chance to have me at their mercy like this very often, and I think they wanted to make the most of it.

Dan finally must have decided to take it easy on me. I think as I began to turn pale green he realized there could be distasteful physical repercussions for him and Jim if I truly got sick. I remember bumping along in the frigid air as Dan abruptly changed the subject and began regaling us with stories of what an impoverished hick he had been when he first came to New York. He'd hitchhiked there from Texas with no money and even less sophistication, and he confessed that he'd fled the Stork Club in shame after asking naïvely whether he'd have to pay for a coat check and getting barked at by the man working the door. We laughed at the ignorance and innocence of our youth.

Dan and I didn't know that our trip to Afghanistan would begin a process that brought another inexperienced young man to the wilds of urban America. We didn't know that this would be a journey that changed lives. At that point, I was only worried about my own.

When we reached the airspace over Baghram, our pilot told us he was going to approach in a fast spiral to offset the Taliban antiaircraft fire that was still being heard in the surrounding hills.

As we lost altitude, our windows cleared and we hurtled round and round, spinning toward earth. I saw flashes of broken and battered Russian planes, sprawling steel carcasses without wings or windows that were tossed like broken toys on the ground below. It was a fitting welcome to a wild place, a rustic reminder of the last superpower that had come here with big plans and high hopes.

I had already decided not to wear a head covering or a scarf, and for God's sake, I was not going to wear a burka. How could I get camera crews—or anyone, for that matter—to listen to me when I had my head in a blue sack? Still, I was a little nervous that walking around with my face and blond hair hanging out would create resentment.

In Saudi Arabia, during the first Gulf War, I hadn't worn a head covering, but then I had been switched twice by the self-important and self-righteous virtue and vice police, old men who carried bundles of raggedy sticks to wield on anyone they felt was breaking their strict interpretation of what constituted appropriate clothing or behavior.

The first time I was switched, it was for flaunting a portion of my brazenly naked wrist. It seemed my long sleeve didn't cover every single smidgen of skin down to my watch. About an inch of my lower arm was showing, something that apparently constituted a pornographic violation of their standards.

By the time I received my second switching, I seriously considered turning the tables on the rail-thin old goat of a man who had smacked me. I figured I could take him, but I knew it would probably be very bad for international relations if an American woman wrestled an old Saudi man to the ground and pulled his dress over his head. Instead, I held my temper, and frankly, I have often wished I'd let him have it.

As a woman, I didn't know what to expect in Afghanistan. How would I be treated? It's something men in news never have to deal with, and I envy them the freedom to just get off the plane and get to work without weighing the pros and cons of showing some kind of public supplication. I've never been any good at that, and the fact that in parts of the Muslim world it is exclusively gender-based galls me. Hopeless, irretrievable American thoughts, I know, but I just can't go along with debasing myself and playing dress up because someone believes that I and everyone like me are either beneath them or have to be protected from personal freedom.

When we landed, we were greeted by a group of men from the Northern Alliance. They were small and dark and their smiles of greeting flashed incredibly white teeth. I would soon learn that everyone in Afghanistan seems to have either beautiful teeth or no teeth at all. They are not a people who do things halfway.

The Northern Alliance welcome wagon looked as though they had just stepped off the battlefield, wearing camouflage jackets and the striking wool hats made popular by their slain leader Massoud. No one checked our passports or our identification; we were just bundled into a waiting minivan for the drive to Kabul. Talk about clearing customs quickly.

As we passed through the small village outside the airfield, a young boy came up and pressed his face to the outside of the passenger window where I was sitting. He looked directly at me, staring at first, then pounding on the window, then spontaneously breaking into a huge grin. This kid wasn't angry at me for not covering my head. He seemed thrilled. The world was finally coming to the aid of the people of Afghanistan, long abandoned and oppressed, for years ignored and under siege. The tragedy of September 11 had given birth to the Afghan Fourth of July.

We sped into Kabul through the empty plains that had once been fertile fields, past abandoned and burned tanks, past markers warning of live land mines, past empty freight containers, once used as hideouts for fighters and now taken over as homes for whole families.

When we got close to the city, I saw what looked like piles of filthy blue rags tossed onto the roadside. A thin, dark hand shakily extended from one of the piles, palm up. It was a woman, then another, and then another, each clad in wretched blue burkas, collapsed and begging beside the road, hoping someone in a passing car would toss them a coin or otherwise show some compassion.

Our driver explained casually that the beggars were war widows who had lost their husbands to the nonstop fighting of the past twenty-five years. With no one to help them and no way to work, begging was their only option.

We roared past, flinging dirt and tossing gravel in our wake, leaving the abandoned women literally in the dust. In Afghanistan, it seemed that around every corner there was always another beggar, or a child struggling with a broken bike, or an old man suffering some kind of paralysis dragging himself through the streets, or a whole family that showed signs of having suffered years of malnutrition. Kabul itself was as battered as its residents. Buildings there had been blown to bits, hit again and again: bombed first by the Russians, then by factional fighters, by warlords, by the Taliban, and then by the Americans.

War without end had created a skyline of windowless buildings that overlooked the city with blank eyes. Silent memorials to the futility and cruelty of constant war, they stared down on a people who had suffered too much, for too long.

Afghanistan ached with so much damage, so much loss, that one person's problems were quickly eclipsed by the next person's catastrophe. Individual tragedies were lost in a sea of despair, a world of overwhelming need.

We drove to the Intercontinental Hotel, built on a hillside overlooking the city. It may have been a beautiful building once, but now it looked like a gigantic shack that had been used for target practice. The sides were pockmarked with bullet holes; the windows were shattered; chunks of the building were missing. The trees around the hotel had gone without water or care, growing twisted and withered after decades of war.

When we checked in, the man at the dark and filthy front desk handed us a bucket. That was the toilet. There was no electricity and no water. No room keys were necessary. Most of the doors were damaged and could be opened with a stiff shove.

We marched up the stairs to where the CBS offices were set up. A generator was powering computers, and satellite phone lines linked us to the CBS system in New York. It was squalid, but it was our new home and we got a huge welcome from the other CBS people already there. It was always good to arrive in a war zone and see our friends

from previous wars, previous years waiting. There is an incredible camaraderie that comes from working in a situation like that, and there is
a mutual respect among those of us at CBS who have done it before
and are willing to do it again.

Standing outside our room that first day were our newly hired trans-
lators, already picked up at various businesses in Kabul to help us get
around and understand what was going on. They spoke varying degrees of English. One kid named Rafi had read and memorized the entire Oxford dictionary. The only problem was that his dictionary had
apparently been printed around 1937. He entertained us by constantly
using ancient phrases such as "shake a leg," "cut a rug," and "hunky-
dory." Money was "moola" or "jack." Coffee was "joe."

Rafi had waited years to have the chance to hone his English and
use those hip phrases, only to find that we Americans didn't necessarily
know what the hell he was talking about. We had to get his dictionary
to look up some of his more obscure slang references.

Another translator did not appear to speak English at all. He just
tried to understand what we were saying and then used hand signals to
communicate with us. It's amazing how well that can work in an emergency.

The best translator was a thin bearded young man named Wahid.
Only twenty-two years old, Wahid had been studying to be an engineer
until the incessant bombings, the lack of electricity, and the practical
educational limits at the University of Kabul caught up with him. He'd
gone to work for the Red Crescent, the Islamic version of the Red
Cross. That's where he was found and hired by a CBS staffer a few days
prior to our arrival.

Wahid's English was wonderful and I quickly nabbed him as the
person to work with us. He even had a great sense of humor.

When we arrived after thirty-six hours in the air, without any real
sleep for ages, we found that Dan had to immediately do an interview
with Abdullah Abdullah, then an up-and-coming member of the
Northern Alliance, who would eventually become part of the new
Afghan government. We dragged ourselves out to the location, completely beat from too little sleep, too much flying, and what felt like no
oxygen content in Afghanistan's high-altitude air.

Dan was so fatigued that he kept referring to Abdullah Abdullah as

Mohammed Mohammed. I was so fatigued, I only caught it about half the time. But Wahid was in stitches—there's a phrase that Rafi would appreciate—as Dan lurched through the interview, fighting valiantly to keep his eyes open and the interview subject's name straight. I have to admit I was of very little help.

When we finished, Dan got up and with great seriousness announced, "That's the worst goddamned interview I've ever done." Actually, it *had* been terrible. I don't even know what the poor man said to us or how we used it. Sometimes, just pushing on through fatigue is the hardest part of the job. Learning to laugh at your own imperfections may be the most important part of surviving in this work. By the end of the trip, after a number of good stories and lots of good work, even Dan was roaring with laughter over his jet-lagged interview style and the bewilderment it must have caused our poor victim.

For nearly two weeks, we spent every day with Wahid. His help was invaluable as we gathered interviews on what was happening in the city, how the Afghans were reacting to Americans, and what they thought of the ouster of the Taliban. He translated and did much more, giving directions, telling stories, pointing out good places to get beautiful or graphic shots, setting up interviews, and generally keeping us from inadvertently killing ourselves.

I remember vividly standing on the roof of a van in the teeming marketplace at the center of the city, overseeing a stand-up Dan was doing in the crowd below. A gang of young men decided to have some fun at our expense and started rocking the van violently. As the van swayed from side to side, I looked around at the throngs of people laughing and pushing the vehicle, and for the first time while I was there, I felt a twinge of fear that things might get out of control.

We couldn't get our shot if the camera wasn't held steady, and by now the van was being *heaved* back and forth. We weren't getting a darn thing done and I was really getting uncomfortable being tossed about standing above a not-entirely-friendly crowd. I looked beseechingly at Yusuf, our dark and surly older driver, who spoke no English. Actually, he rarely spoke at all, just grunted at us disapprovingly.

Now, Yusuf began shouting at the young men shoving the van. God only knows what he said, because it just seemed to escalate the situation. He then began attacking people around the van, tossing aside women and children in an effort to force the young men away. I saw him push to the ground a small child using battered old crutches. In desperation, I shouted at Yusuf to stop, but he didn't understand what I was saying.

Yusuf had made things much, much worse by acting like a wild animal. Truth be told, I think the old guy was horrified to be accompanying the kind of poorly behaved woman who would stand on top of a van, completely uncovered—no burka, no scarf, no sense of decency—in the first place. It was sort of the Islamic equivalent of standing naked on a ladder in the middle of Times Square and then complaining because you've attracted unwanted attention.

Wahid raced to the van and calmed things down, pulling Yusuf back into line and joking with the young men, ultimately getting them to back off long enough so that we could get our work done. It wasn't the first time he'd saved the day for us and it wouldn't be the last.

When we went back to Afghanistan in January, Wahid was once again waiting and he worked with us for weeks, facilitating our conversations and making sure we got access to anyone and everyone we needed for our stories for 60 *Minutes II.*

On our second trip, we examined the extensive Al Qaeda training camps that had been set up in Afghanistan and we did a profile of Hamid Karzai, a man none of us really expected to live long. I remember titling it "The Hardest Job in the World." Dana Roberson was with me this time and we came to count on Wahid's help and cheerful assistance.

Dan, Wahid, and I became close enough that by the time we were preparing to leave, Dan pulled me aside and we talked about whether Wahid would want to come to school in the United States. We both thought he was such a bright kid. It was sad to think of him staying there, his mind and his future at the mercy of politics, religion, and the rush of world events. Who knew what the future held for Afghanistan?

Wahid was thrilled at the prospect of college in America, and together the three of us forged an alliance that has outlasted the war, stretched beyond the boundaries of both of our countries, and made a difference in all of our lives. Dan and I were able to arrange for a large scholarship for Wahid at Southern Methodist University, a wonderful and incredibly generous school in Dallas. His grades were quite good, and his letters of recommendation were persuasive, if I do say so myself. My husband and I renovated the apartment above our garage. And in August 2002 Wahid arrived in the United States, exhausted, exhilarated, and ready to embark on the adventure of his life.

Wahid has now been here more than three years. This December, he'll be getting his master's in civil engineering with a grade point average that would make any parent proud. He wants to help rebuild his country and others ravaged by war and corruption. Wahid has even talked about getting a dual citizenship, an acknowledgment of his deep feelings for both his homeland and the country that has so warmly welcomed him and given him a world-class education.

He has given my family an education as well. My young son is now familiar with Muslim holy days, including Eid and Ramadan, which my son calls the starving holiday. He's never forgotten the time we had to hold Thanksgiving dinner until Wahid got the official word online that the sun had gone down and we could finally eat.

We've spent three Christmases with Wahid, each of which he proclaims as being his "best Christmas ever." Of course, that is also what he said about his first Christmas ever. We've cried together as a family watching It's a Wonderful Life, his favorite movie. And my husband and I have had a crash course in parenting a young man, spending more time talking about etiquette, dating, and sex with Wahid than we ever thought we would with a teenager before our son hit high school.

Dan spent tens of thousands of dollars on Wahid's tuition, something he is extremely reluctant to talk about. He has always said, "It isn't good work if you brag about it." Well, he may not tell, but I will. Dan's generosity and commitment changed a young man's life, and for that he should be endlessly praised. His behavior toward Wahid is a strong barometer of the kind of person Dan is. I consider myself lucky to have seen it, and it is important to me that other people know it. Dan Rather is, plain and simple, a good man.

Southern Methodist University was unfailingly open and encouraging, both before Wahid came and in the years since. He is the school's one and only Afghan student, and I think SMU is as proud of him as we are.

Sometimes, if we are lucky, we get an opportunity to change the world, one soul at a time. I feel so blessed that Dan and my husband

and I were able to seize the chance to make a difference in one life. If I never do anything else of consequence in the years I have left, I can always say that I did this. We saw a deserving person who needed help and we said yes.

It was an improbable, impulsive, and very American thing to do. I know that no one in Wahid's family will ever misjudge the character of this country. To them, the United States is a place of great promise and great kindness.

I wish there was a way to create this kind of bond with more young men and women in countries such as Afghanistan, Pakistan, and Iraq, where for too many poverty, limited education, and the lack of opportunity combine to create a dark hopelessness that often expresses itself in religious extremism. For some, it leads to hatred of the West, in part because people in those places believe we in America don't share with them, don't respect them, don't care about them. I only wish we could have helped more of the people we met live up to their potential.

Visiting refugee camps filled with war victims, and the world's far corners, where poverty is overpowering and people are lost, can be haunting. I will never forget some of the things I saw right after the first Gulf War.

A group of us drove across the border from Kuwait in small convoys, entering villages in southern Iraq that looked like movie sets for *The Flintstones*. They were demolished by bombing and forgotten by everyone else, their problems cruelly ignored by Saddam and plain overlooked by the Americans. At one village, a mob of children waited for the cars passing through. When we entered, they surrounded us, banging on the windows, crying out, and repeating endlessly the only word they seemed to know in English. "Milk," they chanted. "Milk." They were thin and hungry and alone. No adults were in sight. I assumed their parents had told them what to do and then waited inside their small stone homes watching. I hope their parents were there.

Twelve-year-old girls held up infants, some of them appearing to be only a few weeks old. The girls pushed the babies at our cars as we came through, shouting again and again. "Take the baby," they said. "Take the baby."

I cannot let go of the memory of driving straight through without stopping, rumbling past the group of dirty and anguished young faces, kids who were already without hope at the age of ten. We sat in air-conditioned comfort, with full stomachs and big salaries and the secure knowledge that we were going home to a place where the electricity worked and the water was pure and the grocery stores were open twenty-four hours a day. I don't know when I have felt so bad about my inability to help or so grateful to have been born in America. I still think about those babies now. They should be about sixteen years old, if they survived malnutrition, Saddam's barbarity, and all the bombing. I wonder if they are helping the American soldiers in Iraq or plotting against them. I wonder what kind of person I would be if I had grown up like that.

Memories of Afghanistan stay with me as well. I think about the people we met, about what has become of them: The young woman who marched into the beauty shop, lifted her burka, and announced to me, "I want job." Or the father and son who cooked for us at the house where we finally moved after a brief stay in one of the world's worst hotels. Their food, systematically and without fail, made everyone in the house sick, terribly sick. Our American bodies were unable to handle the unfiltered water and unsanitary food they'd been eating for years. But their carefully prepared and attractively laid out food was more than many in Afghanistan got to eat.

I wonder about the poor little man we all called Woodman. He had been hired after he stepped in front of a CBS car and got knocked down and half run over. My colleagues felt so guilty, they brought him to the CBS office and hired him to stock our woodpile and help keep our furnaces going to combat the brutal cold.

We also called him Advil in recognition of the lone English word he spoke. He would say "Advil" to us when he held his hand out, hoping to get another hit of pain reliever for his hurt leg. That was the only medical care he wanted and pretty much the only medical care available for such a slight injury when we first came to Afghanistan. The hospitals were too full of the most desperate cases.

I wonder, too, about how the country is doing. I hope I have a chance to go back. Wahid's mother and seven brothers and sisters are there. Perhaps someday we'll all make the trek together. I would love for my husband and son to see Afghanistan. It's the wildest place I've ever been, a world where the people are charming, the views are breathtaking, and the thin air is charged with great promise and absolute terror.

When we were leaving Afghanistan for the first time, I saw something that summed up the country perfectly. As we raced toward Baghram across the open plains bracketed on both sides by towering mountain ranges, I saw in the distance a huge animal racing toward the road. It was crossing the flats at lightning speed as though it were aiming itself like a missile right at our Jeep. It reached the road just as we were coming by, and we saw it was a massive wolf, something I'd never seen in the wild. It was much larger than any wolf I'd seen in captivity.

It crossed in front of us like a gigantic and ferocious runaway cast member from *Little Red Riding Hood*, its hair standing up on its back, making it look even larger. Its eyes were fixed directly into the windshield, into our eyes. Its mouth was pulled back in an awesome snarl. It was beautiful, terrifying, and inexplicable, a living, breathing metaphor for its homeland.

This face-off between a wolf and a wide-eyed group from the West seemed to symbolize the lack of trust, the fear, and the unfamiliarity that repeatedly keep one side of the world, one side of a war, from identifying with the other. The tragedy that such a lack of identification can lead to was the lesson I learned in spades from my next big story. Dan Rather and our team at CBS, along with a handful of profoundly disturbing pictures, broke wide open the dark tale of prison abuse at Abu Ghraib.

CHAPTER 8

Dan Rather, Dana Roberson, and I were first teamed up by Jeff Fager and Patti Hassler in the summer of 1998 as *60 Minutes II* was getting off the ground. In the months and years that followed, we became a true team, not just colleagues but good friends who enjoyed one another's company and knew we could count on one another's consistently fine work.

I was so proud to produce for Dan. Not only was he a great reporter, but he was a hard worker and, on and off the job, one of the kindest, most self-effacing people I've known. We developed a close working relationship and quickly became inseparable on our stories. We trusted each other.

Dana became like a sister to me. All right, more like a younger, prettier sister who happened to be African-American. Working with her was like working with a best friend. We'd stay up late, get up early, and drive ourselves into the ground trying to get a story just right. We also laughed ourselves sick on a regular basis. People in nearby offices regularly poked their heads into Dana's cubbyhole, long faced and serious, and asked, "What's so funny, you guys?" Our laughter was our way of saying we loved our work and we loved working with each other.

All three of us felt terribly lucky. And in 2003 we were in the middle of a great professional run.

In the spring, we had done a full hour on our Wednesday broadcast about the Apache helicopter pilots shot down in Iraq, getting first-ever interviews with both men. It was no small feat, because every news or-ganization in the country had been chasing the men trying to wheedle, cajole, or somehow finagle that exclusive sit-down talk.

In October, we made news again with the first videotape ever broad-cast of three American contractors being held hostage by communist guerrillas in Colombia.

By December, Dana, Dan, and I got our arms around a story so mind-boggling that even we could scarcely believe it.

Ever since Strom Thurmond's one hundredth birthday in Decem-ber 2002, Dana and I had been obsessed with tracking down the truth about a tale that had persisted not just for years but for generations. The legendary southern senator supposedly had fathered a child in his youth by a beautiful black woman who'd worked in his family's home. The rumors simmered in the black community in South Carolina for most of the twentieth century, through Thurmond's rise to the gover-nor's office, his elevation to the U.S. Senate, and the action for which he will be most remembered—his passionate and divisive filibuster against civil rights legislation.

While whites tended to dismiss the story because of Thurmond's his-tory as a segregationist, many African-Americans were convinced it was fact. They and their families knew firsthand the hypocritical truth about racism and what had really happened behind closed doors in many southern homes. After piecing together information from dozens of sources, we became convinced ourselves.

We talked with many people who claimed to know the daughter, whose maiden name was Essie Mae Washington. Many of them had ties with her going back to their days at South Carolina State College, an all-black school. We were told that after leaving school she had mar-ried a man with the last name of Williams and many of her old friends had lost touch with her.

I talked with Marilyn Thompson, then an investigative editor at *The Washington Post*, and Jack Bass, who together had written a biography of Thurmond that included information on his purported daughter. Thompson and Bass also believed the story to be true but had no luck in getting Strom's daughter to come out of hiding.

Marilyn Thompson and I talked a great deal about what arguments might be used to bring Essie Mae out into the open. To both of us, her story had become a kind of journalistic Holy Grail, something we believed but couldn't prove. Marilyn was taking a break from work but was generous enough to spend the time to share her information and insight with me. She had spoken with Essie Mae years earlier, and while Marilyn hadn't gotten a confirmation, she felt that there was hope that someday Essie Mae would tell the whole tale. I felt very lucky to have found a phone friend who believed in the story as much as I did.

Still, none of us had come up with proof. None of us had been able to persuade Essie Mae, then in her late seventies, to sit down and tell her story on the record.

By the time Thurmond died in June 2003, the year after he finally retired from the Senate, Dana and I had found Essie Mae Washington-Williams. We tracked her down through property records, and I spoke with her by phone. Within days of that call, Dana and I were sitting in a hot car outside her home in Los Angeles, trying to get up the nerve to knock on her door.

Mrs. Williams, a grandmother with a large extended family, lived quietly. One of her daughters and a grandson lived with her, and every one of her family members seemed very protective of their elegant, elderly matriarch.

When I'd called her at home, Mrs. Williams dismissed the Thurmond story without really denying it. "I don't want to discuss that," she said. "That's just a lot of loose talk that's been going around for years." Why had all the talk focused on her? She said she didn't know, but she was "not going to discuss it at all," certainly not with me.

Before she very politely hung up on me, she made one thing clear: We were *not* to come to her home. She wanted to be left alone.

She seemed so sweet, so warm and kind. That made it hard to disobey her, to disappoint her. But we had to. We were sorry to intrude, so terribly sorry, but Dana and I couldn't make any other choice. We were powerless in the face of such an incredible story. We became journalistic zombies. We simply could not stay away. We had to see her, talk with her, beg her to come forward.

So there we were on her quiet California street, surrounded by ranch-style homes with palm trees and tidy lawns. Curious neighbors watched our car with suspicion as we circled round and round and tried to figure out what to say when we went to the door. Some of the neighbors had seen us go by so many times that we finally waved, trying to look casual. To them, we must have appeared to be friendly, amateurish burglars casing the block.

In the backseat we had a floral arrangement so large and ornate, so carefully constructed, that it looked like an ancient Inca offering in a religious ceremony.

Dana and I didn't do this kind of thing very often. Our stories tended to focus more on issues than on individuals. But we also had to be able to persuade people to talk publicly, whether they were whistle-blowers or others with important and intimate stories to tell.

Unlike the morning shows, such as *Today* and *Good Morning America*, *60 Minutes* and *60 Minutes II* did not have teams of assistants called bookers who surrounded a story, got to know the principals, and reeled in big and little fish on a regular basis. Instead, CBS offered up a pair of sweaty-faced, well-meaning women with a genetic inability to take no for an answer. Oddly enough, sometimes that worked.

The flowers we brought were pretty typical in this kind of a situation, although ours were unusually elaborate. For television news producers, flowers had become something of a pagan ritual. You'll know you've become a big story when the flowers and producers start arriving. Fruit baskets are also a producer favorite. Touching notes and phone calls from a correspondent who's covering a story are also regular offerings.

Dan would only make those kinds of calls under duress, only when he had to. He would say, "You know I'm not any good at this." In actuality, it probably didn't matter what he said. Just hearing his voice on the phone is a big deal and helped make it clear that we were serious about getting the interview and treating the person's story with care.

In a competition where everyone goes after the same thing and only one team can finish first, it helps to be creative. Once, after I saw that every other producer on earth was sending a prospective interviewee flowers, I sent a tree. Well, it was a small tree. But I convinced myself I wasn't simply seeking favor with a more spectacular gift; I was trying to communicate something more lasting, something with more gravitas. It's amazing how well I could rationalize things when I was kissing up. By the way, the tree thing worked. We got the interview.

In the television news business, these exclusive interviews are called gets, the successful lassoing of a subject everyone else wants to snare. It could be Hillary Clinton's first interview after the impeachment hearings or a talk with Jessica Lynch, the wisp of a girl who for a short time became the country's most famous female soldier. It could be an interview with Gary Condit, Michael Jackson, or the runaway bride. Whoever it is, for a brief window of time that person will be pursued with a ferocity and single-mindedness not usually seen in polite society.

I can say this as a longtime news producer who has had her share of big gets: There is no lover so ardent or tender, no friend so true, no human being so helpful, as a producer trying to get an interview subject to say yes.

Except for a participant in make-out sessions in the backseat of a Chevy, no one will ever be so smothered in furtively whispered promises, so cradled in lustful embraces, so thoroughly seduced, as someone whose story has become important to television broadcasts. It is shameless, competitive, and sometimes hilarious. And Dana and I were almost as bad as our competition. I say "almost" because this is my book and I refuse to acknowledge that we behaved as inappropriately as others. But it might have been close.

At least we didn't get into a near hair-pulling slap fight the way two competing female television news producers supposedly did in the front yard of one of the Apache helicopter pilots. At least we weren't taken into custody by police for shrieking in the background of a competitor's live interview after losing out on the get.

But we used what we had and something many other broadcasts didn't: a years-long reputation for doing a story in a straightforward, dignified manner. We could promise our interview subjects a story that wouldn't include scary music or re-creations or the sensational touches other broadcasts employ. Some of the time that worked for us; some of the time that probably hurt us.

People tend to think of the media as monolithic, a group that moves as one, people with the same objectives and the same opinions who compete in a friendly, sporting manner. This is not the case. The media's harshest critics have nothing on actual members of the media when it comes to bashing reporting, complaining about a lack of fairness, or calling foul on one another's techniques when it comes to getting a story. That's part of what happened to us when other media criticized our Bush-Guard story.

In fact, there are divisions within the media and then within each of those groups. Television can be broken into prime-time magazine shows, morning shows, cable news, interview shows like Larry King's, and the evening news.

Print is another category with subcategories of its own. The five-hundred-pound gorillas include *The New York Times*, *The Washington Post*, and *USA Today*. Magazines make up another category, with *Vanity Fair*, *Newsweek*, and *Time*. Local daily newspapers are another separate group.

Print and television are frequently at odds, with people from each camp eyeing the other with suspicion. Print people tend to believe they are doing old-fashioned journalism the old-fashioned way, no bells and whistles, no heavy equipment, no vanity.

Television is often the bane of some print journalists, who disdain broadcasters as pretenders who sweep into a story, all hair and lip gloss and glamour, wielding cameras, exuding a specialized clout, pushing to the front to get the best pictures, and dangling tempting access to television celebrities as a way of luring in would-be interviews.

Some of those criticisms are based in fact. The American public, currently obsessed with fame, is more interested in talking to somebody they've watched on television than to a person they don't know working for a publication they probably don't read. The promise of a story presented with great depth is often not as appealing to interview subjects as a trip to New York and a chance to have their picture taken with someone their friends will recognize.

That may be a sad fact of American life, but it is a fact, and in television we took advantage of it.

This time, Dana and I were working without any real competition as we struggled to Mrs. Williams's door with our overdone basket of blossoms. We knocked and peeked gingerly through the foliage when a man answered. It was her grandson, Justin. We asked if Mrs. Williams was home, and he called out, "Grandma, are you here?" From a back room we heard a curt, "No." Uh-oh.

Justin asked why we were there and I found myself stumbling to explain what we were after. Dana wisely wasn't saying a word. I continued to blab. "Well, uh, some people, um, say that maybe, uh, your grandmother is the daughter of, um, someone famous," I stammered.

"Really, who's that?" he countered, seeming to enjoy our discomfort.

It suddenly seemed so ridiculous that I felt like laughing. "It's, um, someone in politics who, um, died recently," I said. My God, I sounded like a contestant on *What's My Line?*

I was acting like Justin didn't know. He was acting like he didn't know. But I didn't know whether he really didn't know and I didn't want to spill the beans on an old family secret. He kept pressing. I finally blurted out, "Well, you're not going to believe this, but your grandmother's father is supposedly Strom Thurmond."

The grandson's face registered no emotion. "Really? Hmm," he deadpanned. "I hadn't heard that."

That's when we knew, really knew, it was true. If someone had told me that Strom Thurmond was my relative, I would have fainted or fallen down. This young man had taken the incredible in stride, as though I had informed him the sky was blue. Of course it was. He knew it all along.

Dana and I limped away in defeat for the moment, only to come back again and then again over the next three days. We brought flowers; we sent food; we talked to Mrs. Williams on the phone; we begged. We were insufferable. One of Mrs. Williams's daughters, Wanda, finally caught us lurking outside the house and ran us off. Her mother was adamant. She was not going to talk.

Finally, completely deflated, I wrote Mrs. Williams a long letter and poured my heart out. I told her I just wanted to talk with her on the phone one more time and I would never bother her again. She called on my cell phone as Dana and I were driving aimlessly around Los Angeles feeling hopeless. This time, Essie Mae and I really talked. She was a former teacher and I pleaded with her to consider teaching the country an invaluable history lesson, to give her children their rightful place in southern political royalty. I told her she had a chance to change the world simply by using her clear, confident voice to speak up and to speak out. I flat out begged her—after all those decades—to take that opportunity. He was dead now. Hadn't she kept his secret long enough?

To my dismay, she started crying, quite softly. I felt like a thug. Mrs. Williams said she appreciated what I was saying, but she had to work this out with her family. "I have to tell my children and my grandchildren the whole truth before I tell anyone else," she said, and she had to be ready to face the inevitable fallout from revealing a seventy-year-old secret.

I hung up reluctantly after she promised to call me when she was ready. She made me promise to leave her alone. I knew this time I had to keep that promise.

Dana and I had to go back to Dan and our bosses in New York and report that our entreaties hadn't worked. In a way, it wasn't the problem it might have been because I wondered if Jeff Fager, our executive producer, really believed in the story in the first place. I had the strange feeling that he thought Dana and I were chasing some kind of fantasy that he would indulge for a while, hoping we came out the other side, sane once again.

Whenever Jeff asked me how the story was coming along, there was something in his voice that made me feel he might as well be asking about our exclusive space alien invasion report. How were we doing with our search for a real-live mermaid? Strom Thurmond has a biracial daughter? Come *on*.

It would be months before I heard from Mrs. Williams again. My phone rang late on a Friday night in mid-December. It was Marilyn Thompson from *The Washington Post*. "Essie Mae is talking," she said. "I just did an interview with her and she wants to do her first television interview with you." I was thrilled for Marilyn. She had a much longer history on the story than we had. I knew what it felt like to chase something for years and finally get it.

The first on-camera interview was nothing to sneeze at. I called Mrs. Williams and we agreed to do the interview right away. Dana and I made the countless arrangements to make sure that Dan got there, that camera crews were lined up, that our location was big enough for all of our gear. I began writing questions for Dan. That's typically what a producer does, but in this case it was even more important. I had spent a fair amount of time talking with Mrs. Williams. With our extensive background on the story, Dana and I tried to come up with good questions that covered all the bases.

Our interview was set for Sunday afternoon. We all planned to fly to Los Angeles early Sunday morning, taking advantage of the time-zone difference to stay at home as long as possible.

When I got up and started packing, though, I turned on the TV and saw my carefully laid plans go up in smoke. Saddam Hussein had been found and captured in Iraq. Dan was on the CBS set in New York anchoring the network's coverage and he would have to be there all day. I had to come up with Plan B.

I asked Mrs. Williams to fly to New York that day. Luckily, she was understanding and agreed to change her plans for us quickly. We did the interview the next day, and although her story broke in the shadow of a tyrant's capture, Essie Mae captured the nation's attention and became a focus of conversation for weeks.

Essie Mae Washington-Williams coming forward did just what we had imagined. Seeing her, hearing her talk about the secret relationship she had with her father, was bittersweet. Any man should have been proud to present her as his daughter. The fact that Thurmond wouldn't do that but would help her financially was sad. Their life of devotion and denial was a metaphor for the long American history of hidden interracial relationships, the intertwining of family trees unacknowledged for generations. Talking about it openly, admitting that we all, black or white, are literally "family" couldn't be more important to us as a country.

Our story on Essie Mae ran on December 17. For Dana, Dan, and me, it was the perfect Christmas gift. We were at the annual *60 Minutes* holiday party the next night, and I remember it as one of the happiest nights of my professional life. We were roundly congratulated on our work and full of hope about what the new year would bring.

The big blowout was held on a CBS soundstage on West Fifty-seventh, so none of us had to go far from work to get to the party. There was a jazz band, great food, and so many familiar faces. I recall spilling wine on Victor Neufeld, getting a huge hug from Jeff Fager, and having my first real conversation with Josh Howard, who was going to be my new boss when Jeff moved to the Sunday show. Dan and his wife, Jean, were there, both of them beaming. There was nothing like the afterglow of a good story. Dana and I danced with the maintenance men, ate too much, and drank just enough to get silly but not so much that our names joined the long list of 60 Minutes staffers who live in Christmas party infamy.

The revelation that Essie Mae was Strom Thurmond's secret daughter was nearly a perfect story, a stunning revelation that also led us to think deeply about important issues. That is not always the case in stories that are the focus of great competition.

I remember precisely when I realized that things in the news business had changed for the worse.

In March 1998, just before going to 60 Minutes II, I was still working on the CBS Evening News. Correspondent Bob McNamara and I, along with a small team of photographers, editors, and technical people, were sent to Jonesboro, Arkansas, to cover another in a series of horrific school shootings.

Mitchell Johnson, thirteen, and Andrew Golden, eleven, had amassed an arsenal and hid their weapons in a stand of trees outside their middle school. Then the boys pulled the fire alarm. As students and staff poured outside, the two boys began shooting, ultimately killing four children and one teacher.

There was videotape of the immediate aftermath, wrenching images that were hard to watch. Desperate parents ran into the school looking for their children. Some emerged hysterical after hearing that their little boy or girl had been hit and was dead or badly injured. To be the parent of a victim—or the parent of one of the shooters—was awful beyond comprehension.

Overnight, Jonesboro became a magnet for the media. The school where the shooting took place was circled by outsize satellite trucks. The city's restaurants were overrun with reporters. There didn't seem to be a street corner or a city building, a church or a shopping mall, without a camera.

The media were no longer covering the story; we were smothering it. The networks, twenty-four-hour cable news, local stations, prime-time programs, morning shows, talk shows, radio, newspapers, magazines, hangers-on, gawkers, police geeks, and, last but not least, reporters who covered the media. We all joined the moving circus that traveled from one end of the country to another, one crisis to another. Jonesboro was the latest stop on an endless itinerary. The main characters in this story were red-hot right now. They would soon be replaced by new characters, a new story line, a new headline.

In Jonesboro, I saw that this saturation coverage was beginning to change the people who were part of the story and, ultimately, change the story itself. Soon after the shooting, everyone in the media was interested in talking with the parents of the children who pulled the triggers. Tragically but routinely, we'd all covered victims countless times. That had become an unavoidable aspect of news coverage.

Now another dimension was becoming standard in the attempts to tease and tempt viewers into our respective tents. We all began competing to tell the stories of the perpetrators. In Arkansas, that meant getting access to the parents of the two boys. Mitchell Johnson's father made it easy. He checked into the hotel where most of the reporters were staying. A long-distance trucker, Scott Johnson wore his dark hair in a loose ponytail. He appeared regularly in the lobby, resembling an unlikely movie star surrounded by news producers, each vying for a promise that Johnson would do their program first.

I heard that Johnson had agreed to do the *Today* show, but so far he hadn't been on. As a producer for an evening newscast I could not compete with what a high-budget morning show offered: a flight to New York, a night or two in a fancy hotel, a chance to be interviewed by a news star/host. But even if Johnson had already made a deal, it couldn't hurt to ask him. That morning in a motel restaurant, I gave it a go.

Scott Johnson was seated with several other family members, eating breakfast. A lit cigarette smoldered right beside his bacon and eggs as I walked up to the table. "I'm sorry for intruding," I began. "My name is Mary Mapes and I'm a producer for the *CBS Evening News*. I'd like to talk with you about doing an interview. I know this is a hard time for your family, but I'm really hoping that . . ."

He cut me off in midsentence. "I've already decided what I'm going to do," he said.

I knew it. He was going with the *Today* show. Still, I pressed on. "Would you mind telling me who you're going to talk with?"

"I'm going with NBC," he said.

I had to know. "Do you mind if I ask why you made that decision?"

He turned to me and said two words flatly: "Market share."

I must have looked at him as if I'd never heard the term. I'd just never heard it from someone who ought to have more important things on his mind.

Johnson went on. "They've got the best ratings in the top ten cities and the most coverage nationwide."

I was flabbergasted. This guy's kid had just killed five people and he seemed to be calculating how he could get the most coverage, the biggest audience to watch him discuss the murders. I was simply stunned.

It had come to this. Someone caught up in tragedy in a tiny corner of Arkansas was gauging market share like a media mogul instead of a man in the midst of a nightmare.

But I also had to examine my own role in what felt more than ever like a news carnival. We were all playing the same game, tripping through a house of mirrors, even if some of us thought we were above participating in the sideshows.

Nonstop media saturation was soaking the country to the point of drowning in celebrity culture, sensationalism, and cynicism. I left the table feeling like I didn't want to do this anymore. I didn't want to spend my life putting attention-seeking people on television. I didn't want to fight over interviews with next-door neighbors who knew next to nothing about the quiet man they lived beside who one day blew up a building or murdered a child or started shooting at a shopping mall. I didn't want to be part of the freak-of-the-week show. If this was where television news was going, it was going to go there without me.

I wasn't sure what I might do instead, but I was relieved to get a call a few months later from Jeff Fager, my former *Evening News* executive producer, who was setting up a new weekday edition of *60 Minutes*.

Like most of America, I believed that the *60 Minutes* franchise was different from anything else on television. The tradition of excellent reporting, the freedom to spend time on projects, the chance to do real investigations—all of those elements were important to me.

It was under Jeff Fager and Patti Hassler on *60 Minutes II* that I would do my best work, including breaking a story that is still reverberating more than a year and a half after it aired. Dana, Dan, and I were the first to report the incidents of prisoner abuse at Abu Ghraib, the Iraqi gulag turned American-run prison. We were the first to get the pictures that shocked the world. And we were the first to show that soldiers stationed there were operating under a deeply flawed and chaotic command system, where no one seemed willing to take responsibility.

In February 2004, the three of us had just finished a story on the Green River Killer, the country's most prolific murderer. Ironically, it was a story I had first covered when I worked in television news in Seattle more than twenty years earlier. It had taken that long for police to catch up with and convict Gary Ridgway, a sexual sadist who had terrorized the Northwest for years, methodically killing close to fifty women and abandoning their bodies in clusters throughout the region.

After his arrest, Ridgway spent months taping interviews with police and we used the tapes to look inside the case and the killer. Ridgway wasn't terrifying in appearance. His public behavior did not seem aberrant. If anything, he seemed a little slow. But as Tom Jensen, the detective who worked the case longer than anyone else, put it, Ridgway "was a serial killing savant."

Watching hours and hours of tape-recorded conversations with this guy was awful. He detailed the killings, the things he had done with the bodies, how little regard he had for the women, the way he had unceremoniously dumped them as though they were trash.

Those of us working on the story felt like we needed a shower at the end of each day, maybe even an exorcism. As we wrapped up our serial killer saga, Dana got a phone call that altered our focus for months and part of the country's for much longer.

Dana and I have made a habit of staying in touch with people we've dealt with on previous stories and with whom we've developed strong connections. Sometimes they'll call for old time's sake, sometimes because they come up with interesting tidbits that can help us on another story down the road. Sometimes we'd call them to see what was up.

That was the case with this particular person, a very unlikely outlet for information having to do with the military. We never could have guessed this source would come up with something so startling, but because of happenstance and geography, this individual had a nugget of information that helped us get launched on a momentous story. What we uncovered led to Senate hearings and a number of official investigations, raising serious questions about American policy regarding prisoners of war, questions that stretched from the abuse of detainees in Iraq, to the deaths of men in custody in Afghanistan, to the questionable practices developed at Guantánamo Bay for prying information from captives.

Here was our original tip: American military officials were investigating reports of abuse at Abu Ghraib. We were told that a number of U.S. soldiers were involved and that an extensive collection of photographs, taken by the soldiers, was part of the investigation.

We were not told who the soldiers were, where they were from, or what they had done. All we knew was that the unit had already come back from Iraq and the soldiers under investigation were left behind in Baghdad.

We knew we could not call the Pentagon with questions because that would sound the red alert and likely end our chances of getting the story. So we turned to old-fashioned, tried-and-true techniques to get the answers we needed. We found there had been a short, generally worded Department of Defense announcement made in Iraq about soldiers under investigation for problems at Abu Ghraib. There were virtually no details given on the case, which was characterized as an ongoing disciplinary action.

With my less-skilled assistance, Roger Charles, our military consultant, set out to find which units had been at Abu Ghraib and when they had been there. We tried to triangulate our information based on dates of duty, types of duty, and which units had already made it home. We came up with several possibilities and began checking units' Web sites to get the names of soldiers we could try to call.

Whenever we talked to individual soldiers, we kept running into walls. Some people would admit to having heard about the case, but they insisted they didn't know who was involved or what had happened. No one seemed to know anything about photos. We kept on, leaving in our wake dozens of confused people who had just happened to answer the phone when we called and were rewarded by being asked a series of nosy and open-ended questions.

In the meantime, we developed a group of sources in another part of the world. Dana and I flew to meet with them, and we flew back the next day, mind-numbingly jet-lagged but happy with our new information. Our sources didn't have pictures, but they did have more details that helped us get closer to the truth.

In addition to this, a man I had befriended reported having had an off-the-record conversation with a judge advocate general, someone who functioned as a prosecutor in military cases. The JAG told my friend that he was familiar with the case but couldn't comment on it one way or another. My friend said that this was a very strong sign that our tip was true, but that the Pentagon was keeping information about this case very close.

In his spare time (not that he had any), Roger worked with Col. David Hackworth on his advocacy Web site, Soldiers for the Truth. Hackworth, a legendary warrior who pulled repeated tours of duty in Vietnam, used his site as an information clearinghouse for military men and women of all ranks and for their families. The site advocated a number of changes in Pentagon policy regarding the war, usually on issues such as up-armoring of military vehicles in Iraq. In return, SFTT received countless e-mail messages of support and chunks of raw information from soldiers in the field, their families, and sometimes people inside the Pentagon.

I wondered aloud if we might use the Web site in a slightly different way. Why not use what information we had to put out an Internet alert on the Abu Ghraib case? I hoped someone, perhaps a friend or relative of one of the soldiers being investigated, would respond.

That's what we did and that's how we broke the story.

Before we put the message out, we believed that the soldiers facing court-martial might be with the 320th Military Police Battalion out of Ashley, Pennsylvania. We were wrong about that but right about our strategy.

We posted a message asking that anyone with information about soldiers in the 320th facing court-martial contact us. Within hours of our posting our alert on March 23, Roger got an e-mail from a man named Bill Lawson. He was the uncle of one of the men being held in preparation for a court-martial.

Lawson wrote that his nephew Chip Frederick was not from the 320th MP Battalion but had been kept behind in Baghdad for investigation in an abuse case. Lawson left a phone number where he could be reached. Roger called Lawson back so fast his fingers nearly burst into flames.

Roger listened to details of Chip Frederick's case and then asked the big questions: Had Lawson heard anything about photographs?

Lawson said that Frederick had acknowledged that pictures were part of the evidence against him. "Chip says that he is in only one of the pictures," Lawson told Roger. "I just hope he's not smiling."

Roger was exultant when he called me. We had found our opening into the story. Now all we had to do was figure out a way to prepare a report that so far had no interviews, little information, no pictures, and no proof. No problem. We would just keep working.

Lawson told us that Chip Frederick called home every day, sometimes at odd hours because of the time difference. Frederick was also under a kind of military house arrest, limited in where he could go and what he could do. He did have intermittent access to e-mail and the telephone. We told Lawson we desperately wanted to interview Frederick by phone or online. We said we could be ready anytime or anyplace and he promised to ask about it when his nephew called that night.

I remember, when I passed that message on to Lawson, I thought to myself it wasn't entirely true that we could be ready anytime or anyplace. At that moment, I didn't know where Dan was, only that he had just returned from Iraq.

Dan's trip there in early March would turn out to be a godsend. Even though we didn't know all the details of the story at the time, Dan was already working on it. He was able to go to the Abu Ghraib prison and interview some of the people standing outside wailing and waiting for relatives. They held up tiny black-and-white pictures of the men they said were being held inside. Others spoke darkly of terrible things going on behind the prison walls. It was a poignant scene we would add to the story later when we dug up the details of what had happened at Abu Ghraib.

For Bill Lawson, our interest in his nephew's situation was good news. He had been looking for help when he saw our e-mail. Lawson had written his congressional representatives and even Bill O'Reilly, trying to get someone to pay attention to the investigation. No one responded.

Lawson believed, with good reason, that the military would prefer to flush away underlings such as his nephew and the others who faced courts-martial. He believed the Pentagon did not want the case to receive any public scrutiny. He was right.

Abu Ghraib would be a black eye for a military program in the middle of a war. Not only would it hurt this country's image in the Arab world;

it also hurt the military's image in this country at a delicate time. The Pentagon would have preferred that the case be settled in complete privacy, without any coverage of the court-martial proceedings. No one at the top of the military wanted scrutiny of the higher-ups who Lawson believed were responsible for what had happened. Most of all, the Pentagon did not want anybody to see those damned pictures.

In late March, we felt we were still a long way from getting the pictures. But in the weeks past, we had been given graphic descriptions of the photos by a handful of people who had seen them or were familiar with what they contained. We could hardly believe what we were hearing. I have to confess that I was shocked at the thought of American soldiers doing the things they were supposedly doing in the photographs: making inmates masturbate, grinning beside a dead body, stacking naked Iraqi inmates in a pyramid, attaching electrical wires to an inmate. It was horrifying.

Through Bill Lawson and Chip Frederick, the details of the case began to become clear. We got the names of the others who were facing charges and began to hear the first rumblings of what would become their defense, that they had been told to do these things by higher-ups or individuals working with outside agencies, ranging from CIA agents to civilian contractors hired by the Pentagon to help with interrogations.

I talked with Chip's wife, Martha, who was an unshakable supporter of her husband. The warden at the U.S. prison where Chip had worked spoke of his employee in glowing terms. It seemed clear that something had happened in Iraq either to change Chip Frederick or to convince him that the usual rules of human interaction did not apply.

I was eager to get him on the phone myself and see what I could find out.

That finally happened on March 25. Lawson made arrangements with Chip for him to call Dan's home number in Austin at a specified hour, which would give me just enough time to make it there from Dallas and allow a cameraman to get there and set up to record a phone interview, which requires wiring the phone.

Everything seemed to be going smoothly by the time I got on the plane that morning. I floated along at thirty thousand feet, confident that we were on the verge of finally getting this all-important interview and nailing this story.

But somehow, when I was in the air, it seemed my carefully laid plans began to fall apart. When I landed I had sixteen phone messages. I remember seeing that number on my cell phone and not even wanting to know what was going on. Nothing good ever came from sixteen phone messages.

There was one from Mark saying that Chip had called my home number by mistake. One from Dan saying the cameraman wasn't there yet. Another from Bill Lawson asking how the interview had gone. Another one from Mark saying that Chip Frederick's wife had called wanting Dan's number. A message from Roger offering another tidbit of information that we could use in the interview. One from the woman who had set up the cameraman, saying he would be late. Another from Dan saying the cameraman wasn't there yet. Oh, my God! There was one from Chip Frederick in Baghdad saying he hoped this was the right number. He was supposed to be calling Dan's home number! Another from Chip's wife saying he had called the wrong number. Another from Dan reminding me that he was going to do his own makeup even though he was still recovering from cancer surgery on his nose. Uh-oh. Another from Mark saying that he hoped everything was going all right and did I need him to pick Robert up from school that day. And on and on.

I threw myself into a cab for the long drive to Dan's, working the phone like a maniac all the way. Jean Rather, ever the picture of calm, met me at the door. I was happy to see her. For whatever reason, Jean always carries with her the illusion that everything is under control. I needed some of that.

In fact, our catastrophes began slowly working themselves out once most of us were in one place. As soon as the camera setup was ready, the phone rang. It was Chip Frederick calling from Baghdad. Maybe this was going to work after all.

Dan did a great job with the interview, using this one-time-only opportunity not just to get Chip Frederick's side of the story but also to gather as much information as possible on the other people involved and where the military was with its investigation, and to garner some insight into exactly what had gone on over there.

Frederick told us that one Iraqi prisoner had died after being questioned by a group from "an outside agency." He said he wasn't sure who these men were working for, but he thought it was the CIA, the FBI, or the Defense Intelligence Agency. Getting information on any of those kinds of operations would be virtually impossible. But knowing that an agency of that type was involved in questioning detainees was crucial.

Frederick painted a picture of a prison that was understaffed and out of control. Handfuls of poorly trained guards oversaw thousands of detainees amid constant mortar attacks from outside the prison and assaults by inmates themselves. He said the Iraqis hired by the U.S. military to help with the inmates smuggled in weapons and drugs and carried messages back and forth between the men in prison. He said that Brig. Gen. Janet Karpinski ran a loose and chaotic ship, not even posting the Geneva Convention rules in the prison. He said she did not make any visits to cell block "A," where he worked and where the worst abuses took place. He said the general appeared to have little or no interest in overseeing day-to-day operations of the facility.

Frederick told us that the inmate who died during questioning was removed from the prison through a ruse. He said the body was wrapped in plastic and packed in ice shortly after death and stored in a shower stall until guards were ready to remove the dead man. Before he was taken out of the cell block, according to Frederick, various soldiers posed with the body, grinning and giving "thumbs-up" for the camera. When the picture-taking fun was over, they brainstormed a plan for getting the body out without causing a riot among the angry detainees.

To keep inmates from suspecting a death, Frederick said, the guards placed the dead body on a gurney and tucked a blanket around it, then put IVs in the dead man's arms and pretended to be giving the man CPR as they rolled him past the cells that held other prisoners.

Frederick recited a litany of grotesque situations at Abu Ghraib, stories that eventually would be told and retold in the press, in Senate hearings, and ultimately in a military court. His greatest concern at the prison appeared to be his own safety. The guards had reason to be fearful. Frederick recounted that he had been the target of gunfire from *inside* the cells. Now, that's a problem in a prison. He said some of the detainees appeared to suffer severe mental illness but had received no medication.

He was candid about some of the tactics the guards used with the inmates, admitting to us that dogs were brought into interrogations because the detainees were afraid of the animals. He said that interrogators from outside agencies had encouraged the guards, who had little or no training in handling detainees, to "soften them up" prior to questioning. He said his fellow guards had complained to General Karpinski and her staff about problems at the prison and repeatedly asked for procedures and guidelines for how they were supposed to handle prisoners. Frederick said none of their questions or complaints was ever answered.

Frederick told us that the military investigation into abuses began when a soldier by the name of Joseph Darby turned over a computer disk full of incriminating photos to an officer. The pictures included shots of naked hooded detainees piled into pyramids and detainees masturbating while Americans mugged for the camera next to them. Frederick admitted that a picture of him sitting on a detainee was part of the cache confiscated by the military. He told us that one picture showed a detainee with wires hooked up to him standing on a box and that the detainee had been told that if he fell off the box, he would be electrocuted.

When our interview finally ended, Dan and I knew we had an important, volatile story, a story that would shake America's understanding of the war in Iraq and raise questions around the world about how Americans were treating the people they were taking into custody.

Dan and I went out to lunch and talked soberly about the fallout of running a story like this. In my experience, there is usually a moment like that in every big story. Before the news breaks, before the world knows what you have been working on, you can sit quietly and talk about the consequences of going forward. It is a necessary gut check that Dan and I had gone through together with some frequency. We knew this was a big story. We knew there would be a big reaction.

Both of us knew that reporting this could and probably would mean harsh criticism of us for raising issues concerned with the welfare of Iraqis rather than the welfare of our own soldiers. As always, as the face on the report, Dan would bear the lion's share of any backlash.

I know few people as fervent as Dan when it comes to honoring the sacrifice and dedication of the men and women who wear American uniforms and risk their lives for those of us lucky enough to be able to merely watch war from the sidelines. Neither Dan nor I wanted to criticize our soldiers unnecessarily. But there are rules in war, rules that Americans want to follow, rules that are in place for our own protection. Rules that ensure that our soldiers won't be treated badly if they are taken into custody. For these reasons and many others, as journalists, we had to keep going.

And we did. Through hard work and the cooperation of countless people inside and outside the military, we were able to track down good information on what had happened at Abu Ghraib. Eventually, I was holding the pictures in my hands.

I got about a dozen photos on Friday, April 9. In Dana's tiny office in New York, we sat grimly and looked at picture after picture. Dan came rushing in from across the street and the three of us huddled around the desk, flipping through the photographs silently. Jeff Fager and Patti Hassler came to Dana's office to see the pictures and had the same reaction we did. They just stared.

No one said a word. We were speechless.

I had known the pictures were going to be bad. We had heard them described in excruciating detail. But when I actually saw them, I remember feeling sick. I hated to see Americans behaving in ways that can only be described as villainous and bullying. Our story would trigger debate over whether any of the Abu Ghraib offenses constituted actual torture. In a sense, that's a rhetorical game. Whatever this was, it was terribly wrong. It had to be exposed and it had to stop.

I remember thinking that any of these young men, wearing hoods, powerless to refuse the demands of their captors, deeply ashamed of what had happened to them, could be someone like my surrogate son, Wahid. They could be good kids. Our sources were telling us that many of the detainees at Abu Ghraib were often imprisoned for little more than driving through the wrong place at the wrong time. They could be young men guilty of nothing more than being caught in a country at war. Even if they were guilty of fighting the Americans, that justification was no cause for this sick mistreatment of inmates.

Our job was to get our story together and get it out and make sure that this abuse stopped.

I began looking for people who could comment on what these pictures represented. My first thought was that Sen. John McCain would be ideal. As a former soldier and a former prisoner of war, McCain could offer invaluable insight. I contacted his office and talked repeatedly to his aides, telling them what we had and how I hoped the senator could help us. In the end, they told me he was going to stay out of this one. This was an ugly story and there was no upside in volunteering to be part of it.

We were able to call on former covert CIA field agent Bob Baer and retired marine lieutenant colonel Bill Cowan, who'd had extensive experience in Special Operations. I'd worked with both of them on previous stories and knew I could count on them to be candid and thoughtful.

We showed them the pictures and then listened as the two men, veterans of both bloody wars and the difficult business of intelligence gathering, including field interrogations of prisoners of war and covert sources, poured out their disgust and heartbreak at what they saw in the photographs.

Baer said it was particularly bad that this had happened at Abu Ghraib, once the grisly centerpiece in Saddam's reign of terror, a place where Iraqis were tortured and killed for decades.

Cowan told us that his son, who had been fighting in Iraq for months, stood a good chance of paying for this kind of ignorant and illegal behavior, that every American soldier would, in one way or another, pay for the rage and despair that this kind of abuse created.

We were still looking for interview subjects who might know something about this story, so Roger called his longtime acquaintance Seymour Hersh to ask if the famed investigative reporter had come across any information about Abu Ghraib. Hersh told Roger he hadn't heard anything about the American-run prison in Iraq but said he was working on a story that involved secret prisons run by the CIA. Roger and I believe this was the first time Hersh heard about the abuse at Abu Ghraib. It would be ironic if we provided the tip that propelled him to work on the story, because in the end, Hersh would become our greatest competitor. Even though we put our story on the air the week before his piece ran in *The New Yorker*, he has been given credit by many for breaking the story of Abu Ghraib. I guess I have no one but myself to thank.

Once our interviews were completed, I began working on the script. At the same time, I finally contacted the Pentagon and told them what we had. I hadn't wanted to call too soon for fear the military would hurt my efforts to get information. The first thing the public relations officer asked me was whether we had the pictures. I know that made all the difference in the world to the military in terms of deniability. When I told him I did have them, he shared that people at the Pentagon "had been dreading this phone call," saying everyone working there knew this was a hard story to keep under wraps.

But the Pentagon had lots of options available as far as delaying the story, and over the next two weeks military officials would take advantage of every one.

We told the Pentagon that we planned to air the story on April 14 and asked for someone who could be interviewed on-camera about the Abu Ghraib case. The public affairs people immediately began backpedaling, saying they didn't think they had anyone available who could speak authoritatively on the subject. They begged for more time.

While I was waiting for the people at the Pentagon to make up their mind, I had to do something on the Abu Ghraib story that has never been part of my producing experience, before or since. Obviously, the pictures had to be doctored. There was lots of nudity, and none of that could go on the air, at least not on CBS.

Someone had to personally oversee the process. So I went to the control room across the street from the *60 Minutes* office and carefully, with the help of a technician, digitally erased all the genitals in the pictures. We tried pixelating them, fuzzing them, blacking them out, finally settling on a combination of blurring and smearing. It was an odd feeling. Again and again, we would isolate someone's crotch and systematically erase every bit of his manhood. I felt these detainees had suffered enough and now look what I was doing. I remember telling my husband that he wouldn't believe how I had spent the day.

But it was easier to digitally neuter dozens of men than it was to deal with the Pentagon. We were still faced with airing a story that had no official response from the administration. This was further complicated by the fact that we would have to report that the Pentagon hadn't denied the story or refused to speak, but had simply asked for more time to get an appropriate person to comment on-camera. We wanted to have either a real response from the military or a flat-out "no comment."

We went back and forth about what to do until Wednesday afternoon, when the story was killed for that night. Jeff Fager made the call to hold the story for what I thought were good reasons, opting to wait until we got a Pentagon reaction. I had not seen any interference from the corporate offices or heard anything about Andrew Heyward having great hesitation about airing the story, which is not to say I would have been privy to pressure like that.

I remember leaving New York that night and getting a phone call from Dan as I arrived at the airport. He was incensed that the story had been put off. He told me, "Just walk away. Just walk away. You have done great, great work, but they're not going to run it and the best thing to do is walk away without looking back." He was unusually peeved at the decision to hold the story.

I told Dan that I believed very strongly that the story would run the next week and tried, without success, to talk him out of his funk. In retrospect, I wonder if Dan knew something that I did not.

By the following week, we had more details on the abuse at Abu Ghraib. We had been given information that was part of what would soon be called the Taguba report. Prepared by Maj. Gen. Antonio Taguba, the report was an unusually blunt finding of fact after an internal military investigation into practices at the prison.

The parts of the report we had, among other horrors, outlined the rape of a young man at the prison by a civilian contractor brought to Iraq by the United States to work as a translator. The report named other civilian contractors working as interrogators, including a man who called himself Big Dog.

We modified the story and prepared for air again. We still wanted someone from the Pentagon to go on-camera. This time, we were promised a relatively low-level person within the public affairs office who apparently had some knowledge of the case. It was not ideal, but we agreed. The Pentagon would not schedule the interview until Wednesday morning, the day our story was supposed to air. That was cutting it close, but we agreed again.

Tuesday morning, the phone rang at Dan's house and the ground began to shift once more. On the line was Gen. Richard Myers, the chairman of the Joint Chiefs of Staff. He told Dan that he was calling personally to ask that the story be postponed once more. Myers said there were "deep, deep national security reasons to hold this piece."

He implied that the American military's actions in Fallujah would somehow be compromised if we ran the story.

The battle for Iraq had been so swift and the outcome so certain. But now, as we prepared to report what had happened at Abu Ghraib, the American victory was beginning to unravel. The city of Fallujah had become a flashpoint after a handful of contract security workers were killed in an ambush and their bodies were dismembered and displayed in the streets.

Now the U.S. Marines were in the city, suffering and dying in the brutal *almost* hand-to-hand combat that marked the battle for control of Fallujah. The thought that we could hurt those American soldiers was devastating.

After speaking with Myers, Dan called me and said he was conflicted. The journalist in him wanted to go with the story; the patriot in him was worried that if we did we might be hurting the country in ways we could not clearly see. There was a war on; there were soldiers in harm's way. "The chairman of the Joint Chiefs doesn't call every day and it is not something that can be dismissed out of hand," Dan told me. Still, he said his inclination was to go with the story.

Our whole team met later that day with Jeff Fager and Patti Hassler. As a group, we decided to send Dan down to Washington on Wednesday to do the interview. We would make a decision late in the day about whether the story was going to run.

By late morning on Wednesday, April 21, Jeff was leaning against running the story, for a variety of reasons. The primary problem was that we didn't have an interview with a high-level person at the Pentagon. What good would a public affairs person be if that individual didn't know the details or was unable to discuss an ongoing investigation? Shortly after Dan landed in Washington, the Pentagon abruptly canceled our interview. Now, we had nothing.

Jeff canceled the story again. By this time, we were wrung out. Dan was on his way back from Washington. All of us were cranky and unhappy, including Jeff, who had made the call to stand down.

Dana, Roger, and I began calling our sources to tell them we were waiting at least another week, until the next airing of *60 Minutes II*.

Roger spoke with Bill Lawson, Chip Frederick's uncle, who told him that he had prepared one hundred stamped and addressed envelopes with details of his nephew's case for other news organizations and editorial boards. He planned on sending them out after our story aired. Now he said he was prepared to mail them that night, whether our story ran or not. He was worried that CBS would ultimately back down and not run the story at all.

We asked Lawson to wait one more week and he agreed. Again we met as a group and talked over what to do. Fager briefly considered whether we should team with *The New York Times* to do the story, which I didn't necessarily want to do. We had done the research; we had the goods; we had found the story. Why should we hand everything over to someone else?

We were worn out. I decided to go home rather than stay in New York, waiting for another week. There was no point. We had as much as we were going to get without the Pentagon's help. I was as ready to air as I would ever be.

I flew out of Newark that night. It was late and my head was spinning. I stopped at a news kiosk and bought as many home-decorating magazines as I could, hoping they would give me a nice break from the less-aesthetic decisions I was struggling with at work. There was a Dick Clark café right by my gate, so I settled into a chair, ordered a glass of wine, and began flipping through my magazines. I needed to decompress.

Of course, my cell phone rang after I had looked at only one page of my glossy decorating porn. It was the Pentagon public affairs person again. "Rock Around the Clock" was blaring in the restaurant and I could barely hear what he was saying. I made out this much: His bosses were upset with some of the questions other reporters were starting to ask. Had we shared our information or pictures with anyone else? Of course we hadn't. I told him I would call Jeff Fager and have him call to reassure him.

When I reached Jeff, he exploded. "Goddamn it, why do you make everything such a big fucking deal?" I was taken aback. Not only was he seriously yelling at me, something that had happened only rarely in our years together, he sounded really upset as well. I might have been dense up to that point, but even I was able to discern that for Jeff, there had been a great deal riding on the decision to hold or go with the story. For him, it had become a no-win situation.

If we ran the Abu Ghraib story, we would face the criticism and fall-out we knew was coming. If we held it, we would feel like we were backing down and we faced the prospect that someone else might get the story and go with it. The Pentagon might even do a preemptive strike and release the information itself. We were all miserable.

That weekend at home, it became clear who was asking the bother-some questions at the Pentagon. Sy Hersh called me and said he was working on the story, too. He asked if we were going to run the story next week. I said I thought we would. I was very leery of Sy because, God love him, he is *always* working. If you weren't careful, even the most casual conversation would find its way into print. I was braced for him to do a story outlining the Abu Ghraib scandal with a brief and embarrassing sidebar on the lack of spine at 60 *Minutes II* and CBS News, including inane and mindless quotes from me. I couldn't even think about it.

On Monday, I was back in New York. Everything was on-track for us to run the story that Wednesday. Out of the blue, Jeff Fager got a call from Lawrence DeRita, a public information person at the Pentagon, who angrily accused us of giving the pictures to Sy Hersh. I ran up to Jeff's office and stood listening outside the door. Jeff was yelling into the phone. This was rapidly spinning out of control. Roger Charles told me sagely, "Sy Hersh is getting us all in trouble."

Sy has a history of getting everyone in trouble. I'm sure it is a source of pride. But the only way out of this circle of angry phone calls, disap-pointed sources, and endless worry was to run the damn thing. Fager called the Pentagon back and told them we were running it Wednesday regardless of whether they cooperated with us.

We were set. I continued to tweak the script and we debated how to characterize the Pentagon's response.

The Pentagon called again after what had to have been a great deal of in-house debate. They were going to arrange an interview for us with Brig. Gen. Mark Kimmit, the smooth Baghdad-based face and voice for the American military action in Iraq. We were home free.

Tuesday morning, we did the interview. I watched the live feed from Baghdad feeling good. I don't know if Kimmit was actually great or I just thought he was great because he answered Dan's questions so straightforwardly. We had it. After weeks of fighting the Pentagon, the calendar, the competition, and one another, we finally had it. The

Pentagon was publicly confirming that our story was true, that the information we had chased so long and so hard was accurate.

Everything else was almost anticlimactic. We ran the story on April 28, and the next day there were mentions of it in a number of newspapers. It didn't make a real splash until the European press began to buzz about the story a couple of days later.

Then, American newspapers and networks began to cover it heavily. More than a year and a half later, they still are. The reverberations of our Abu Ghraib story are still being felt. If we hadn't aired it, if Sy had not followed us, if the Europeans had not been outraged, the debate we have seen over American policy toward prisoners and detainees might not have taken place. That would have been a tragedy.

I have always been proud to be a citizen of a country that is a moral leader. Sometimes maintaining that position means looking in the mirror and acknowledging that we can do better. I am proud that our work at *60 Minutes II* was part of that process.

The other fascinating element I took away from the Abu Ghraib story was how digital cameras, computers, the Internet, and other new technology have altered any country's ability to keep dirty little secrets. Without the pictures, there would not have been a story, certainly not as big a story. There would not have been an admission by the Pentagon that American soldiers had abused the rights of Iraqi civilians inside Abu Ghraib. Without the Internet, communication between a worried soldier and his supportive family would have been slower and less complete. Without CBS's technical abilities to do satellite interviews, to get into and out of Iraq quickly, to draw millions of viewers, nothing might ever have been known about the secrets of Abu Ghraib.

But there is a downside to a digital world. We may all be better at exposing secrets and running down information, but we are still beholden to the human weaknesses that lead us to use our new abilities in dark and irresponsible ways. Just as the latest in digital equipment was used at Abu Ghraib to record old-fashioned cruelty, the World Wide Web was tapped to snare us in old-fashioned dirty politics.

This new technology, so crucial to getting and telling the Abu Ghraib story, was about to bite us all in the ass.

CHAPTER 9

The revelations of abuse at Abu Ghraib would be my last story with Jeff Fager and Patti Hassler. Jeff's long-anticipated move to replace Don Hewitt as executive producer of the Sunday *60 Minutes* broadcast took place shortly after our season officially ended in May 2004. It was not surprising that Jeff wanted to take his right hand, senior producer Patti Hassler, with him to his new job. Like Jeff, Patti was an alumnus of the legendary Sunday program, and being entrusted with the top spots there was a strong and much-deserved endorsement for the two of them. I was very happy for my colleagues. But like the rest of the team at *60 Minutes II* who had worked for them, I was a little worried about the future of our Wednesday broadcast when they left.

Josh Howard, a senior producer under Don Hewitt for years on the Sunday show, stepped into Jeff's executive producer position at *60 II*, which was how we always referred to the show, even after CBS officially changed the name to *60 Minutes Wednesday* late in 2004. Patti was replaced at *60 II* by Mary Murphy, who had worked at CBS News in a variety of producing positions over the years.

I had not worked with Mary or Josh previously, unless you count an unforgettable night she and I spent in the middle of a Texas hurricane in the early 1990s. She was working for the *Morning Show* and I was working for the *Evening News* when we were sent as part of a larger CBS team to cover a storm moving in fast on the Gulf Coast. The two of us reached Houston late in the day and together we rented what we were told was the airport's last available car as the storm closed in. The vehicle was something ridiculously small and light, maybe a Honda Civic hatchback. Not what you'd want to navigate through hurricane winds. Typical for CBS producers, we were more terrified of our bosses than any big storm. Mary and I just kept going, driving through the gathering darkness into the jaws of the storm. High winds whipped around us and rain pounded our sad little Hot Wheels car.

We'd crept almost to Galveston when we finally conceded that we had to pull off. We couldn't see a damn thing ahead of us anymore. The rain was coming down in sheets and neither of us could tell whether we were driving down the freeway or into the ocean. We limped to the parking lot of a dumpy, abandoned, low-slung motel and wedged our car into what seemed to be a protected corner where we could wait out the storm.

Listening to the radio and eating Ritz crackers, we talked and waited for hours, taking breaks from time to time to call our friends and families on cell phones and terrify them with updates about being trapped in a huge storm, helpless and alone. How thoughtful of us. If my son one day does something unthinkable like that to scare me, I will richly deserve it.

When the eye of the hurricane passed over us and the winds calmed, Mary and I set out for Galveston again, and this time we made it to the safety of CBS's temporary offices in a large, empty hotel on the beach. There our fellow newspeople were camped out in the dark, dank lobby, eating all manner of snack foods and riding out the storm.

Junk food was a hurricane ritual for news crews. The food is usually squirreled away by male photographers, producers, and soundmen who hit the grocery stores in the hours before the hurricane makes landfall. The stockpiling starts out as a good idea: In a hurricane's wake, restaurants won't be open, hotels won't be serving food, we'll be working nonstop, and there will be no electricity, so everyone needs to have handy, nonperishable food. The problem with sending the guys shopping is that they invariably buy the worst kind of junk and lots of it. Throughout the coverage of any big storm, television news teams work like fiends, fueled by a massive stash of sickeningly sweet and over-whelmingly salty snack foods. Why battle only the elements when you can do it while fighting off severe digestive problems from eating junk? No wonder we always returned from hurricanes sick and bone tired.

When I was new at CBS, covering the aftermath of Hurricane Hugo in South Carolina in 1989, a helicopter approached and hovered low over my crew as we worked in a badly damaged area outside Charleston. I recognized the person in the passenger seat as longtime CBS cameraman Clarence Gibbons. I desperately hoped the helicopter was going to land so I could climb onboard and get away from the swampy, bug-infested, thoroughly miserable area we'd been working in that day. I also needed to go back to our temporary headquarters at a local hotel, look at the tape, and start writing my story.

Sure enough, the chopper descended ever closer as my excitement and sense of relief grew. Then to my dismay, Gibbons reached out the chopper's open door and let loose a shower of Moon Pies for those of us on the ground. He saluted as the craft soared off into the ether.

That was it. That was what Gibbons moved in close for. I wasn't going anywhere. But I was going to be gorging on Moon Pies for the rest of the day.

If you haven't experienced this southern snack delight, it's a chocolate-covered marshmallow-filled cookie sandwich. Just the thing to keep you going when the humidity is so bad you feel like you're underwater and you're not sure where your next meal will come from. I'm sure Gibbons felt he had performed a kindness, but the sweet absurdity of his gesture left me dumbstruck and laughing. For journalists pulling devastation duty, whether triggered by a tornado or a flood, a hurricane or an earthquake, junk food is truly the coin of the realm.

In my years at CBS, I joined the junk food routine so many times that, I swear, when the wind and rain kick up, I start craving Ho Hos, honey-roasted peanuts, and malted milk balls. Maybe even a Moon Pie. Those were the days.

When Mary Murphy and I met with Josh Howard in June 2004, our hurricane days were long gone. We were all dressed in decent clothes, sitting in Josh's office, talking about the stories I was working on for the coming year. I had big plans of my own and outlined a handful of stories that I was prepared to do if they approved.

One of those stories, which sprang from my vantage point in Texas, was about George W. Bush's early years, encompassing both his time in the Guard and the beginnings of his business career.

A Houston businessman by the name of Bill White believed that he had documents that would prove the Bin Laden family had invested at least fifty thousand dollars in Arbusto, the start-up oil operation that Bush put together in Midland, Texas, in the mid-1970s. There was quite a bit of media interest in the documents Bill White had. He'd been speaking with a variety of publications and producers, from *Vanity Fair* to Michael Moore. I was eager to get to the bottom of the story and see what was there, if anything.

I brought Mary and Josh up-to-date on what I had been able to find out about the Bush-Guard story in the past and shared with them what I thought might be the most fruitful areas to dig in that summer.

Bush would be challenged for the presidency by John Kerry, a Democratic senator who served in Vietnam, then came home to join protests against the war. At that point, none of us had heard of the Swift Boat veterans. There seemed no question about Kerry's solid military credentials. This would be a face-off between two Vietnam era veterans, men who had chosen very different ways to serve their country during the war. I thought it would make for a fascinating race, particularly given the ongoing war in Iraq.

Josh okayed my hiring Roger Charles to help search out more National Guard records and told me I could hire another associate producer, Lucy Scott. Lucy had worked at CBS News years earlier and was a respected, thorough newswoman. She was also based in Dallas, where she was a journalism instructor at Southern Methodist University.

I needed the help because Dana, my buddy and associate producer, was about to have her second baby and would be on maternity leave by the time our stories started airing in the fall. Josh and Mary seemed excited about the stories I had planned and couldn't have been more supportive in providing me with help and encouragement.

Roger, Lucy, and I divided up the work in the only way that made sense. Roger was going to hunt for records. Lucy was first going to get up to speed on the story, which was no small feat. I was going to try to get Ben Barnes to finally do that interview on his claim of helping get Bush into the Guard, and I would go back to some of my original sources and see if I could get anything new from them.

All three of us were going to work on getting and analyzing the documents that supposedly laid out the Bin Laden links to Bush's early business dealings.

In mid-summer of 2004, I began to get e-mails from Mike Smith, the young researcher who had worked with me on the Bush story in the summer of 2000. He had been hired as a producer on a German documentary about President Bush and the Bush family and felt they had gathered some new information in the interviews for that doc. He thought there might be a way to incorporate some of that into a story for 60 *Minutes*. I agreed and brought Mike onboard to join our working group.

Our rambunctious little working group talked constantly, comparing notes, cultivating sources, and unearthing and interpreting thirty-year-old military records. We compiled what we believed constituted Bush's entire military record or at least everything that had survived over the years. We had long lists of members of the Texas Air National Guard during the president's years there. We had rosters of his class at Moody Air Force Base in 1968 and 1969. We went back to old sources and tried to develop new information. We did what reporters do. We dug.

Bush was finishing his first term and running for a second. He had guided the country after the terrorist attacks of September 2001. He had taken the nation to war, first in Afghanistan and then in Iraq. Ironically, as commander in chief he was depending on National Guard troops to fight in ways that no other president ever had. Answering the questions about his own military service in the National Guard, questions that remained after three decades, had never seemed so pertinent or important.

Many Americans believed Bush had served honorably; others believed he had used privilege to avoid combat and then failed his obligations by leaving the Guard under circumstances that had never been adequately explained. Still others thought that Bush had done nothing worse than countless other Americans of means did during the Vietnam War: He had pulled whatever strings he and his family could to avoid combat, and who could blame him?

I knew how much smoke there was surrounding his record and how much evidence existed to show that his service had been, at the very least, cut short. This time, I was determined that if there was anything substantive behind the story, we were going to do our best to find it.

One of the longtime theories whispered about Bush's departure from the Guard was the notion that he had experienced a close call as a pilot, lost his nerve, and quit flying. We checked out accident reports in F-102s nationwide, with an emphasis on incidents in the Southwest region. We found at least one plane that plunged into the Gulf but nothing that appeared to have links to President Bush. What the accidents and deaths did underscore for us was the dangerous nature of flying, even stateside. The F-102 might have been "low and slow," as pilots called the old planes compared to the subsequent generation of fighter jets, but to sit alone atop that kind of power, to keep control at those speeds, at that altitude, in darkness and daylight, was a demanding task. Texas Air National Guard pilots, including George Bush, were men who entrusted their lives to their powerful planes, to their ability to fly them flawlessly, and to one another.

One of Bush's pilot friends told us that the future president had been deeply unsettled by the loss of some of his Moody Air Force base classmates who were killed in Vietnam. We talked to countless airmen who trained at the Georgia base with Bush and we found the names of pilots from the program who had died overseas. Many of them had been sent to war immediately after they completed training. Some of them died while serving as navigators, others as pilots in small Cessnas doing dangerous aerial runs to track movements of the elusive Vietcong, a deadly job known as "forward recon." Too many of these brave men died, as in any war. Nothing drove home the depth of that loss like reading the thirty-year-old obituaries of young kids who never came home. It was heartbreaking.

I checked the Vietnam War Memorial to see how many of the men listed there shared Bush's birth date, July 6, 1946. Their fates could be interpreted as a kind of "what if" indicator, one measure of a war's cost and what might have happened if the future president and others had not been able to get into the Texas Air National Guard. There but for the grace of God.

Twenty-five men born the same day as George W. Bush died in Vietnam. Their dates of death and enlistment offer a compelling counterpoint to the president's military career.

In May 1968, just about a week before young George Bush would get the formal backing of Texas Air National Guard colonel Buck Staudt, a young marine named Thomas Michael Casey, Jr., began his tour of duty in Vietnam. Nine months later, when Bush was at Moody receiving coveted and expensive pilot training, Casey was cut down by small-arms fire in South Vietnam.

In the summer of 1969, about the time George W. Bush was flying out of Moody for his onetime date with presidential daughter Tricia Nixon, another man who shared his birth date was fighting for his life in Vietnam. Lawrence Raspberry, a black man from Alabama, was shot to death in South Vietnam on June 30, 1969.

In 1970, when Bush was pulling weekend duty at Ellington Air Force Base and living in Houston at the Chateaux Dijon, he was known among his friends as someone who never lacked a date. At that same time, on the other side of the world, Raymon James, Jr., who shared Bush's birthday but little else with him, had drawn the short straw. He was completing a thirteen-month stretch in Vietnam. On November 10, 1971, he died in a helicopter crash.

Such comparisons could be done with anyone who served in the National Guard or got a college deferment or didn't do active duty in Vietnam. That includes a significant chunk of the males in Bush's age group. What's different about the man who became president is the way he consistently used his brief military career to boost his political prospects and, during his years in office, the way he has used the National Guard to implement his foreign policy vision.

In his unsuccessful 1978 run for Congress in Midland, Texas, Bush's first attempt at public office at age thirty-two, his campaign literature reportedly described him as a "former air force pilot," rather than a one-weekend-a-month Air National Guard pilot. His father's 1987 autobiography, written to promote George H. W. Bush's 1988 candidacy for president, also stated that his oldest son had been in the air force.

"Now 'little' George was flying jets in the air force," his father wrote in recalling the early 1970s.

That characterization wasn't true, but the air force references and fudging on how long he served in the Guard constitute conceits that, once put out there by the family, kept popping up in Bush books and campaign literature. Before his 2000 presidential run, George W.

Bush's autobiography, *A Charge to Keep*, written with the help of long-time aide Karen Hughes, claims that after completing training in June 1970, Bush "continued flying with my unit for the next several years." Again, not quite true. He flew for less than two years before requesting the transfer to Alabama, giving up his pilot slot.

The president's dramatic flight onto an aircraft carrier in May 2003 to announce the end of "major combat operations" and declare "Mission Accomplished" in the Iraq war was the ultimate marriage of his brief military background and modern political mythmaking. The president looked great in the flight suit addressing America and its forces. But when he was being paid to wear it, fly planes, and protect the country, that military outfit and the obligations it entailed apparently couldn't compete with the chance to work on a Senate campaign in Alabama.

For years, Bush presented himself as a former fighter jock. By all accounts, he had the jock part nailed. What's been much more difficult to pin down was the degree of his desire to stay in uniform, to stay in the pilot seat, to fight for his country. As he ran again for the highest elective office and four more years as leader of the free world, I wanted to figure out what had happened to Bush's written promise to work for the country as a National Guard pilot until 1974. According to Bush's military records, he'd stopped flying in 1972. Raising questions about the record is not partisan; it is plain old reporting, searching for the why, what, when, where, and how of a story, dredging up the details, getting at the truth.

In some cases, digging deep reveals that there's no story there, at least not a story that's ready to be reported yet. That's what happened with the cache of business documents that Bill White had.

White was a former business partner of James R. Bath, a colorful guy who'd been a pilot in Bush's Guard unit and later became the Texas financial representative of the Bin Laden family. White believed he had documents showing that Bath's fifty-thousand-dollar investment in Bush's start-up oil company had actually been Saudi money. It would have been provocative to say the least, if it could be proved that the president had longtime financial links with the family of the man who masterminded the attacks of September 11, 2001.

I spent a day with Bill White and his warehouse of material. Roger Charles spent forty-eight hours looking at the paperwork that White had collected. In the end, neither of us believed that White's documents, although interesting, contained a smoking gun or anything that we could make into a real story. The documents suggested things, but they were only starting points. Ultimately, I didn't think they brought anything new to the discussion about the financing of Bush's first business.

I decided to move away from that story and on to several others. Most had nothing to do with the president or politics. I was still trying to finagle an interview with Harper Lee, my favorite author, a profile that Dana and I had worked to get for more than six years. I was also investigating an offshoot of the Abu Ghraib story. And I was toying with a couple of lighter pieces that would balance our workload for the year. I loved doing stories that were simply fun to report, fun to watch, and were unrelated to prison abuse, backroom deals, or politics.

Our all-time favorite had to be a profile of George Clooney we had produced a couple of years earlier. Dan's wonderful makeup woman, Christina Bryce, teased Dan mercilessly about how we were going to ignore him once George came in the room. As it turned out, we weren't kidding. Clooney was very handsome, terribly charming, and surprisingly funny. Dan was . . . well, he was Dan.

Before George arrived, we women admitted that we had either purchased new underwear, turned our wedding rings around, ditched our glasses, or changed our makeup specifically for this shoot. We thought that was a hilarious comment on our pathetic vanity and optimism. Dan was horrified. Eventually, our constant gushing about Clooney made Dan start to feel self-conscious. At one point, we had to take a shot of Dan and Clooney walking away from the camera. I adjusted the wireless mike that was clipped to Dan's belt and he whispered to me, "Does my rear end look big when I'm walking beside this guy?" I comforted him by telling him not to worry about it. "No one is looking at your rear end, anyway," I told him truthfully.

When we finished the interview and our little group left the location, piled into one car, Dan tried valiantly but hopelessly to make us stop talking and caterwauling about George. When one of us, probably me, said something particularly crude and unladylike about George, Dan covered his ears, pretended to sing, and shouted that he didn't want to hear, didn't want to know. We laughed all the way back to the office. Dan used to call our group his all-girl orchestra, and we had an awful lot of fun together.

The Bush story was not, by any stretch of the imagination, fun. It was, however, important and we stayed on it.

By summer of 2004, the Texas gossip grapevine was beginning to reverberate with word that someone had new documents involving George W. Bush's Guard service. I kept hearing about an unusual number of national news organizations chasing the story in Texas. Many times when I would call sources, they'd tell me they had just gotten off the phone with someone from *The New York Times, Vanity Fair,* or *USA Today,* or from a freelance reporter working on a Bush story.

Our group traced the document rumors back as far as we could to a woman in San Antonio who ran an anti-Bush Web site and seemed to talk on the phone approximately twenty-four hours a day—maybe more. She went by the name of Linda Starr and she served as a de facto clearinghouse for reporters chasing information, rumor, and innuendo about Bush's military record. I didn't have a great deal of trust in partisan Web site operators, but Starr claimed to have some insight into where these documents were and what they contained. Like other reporters on the story, I listened to her accounts and kept trying to separate the truth from the chaff.

In August, Starr suggested that I contact Bill Burkett, a cantankerous cattle rancher who lived in the wilds of West Texas. I knew a little bit about Burkett, and a Google search gave me the public version of the rest of his background. There were all kinds of Internet hits on Burkett's involvement with the Bush-Guard story in previous incarnations. Only months earlier, in February 2004, Burkett had gone public with a tale about witnessing what he called a "scrubbing" of Bush documents at Texas National Guard headquarters in Austin in 1997 while Bush was governor. Any destruction of Bush's Guard records had never been confirmed. One of the people Burkett relied on to back him up had denied all knowledge, leaving Burkett and his claims to twist in the wind. He was generally viewed by the press as an anti-Bush zealot. That is how I regarded him, too. Still, reporters from many news operations continued to talk regularly with Burkett because of what he might have or could provide access to.

I sent Josh Howard an e-mail shortly after my first conversation with Burkett. I had always kept my bosses updated on my stories' progress and I particularly wanted my new boss to know about this story and our search for any Bush documents that hadn't been made public.

I said that I had made contact with an ex–National Guardsman who had spent several years working at Camp Mabry, State Guard head-quarters, in Austin, Texas. I told Josh I believed that this man was the person who had the documents and that I believed he had been in a position to obtain them during his time in the Guard.

Burkett had worked at the Austin headquarters for some time and was part of an internal attempt to report and correct the Guard's ongo-ing battle over ghost soldiers, nonexistent soldiers who were listed on paper for the purpose of padding numbers for funding requests. The phony counts had been a problem in the Texas Guard since the 1970s and were a major part of the corruption that Guard leaders tried might-ily to clean up in 1980.

Burkett had left the Guard in the late 1990s, forced out in what ap-peared to be another of the organization's seemingly constant and toxic personnel purges. I knew that Burkett didn't like Bush. Though Burkett had started out as a Republican and Bush supporter in the early 1990s, I knew that he had been badly disillusioned when he saw that as gover-nor, Bush didn't really do what Burkett thought was needed to change the Guard system. I knew that he was bitter over what he felt was unfair treatment when he filed medical claims about a neurological problem he said developed while he was stationed in Panama for the Guard.

But bitterness, medical problems, political differences, and an angry departure from a workplace don't disqualify someone from serving as a source. In fact, those often are defining elements for a whistle-blower. I decided to keep talking to Burkett.

Burkett's reputation as difficult to deal with was well deserved. He was finicky, thin-skinned, rigid, and quick to get huffy if he felt he was being patronized. He was also thoughtful, smart, funny, and frank. And he seemed to have an absolutely unbending sense of ethics, a righ-teous, sometimes self-righteous indignation when it came to right and wrong—a classic, uncompromising characteristic for a whistle-blower. I thought he was paranoid when he talked about the retribution that would rain down from the radical right if a news organization did a report questioning the president's military record. He turned out to have a better grasp of the ferocity of current political firefighting than I did.

Mike Smith seemed to be a better fit with Burkett than I was. The two spoke the same language and Mike had the patience to listen to Burkett for hours. I did not. I was also capable of rubbing Burkett the wrong way without intending to. And if he had documents or knew where they were, I wanted them. I didn't want my impatience or my inability to hold my tongue to keep us from getting the papers, if they existed.

Mike became the point man for us with Burkett and, in conversation after conversation, he and Burkett talked about the documents. First they discussed them in theory, then as something that truly existed, then as something Burkett might be able to get his hands on, then as something he might be able to show us.

Burkett told Mike that the documents' destination was being decided by a group of current and former military men who were brainstorming what should be done with them. He said he couldn't make any agreements without consulting these men. We urged him to give us more information about this group. He didn't at this time, but as the months went on, we found out these men did exist. This was a handful of retired military men, some of them high-ranking, most of whom lived in Texas. They were not Bush supporters and all of them had strong opinions about Bush's record in the Guard. In the weeks and months prior to Burkett's turning the documents over to us, they were in frequent contact with him to discuss what to do with the papers. I don't know that these men were the source of the documents. Burkett referred to them as a sort of advisory council.

I felt that if Mike could get Burkett to promise to bring us a sample of the documents to a meeting, we would end up taking them home. We didn't discuss with Burkett whether the papers were originals or copies. We didn't talk about what they contained. Mike just kept pushing for a meeting where Burkett would bring us some papers.

While Mike was talking with Burkett, I checked into Burkett's credibility. One of the many people I talked with was Jim Moore, the author of two books on Bush, one of which was *Bush's Brain*, a profile of Karl Rove written with veteran *Dallas Morning News* reporter Wayne Slater. Moore's most recent book was *Bush's War for Reelection*, in which he wrote at length about Bill Burkett's claims, as well as his character.

Moore told me that Burkett was "the real deal, not a liar." He went on to say that he included 120 pages on Burkett in his book because he thought Burkett's information was so important. Moore recounted Burkett's story of the scrubbing of Bush's records. "He saw what he says he saw," Moore concluded. Moore also believed there were other documents floating around in Texas. "My belief is that it is some former officers in the Texas National Guard," he said. Moore noted that there had been so much infighting in the Guard, so many threatened lawsuits citing racial discrimination, so many political battles and turf wars over the years, that document hoarding and leaking was inevitable. I certainly agreed with him on that possibility. I'd never run across an organization whose members had such deep-seated resentment toward one another or suffered such petty political divisions as the Texas National Guard. Guardsmen had been forced to align themselves with one clique or another, this power base or that for decades.

Finally, late in August, Burkett agreed to get together with Mike and me. We would meet in Clyde, a small town not far from Burkett's home, on Thursday, September 2. By then, I had talked at length with Josh Howard about Burkett and his background, describing him and his life in detail. As a result of the illness he says he contracted in Panama, Burkett has seizures fairly regularly. Sometimes the seizures were severe enough that his ability to speak would be impaired for a few days. Our talks and our ability to schedule a meeting were always at the mercy of his doctor visits and medical condition.

Shortly before meeting with Burkett, I sent another e-mail to Josh updating our work: "We can do at least a preliminary sort of verification on them, since we know Bush's records so well . . . If docs check out, you might want to consider this for the 29th [of September]. Keep everything crossed."

I wanted to have time to do the best verification possible on any documents. I assumed I would have weeks to check and recheck, write and research, as well as prepare for any backlash we might face from the White House in doing our report. I didn't imagine that I was setting myself up for a story that would blow my career to smithereens. When I wrote that e-mail to Josh, I was on top of the world. I thought

I was on the verge of getting something that countless reporters were looking for.

On September 2, Mike and I were supposed to meet Burkett and his wife, Nicki, at a Whataburger, a Texas hamburger haven just off a desolate stretch of highway, at 12:30 P.M. Mike and I got there at 11:00 A.M. With an hour and a half to kill, we ate, sat in the car, people-watched, drove around, fidgeted, listened to the radio, ate some more, talked about old movies, and agonized over whether the Burketts would show up. Complicating matters, we realized we didn't really know what they looked like. We hadn't set up a secret signal or an identifying action so we would be able to recognize each other. But we knew their approximate ages and that he had medical problems.

So we sat outside the drive-up window in our rented white SUV and sized up the middle-aged couples walking in and out of the hamburger joint. We paid particular attention if the man was limping or otherwise displayed frail health.

That narrowed the field to virtually every couple that went into the place. Either the entire customer base at this burger stand fit the same description or something they were serving in there was creating medical conditions in men and aging the women. Mike and I had just about given up on our quest when a blond woman with a deep tan and a huge smile came over and knocked on our window. I recognized Nicki's voice from our phone calls.

Burkett stood behind her and motioned for us to stay in the car. He wanted to drive to another location. We followed as the Burketts led us under the freeway, around a corner, and into the parking lot of a big family-owned pizza place on the opposite side of the road. Bill and Nicki were hungry and ordered pizza as we sat at a table in the back, sipped sweet tea, and started talking in earnest.

Burkett had carried in a towering stack of file folders, notebooks, and thick, legal-sized envelopes, limping along over protests from the rest of us. We pleaded to help him, but he loudly insisted that he could carry the load himself.

Bill Burkett flipped open a notebook and began talking about his history in the Texas National Guard. He was animated and funny as he recounted his version of what had happened to him. He blamed his problems on his insistence on fixing the ghost soldier issue, something that the governor's office didn't want to hear about or do anything about, he said. Burkett said his passion for setting things right led to his isolation in the Guard command structure and that isolation led to his eventual removal from his position.

I believed the Burketts viewed themselves as martyrs who had suffered for Bill's sin of daring to speak the truth. I knew that life was often more complicated than that, but my lack of complete acceptance of Bill Burkett's worldview did not negate his value as a whistle-blower. Many see themselves as martyrs. They have to in order to work up the passion and the courage to break ranks with former colleagues and come forward with damning information.

Bill Burkett clearly reveled in telling his tale of woe to a new and rapt audience. Mike and I took copious notes and asked questions. Finally, after what must have been ninety minutes of backstory, my eagerness got the better of me. "Did you bring us anything?" I asked.

Burkett reached into a blue paper folder and pulled out a white sheet of paper with a few paragraphs typed on it. I saw the heading "111th Fighter Interceptor Squadron" and the date "01 August 1972." I knew that was the date referred to in the official record as the day Bush's commander suspended the young first lieutenant's flight status.

Burkett handed the document to me and watched Mike and me read it, our heads huddled together, our lips moving. We exclaimed at what was there. This memo said that Bush was being suspended not just for "failure to meet annual physical examination [flight] as ordered." It said that Bush also was being suspended for "failure to perform to USAF/TexANG standards." That was new. And it was big.

The document said that the officer "has made no attempt to meet his training certification or flight physical" and that the officer "expresses desire to transfer out of state including assignment to non-flying billets." The official story had always been that Lieutenant Bush wanted to go to Alabama to work in a local political race, but this document's statement about Bush making "no attempt" to meet his certification or to get his physical sounded bad and presented a new context for long-ago events.

The document also referred to Bush's pilot position as "critical." If that was true, then the long-held claims by the Bush camp that he had been no longer needed as a pilot were untrue.

I read the paper again. And again. And again. I knew Jerry Killian had been dead since the 1980s. We'd often said that he had been in the perfect position to know what had happened, but there was no way of getting Killian's version. Maybe now we had. *Maybe.*

I looked up and told Burkett my greatest fear was that this was a political dirty trick, something that one side or the other might pull to hurt either the president or the newspeople who ran with the document. It amounted to a test question. I didn't know what Burkett knew or whether he could be trusted.

Burkett looked hurt and genuinely shocked, as though the thought had never occurred to him. "I can't believe someone would hate me that much," he responded.

Either he was a hell of an actor or he was telling the truth. Personally, I believe he'd never considered the possibility that someone would try to trick him.

Then Burkett handed over another document. This one also contained information that was damning to the president. We began to talk about taking the documents with us to start verifying them. I reassured the Burketts that the memos would not be used in any story until we had document examiners analyze and approve them. I told them we planned to parse the information in the memos for accuracy against Bush's official record. That would include comparing dates, addresses, names, and specific references with known documents. We wanted to have complete confidence that this was the real thing—authentic memos written in the 1970s and photocopied for us. I was eager to begin digging to see whether I could get independent confirmation on the content of these documents, through corroboration from the Killian family or from other colonels, pilots, and commanders who had been in Bush's unit.

I couldn't wait to get up from the table, take the documents, and get out of there. I didn't grill Burkett on where he had gotten them. I knew him well enough to worry that if I gave him time to take the documents back, he was fully capable of doing just that. His moods could change very quickly. And I couldn't let that happen.

Nicki and Bill began to discuss all the reasons that they shouldn't let us have the documents. Nicki was frustrated. She spoke with anguish about everything that had gone wrong with their lives since Bill had begun to speak out about the Guard and President Bush. She finally got a small picture out of her purse and placed it on the center of the table. It was a snapshot of a little blond boy. "This is why I don't want you to take the memos," she said. "This is our grandson, and I don't want him to be hurt by this." I didn't understand exactly what she meant, but I did my best to assure her that we would protect her and Bill and that we would maintain complete confidentiality about where we had obtained the papers.

I told her that she could trust me, that I had been in a court battle years earlier to protect my notes and avoid identifying sources. I said that CBS and I were prepared to do it again. I begged the Burketts to let me have the papers, using every argument I could think of to make my case. Duty to country, honor, guilt, honesty, motherhood, military experience. Anything, everything.

Eventually, Nicki sat back and looked at her husband for a long time. She had tears in her eyes. She put her hands on her chest and then brought them forward, indicating that this was a decision of the heart. She told him to do what was in *his* heart. He sat silently for a couple of minutes, his head bowed. Then he looked up. "Okay, you can take 'em," he said. "But I'm not vouching for these. I'm just the person who was given these. You have to get some experts of your own to look at them." That was no problem. I was already making phone calls in my head.

At that point, you could have put everything I knew about document analysis and authentication on the head of a pin and still had room for the state of Texas. Soon enough, I would learn the ins and outs of an obscure process that is great at raising doubt but doesn't lend itself to establishing anything with absolute certainty.

I just wanted to get in the car and get going. Mike and I said our good-byes and our thank-yous, told the Burketts we would be in touch, and pulled out of the parking lot in silence. We drove about ten feet and then began to whoop. At last, we might have something we'd spent years looking for. We might have real answers, real documentation. We sped out of town happily, not knowing that the precious cargo we carried, the two pieces of paper we'd sought for so long, had set us on a road that led to nothing but trouble.

CHAPTER 10

We sped away from dusty Clyde, Texas, that Thursday afternoon as if we were being chased. Clutching the two memos, Mike Smith and I careened toward the comparative metropolis of Abilene, aiming our rental SUV at a Kinko's we knew was waiting there. Our first order of business was to fax to New York the two Bush National Guard documents that Bill Burkett had handed us. I wanted Josh Howard, my new executive producer who had just arrived after years at the Sunday broadcast, to see what we had. Plus, we needed to fax the documents to Washington so Roger Charles could begin taking them apart, looking for potential errors in information, format, wording, or military jargon. I also wanted Roger, our longtime military consultant, to begin the meticulous task of comparing the new documents and their dates with the information in Bush's official record. From the moment we saw them on that September 2, our overriding concern was whether these new pieces of paper really represented the truth or a new piece of the truth.

I called Josh's office, got his fax number, and told him that two memos were on the way. While he was waiting for them to come in by fax, I explained to him what the documents said and what that meant for the story. I had gone over with Josh many times what I knew about Bush's career and the odd way it had petered out, leaving a gap of at least a year in which he didn't fly, didn't drill, and didn't leave any footprints of military service. Finally, Lieutenant Bush had reappeared for just a couple of months of drills before leaving the Guard in the summer of 1973, nearly a year earlier than he had promised. Once again, I quickly recounted to Josh the documents that were already publicly known, then laid out for him the significance of the wording in these new memos. One of the new documents, dated May 4, 1972, and signed "Jerry B. Killian," Lieutenant Bush's commander in the early seventies, ordered Bush to report within ten days for his annual physical examination, a flying requirement. We already knew from Bush's official record that he was suspended from flying for not taking his physical. The second document, dated August 1, 1972, and titled "Memorandum for Record," said that Lieutenant Colonel Killian ordered Lieutenant Bush suspended from flying on that date and that Bush had "made no attempt to meet his training certification or flight physical." The memo also called for a flight review board and said that Bush's transfer to Alabama that May had not been allowed. Killian's initials were signed above his name.

At first, Josh didn't seem to think the memos presented anything new. It was a reminder to me that he had not really paid attention to the Bush-Guard story over the years, so a twist or turn in what had already been made public didn't mean much to him.

Roger, on the other hand, was excited about what the memos revealed. Because he was intimately familiar with Bush's record—perhaps most of all because he was a Vietnam veteran—he knew the significance of what these new documents said about President Bush's military service.

Now we had to build our own confidence in the authenticity of the papers. At this point we had two documents, and although we didn't know it yet, we would soon get four more. The memos appeared to be typed in the same font or character style, presumably on the same typewriter. Some of the documents bore a signature or initials for Jerry B. Killian. Roger immediately got down to dissecting the first two documents while Mike and I started the drive back to Dallas.

On the way I called Dan Rather, who was working at the Republican convention in New York and anchoring the *Evening News* from there. I talked with him briefly and laid out what we had. He thought the memos, if genuine, were important. We also brainstormed a little bit about the upcoming weekend, because Dan was planning to head straight from the convention to cover a hurricane that was about to hit Florida.

Like a moth to a flame—or a tornado to a trailer park—Dan was drawn to hurricanes. More than drawn to them, really; he wanted to drop everything when a big one was bearing down on the country's coastline. Dan simply had to be there when a storm made the sky bubble like boiling water, when the wind went on the attack, when the rain cut through your clothing like one hundred thousand tiny ball bearings. He loves storms the way Romeo loved Juliet. Anyone who worked with Dan knew that and had to accept it. Sometimes you even had to go take part in a hurricane run with him, despite the fact that your enthusiasm could never match his. Believe me.

Dan told me that after my phone call about the first two memos he immediately called CBS News president Andrew Heyward and outlined for him what we had in our possession and what we thought the documents meant. Dan wanted Andrew to get involved. He wanted Andrew's support on a story that promised to be both high-profile and provocative. Dan said that Andrew agreed wholeheartedly that this story was important and that he would be involved.

Yvonne Miller, a *60 Minutes II* associate producer in New York who was filling in for Dana while she was on maternity leave, got the faxed documents and I asked her to begin looking for document analysts we could use as paid consultants to examine these things.

The first thing we found out from the analysts was that without originals, there was no way we could ever date the documents physically and be *100 percent* certain from the pages themselves that they were produced in the 1970s. A test that pulls fragments of the ink out of the paper and analyzes its precise makeup can give you an idea of when the ink was manufactured and how it was applied to the paper. That wasn't an option for us. These were photocopies of the originals or, more likely, photocopies of photocopies.

That did not negate their value, by any means. Having only photocopied documents was not a showstopper and we had no reason to think that this factor, in itself, should bring our story to a screeching halt. Most news reports involving documents in the long history of journalism—whether the Pentagon Papers or simple garden-variety court records—are based on copies of documents, not the originals, and there are many effective and definitive ways to test the authenticity of what's on a page of paper other than sampling the ink or the paper. What was most important to us was finding information that would validate or negate the documents and what they contained. Scientific proof isn't the journalistic standard in such a case. Solid, compelling evidence is. If we didn't have good reasons to believe in the memos, they would never see the light of day.

Analyzing the content of the memos, comparing each detail of information with the official records, getting corroboration from anyone else associated with Bush's unit—those were the things that could give us a sense of whether these memos were the real thing.

On Friday, the day after we received the documents, I talked with Josh about the potential airdate for our story. Which Wednesday night should we shoot for? I had envisioned running a story on September 29. It was already September 3, but I thought I could have a great story by then.

It turned out there were some stumbling blocks. Our time slot on September 15 would be taken over by a Billy Graham crusade in about a third of the country, Josh said, and *60 II* would be preempted on September 22 because of an hour-long Dr. Phil special. So our choices, Josh said, were really the eighth—my God, that was just *five days away*!—or waiting another three weeks until the twenty-ninth, the date I had initially assumed we would aim for. After all, we had an incredible amount of work to do.

The bottom line was that the story's airdate was determined not by its newsworthiness, not by the amount of time we needed to get it ready, not by anything our competitors were doing. Our airdate was decided by an unholy confluence of Dr. Billy Graham, Dr. Phil McGraw, and the network forces that reduce news to a commodity. When the story ran was decided by a cocktail of religion, self-help rhetoric, and ratings. These kinds of programming dilemmas and compromises are a fact of network life, as much as I might wish it were otherwise. I had long ago grown accustomed to the demands of other broadcasts, other stories, and other considerations affecting when—or even if—a story of mine would go on the air.

When talking about deadlines and airdates, we sometimes kidded,

"Let's pretend." At least that was the phrase that Jeff Fager, Patti Hassler, and I used, meaning that we would aim for a certain date and work as hard as we could, mindful that stories often need more work and get delayed, sometimes for weeks. Often, too many stories would be prepared for one broadcast than could run. Sometimes as late as the day of the broadcast, Jeff would choose which reports he wanted to air right away. The others would be held for later airdates.

Those of us working the Bush-Guard story at 60 II already knew that many news organizations were chasing the president's National Guard documents and that they could essentially do a story at any time, compared with our restrictive weekly schedule. In sizing up our Bush-Guard story—Josh's very first as executive producer on 60 II—Josh wanted us to push as hard as we could and get it on the air as soon as possible. That meant getting a thousand things nailed down in just a few days so the story could make the September 8 broadcast.

I agreed to the immediate deadline that Josh wanted and I joked that I would "pretend" the story was going to run on the eighth knowing I really had my work cut out for me. But I had never missed a story deadline in my life, whether crashing a story—working frenetically to get it finished—for a daily newscast or cramming two weeks of work into a few days to complete a story for 60 Minutes. I was a team player and I was proud of it. I particularly wanted to please my new boss.

Besides, I had almost lined up the Ben Barnes interview, which would be a big part of any story we aired on the eighth. If we didn't get that, we wouldn't go ahead with the story. If we did get the interview, we could use only Barnes in a story if we didn't feel solid enough on the documents. We had some choices.

I felt it was going to be very rough, but possible, to make a September 8 deadline. I'd already set in motion the countless details of producing and the supportive elements of reporting that would go into getting this piece on the air—everything from arranging the editing to planning the graphics, along with writing and recording the script.

By Friday night, I had lined up Robert Strong, the Texas college professor who worked at the Texas National Guard headquarters in Austin as a clerk until the early 1970s. He was an articulate witness on the nature of the Texas Guard at the time the president served and was very familiar with the ins and outs of communication within the Guard system. While he didn't know Bush as a young lieutenant, Strong knew the personalities of most of the other men involved, including Jerry Killian, the man who supposedly had written these memos. We had actually flown Strong to New York and interviewed him in 1999, but we had not done the story then and had never used the tape. He had given us lots of details on the problems in the Guard in that first interview. Now, I had new specifics I wanted to ask about.

This time, we were going to interview Strong in Austin on Sunday night, if I could get Dan out of the storm, out of Florida, and to Texas in time. I started checking the Weather Channel compulsively, watching the progress of the hurricane that Dan was courting this time. Frances was the latest in a quick succession of storms to pound Florida, and it looked as though she was as powerful as the rest of them. It was bad news for Florida and a serious complication for anyone trying to travel in or out of the state. We had to figure out where Frances was *not* going to be on Sunday and try to get Dan there so he could get on a plane, get into the air, and get away.

On Saturday afternoon, while seven-year-old Robert attended a children's birthday party at a friend's place, my husband and I broke away and dropped off copies of the two memos at the North Dallas home of Linda James, a document analyst who happened to live nearby.

James lived in a ranch-style home and used her front room as an office. She told us that she had become a document examiner after watching *Perry Mason* as a kid and that she had testified at trials for years. She looked at the memos briefly and said she was going to need more time to glean information from them. I mentioned that we were using a handful of analysts and she asked who else was involved. When I told her we were consulting a San Francisco examiner named Marcel Matley, she brightened and went to her bookshelf, pulling out his writings. "Oh, he is the best!" she exclaimed. "I have all his reference books and I use them to make my comparisons." That made me feel good about Matley and I thought it might bode well for getting a consensus one way or another on the memos.

I have to admit, however, that I was not entirely comfortable with the whole document analysis industry. It seemed to be a kind of black art that boiled down to subjective judgments on the part of the examiner. We needed the analysts to look at both signatures and typeface.

Was it too much to ask that they could be completely versed in what seemed to be two very different disciplines? I didn't have the experience to know what we could expect or how much confidence we could have in these supposed experts, who regularly offered their paid professional opinions as expert testimony in court.

I did know that document analysis is a very contentious and adversarial profession, that for every analyst swearing that a signature is probably real there can be another analyst waiting to come forward to testify that the signature is probably false. I worried that the examination of the new memos would come up a wash, with no clear-cut conclusions.

I was used to trusting reporting more than people who looked at letters magnified many times, who gauged the arc of a signature loop, who checked for an extra squiggle or a missing crossbar. I trusted people familiar with the military, the men involved, and the situation in the Guard at the time.

On the night we had gotten the memos from Burkett, Roger Charles sent me an e-mail that stated that he had found in the memos "a couple things that make me feel better." We had all approached the new memos with the mind-set that they could be frauds. We had to begin that way and force the memos to prove to us that they were real. The more Roger examined the details in them, the more convinced he became of their authenticity.

I continued talking with Ben Barnes that weekend, trying to set up a time and date for an interview. The former Texas lieutenant governor had promised he would talk with us, and this time he had another reason to finally sit down. A few weeks earlier, a piece of video began circulating on the Internet that basically broke the ice on his claims about getting Bush into the Guard.

Barnes had been a fund-raiser for the Democratic Party for some time, speaking to groups, pitching candidates, and pumping up donors to vote with their dollars. He had recently spoken to a gathering of Democrats in Austin and told them about a visit he had made to the Vietnam War Memorial in Washington. He said that seeing the wall of endless names, the mementos left by families still grieving, the enormity of the pain that the Vietnam War had caused, made him think back to his own role in that divisive conflict. Barnes told the audience he was ashamed that, while publicly touting the war as a just cause, he had privately helped young men avoid service in Vietnam. He said that he had helped President Bush and others avoid combat by helping them get into the much safer Texas Air National Guard, where their chances of being sent overseas without volunteering were virtually zero. Barnes added that he was sorry for his complicity in helping some people stay out of the war when so many other young men had no choice but to comply.

Among the many changes in the world since Barnes last ran for office in 1970 was the proliferation of video cameras and the rise of the Internet. There was no longer such a thing as speaking to a group privately. Someone at the Austin gathering had taped Barnes's speech and that video started showing up on Web sites. Barnes's ability to deflect the story as he had done in years past was gone overnight. Now he either had to stand behind his words or look as though he was afraid to speak out. Worse yet, he might look as though he hadn't told the truth to the dozens of people in the room.

Also irritating to Barnes, still a high-powered player in Washington political circles, was the quality of the video clip itself. He thought the bad lighting and spur-of-the-moment setting were unflattering to him. He laughed when he complained to me, but I could tell he meant it. "I'm all sweaty and I'm wearing a terrible-lookin' shirt and I look just awful," Barnes said in his Texas drawl. "Gawd almighty." High school girls have nothing on politicians, retired or otherwise, when it comes to vanity. Barnes said he wanted the opportunity to speak in depth about the subject, answer questions, and finally bring to a close the whole matter of helping Bush, why he did it, and how he felt about it now.

I pushed Barnes into scheduling an interview with us on Tuesday, even though he was still going back and forth about whether he should follow through. This time, I had a strong sense he was finally going to say yes.

When I talked to Dan on Saturday night, he sounded weary. Covering a hurricane can really knock the bejesus out of a person, and as much as Dan likes those wild and woolly storms, he's only human. No sleep, no decent food, the trauma of seeing severe damage to a beautiful place, spending day and night talking with so many people who have lost so much. The nonstop work, once again, had taken a toll on him, too.

Dan called to tell me he had left New York with nothing except "hurricane clothes": jeans, shirts, and a damned safari jacket that I have considered my mortal fashion enemy for years. I didn't like it. I have never liked it. And I *really* started to hate it when other smart-aleck media people began joking about network anchors and big-shot reporters and their bad habit of wearing safari jackets every time they left Manhattan. Dan, on the other hand, loved his battered and bedraggled safari jacket friend.

I thought I had gotten free of it once, a few years earlier, when it had started to look particularly tattered and torn. Dana, Dan, and I were changing planes in Brunei or some other godforsaken place on the way back from God-knows-where. While we waited for our flight, Dan told us that he thought it was time to finally put the old jacket out to pasture. Dana and I nodded sympathetically but behind his back exchanged gleeful looks. Then Dan added, "But I've found this great tailor, thank God. He's already measured every part of my jacket and he's going to use old fabric and the same buttons and make one *exactly* like this one." Gee, Dan. Great news.

Well, Dan wasn't going to wear his new/old safari jacket to do an interview on this story if I could help it. I called an acquaintance in Austin and had her buy a jacket, shirt, and tie that Dan could wear on-camera.

On Sunday morning, Mike Smith called me with a new development. Burkett wanted him to come back to West Texas. He had more memos he wanted to hand off. He seemed to want to be rid of them all. Mike sped toward his meeting while I continued to set up our shooting schedule.

As I was leaving for the airport to meet Dan, Mike called to say he had four more documents in hand. He faxed them to me quickly. I was astonished when I saw this second group of memos. One, dated August 18, 1973, had jots of handwriting in a few places and the heading "CYA," the old shorthand for "cover your ass." Its subject: the internal controversy over Lieutenant Bush's annual performance rating in light of his yearlong absence from the Texas Guard. On a typed page titled "Memo to File," purportedly written by Killian, the lieutenant colonel stated he was under pressure from a former commander to "sugar coat"

Bush's performance in a training report. "Bush wasn't here during rating period and I don't have any feedback from 187th in Alabama," the memo said. Killian said he would "backdate but won't rate" Bush on his "OETR," short for "Officer Effectiveness Training Report." This was potentially huge.

Here, in black-and-white, was what seemed to be a missing piece of the puzzle in Bush's official records. Over the years, I had compiled from state and federal agencies a set of Bush's official documents that was as complete as possible, using Freedom of Information Act requests. Those official records, which I had pored over again and again, included an odd page from what appeared to be a form for an Officer Training Report for Bush dated May 2, 1973, three months before this new "sugar coat" memo.

The May report by Lieutenant Colonel Killian and Lt. Col. William D. Harris, who rated pilots in the 111th at Ellington Air Force Base in Houston, did not rate Bush, as required. It simply stated, "Lt. Bush has not been observed at this unit during the period of report." Bush had left his unit in Texas supposedly for Alabama one year earlier, in May 1972. Bush was to work on a local political campaign in Alabama while continuing his Guard drills there. His two previous annual performance reviews were done each May, and they had both been pretty darn good.

I had always wondered why this nonrating document from May '73 was part of Bush's official Guard file. It made no sense. It would have been like having Moody Air Force Base in Georgia, where Bush did his initial training, write a report on him a full year after he had transferred to Ellington. It was akin to asking a teacher to grade a child's schoolwork a year after the kid transferred to another school. Obviously, the child's new teacher should hand out the grades, not the teacher responsible for the previous year.

So why didn't the 187th at Dannelly Air National Guard Base in Alabama—where Bush was supposedly doing his drills after May 1972— file his annual rating report in May 1973? Or at least some portion of it? If the 187th *had* written a report, why wasn't it in the official file? And why had Bush's original unit been asked to write a report, as well? Perhaps, in these new documents, we had found part of the answer.

If the new memos were real, then there had been pressure on Killian to write a report on Bush—and write a good one—because Bush had not attended drills at the 187th. That unit had not written a report at all, perhaps, it appeared, because there was nothing for the 187th to report.

This explanation made sense in light of the oddities in Bush's official documents. It also made sense because we knew there had been no paperwork found in Alabama indicating that Bush ever showed up there as he had promised he would while he was working on the U.S. Senate campaign of Winton Blount, a friend of Bush's father. No one had ever stepped forward with a verifiable firsthand account of seeing Bush on the base or doing anything to live up to his pledge to do his duty and perform his drills in Alabama.

Spokesmen for George W. Bush have previously offered a variety of explanations for why there is a gap of more than a year in the president's Guard service. They said that when he made the decision to go to Alabama, the president knew that his plane—the F-102—was being phased out. This was true, if a bit premature. The F-102 was flown in drills out of Ellington until 1974.

Spokesmen have also said Bush quit flying only temporarily so he could work on the Blount campaign. They said he didn't take his physical that May because he knew he wouldn't be flying in Alabama, an explanation that implies he would return and fly again later, something he did not do.

The president's people have always emphasized that he had his commander's permission to leave Texas, to stop flying, and to make up drills later in 1973. They repeat again and again that he was honorably discharged. But there has never been a simple, consistent message about why Bush left the Texas Guard, why there is no record of his making up drills in Alabama, and why he didn't return to Texas immediately after the Blount campaign ended in defeat that November.

Was it possible that elements associated with the Texas Air National Guard pressured Killian to write an annual report rather than let there be a lapse in Bush's paperwork? If so, who was behind it? Who was protecting Bush? I knew that having the appropriate documents filed at the appropriate time was gospel in the military. Missing an annual report, including a physical examination, would be a major no-no. Missing the regular Guard drills could get a Guardsmen sent to active duty, even sent overseas.

Was it possible that in this case the Texas Air National Guard decided to cover up the failings of a young man with powerful connections? People who served in the Texas Air National Guard were forthcoming with tales of other young men of means who were given special treatment during their time in the Guard. Any reporter covering the Bush-Guard story had heard stories about men sent to Vietnam for missing drills. I personally knew of one man in the Texas Air National Guard who had to move heaven and earth, calling in high-powered political help to stay in the United States after missing two drills. What had happened with Bush? Was there another explanation? My head was spinning.

The other three documents that we had just obtained were almost as explosive. In a memo dated February 1972, Jerry Killian asked to be updated on flight certifications for Bush and, interestingly enough, James Bath. Flight certifications were required for all pilots and involved meeting rigorous performance standards successfully, along with passing a flight physical, a medical exam that was much more thorough than the standard physicals given for nonflying personnel.

Six months after the memo's date, Bath was suspended from flying at the same time and for the same reason as Bush. That's in the official record. I also knew, although this wasn't yet public knowledge, that for about six weeks starting in February 1972 Bush had been bounced back to a training plane for reasons that are unclear. At the same time, he appeared to be having trouble landing his F-102. In mid-April, Bush quit flying altogether. With more than two years of flying still required on his commitment, he climbed out of his F-102 and never flew a military plane again.

Very few other people had this information. A story was about to be published by the Associated Press and reporter Matt Kelly, outlining Bush's flawed flight performance in February '72. But it wasn't public yet. We now had found a document supposedly from that very time, in which Bush and Bath's commander requested their flight records. If the document was forged, how would someone have known that February would be a key time to date a dummied-up memo portraying Killian as concerned about Bush's flight certification? Instead, that detail of timing seemed another unmistakable confirmation of the memos' content and authenticity.

Another of the four newest documents was titled "Memo to File," just as one of the first two had been. It appeared to be the sort of note that someone might make to keep for his own records. The memo, dated May 19, 1972, and without a Killian signature or initials, said that in a phone call from Bush they "discussed options of how Bush can get out of coming to drill from now through November.

"Says he wants to transfer to Alabama to any unit he can get in to," the memo continued. "Says that he is working on another campaign for his dad."

The phrase "another campaign for his dad" caught my eye. In January 1970, right after Bush transferred to Ellington to fly the F-102, his father had announced he was running for the U.S. Senate. In fact, George H. W. Bush was running against Lloyd Bentsen, who also had a son in the 147th. George W. Bush, dressed in his National Guard flight jacket, made campaign appearances for his father, gave speeches as his father's surrogate, and traveled the state to pitch his dad as the right man for the job in Washington. It made sense that a commander who had already lived through one campaign might reference this latest request as "another campaign for his dad." To me, it was another small point, another layer of texture in the new memo that rang true.

Another new document, dated June 24, 1973, and signed "Jerry B. Killian," was addressed simply to "Sir," someone above Killian in the National Guard food chain. The memo recounted that Killian "got a call from your staff person concerning the evaluation of 1st Lt. Bush due this month." The memo's date indeed matches when Bush's evaluation would have been due. "His rater is Lt. Col. Harris," the memo said, also correctly. "Neither Lt. Col. Harris or I feel we can rate 1st Lt. Bush since he was not training with 111 F.I.S. since April, 1972. His recent activity is outside the rating period." I knew from his official documents that after being gone from Ellington for a year, Bush suddenly reappeared there in late May 1973 and began drilling, even though he was still suspended from flying. His official record does not show that he made any attempt to retain his flying status. These memos, at least from a quick reading, did not veer from the information I had gleaned from the official record. I was convinced we had even more good material for a story.

I bundled up the four documents faxed by Mike, put them in my briefcase with the two copied pages we had gotten from Burkett earlier, and headed to meet Dan and catch our flight to Austin.

When I saw Dan that Sunday afternoon at the Dallas–Fort Worth airport, I was glad we'd bought new duds for him. He looked rough, like someone who had been battered by high winds for a few days. He looked so unlike his cleaned-up on-camera self that no one came up to him to ask for an autograph or compliment him on a story he had done or just to talk, as often happened. No one knew who he was this time.

While we sat waiting for the plane, I handed him the memos and he read them quietly, pausing now and then to ask a question or clarify a point about Bush's official record. Dan didn't characterize his feelings about the documents or their implications for the president. He said he was eager to see what Roger found in his analysis and what the document and signature examiners said when they spent some time with the papers.

Dan was all business when it came to getting ready for the interview with Robert Strong, whom he remembered from a few years earlier. On the plane, we talked about what the memos might mean. Dan, ever cautious, warned against jumping to conclusions. I told him I couldn't agree more, but that Roger already was finding reasons to believe in all the memos' authenticity and that my quick comparison with the official documents had given me some confidence, too.

We landed and raced to the hotel where our camera crews were set up. Dan changed his clothes and I showed the collection of memos to Robert Strong. Strong had left the Guard about the time that Bush left to go to Alabama. He eventually became a college professor in Texas, teaching—among other subjects—ethics.

Strong is a man who chooses his words carefully. He looked at the documents for a long time and quietly sat thinking. I remember watching him shake his head back and forth. I wasn't sure what that meant. Did he think the documents were wrong? Was he disgusted with the Texas National Guard? With us? I didn't want to ask him too many questions before we did the interview. I wanted his responses to Dan to be as fresh and straightforward as possible.

We sat down and Dan started the interview, asking first about some of the people in the Guard in the early 1970s. Strong told Dan that he had known Jerry Killian "quite well personally. Actually, I flew in the back-seat of his T-33 a couple of times going back and forth to Houston."

Dan asked Strong about the documents' authenticity: "Is there any doubt in your mind that these are genuine?" Strong was no document analyst, but his years in the Texas National Guard, his familiarity with its personalities and patterns of behavior, gave his opinion weight with us.

"Well, they are compatible with the way business was done at that time," Strong said. "They are compatible with the man that I remember Jerry Killian being. I don't see anything in the documents that is discordant with what were the times, what were the situations, and what were the people involved."

Dan asked Strong what he thought Killian was trying to do with this series of memos.

Strong answered quickly and was very clear. "I think, first of all, he was trying to get duty performed that was supposed to be performed. And I think he was trying to protect himself because of the political environment in which he found himself, dealing with the different individuals involved."

Then Strong laid out what seems to have been an ugly truth about the Texas National Guard at that time—that it was not simply a military organization. It was an amalgam of the worst kinds of Texas politics and cronyism. Robert Strong's voice quavered when he spoke. "It verged on outright corruption in terms of the favors that were done, the power that was traded. And it was unconscionable," Strong said. "From a moral and ethical standpoint, it was unconscionable."

If there was a dirty little secret about the Texas National Guard, it was not just that George W. Bush and others received favorable treatment getting into the Guard during war time or getting out of the Guard without doing their duty—though I certainly believe that was the case with the president and a number of other blue-chip young men. The real story of the Texas National Guard—particularly during Vietnam—is that the system was a fully functioning political hothouse, populated in part by men who built careers by passing out favors, aligning themselves with powerful protectors, ignoring those without money or connections, and courting those who had them.

Like the old saying about war itself, the Texas National Guard during the Vietnam era was an extension of politics by other means, a place where Democrats and Republicans, movers and shakers, old boys and young men, built a private society. And you couldn't get in unless they wanted you in. Often, they didn't want you in unless you—or someone close to you—could do something for them.

When Strong's hour or so interview was wrapped up, we headed back to the airport, piled onto a plane, and began the long trip through the night back to New York. After we took off, we talked animatedly for a few minutes and then, one by one, passed out. Nearly our whole group was there: Dan and me, Mike Smith and Lucy Scott. Only Roger was missing. We were too tired to talk but too wired to sleep well. We arrived in New York early in the morning. I staggered into my hotel room at about 6:00 A.M. and fell onto the bed.

Within a few hours I was up again and getting ready to go to work. It was September 6, Labor Day, yet another holiday on which I would work that year. The Abu Ghraib story had kept me from celebrating my anniversary, going on a spring break vacation, having my birthday at home, and spending Mother's Day with my family. It had been a good year for news and a bad year for holidays. I vowed that this would be the last holiday I would work for a long while. Ironically, that would turn out to be one promise to myself that I actually kept, just not in the way I expected.

As those of us working on the Bush story got to the CBS building, we packed into Dana's small cubbyhole of an office. I always worked there beside her when I came to New York. I knew that other producers who didn't live in New York had their own offices waiting for them when they came to the city to work, but I didn't really want one. Dana and I always liked sitting together and enjoyed the periods when we could exchange information without being even a phone call apart. It made work more efficient and it certainly made it more fun.

Now that Dana was on leave, I took over her office. Yvonne's little room was right next door, so it was convenient for us. By the time Mike Smith, Lucy Scott, and I arrived, Roger Charles had landed on a flight from Washington and he was headed in, as well. Dan called and said he would be in shortly.

We were quite a disparate group. Mike was always tired, his eyes constantly half-closed with fatigue, his ponytail in disarray, his clothes disheveled, because he had been up half the night working on whatever story was bedeviling him at the moment.

Lucy was perpetually well-dressed, professional, and prepared to work her heart out. Yvonne was eternally helpful and eager to laugh. Roger Charles approached every story as though it were a military operation. "There was no room for error, lives were at stake."

Dan was the heart of our little club, the patriarch of our group who passed out pats on the head, hugs and corrections, the man who asked questions, offered encouragement, and kept us going because we felt that "Damn it, if Dan could work this hard and this long, so could we."

Everyone was there that Monday morning. Except Josh Howard and Mary Murphy, the program's two top managing producers. They both called and sent e-mails, but it soon became clear that they were planning on enjoying Labor Day with their families and friends. I e-mailed Mary, telling her that we were doing interviews with a document analyst that day, getting ready to interview Ben Barnes and generally facing an overwhelming amount of work.

She wrote back, telling me that she had high hopes that we could get everything done and asking me to call her if I needed her help.

I have to say I absolutely expected that Mary Murphy, as *60 II*'s senior producer, would be in the office that day. I was very surprised that she wasn't there. It was a holiday, of course. But those of us on the producing/reporting/research team were there and if I had been the broadcast's senior producer, I would have wanted to be there to have input as early as possible when a story this provocative and this important was being prepared. I knew that if Jeff and Patti were still in charge of the program instead of having moved to *60 Minutes Sunday* that summer, Patti would have been sitting in the office tapping her foot when we arrived. She would have stayed with us all day and all night. We would have been in constant contact with Jeff, who would have celebrated the holiday by yelling at us each time we called him. But there was no way he wouldn't have been on top of the story and intimately familiar with its nuance and detail. Jeff would have been virtually in the room with us. Patti would have made sure that everything we did met her demanding standards and then some. None of us would have had a carefree holiday, but we *all* would have had confidence in the story when it went on the air. We *all* would have had our fingerprints on it, a strong grasp of the facts behind it, and we *all* would have been able to fight for the story ferociously if it came under fire. I was puzzled that Josh and Mary had made different choices than I was used to, but I didn't know what to do. I couldn't order them to come into the office. I didn't want to begin a working relationship with someone by overstepping or appearing overly needy. I told myself that they must just do things differently and that I had better get used to it.

Television is a collaborative medium and no one is so good, so smart, so superpowered, that they should be burdened with overseeing every detail and taking sole responsibility of a controversial story. The tremendously short deadline that I had been assigned, especially given the weight and complexities of the story, made the burden even more crushing. We did not have the kind of support from our new executive producer and senior producer that I could always count on from Jeff and Patti. Our new bosses did not have the kind of connection to the Bush-Guard story that they should have had. I believe the lack of personal and professional investment in the story by Josh and Mary, glaringly apparent on Labor Day, set the stage for everything that followed.

Strangely, the higher-up who called in the most that Labor Day was Betsy West. This was a first. I had never known Betsy, whose job was vice president in charge of prime-time news programs, to get so involved in a story. Her work on *60 Minutes II* had always been limited to viewing the edited story after an initial screening and approval by the executive producer.

Story screenings at *60 Minutes Sunday* and *60 II* were fairly ritualized affairs. Each broadcast had its own screening room, which reflected the different natures of the show and the people who worked on them.

The *60 Sunday* room was older and looked like a small, somewhat scruffy movie theater, complete with bucket chairs and a gradually rising floor. It was presided over by Don Hewitt, who acted like a miniature Louis B. Mayer, grandly calling for a look at the dailies done by one of the lesser individuals who toiled at his studio. The story's producer, the on-air correspondent, the editor who physically puts the audio and video of the story together, and the broadcast's senior producers and managers who oversee each story that goes into the broadcast, as well as shaping the show itself, would file into the space, dim the lights, and watch the videotaped story together.

It was when the lights came up that things could get hairy. Don Hewitt had such a reputation for savaging the producers responsible for stories that screenings were events to be approached with some measure of dread. When I did my story for 60 Minutes Sunday on Karla Faye Tucker, I had heard so many dire warnings from so many other producers that by the morning of the screening I was terrified. I wasn't sure I could trust my ability, my writing, my years of work, enough to get me through the screening alone. I did what every self-respecting, no-longer-very-religious granddaughter of a Methodist minister does when things get tough. I threw myself onto the bed at my hotel that morning and prayed passionately and fervently for deliverance. I prayed that I would survive. I prayed that I wouldn't be leaving the screening room in pieces. I prayed that Hewitt would approve the story. It apparently worked. Or my work worked. When the lights came up, Hewitt barked, "It's great," followed by a head-shaking, foul-mouthed appreciation of the kinds of things that happen in Texas, and ending with: "Jesus Christ!" Actually, I had known we were okay about halfway through the story, when the story introduced Karla's new husband, the minister, and Hewitt had howled loudly, "Oh my God, he's a goddamned preacher."

Hewitt liked the story very much and it aired with very few changes, but I will never forget how afraid I was.

The 60 II screening room was a more modern and casual place that reflected Jeff Fager's less imperial approach. There was a large flat-screen television at one end and a great sound system. Facing the screen was a long table where Jeff and Patti and Mike Whitney, the senior producer in charge of the more technical aspects of the show, watched and made notes. Chairs along the walls were available for everyone else who worked on the story. Sometimes there was a lot of laughter. Sometimes there was harsh criticism. My experiences in this room were always fair. Most of the time, Jeff wanted changes in the story or Patti had suggestions she thought might help the piece. We would make those changes and then hold another screening that included Betsy so she could sign off on the piece before it aired.

Betsy would often have a suggestion, usually nothing that required major surgery. In my experience, though, she had never been involved in the nuts and bolts of news gathering, interviewing, writing, or editing a story.

When Betsy called repeatedly on Labor Day with questions or suggestions, I came to believe that she was doing this as a surrogate for Andrew Heyward. I had always gotten along well with Betsy, and on this story I felt that if this was what my supervisors wanted to do, that was fine. At that point, I appreciated the interest of an executive-level person. This story was starting to get lonely.

I spent part of the day talking on the phone with the document analysts who now had copies of the first two memos. Yvonne had copied the faxes she'd received from us on Friday and immediately sent them out via air courier to Jim Pierce in Los Angeles, Marcel Matley in San Francisco, and Emily Will in North Carolina. She also sent them several sample Jerry Killian signatures assembled from the stack of official Bush records we had received from the government over the years.

Emily Will and I had an unusual conversation that Monday, a talk that raised questions for me about how well-suited she was to be working on this project. I called to see how her analysis was going and she told me she had a problem with the documents. Concerned, I asked her what the trouble was. She said that she had done research on the Internet about President Bush's military record and found that he had been in Alabama at the time these documents were written, so there was no way they could be true.

I was taken aback. Will wasn't supposed to be doing research on her own about the facts of the story. She was supposed to be looking at the memos' typeface and signatures for signs of authenticity or forgery. Just because Lieutenant Bush was supposed to have been doing Guard duty in Alabama—and there was, of course, no record of his ever reporting there—didn't preclude his Texas commander from writing these memos. In fact, the new memos meshed extremely well with the official record. I told Will that we could handle the information end of the investigation and asked her to confine herself to what she saw on the face of the documents. I recall her telling me, "I always work on the whole thing." She saw her job as doing research and reaching conclusions on the total package, she said.

Document examiner Jim Pierce, the man who probably had the most experience, told me he had just gotten started on the two documents we'd sent him but so far saw nothing amiss. He wanted to keep looking. Linda James, down in Texas, told me she needed to see originals in order to make a final judgment. *Well,* I thought, *I would love to give them to you, Linda.* Unfortunately, I didn't have them and I sure didn't know who did.

James would later tell the investigative panel that she *may* have told me that she was concerned about the superscripted "th," although she "was not certain" she had actually brought that up. She told the panel she needed more examples of Killian's signature to make a professional judgment about our memos.

Marcel Matley was making the long trek from the West Coast to New York so he could look at the photocopies we had and compare them with the many Killian signatures from official records.

While we waited for Matley to arrive, we tried to come up with someone we could interview who could speak with authority about the National Guard, its role in the Vietnam War, and the propensity for politics to seep into the determinations of who got into the Guard and who got turned down.

Roger called his friend Col. David Hackworth, a man who had spent nearly four years in combat in Vietnam. Roger asked Colonel Hackworth, the country's most decorated living soldier, if he would be willing to look at our documents. Once again, the battered old warrior was willing to speak out about the multiple inequities in the draft system during Vietnam. Hackworth said he believed that the president had probably dodged service in Southeast Asia by going into the National Guard. But Hackworth told Roger he admired Bush for his inherently risky service as a pilot, although he said he had serious questions about why the future president had walked away from his responsibilities to Guard and country when so many others were risking everything in Vietnam.

Hackworth agreed to come in and look at the documents we had found and give us his informed opinion, based on years of military service, about whether they seemed real. It meant a great deal to me that he would come in for an interview, not only because it was a holiday but because Colonel Hackworth was in the middle of another fight for his life. He had battled prostate cancer into remission, only to have it reappear in his gallbladder and lungs. Now he was in the process of having chemotherapy.

Marcel Matley arrived first, worn out from his cross-country flight but anxious to look at the documents we had. The first thing he told us was that the photocopies we had originally sent him over the weekend, which were made from the faxes we sent to New York from the Abilene Kinko's, were not nearly as good as the ones he was able to look at now in New York. For the first time, he was seeing photocopies that had not been faxed. The other analysts also were working with copies of the faxed documents. Faxing, we would learn, to our great detriment, destroys much of the detail and subtlety of a printed document, making letters and characters much less distinct or even turning them to mud. Faxing also significantly changes the proportion of the document and the typeface, a factor that would prove incredibly destructive to us in the days ahead.

We had collected more Killian signatures from the official records and laid them out for Matley. He immediately went to work, enlarging the "official" signatures, as well as the signatures on the new memos, and attaching all of them to the wall. They were large enough to see from the other side of the room. He didn't mark which signatures were from the new memos or the official record. His approach was to try to determine if one person did all the handwriting. Matley went over each signature meticulously, looking for consistencies, inconsistencies, and impossibilities.

The new memos contained two signatures and one set of initials, along with some other peripheral initials and markings. We left Matley alone for hours to pore over all six memos and evaluate the signatures, the typeface, and the writing on the periphery of the documents, and to take measurements and make notes.

In the meantime, Colonel Hackworth arrived at our offices, right on time and looking polished, as always. On this visit, though, his hair was nearly gone and his face was thin. He was beginning to look frail, a hard thing to accept in someone who had always been so fit and full of fire.

Colonel Hackworth plunged right into the documents, examining each memo line by line, looking for signs that something wasn't right. After reading and rereading them, letting his attention linger on each one, he leaned back and let out a long breath. "He was AWOL," Hackworth said flatly, echoing the harshest critics who considered Lieutenant Bush absent without leave from his unit from spring of 1972 to late May 1973. I had never heard Colonel Hackworth talk this way about the president, the man he always referred to as the commander in chief. Colonel Hackworth didn't always agree with any president's policies, but few people were more aware of command.

During the interview, Dan asked Hackworth about Vietnam and whether there were preferences given to some people either in the National Guard or in regular service. Hackworth told us that when he worked in the Pentagon during the Vietnam War he regularly received phone calls from congressmen and senators and political operators trying to persuade him to keep their children or their friends' children out of harm's way. He said he always refused but that others participated in that kind of favoritism. He said it was standard operating procedure during Vietnam for people with political influence to try to affect placements or assignments for well-connected young men.

Dan asked him what he made of the memos. "I think they are the clearest indication that the president of the United States was AWOL at a particular time when he and his handlers are saying, 'No, he was present for duty,'" Hackworth said. "But where is the evidence that he was? Where is one person to come forward and say, 'I was with him on duty in Alabama'?" Hackworth left our offices disgusted anew at what he saw as the inequity suffered by American soldiers who fought and died in Vietnam. As someone who had been there, as someone who had seen men wounded, dead, and dying, Hackworth offered views— of these new memos and of the everlasting unfairness of Vietnam— that meant something.

By the time we escorted Colonel Hackworth out, Matley was ready to talk with us. His interview was going to be a challenge. Matley spoke in the qualified and legalistic jargon he used in his courtroom testimony, not in the clear, snappy sound bites that television news producers and audiences prefer. But Matley had the experience, had spent the most time with the documents, had seen the highest-quality copies, and had made a determination about their validity.

He told us, first of all, something that we already knew, that the documents could not be "authenticated," in a legal sense, because the ink could not be tested for age. He did say, however, that he saw nothing in the typeface that was out of line with what could have been created on a typewriter at that time. He said he assumed these were reliable copies of authentic documents. Then, he turned to the signatures, which he felt contained good information that he could use to make a determination about their validity.

He found a preponderance of evidence that all the signatures and initials had been done by the same person. Matley singled out one signature, on the memo dated June 24, 1973, as showing some conspicuous differences but determined that there were also what he called inconspicuous similarities between that signature and others known to have been done by Jerry Killian. He said that the stress indicated by the contents of the document, in which Killian noted to a higher-up that he felt he could not rate Lieutenant Bush after Bush's long absence, was enough to create a situation where the signature could vary slightly.

Matley explained this as best he could, but I have to confess that it was not riveting television. Dan asked Matley questions, repeatedly trying to get him to speak in a language someone other than lawyers could decipher. It was tough. Finally, Dan essentially asked him, "Are you saying that if I present these to the American public and say that, to the best of our knowledge, these documents were all signed by the same man, I am going to be on safe ground?"

Matley finally answered simply: "Yes."

It was the best we could get in terms of clarity, but we all felt comfortable with Matley's assessment of the signatures and the typed documents, and he seemed very comfortable with his findings.

None of us realized we were just days away from getting our heads handed to us in a ferocious political attack unlike any we'd ever seen.

We saw Matley out of the building and talked about how we could get other confirmation on the documents when the two men who would know for sure had already been dead for years. Lt. Col. Jerry Killian had passed away in 1984. His partner at the 111th, Lieutenant Colonel Harris, had also been dead for some time. I had already spent much of the weekend trying to reach the one man still alive who I believed was certain to know whether these documents were real or not.

Gen. Bobby Hodges had been commander of the 147th Fighter Group at the time these memos were supposedly written. He was Killian's supervisor, the man whom I believed Killian was addressing as

"Sir" when he wrote the June 24, 1973, memo saying that he could not do Bush's evaluation.

For days, there had been no answer at Hodges's home in Arlington, Texas. Then on Monday afternoon, a woman picked up when I called and said that Hodges had been at a weekend bridge tournament and would be home any time. I told her that I would call back that evening.

Dan and I began talking about how to lay out the story and both of us were eager to hear what Hodges would say. Dan finally went home to prepare for his interview the next day with Ben Barnes. I promised Dan I would call him if and when I talked with Hodges.

Roger Charles was sitting in the corner of the room. Mike Smith was on the couch. I told them to stay and listen to the conversation from my end. "Wish me luck," I said as I picked up the phone and dialed Hodges's number.

General Hodges answered almost immediately. I told him who I was and asked if he had a moment to speak with me about some old memos that I had come across from the 111th Fighter Interceptor Squadron, a company once under his command. I told him that these documents appeared to be from the personal files of Lt. Col. Jerry Killian.

I asked Hodges if I could read them to him, and he said he would listen. I read the first memo, then the second, the third, and on until the end. The retired general listened to every word from each of the six memos. He didn't interrupt me once. He didn't ask any questions, didn't grill me on where I had gotten the documents or whether they were hand-written or typed. He was very quiet.

When I finished reading, I asked if the memos were familiar to him. He said they were. I knew that Hodges was a strong supporter of the president and that he wouldn't want to hurt George W. Bush politically or in any other way. But I thought Hodges was also a man who would answer a question candidly rather than shrink from it. He could be defensive and combative, but he didn't seem to be a man who would obscure the truth. That made his candor rare.

Hodges told me that "Jerry was mad at Bush leaving," that "Killian was miffed because some of his pilots were [rotating] out rather than go to the F-101." Hodges said that with Bush, here was "one who missed his physical, [which was] no big deal," but that "Jerry was miffed."

Hodges also said he told Killian, "You can't treat weekenders like full-timers." He told me that Killian was a "hardnose, an overboard hardnose." Hodges went on to say that Bush "went to Alabama with everybody's blessing." I didn't understand how he could say that after he had just told me that Killian disapproved, but this was just another in a long series of contradictions in this story. Here was a Bush supporter, his former commander, telling me that he was familiar with the details in three-decade-old memos that reflected poorly on the pilot who became president: Killian's anger with Lieutenant Bush for making no effort to take his physical or maintain Guard standards; his frustration about Bush wanting to go work on another political campaign; Killian ordering Bush to get his physical and, finally, suspending him from flying for his refusal. This was weighty testimony as we assessed the evidence posed by the newly discovered memos.

As we talked, Hodges's tone soon changed and he again sounded like the Bush backer he was. "I hate to see anything written about this, taking Killian's word," he said to me chidingly. Doing a story on the memos "would be wrong," he said. "You're trying to make news, trying to create a problem here when there isn't one.

"Using someone's personal notes, that's going overboard," he said. General Hodges never said a word about a possibility that the Killian documents might be fabricated or somehow wrong. At no time did he question any of the information in them.

As we continued to talk, he tried to persuade me to just drop the story. I offered to show him the documents, but he said he didn't want to see them. I also asked if he would speak with us on-camera, but he declined.

"Everything [was] black or white" for Killian, General Hodges said near the end of our conversation, adding, "Killian thought he was trying to do his job the best he could."

The general offered me a final warning. "You're creating a situation."

No kidding. I looked at Roger, who was sitting behind me smiling at what he could tell was a flat-out corroboration from Hodges. I told Hodges I would think about what he said and call him again in the morning. When I hung up, I was satisfied. I had a confirmation from someone in an ideal position to know, someone who supported the president but had told the truth anyway.

Roger and I did high fives and everyone working on the story rushed into the room when they heard us yelling and laughing. We all felt we had it. Through a respected document analyst, we had the best authentication we could get from photocopies and signatures. We had meshed the official records with the new memos and found that they fit superbly. And now we had a strong confirmation from someone who had been there, a firsthand witness. I had a three-legged stool on which to support the story, and three-legged stools don't wobble. We were there. I called Betsy at home and told her about the corroboration from Hodges. She was pleased, too.

I called Dan at home and told him we had it. He felt satisfied. So did I. It had taken a long time, but I felt we were on the verge of reporting what had really happened in the messy middle of George W. Bush's career as a pilot.

After days of nonstop work, I felt I could relax a bit. What could possibly go wrong now?

CHAPTER 11

Our reporting team was at the office early on Tuesday morning, even though some of us had gotten very little sleep. I had been up half the night working on the script, laying out the narrative, choosing sound bites, and determining how the story would flow. I'd probably had a luxurious three hours of sleep, a schedule that wasn't unusual for me when I was crashing a story. Overnight, I'd sent Josh a stream of e-mailed scripts with various approaches, hoping he would look through the numerous versions and find one that he wanted me to go with.

In my years at *60 II*, I had grown accustomed to this drill, working long hours, e-mailing scripts, and then waiting for the phone to ring. It would always be Jeff Fager or Patti Hassler, the yin and yang of copy editing, on the other end of the line. Patti would gently suggest some alternatives or an addition I might make. Jeff's approach was different: I would have written an opening to a story that I thought was profound and poetic and perfect. I'd e-mail it to Jeff and the phone would ring. I would know instantly it was Jeff. "That's not how it should start. Mary, Jesus Christ. Stop preaching. Nobody wants to hear that." Sometimes, he'd be more diplomatic: "What the hell are you thinking?" I have to admit that, more often than not, Jeff was right. But don't tell him that. He'll become even more unbearable than he already is.

I always respected Jeff's and Patti's leadership and I missed them both on this script. Josh sent back to me an occasional e-mail Monday night and Tuesday morning, saying things like "I love it" or "The script looks great." I was unaccustomed to this terse, unquestioning, unde-manding response and it made me nervous.

I knew that even the best stories and scripts need input from an in-sightful, inquiring editor, rigorous attention, genuine critical analysis, not just a rubber stamp. Shouldn't someone be asking me questions? Maybe even yelling a little? I missed the yelling.

Nevertheless, I kept plugging away, while everyone else working on the story stayed on top of their various responsibilities. Yvonne was handling the document analysts and making sure the details were set for the Ben Barnes interview scheduled for that afternoon. Roger con-tinued to work military sources and angles. Mike stayed in touch with Burkett just to let him know the progress on the story and talked to a couple of other sources including Gen. Belasario Flores, the retired Texas National Guard leader who had important information on how the Guard operated in the 1970s.

Mike and I also talked over what to do about Gary Killian, Jerry Kil-lian's son. I had talked to him once and Mike had spoken with him a couple of times. Even before we got the documents from Burkett, Mike talked with Gary Killian because his father had been such an im-portant figure in Bush's Guard history. Mike asked Gary Killian if he had any of his father's old military paperwork. Killian said that he and his father had not been close, that he had no paperwork and didn't even know much about his father's time in the Guard.

Shortly after we got the documents, Mike called Gary Killian again. This time, Killian's attitude seemed to have changed. He asked if we were working on "a Bush-bashing story." We were examining Bush's record in the Guard, Mike explained. Gary Killian said he had heard from Dean Roome and Maurice Udell, two of Bush's old pilot buddies, that something was in the works involving what he again called a Bush-bashing story, a phrase he used several times in the conversation. We believed that with all the scuttlebutt in Texas that new Bush documents were about to emerge, Roome and Udell might have sought out Killian to make sure he was on-board with the Bush team and ready to refute any negative story that might be developing. We believed that Gary Kil-lian was probably going to be hostile to any story we did.

Lucy Scott was helping us with everything in New York and staying in touch with her sources in Texas, including Gen. Buck Staudt, the legendary foulmouthed Bush loyalist whose clout in the Texas Air National Guard was so complete that it outlasted his career. We were told that years after Staudt retired he could still strike fear into people's hearts simply by stopping by the unit's headquarters.

Lucy had met and befriended Staudt earlier in the summer, spending time at his home in Texas looking through his photographs, talking about the old days, and watching FOX News, which seemed to blare from his television set around the clock. Staudt was in his eighties and had lost his wife. He seemed lonely.

We had started letting our sources and contacts know that we were planning to air the story that Wednesday. We planned to contact the White House by Wednesday morning, at the latest, for the administration's comments about the new documents.

Reporters never want to get a comment on a big story too soon. That meant you ran the risk of the White House or whomever the story focused on going public, stealing your thunder, getting out in front of the report. The Clintons and their advisors were the absolute best at this. We all felt the Bush White House was a public relations force to be reckoned with as well.

I was confident, though, that before Tuesday ended, the White House would contact us and ask what was going on. I believed there was no way that longtime Bush backers like General Staudt or Gen. Bobby Hodges would get wind of our story and not share the "intel" with their friends in Washington.

Mary Murphy sent me a note Tuesday morning, asking how the story was coming along. I wrote back with typical understatement: "Total meltdown. All sweaty. Very bad hair. Got confirmation on the docs last night from a longtime Guard Bush backer. Gee, they're not just juicy, they're TRUE. See you in the office." Mary told me that she wouldn't be in until late that day. She was taking her kids to a school orientation.

Once again, I was mystified at the lack of involvement by the broadcast's top producers. I know how hard it can be to balance the demands of work and parenting, but we were up to our necks in a complex, controversial story that was supposed to air the next day.

I knew our reporting was on solid ground. The phone interview with Bobby Hodges did more than confirm the basic facts of the memos for me. It made the possibility of any forgery or political dirty tricks in creating the documents seem much, much less likely. How would any forger have known Jerry Killian's feelings and actions regarding Bush's performance? Why would General Hodges have told me that the memos were familiar to him if they were forgeries designed to play a role in a political campaign? I continued to work on the script feeling that we were going to have an airtight story ready to go for the following night.

The office we worked in was starting to show the ill effects of non-stop habitation. I was glad Dana wasn't there to see what we had wrought in her work space. The wastebaskets were full of yesterday's lunch and dinner leftovers and last night's midnight snack. The windowless room, always either too hot or too cold, had a way of absorbing the aromas of whatever had been eaten there. On this morning, it reeked of Caesar salad that smelled like it might have been served to Caesar himself, Chinese food gone south, Indian curry that had lost its punch, and half-empty cartons of milk, grown surly overnight. We weren't just preparing a story; we had our own hazardous biological experiments under way.

The L-shaped metal desk was covered in notes, copies of the memos, interview transcripts, shot logs of videotapes, Bush's official records, and archive tapes with recordings of various scenes and events that we might want to use in the story. People were running in and out with more tapes, more notes, more mess, trying to anticipate what we might need. We could conceivably use pictures of the president landing on the aircraft carrier for his infamous "Mission Accomplished" pronouncement. We might want to include old pictures of his first debate in the Texas governor's race, where he was asked pointed questions about his Guard career. Might as well keep them handy. How about old video from Vietnam? Pile it on.

The battered furniture in Dana's office, a collection of castoffs that none of us would ever have in our homes, was looking particularly bad. The scruffy, stained seating area was drowning in high-tech and lowbrow debris, a sea of laptops and cables, cell phones and beepers, notebooks and binders, important papers and paper plates.

Adding to the chaos, the office equipment at CBS was almost hysterically out-of-date, or at least so out-of-date that the constant failures and complications could make anyone hysterical in the hours leading up to deadline. On some level it was exciting to know that when you answered the office phone you might be using something that Edward R. Murrow had actually spoken into. On the other hand, it would have been nice to have upgraded equipment that could have prevented the recurring problems we had with our telephones, printers, laptops, and fax machines.

The phones were a real sore point. CBS's executives had good phones, with several lines, speakers, lots of red lights, and the exotic capability to put a call on hold. The producers' office phones, particularly those on the eighth floor, tended to have large square buttons that often got stuck or broke off when you tried to click over to another call. The phones themselves were an odd flesh color, something like a vintage caucasian Barbie doll. And our weird old skin-colored phones were about as useful for communicating as a Barbie phone. Without exception, I could call Dana's office from my cell phone from the middle of nowhere and it was *her* phone that would have trouble. "Can you hear me? Hello. Hello? Dana? Oh, crap."

Our temperamental office tools invariably made crashing a story harder than it had to be and were part of the charm of working at CBS News. We didn't have the best gear. We had the best people. Or at least that was the propaganda, and I wholeheartedly believed it. I was proud of us.

My laptop computer screen had a thick black horizontal line running through it. A lot of the letters on the keyboard were rubbed off from my years of furious typing, pretty much ensuring that no one else would ever want to use it. And my laptop couldn't seem to communicate consistently with the printer or with other computers on the CBS system. None of this was a real problem until the minutes to airtime were ticking away like a watch on a time bomb.

When I arrived Tuesday morning, I knew that in just a few hours it would all start happening again. The clock would turn on me. I would have to outrun, outplay, and outplan time itself as the sands dwindled in the top of the hourglass. I'd done it many times and I felt confident that I could do it again, even though this story was complex, even though I didn't necessarily want this story to air so quickly.

How we would get an official response from the White House was Topic A for the day. Dan very much wanted to fly to Washington Wednesday morning and interview whomever the administration made available. Josh, Dan, and I agreed that the plan made sense and Josh started talking with Janet Leissner, our Washington bureau chief, about how to make it happen.

Early Tuesday afternoon, Ben Barnes showed up with his public relations person, Karen Hinton, who has a fabulous sense of humor. Thank God. Having a worried, grim-faced PR person hovering in the background, trying to keep a client from saying anything interesting, can kill an interview.

Ben seemed ready to go but still a little worried about what the fallout might be for him. I should have had him worry for us. Instead, I told him that all he had to do was tell the truth, answer the questions, and he would never again have to talk about Bush or the National Guard or his own behavior during Vietnam.

When Dan and Barnes sat down for the interview, I remember thinking that I had worked for a long time to get to that moment. It had taken me years to get these two men in the same room with cameras at the ready. For any reporter, there are few things as maddening as a person who repeatedly tells a fascinating and provocative story off the record and then refuses to do so publicly. That's what Barnes had done in talking about Vietnam and the National Guard with a number of reporters over the years.

Shortly before the tape rolled, Barnes told me that he had originally intended to do this interview with the late David Bloom, an NBC reporter who died suddenly while covering the early stages of the Iraq war. I would have gladly lost out to the hardworking Bloom, who I knew had spent years calling and cajoling Barnes as I had.

Dan was more than ready as the interview started. He began with some small talk about the early days of Barnes's political career, his election as Speaker of the Texas House at the tender age of twenty-six, and his close friendship and political alliance with Gen. James Rose, the head of the Texas Air National Guard in the 1960s.

Dan then cut to the heart of the story. "Tell me the truth, the whole truth, about what happened with George W. Bush and the draft and the National Guard. Start at the beginning. Take me right through it."

On-camera, Barnes seemed at peace with going public. "Well, first of all, I want to say that I'm not here to bring any harm to George Bush's reputation or his career. I was contacted by people from the very beginning of his political career when he ran for governor and then when he ran for president and now that he's running for re-election . . . and I've been quoted and misquoted. And the reason I'm here today, I really want to tell the story and I want to tell it one more time and get it behind us.

"This is what the truth is about, the time in which I served and the role I played."

Okay, this was it. What was he going to do? We all leaned forward, listening closely, waiting to see if Barnes would be as candid on-camera as he was in private conversation. And he was.

"Sid Adger, a friend of the Bush family, came to see me and asked me if I would recommend George W. Bush for the Air National Guard," Barnes said. "I don't know whether my recommendation was the absolute reason he got into the Guard. He was a congressman's son. He graduated from Yale. He was a person that would have been eligible."

Barnes talked about why a recommendation from the politically powerful was so important. "There was a long list of people waiting to be, or hoping to be a candidate for the Air National Guard or the Army National Guard," he said. "That was one route that young men had to go to, or that was available to a very special few, to be able to avoid being drafted and being able to avoid going to Vietnam."

Dan broadened the questioning as to how widespread this was during the Vietnam War. "You said you did this for others," Dan said. "Had you done it for others before, asked for what we would normally call preferential treatment?"

"I'm sure that I had done it previously," Barnes responded. "I know I had done it for others, I'm certain."

Dan didn't want to put words in Barnes's mouth, so he went back at the question again. "I used the phrase 'preferential treatment,'" Dan said. "Perhaps I shouldn't have. Would you describe it as that? A request for preferential treatment?"

Barnes didn't hesitate. "Oh, I would describe it as preferential treatment. There were hundreds of names on the list of people wanting to get into the Air National Guard or the Army National Guard. I think that would have been a preference for anybody that didn't want to go to Vietnam, that didn't want to leave. We had a lot of young men that left and went to Canada in the '60s and fled this country. But those that could get in the Reserves or in the National Guard, that meant that they could serve and get their military training. And chances were that they would not have to go to Vietnam."

Barnes continued. "I got a lot of young men from prominent families in Texas into the National Guard. Not that I'm necessarily proud of that.

"But I was a young, ambitious politician doing what I thought was acceptable, that it was important for me to make friends."

Barnes went on to say that he was ashamed of what he had done during Vietnam, that he was "very, very sorry."

It was one of the few times in modern American history that one of the men who pulled strings for the powerful, a politician who did favors to get favors, had the guts to sit down and tell it like it was. I thought the strength of Barnes's speaking out was really in what it revealed about privilege and power beyond George W. Bush. The strength of the story was in what it said about our country and the way we were torn apart by a war abroad and a war at home, where class differences could determine who would fight and who would stay safely behind, who would live and who would die.

When Barnes had gone, Dan and I met with Josh to talk about what we had in hand for the story. Josh told us that Jeff Fager had gotten a phone call from *The New York Times*, which had also been pursuing the Burkett documents. The editors knew that we were doing a story on Bush and the Guard the following night and wanted to know if they could go in with us and report the story at the same time. Josh laughed and said he had told Jeff to turn them down. Dan and I did not disagree.

Dan and I were concerned about having time to get everything nailed down by the next night. Dan asked Josh if we could run the Barnes interview on Wednesday night and follow up with a report on the new documents on *60 Minutes* Sunday night. Josh turned that down flatly, saying there was "no way we could do that politically." That's a small "p" in "political," as Dan would say, a reference to the fact that this had to do with CBS internal politics, not Republicans or

Democrats. The competition between the two broadcasts and the alchemy involved in which correspondents belonged to which show and which ones could cross between the Sunday and Wednesday programs was a witch's brew that few understood. I didn't want anything to do with a wrestling match over turf, but I vastly preferred splitting our story between Wednesday and Sunday to buy more time and to work with Jeff and Patti again. At that point, we still had the option of waiting a week and airing a story about the new documents on *60 II* in eight days. But Josh felt boxed in by our upcoming preemption in many cities in the following weeks and didn't want to put off the documents story that long. He was also worried about being beaten on our own story by one of the many other news outlets chasing after the documents.

After Josh left, Dan and I talked briefly about speaking to Jeff privately, but we decided against it. We thought that wouldn't be playing fair with Josh on our first story with him. So we battened down the hatches, strapped ourselves in, and resumed the chaotic marathon of crashing the whole story for the next night.

Yvonne brought me up-to-date on the document analysts and what they were saying. It seemed that not much had changed, but Emily Will was raising questions about whether the little "th" in "111th" was available on typewriters in 1972. In the overblown, misguided debate about a tiny symbol that was to come, we would soon come to know that the "th" is known as a superscript and that superscripts were on many typewriters in the early 1970s—despite the arguments of partisan critics.

I called Marcel Matley, who was back in San Francisco, and he said he was certain that superscripts were in use on a variety of typewriters at the time, particularly customized machines purchased in special contracts by the military, among others.

When I told Emily Will what Matley had said, I remember her telling me, "I defer to Marcel on this." But she didn't entirely drop her concern. Hers was a good point and exactly the kind of thing a document analyst ought to be asking about. What Will and Matley and the others didn't know was that we had solid information on the content of the memos in relation to known documents, as well as corroboration from someone who was there when Killian had trouble with Lieutenant Bush. In that context, if Matley said there was no question that the little "th" was available, especially on military typewriters, in the early '70s, and other analysts said he knew best, our confidence remained high.

Dan came over to make some changes, record narration of the script sections that I had written, and talk about our progress in preparing the story. I met with our graphics person, Bruce Jensen, in Josh's office and talked about doing a visual element to show that the new documents meshed with the dates and data in Bush's official record. What I had in mind was a graphic that shuffled the new memos into sequence with the official documents, showing that the two sets complemented each other and seemed to be part of the same story. There was no contradiction or discrepancy. Bruce was adamant that he was not able to do something that complex so quickly. We went to Plan B, a simpler way of telling the story without intricate graphics. Unfortunately, our story as televised would not be nearly as compelling or authoritative in demonstrating the many ways that the new and the old documents fit together. Our video editors were working away and I continued to labor over the script.

Late Tuesday afternoon, Josh called me to his office. The White House had called asking what we were working on for the following night. The word was that we had a story on Bush's Guard service. I wondered what had taken so long.

Josh, Betsy, and several others decided that Josh would read the memos over the phone that night to someone at the White House, as soon as the Bush people agreed to an interview in the morning. From what I understood, that exchange happened later Tuesday evening. I wasn't there. I was downstairs in Dana's squalid office working on the script.

By Wednesday morning after another mostly sleepless night, I had a script hammered together that I believed would get us through much of the day. I knew I would have to make major changes once we received reaction from the administration.

We knew that Dan Bartlett, one of the White House media masterminds, would be speaking for the president about the documents. What we didn't know was who would do the interview for CBS. A massive rainstorm had moved onto the East Coast, engulfing New York and Washington in a heavy downpour that would last most of the day. There was no way that Dan could get on a plane and run the risk of not being able to get back to New York for the evening newscast or to do the taped opening of 60 *Minutes*. The train was an option but was too slow.

Our news executives decided that White House correspondent John Roberts would do the Bartlett interview. I e-mailed questions and spoke with John briefly, telling him that I was prepared for the White House to say the memos were fakes. I thought that was their only possible po-litical strategy, to deny everything. It also fit with Bush überadviser Karl Rove's take-no-prisoners media policy, a tendency to attack the mes-senger if the White House didn't like the message. It turned out I was right about the tactic but terribly wrong about the timing.

Roberts went to speak with Bartlett late Wednesday morning. It seemed like hours until he came out and called me back with the offi-cial response. Bartlett did not point to the documents as possible fakes or say he didn't believe them. He took a different tack, contending that the documents merely confirmed much of what the Bush camp had said for years. The fact that the story was coming out now, he said, was nothing more than politics.

"Well I think, generally, it's obvious that it's election season now," Bartlett said on-camera as the interview began. "Every time President Bush gets near another election, all the innuendo and rumors about President Bush's service in the National Guard come to the forefront.

"It's not surprising that people like Ben Barnes, longtime activist, Democratic activist, who is a vice chairman of John Kerry, would be making these recycled charges of President Bush."

John Roberts pushed right back, refusing to let Bartlett dismiss the documents as simply politics as usual. "What about these two official documents signed by Jerry Killian is rumor and innuendo?"

Bartlett seemed to be caught flat-footed. "Well, it's impossible for anybody to read the mind of a dead man. Killian writes memos to him-self in this file."

Roberts cut in. "I'm not talking about the memos to himself. I'm talking about the two official documents."

Roberts and Bartlett jousted over two documents in particular. The May 4, 1972, memo in which Killian ordered Bush to take a physical and the one dated August 1, 1972, that suspended Bush from flying for failure to take his physical, among other things.

Roberts said to Bartlett: "This first document, dated fourth of May

186 | MARY MAPES

1972, specifically says, 'You are ordered to report for a physical examination.' So he either ignored or didn't fulfill a direct order, not an option."

Bartlett answered: "In fact, the memorandum shows, the other memorandum in your possession shows, that he spoke to the commander who made that order to talk about his personal situation in the fact that he was going to Alabama. So at every step of the way, President Bush was meeting his requirements, granted permission to meet his requirements. And that's why President Bush received an honorable discharge."

Bush indeed was honorably discharged, but that didn't eliminate the possibility that he hadn't completely fulfilled his military duties. If the Texas Air National Guard was flexible enough to let a pilot walk away from his commitment when he had more than two years remaining on his promise to perform, it could certainly be flexible enough to hand out an honorable discharge to the same man.

Bartlett pushed the honorable discharge argument again and again: "He's proud of the fact that he was honorably discharged, and the fact that people are raising politics at this time is part of the game. But it doesn't ignore the facts, and the facts are there in his file. He met his requirements, he satisfied his commander's requirements, and that's why he was given an honorable discharge."

Roberts asked the question I had been waiting for: "Is your suggestion that these documents, at least a couple of them, could have been fabricated?"

Bartlett didn't bite. "I'm not saying that at all. I'm just saying that the fact that documents like this are being raised when, in fact, all they do is reaffirm what we've said all along is questionable.

"It's not a coincidence."

It was fair to say that the interview had not been a strong performance by Bartlett. As we watched the tape being fed in from Washington, many of us had a similar reaction. Boy, this could be a real problem for Bush. After all these years of unanswered questions about the president's Guard career, sending out a spokesman to keep repeating that Bush had been honorably discharged wasn't going to cut it. Not when the nation had National Guard troops in harm's way at this very moment on the other side of the world.

I selected the portions of the interview that best made Bartlett's points and had them taken to the editors, along with instructions for where we would lay them into the story.

The script from which we were editing began with the new documents and included a number of caveats regarding what we knew about these memos. It included a thorough history of Bush's performance as a pilot prior to the time these memos were supposedly written. I thought that was only fair. In Bush's evaluations before his missing year, he had gotten good marks. Lieutenant Colonel Killian's two previous evaluations of Lieutenant Bush had bordered on glowing.

This is a passage from an original script for our story:

In 1971, Colonel Killian signed off on a report saying, "Lieutenant Bush is an exceptionally fine young officer and pilot," who "performed in an outstanding manner."

In May 1972, Bush's performance report was also very complimentary. Colonel Killian signed a statement saying that the future president was "an exceptional fighter interceptor pilot and officer."

About two in the afternoon, we had our first screening and, as we sometimes did with crashes, we viewed the story in the editing room in two sections. Our whole team was there. Betsy came down to watch, as did Josh and some of the eight or so others who were regularly involved in making sure that questions and answers from interviews were not taken out of context, that the writing was up to snuff, and that technical details were in order.

The story was too long. My memory is that it ran about sixteen minutes, at least three minutes longer than we were slated to run. As Josh watched, I could see he wasn't happy.

The section quoting from the new and old documents and showing how they folded together was not exciting or visual. I thought it was important, however. Those details were the only way to demonstrate not only Bush's praiseworthy performance in 1970 and 1971, but that something had drastically changed in what turned out to be his last two years. Going through the documents might be tedious, but it was necessary to let viewers understand how these new memos meshed with the official record, which was compelling evidence for their believability.

The first version of the story also included an interview with Marcel Matley and an explanation of what he did to check out the signatures. We had him on-camera saying he found that the signatures on the new documents were made by the same person who signed the official records.

When the lights went up, Josh made it clear he wanted the story flip-flopped, with Barnes coming first, followed by the section on the memos. I didn't disagree, but I began to worry seriously about the lack of time we had to make these changes. I started to get that shivery feeling I had when I knew I didn't have enough time to get a story exactly the way I wanted. With the amount of detail we had to plow through, the complicated script, and the technical demands of putting up graphics to illustrate the memos, I did not know how we were going to do it.

Josh also wanted me to drastically cut down the section showing the new documents meshing with the old. In fact, he really didn't want any of that meshing explanation in the piece. I didn't understand his reasoning and I thought he was being heavy-handed. He was making a decision based on style, not substance.

But I felt crushed by the press of time. We were only hours from air-time and he was the program's executive producer. We discussed some options briefly, but the ticking clock was a tyrant. We had to get moving and make some decisions.

Josh decided we should completely leave the meshing evidence out of our story. He thought it was too confusing, too many specifics for viewers to follow, too inside baseball. I balked and then reluctantly agreed in the pressure-cooker atmosphere that was heating up around us. Josh's decision meant that we would undermine our story's credibility, omitting some of its strongest corroborating details. We sacrificed complexity and substantiation for simplicity—and we would pay for it dearly.

But the cutting didn't stop there. Josh also wanted to remove a section from the script where we reported that General Hodges, Colonel Killian's direct commander, had corroborated the memos' content. Hodges's statements to me had strongly supported the documents' authenticity and absolutely had to be part of the script. This was part of what I had written: "General Hodges described Colonel Killian as a 'hardnose' who saw 'everything in black and white.' But he confirmed that these memos were consistent with the disapproval Colonel Killian had expressed about Lieutenant Bush at the time."

Josh told me to get rid of that passage, as well. We had no pictures, no interview, no way to break up the long narrative. It was a style decision that would be another blow to our story's credibility. We were now excluding altogether two of our strongest reasons for believing that the memos were real. Two of the three sturdy legs supporting our story were knocked aside in haste. Those choices didn't change the validity of our report or the questions it raised, but they preempted vital areas of corroboration that could have made a huge difference to viewers when the story aired. Once the firestorm began over the documents' font style, it seemed that no one on the right and no one in the media was interested in that corroboration. Our news executives up the line even lost sight of the value of General Hodges's confirmation, or the importance of the meshing analysis. More likely, the CBS executives never paid enough attention in the first place to understand it or what it meant to the credibility of the story.

Will would later tell the investigative panel that she had absolutely not deferred to Matley and that she had flagged more problems with the documents than simply the superscript "th." For my part, I have no recollection of that: I simply don't recall her raising questions about either proportional spacing or problems with the signatures.

The piece we were left with made it look as though our trust in the new memos rested entirely on the word of document analysts: Marcel Matley and the off-camera support from document analyst Jim Pierce, who had only seen the two original Burkett memos; Linda James, who wanted to see the originals; and Emily Will, who had deferred to Marcel but had questions about the superscripted "th."

I was uncomfortable with the script and, in retrospect, I should have done something I'd never done at work before. I should have said, "No." I should have said, "You'll have to run some other story tonight. I'm not going to crash this. I'm not going to go any further. We have an important, valid story and we're going to make sure we present it as completely and clearly as we can."

But I didn't say those things. Instead, I went back to work on the script as ordered and kept juggling and writing, trying to come up with a format that Josh and, to a lesser extent, Betsy would accept.

Neither of them was comfortable with Hackworth in the story. They felt he was too political and so he was gone, too. Our running time was now closer to what we needed, but in terms of content, our troubles were growing by the hour.

I was beginning to believe that Josh had never crashed a piece. I knew that working on a story right up to the moment of airtime was rare on the Sunday broadcast, but I had no idea that Josh was totally out of his element in putting together a story quickly. Betsy hadn't worked as a story producer in years. But there we were, crammed into Dana's office, watching the clock and trying our best to pull this mule of a story onto the air.

I have never come so close to missing a deadline. God, I wish that for once in my life I had.

The scene that Wednesday night as time grew short would have made sausage making look like an art form. I was hunched over my computer, dangerously close to airtime, while Betsy and Josh struggled to make script changes.

After twenty-five years in television, I had developed an almost phys-ical sense of what I needed to do and when I needed to have it done in order to get something on the air. On this night, I was in pain. I was los-ing control of the clock and losing control of the story.

Everyone was frantic. Two editors were waiting for newly recorded audio tracks of the latest script. Josh and Betsy were having trouble making up their minds. They were putting things in and taking them out in what seemed like willy-nilly fashion. We went back and forth, ar-guing over each change and thrashing about to make decent choices as the minutes ticked away.

Eventually, there was no time to argue the merits of what was being left in the script or what was being left out. They told me, I typed. They asked for a change, I made it. I was on producer autopilot. I felt I had no choice. They were my bosses. I couldn't—wouldn't—miss a deadline.

Everyone else working on our reporting team had fled the small of-fice. The tension in the room was too much for most. Our faces were drained; our hair was matted down; our voices were raised. My laptop kept locking up; the printer wouldn't work; the phone kept ringing; my stomach kept churning. We looked like we were delivering a baby in the back of a cab, complete with screams, tears, and torn clothing.

Dan came in and quickly recorded changes in narration. The editors, white-faced and rightly terrified, grabbed their tracks and ran back to their editing bays to continue slashing the piece together.

We all watched the story one more time, and then Josh said he had to take it. I was later told that the tape of the story was shown to Andrew Heyward. I wasn't there for that screening. I had collapsed on Dana's couch.

The story aired at 8:00 P.M. and, on the broadcast, it looked solid. I began to beat myself up for being so worried. Friends and colleagues called to congratulate me. Dan was pleased. I felt peaceful after an unbelievably long day of stress and fear and worry about what could go wrong. By the barest of margins, it seemed we had pulled it off.

In my wildest dreams, I couldn't have imagined the course I had charted for myself. I couldn't imagine the shock waves that would reverberate through television and journalism and the Internet, through politics and my personal life.

Without knowing it, I had just bitten the top off a grenade and thrown it, sputtering and about to blow, into the middle of my life.

CHAPTER 12

The attack on our *60 Minutes* story gathered force while we slept. An invisible army was moving into position against us before we even went to bed. As we fell asleep, the first shots were fired. The next morning all hell broke loose. That's how quickly this campaign of criticism, however partisan and inaccurate, took root and began to flourish.

The lightning speed of the attack, the overwhelming nature of the echo chamber poised to discredit us, combined with CBS's inability to coordinate an effective, coherent response and the failure of the rest of the media to slow down, do some thorough, objective reporting, and stop repeating the unsubstantiated claims of the blogs, ultimately doomed the story and all of us who put it together.

Sadly, that group included Dan Rather, one of this country's and this generation's premier reporters. The list of victims would also include CBS News itself, for decades a bastion of solid journalism and a fortress for corporate leaders who weren't afraid to fight for the right to report the truth, fairly and aggressively, without fear of recrimination.

By September 2004, CBS's past leaders—men like Bill Paley and Fred Friendly and Ed Murrow himself—seemed to belong to an almost quaint time when public service took precedence over profits, when broadcast journalism was not just another product line. The people who had replaced those old-timers were unable or unwilling, beyond a point, to fight for journalistic principles or for a story. In defense of both the news division and the corporation, however, none of us, myself included, quite knew how to battle back in the face of this first-ever cyberattack on mainstream media.

The bloggers and the Web site operators seemed to have so many advantages. They could rail against CBS News twenty-four hours a day. They could say whatever they wanted without regard for standards of accuracy or balance. They could twist the truth without any imperative approaching fairness or reason. They could launch hateful personal attacks from the comfort of their unconscionable anonymity. They could make cruel and childish jokes, egging one another on like drunks in a bar. The masked belligerents howling for accountability from CBS had no accountability of their own. They were off the leash and running wild. The mainstream media didn't know what to make of this man-made firestorm, and as they tried to figure it out, it blinded them, too. Where there was so much smoke, wouldn't there be some fire?

CBS had to be more responsible than its denigrators, of course, and there was limited airtime, limited resources, and limited vision about how the company could wage a war against a group of aggressive nameless attackers. The volume of their protests and the repetitiveness of their blasts captured the attention of the mainstream press, which has always licked its chops over a good scrap—especially one involving a major competitor—and, given the political climate, most certainly didn't want to be accused of ignoring conservative complaints.

Most important, unlike CBS, the bloggers had no standards or history to protect. They had no standards or history at all. They appear and disappear overnight. Yet somehow, incredibly, no one seriously held them or their claims up to real, legitimate scrutiny.

Part of the problem was the age of some of the facts in question. The companies holding the old IBM or other typewriter trademarks had to tell inquiring reporters that they no longer had anyone on staff who could discuss the finer points of the type fonts used in 1972 or of the proportional spacing both side to side and up and down on a typed page. Although bloggers may have been proficient at digital communication, they were hard-pressed when it came to getting solid information on obsolete technologies. At CBS, we had to search hard to get a straight technical analysis of the documents, and bloggers were working with versions that had been photocopied, faxed, posted on the Internet and downloaded. We then all had to rely on the individual testimony and memory of people who claimed expertise in an adversarial, subjective field.

We at CBS were able to find several reliable and credible authorities who confirmed that proportional spacing and the little superscript "th" *were* indeed available on typewriters in the early 1970s, particularly in specialized applications such as the military, which bought huge numbers of typewriters and could specify what they needed. We put these authorities on the air in defense of our story, but their carefully stated knowledge and experience were disregarded.

Bloggers were already bellowing about fakery with more certainty than a carload of credible, cautious experts could overcome.

Conservatives had quickly decided what they wanted the conclusions to be—that these memos were fakes—and spread their "findings" like wildfire. Their knee-jerk response didn't bother with the extra, objective steps that we had taken, inspecting and analyzing the memos in total and then reaching a judgment. We had done signature comparisons and content analysis and made phone calls to people who had been in Bush's unit. We meshed the old official records with the newly discovered memos looking for overlap, disagreement, or corroboration. To the bloggers and ultimately—almost insanely—to the mainstream media, none of this work mattered. Our critics never addressed the Jerry Killian signatures in any meaningful way or the content of the memos at all. They focused on the fonts and gave birth to the big lie: The documents we had weren't real.

Bloggers felt the truth could be found in the tiny crossbar of the letter "t," the foot or lack of foot on the numeral "4," the blob of ink on the end of an apostrophe. But the bloggers and their "experts" were looking at these minute details on *bad* copies. The versions they inspected had been repeatedly copied and repeatedly faxed, then scanned, and then downloaded, forever altering their appearance in large and small ways. A comparison of the photocopied memos we originally received and the memos as they appeared in the variety of analyses done by bloggers is shocking. They don't look like the same documents and they really aren't. (See Appendix 1.)

Bloggers didn't bother looking at the entire forest—the content, the context, the totality of the documents. They peered through soda straws at individual twigs. They sought their final answers in the least technically sound manner. What they found were minuscule elements they needed to build into whopping lies about the memos, the president's service, and CBS's work on this story. And it all worked.

Accusation, mischaracterization, and blatant inaccuracies migrated rapidly from Blogger World to big media. It was unbelievable.

However the strategy originated, it proved ingenious for the perpetrators. These were their primary initial points in arguing that the new documents could not have been produced in 1972 and 1973. Bloggers said flatly that typewriters didn't have these specialized functions at that time. The blogs quoted various so-called experts, some of them anonymously, some of them by name. None of these self-proclaimed specialists ever looked at any of the memos other than those available to be downloaded from either the White House Web site or the CBS Web site.

The bloggers' experts were obsessed with whether the individual letters in the new memos were proportionally spaced, rather than each letter taking up the same amount of space. They also focused on the memos' use of a superscripted "th," as in "111th," as well as the memos' seemingly curled apostrophes. They declared that the memos were typed in Times New Roman, a font that happened to match a default setting for Microsoft Word computer documents. The font also existed in 1972 and 1973.

Later—much later—each of those arguments would prove patently false, at least to the satisfaction of many, but by then it didn't matter. And we would learn that an array of typewriters had those supposedly impossible specialized features even before the early 1970s. The memos' font was not Times New Roman, recent examination has confirmed. But those accusations and others stuck long enough until more doubts, equally groundless, were raised, held high, used as clubs against us, and then discarded.

The bloggers were merely the starting point. A perfect storm of complicity was brewing with the bloggers and the mainstream media, and the violent crosswinds helped sweep away the solid work, the solid story, we had built.

Other news organizations played a crucial role as the controversy deepened, not as reasoned arbiters of the disputed points but as competitors who saw their own opportunities in another's misfortune.

Some of the competitive criticism of our work may have been done unknowingly, but most of it seemed carefully aimed to do us harm.

Competitors' news reports chipped away at parts of our report at the same time that they swallowed many of the bloggers' arguments hook, line, and sinker: They used blog site sources or found a few experts of their own who doubted that old typewriters had fancy spacing or that tiny "th" or who were suspicious of the memos' type font.

Colonel Killian's son and widow, who were ardent Bush supporters and who weeks earlier had said they knew little about the elder Killian's Guard career, now went public to say they thought the memos were fakes, citing no substantive reasons. Bobby Hodges repeated the charge, citing the Killian family, although the general continued to confirm that Killian had discussed his problems with Lieutenant Bush with him. I was accused, wrongly, of conspiring with the John Kerry campaign in my attempt to get the documents from Bill Burkett. Competitors also mischaracterized the work and conclusions of our document analysts. *The Washington Post* ran a blatantly inaccurate and particularly damaging report that Marcel Matley said he did not "authenticate" the new documents for CBS and had examined only one Killian signature. He had, in fact, found nothing in the typeface or signature to indicate the documents were not authentic, but their authenticity could not be physically proved because they were photocopies.

Each of these issues, individually, could be corrected and knocked down. But together they began to form a wall, brick by brick, that would seal our story's fate.

The debate was reduced to two taunts that rang out like schoolyard mockery. The first might have been funny if it hadn't been so pathetically frustrating: The documents are fake! They're phony! They're forgeries!

The other taunt was equally maddening: Prove the documents aren't fake! Prove they're real! That, as we'd known from the start, was impossible. Only original documents can be tested and proved authentic. We had relied on other tests: witnesses, analysts, Bush's official documents. But in this supercharged climate, I couldn't get anyone, even at CBS, to pay attention to the subtle but important clues inside the old military records. No one was listening to reason, just to the siren song of the supercharged blogs.

Now I know that none of this had to happen. This was an abberation, an ugly moment when mainstream media's credibility problems caused by journalism scandals, the rise of conservative Web sites, corporate interests, dirty politics, and an inattentive public got together and had a horrible party. They tore up the furniture, broke the wineglasses, left cigarette burns everywhere, and had hangovers for weeks. Then everything went back to normal. Or at least it did for some people. The rest of us saw our jobs and our life's work destroyed in a few weeks of chaos and abandon. The reputations we had worked so hard to build were trashed repeatedly by bloggers who sat in the dark and signed off on angry missives with names like Travimoto, steplock, and Big Kahuna. How do you respond to someone who doesn't have the balls to step out from behind the keyboard? How do you win an argument with a cipher?

I didn't know the exact chronology of our demise until long after the shouting and the shrieking had died down. I just knew that on September 9, 2004, everything I had worked for professionally and much of what I believed in personally began to fall apart under a withering hail of virulently partisan e-mails, vicious Internet postings, and untrue mischaracterizations on conservative Web sites.

Just before midnight Eastern time, an anonymous blogger calling himself Buckhead posted a long analysis of our memos based on what he claimed were facts about typography. His screed appeared first on the conservative Free Republic Web site. To the untrained and the undereducated, to those who had lived their entire lives without plunging into the mind-numbing history of American typography—and that included virtually everyone—Buckhead's initial post certainly seemed impressive.

Whoever he was, Buckhead wrote like he really knew his way around the history of type, typewriters, and computer printing.

Every single one of these "memos to file" is in a proportionally spaced font, probably Palatino or Times New Roman. In 1972 people used typewriters for this sort of thing and typewriters used monospaced fonts. The use of proportionally spaced fonts did not come into common use for office memos until the introduction of laser printers, word processing and personal computers. . . .

I am saying these documents are forgeries, run through a copier for 15 generations to make them look old. This should be aggressively pursued.

Buckhead, the self-appointed expert, and whatever unnamed collab-
orators fed him his information were *wrong* about proportional spacing, *wrong* about the type font, and *wrong* about any reasonable—let
alone conclusive—evidence that the memos were forged. But the
avalanche he started had already begun to slide down the mountain,
destroying everything in its path.

Buckhead's midnight call to arms was all that the radical right blogosphere needed to hear. There had never been anything like it, a mo-
bilization of right-wing Internet users to assail a specific news story.
They would use their numbers, their volume, and their sheer insistence
to rip at a respected anchor/reporter, a news program, and a network
that the right wing had caricatured for decades as the epitome of an
elite, liberal media. These were people who still resented Edward R.
Murrow for taking on McCarthy, who never forgave Walter Cronkite
for telling the truth about Vietnam, who were still raging at Dan
Rather for his work on Watergate.

Now their bloodlust had found an opportunity and before Dan
Rather or Andrew Heyward or I even knew what was happening, these
people were on the march, pitchforks, fiery torches, and computer
keyboards in hand.

Bloggers and readers in this activist arm of conservatism were already closely organized around a handful of related and interdepend-
ent Web sites. Their dark and angry little computer kingdom constitutes
the Internet's version of conservative talk radio, which seized a huge
slice of America's airwaves two decades ago with its black-and-white,
blast furnace approach to issues and politics. Now there is an army of
bitter and braying radical conservatives out there doing the same thing
in cyberspace.

Buckhead's hastily reached conclusions and accusations about the
Bush-Guard story were immediately echoed on a bouquet of other far
right Web sites—particularly Powerline and Little Green Footballs—
places that most of the mainstream media had never heard of but
would learn about in the hours, days, and weeks ahead. As regular media outlets discovered these conservative sites and their army of follow-
ers, the bloggers were handed a newfound power that must have seemed
both startling and miraculous to them. Their partisan claims, unsubstantiated as they were to any observer who truly clung to objectivity,

were stated and restated incessantly as absolute, unshakable facts. Their hubris went virtually unchallenged by the mainstream media, which didn't know a damned thing about typeface, kerning, or proportional spacing, either, but tried hard to appear that it did. A few progressive Web sites did some fascinating work, but it seemed that few people paid attention. God forbid somebody could withhold their opinion until they learned something. Skepticism, a supposed hallmark of journalism, was largely forgotten and many reporters quickly and unquestioningly accepted the bloggers' arguments.

Once again, in a graphic demonstration that the media does not work in anything approaching a monolothic way, other big media outlets had their own agendas as the controversy over the *60 Minutes* Bush-Guard story exploded.

Sadly, for some media outlets, the agenda was not independent, careful, thoughtful analysis. Media organizations, even those not planted firmly on the right, who are not motivated by partisanship and still pride themselves on unbiased and fair reporting, nonetheless had a unique bias of their own relating to our story. Just as our *60 Minutes* team believed the story we had presented was a well-corroborated, valid, and accurate report, the other big media, both print and electronic, desperately wanted it to be the opposite. It simply made for a better story.

As in any public discussion, these mainstream media outlets were the forum for much of the debate, though what was happening on the Internet was overshadowing and outrunning the big media as never before. But suddenly, the old-line media companies were once more cast as arbiters of one of their own and, this time, CBS was in their gun sights. The reasons were pure and simple: competitiveness and perhaps a chance to see a competitor suffer the kind of blow they themselves had suffered in recent years. *The New York Times* had Jayson Blair, *USA Today* was embarrassed by Jack Kelley, *The New Republic* was fooled by Stephen Glass. Almost everyone had fought lawsuits, published inaccurate reporting, made embarrassing mistakes. Headlines like this had recently dominated reporting about the media. It seemed competitors decided it was *60 Minutes*'s turn and eagerly stacked wood on our funeral pyre. The problem was that they were wrong. If we had committed errors, they were not the kind of journalistic errors that deserved the death penalty. No one had lied, made up quotes, created stories, or fabricated evidence to cover our trail. We had not committed journalistic crimes.

Our critics on the Web, however, had no such allegiance to the truth. Their interest in this story begins and ends with the radical right. Buckhead, our first anonymous hit man, is no stranger to conservative causes. The *Los Angeles Times* revealed that his name is Harry W. MacDougald, and he is an Atlanta lawyer with years of experience working on right-wing issues.

What made MacDougald such an instant authority on typography and its history? Who knew? Who cared? Certainly not the people who shared MacDougald's politics. They adopted his overnight expertise on typography and everything else without question.

In his day job as a litigator—where MacDougald presumably uses his real name—he is affiliated with two conservative legal groups, the Southeastern Legal Foundation and the Federalist Society, whose agendas reflect a far right approach to litigation and legal questions on a wide array of subjects.

The Southeastern Legal Society, where MacDougald serves on the legal advisory board, has challenged affirmative action and domestic partner benefits for government workers.

MacDougald was also a key player in drafting the petition that eventually won a five-year suspension of Bill Clinton's Arkansas law license after Clinton's misleading testimony in the Paula Jones sexual harassment case. He could hardly be described as a disinterested political observer when he made judgments on the Killian memos.

Call me a cynical reporter, but I am beginning to see a pattern here.

MacDougald's overnight savaging of the Bush-Guard memo was an unqualified success and quickly led to his celebration as a cyber folk hero. Gracious in victory, he has insisted that his fellow cybercitizens share his glory. Freepers, the denizens of the Free Republic site, "collectively possess more analytical horsepower than the entire news division at CBS," he boasted in an e-mail published in the *Los Angeles Times*.

But much of the analytical stuff that Freepers and MacDougald were handing out was more horseshit than horsepower. Much of what MacDougald boasted in his initial e-mail assertion quickly and plainly was shown to be untrue. MacDougald himself later posted a modification, saying that proportional spacing *may* have existed in 1972. Then he waivered on that. Buckhead's back-and-forth was a reflection of the difficulty anyone had in making flat pronouncements of what did and didn't exist on typewriters thirty years ago. But by that time, none of it mattered. The damage was done. There was blood in the water, my blood. The blood of my friends and colleagues.

Within minutes of Buckhead's original posting, Freepers began to repeat and embellish Buckhead's thoughts. Not surprisingly, they all agreed with him, they all agreed with one another, and they all agreed this should be pursued aggressively. Freethinkers they are not. The Freepers and their lockstep like-minded fellow travelers moved as a group, like a school of sharks sweeping toward an unaware and un-armed victim. CBS was like some sunburned, overweight Florida tourist with a cut foot, floundering and flapping in the water alone in the surf. The Freepers swarmed CBS not because it was right or fair but because they could. On Web sites such as Powerline, INDC Journal, Allahpundit, and Spacetownusa, the bravehearts of the blogging world worked anonymously in what appeared to be huge numbers, in unison, to destroy the Bush-Guard story, to uphold one another's wild and hateful claims, to outshout, outargue, and outblog anyone who dared to dis-agree. And on their Web sites there is no disagreement. They hate in uni-son, they speak with one angry voice, they each make themselves bigger by staying as close together as possible.

Their postings, their beliefs that the memos were fakes, and their trashing of CBS spread rapidly across the blogosphere. It was like the monster that ate Cleveland, and by midday that monster was pounding on my office door inside the CBS building.

That's where Betsy West appeared, holding two pieces of paper. One was a printout of one of our memos. The other was a slightly different, slightly cleaner version of the same memo. "Mary," she asked, "what's going on? These blogs are saying that the memo can be re-created ex-actly in Microsoft Word." She looked stricken and held both papers up with shaking hands. I tried to look at them, but I wasn't sure what to say. They did look similar. But I didn't think they were exact. How could a person even tell how closely they resembled each other with-out, at the very least, a magnifying glass? We weren't document exam-iners. "Mary," Betsy pushed, "what's going on?"

I told her I didn't know. I wasn't a typography expert. I was a news producer. I could give her anything she wanted in terms of chapter and verse on the Bush story or go over countless details constituting why I thought these documents were real. I could tell her a story, quote people who knew Bush's record and performance, show her the president's official records and how they agreed with the new memos.

The supposed replication of one of the documents on a computer would prove to be the most damaging allegation against us. It was quick, it was easy, and it appeared deceptively definitive to anyone making quick, uneducated comparisons. The problem was that it proved nothing, other than the fact that computers can replicate all kinds of things. The spacing and characters in the replication were close to the Killian memo, especially to the amateur eye, but they were not precise. It was fraudulent evidence, yet the world believed it.

It is possible, with the right fonts, to replicate an endless stream of documents. That is not an indication that these original documents are not "real." It is a reflection of the fact that computers are incredibly flexible technical tools. The Times New Roman font used for the widely circulated replication does not match the font in the Killian memos. Many of the memos' characters differ from Times New Roman and some analysts have said that the memos' font looks more like Press Roman, a different old font altogether.

There are comparisons of some of the letters in the memos with the Times New Roman version of the same letter at www.truthandduty.com. The differences are obvious and demonstrate that the Killian memos were not produced using this Microsoft font.

In September 2004, I did not have the ability to glibly or quickly knock down this kind of parlor trick. I could not hold up a piece of paper and pretend to prove anything. I was a newsperson who came to conclusions after long periods of questioning, examination of other records, knocking on doors, making phone calls, and talking to people who were there at the time in question. I had looked at this story, off and on, for years. I didn't make conclusions based on the shape of a letter or what I *thought* was the shape of a letter. I didn't have that kind of training and neither did Buckhead.

Inside CBS, we were approaching full panic. Part of the problem was that we suddenly found ourselves in a war and the network didn't fight wars. It didn't know how to fight wars. It didn't have a war room. It didn't have a war mentality. CBS had a press office that released carefully crafted items on upcoming broadcasts, doling out details on what had happened on the week's *Survivor* episode and touting sneak peeks at the triumphant or deeply shaken participants on reality shows. The PR unit created timeless blurbs like this: "Hear from Jennifer, the morning after she lost the Tribal Council tiebreaker," or, "Watch Big Brother: Will Maggie or Eric leave the Big Brother house for good?" Sometimes, they would simply list the celebrities appearing on *David Letterman* that night. The people who do that for a living are not soldiers and their work area does not constitute the kind of war room found in fight-to-the-death campaigns. That's what CBS News needed. What we got couldn't have been further from what we needed.

There are PR people working specifically for CBS News as well, but they were not experienced in the hand-to-hand combat that quickly developed in the backlash against the Bush-Guard story. They were best prepared to answer the usual flood of questions about how old Mike Wallace is and where viewers can get a transcript of a story on Medicare cuts.

One CBS PR man was brought in specifically to help, a confidant of Les Moonves named Gil Schwartz. I'd had virtually no experience with Gil, so I didn't know what to expect. Naïvely, I thought we were working toward the same thing, that we all wanted to defend the story, to come out of this intact. In retrospect, I believe Gil's only job was to make sure that the corporation and the corporate leaders, particularly Les Moonves, came out okay. The rest of us were on our own. In that regard, Gil did a masterful job. In fact, I understand he got a promotion shortly after the debacle drew to a close. I hope he accepts my belated congratulations.

No matter whom Gil was trying to protect, it seemed almost impossible for anyone within CBS to have any impact on the cyberdiscussion or the way that it fed the mainstream press response. On September 10, two days after our story ran, Gil sent me an e-mail. "If we can destroy the 'th' issue, we're way ahead," it said.

He meant that he wanted to address the criticisms of the "superscript," the raised "th" that appeared at several points in the memos. Critics said that it didn't exist at the time the memos were supposed to have been typed. But it *did* exist. We reported this on the *CBS Evening News* on September 10. We had found examples. We just couldn't break through the wall and get people to understand this.

I just didn't know how to convince people that the main criticism being leveled at us was baseless. Facts couldn't do it. People on-camera vouching for the facts didn't cut it for these people. Examples of "th" in old copy plastered all over CBS didn't have any impact. What could we do?

This speculation, that the superscripted "th" could not possibly have been done on a typewriter in use in 1972 or 1973, had begun with Buckhead. And all rational thinking about it seemed to stop there. No one listened anymore.

To prove Buckhead wrong, a number of us had stayed up half the night, going through badly Xeroxed official Bush documents released by the government until we found a small superscripted "th." Roger Charles and a few others sympathetic to our plight—to fairness, really—helped us find still other contemporaneous examples of the precious superscripted "th."

One example of a "th" that we found in official Bush documents appeared to have been typed as early as 1968, and we planned to put it on the air that night and release it online to show our critics that the "th" issue was resolved.

In the meantime, we had already written press releases saying that the "th" issue had been resolved and a handful of reasonable Web sites were posting examples of the new superscripted "th" from official documents. But amazingly, none of it made any difference.

By this time, I was terribly frustrated with the cyberworld's stubborn refusal to accept reality and I barked back at Gil in an e-mail: "For the 1000th time, the 'th' issue is gone. We have examples from the official White House docs. We're set."

Gil decided to lecture his dim-witted colleague:

The problem, Mary, is one of perception. As far as the press is concerned, the "th" issue is not gone. It's very much alive and they have people crawling all over it. If we wait to address the issue until tonight's news, we will DIE in the press tomorrow. Die. . . . As in dead.

You tell me. How do I get the message out RIGHT NOW, as in RIGHT THIS VERY MINUTE, that the "th" thing is no longer an issue? They've got a bunch of "experts." We have nothing. We need to communicate something in the next hour or so if the story isn't going to thunder away from us on a Friday afternoon. Help me out. Gil.

I didn't know what else to do. I had done my job. Now it seemed I was being given responsibility for failing to craft an effective PR defense on behalf of my story. I was failing to convince the bloggers even though we had ample evidence. What could I do? I wasn't superhuman. I wasn't a PR whiz. I knew how to get and tell stories. I didn't have a clue how to launch or win a PR war.

I felt physically sick. I could feel my colleagues, especially at the executive level, turning on me. Josh, Mary, Betsy, and Andrew had grown cold. I had wanted to do this story. I had brought it to them. I had assured them I had it. Now I had caused a big mess. I had been wrong. I was the problem. I hated myself. Sticking together as always at CBS, my executives hated me, too.

I don't know when I have ever felt so lonely or so inconsolable, certainly not over a professional situation. My heart seemed to ache with each beat.

The concept of the Internet as a model of democratic discussion is a sound and attractive one: the free enterprise system applied to ideas and information and elevated by technology to be easily accessible to all. Who could disagree with the value of a forum where issues can be considered, examined, and challenged, an open exchange of thoughts and perspectives for the inquisitive? Blogs, at their best, can do those things and more.

But like an iceberg, there's much more to the Internet than what's on the surface. For all its advantages, it is the innovation that has allowed every form of pornography to run rampant and has made identity theft and financial scams as common as car theft. There's a terrible

206 | MARY MAPES

truth about political blogging, as well. At one time, there may have
been a notion that many blog sites were made up of respectful, self-
correcting communities of concerned citizens who are strictly interested in the truth and will quickly set the record straight on any issue.
That is pure unadulterated horseshit. Far too often, there's nothing
civil or intelligent about the discourse on angry partisan sites. More
likely, bloggers on many partisan political sites cling to their own kind,
nurturing their prejudices, shouting down dissent, and promoting hate-
speak against any presumed opposition. The result can be closer to fas-
cism than democracy. Far from a place where everyone has a voice, the
blogosphere is often about who shouts loudest.

The world of the bloggers is the snakes' nest where personal and professional attacks were spawned against my CBS colleagues and me.
While I was trying to figure out how to defend Dan Rather, my story,
and our record, I suddenly had to deal with the fact that blogs like Free
Republic—those proud defenders of the Constitution—were posting
my picture alongside some choice words.

The first one I saw was early on Friday, September 10. There was a
shot of me from the day in 1999 when I was going to jail in Jasper and
above the photo were the words "Here's the bitch."

A moment later NavyCanDo, a poster on a blog who must be very
proud of himself, wrote: "I'm picturing Sean Hannity right now sharp-
ening his knife to gut this witch. The house of cards is coming down."
A moment later, there was another post about me: "Mapes: feminazi
propagandist."

I am not faint of heart. I can laugh at myself—and even appreciate
the irony of having a perfectly wretched picture of myself bandied endlessly about the Internet. But by the end of that Friday, when I had
been drenched in a downpour of dirty names, filthy ideas, and unfair
characterizations, I didn't have much fight left. There was a mean, sex-
ist tone to it all. This seemed to be a boys' club. And I do mean *boys*.
None of the good men I have been lucky enough to know and include
in my life would ever have behaved this way to anyone, whether they
knew her or not.

I think the majesty and maturity of the bloggers' sentiments speak
for themselves:

God, does she look like an evil lefty sneak.

Somebody wore out a whole bag of ugly sticks on her.

Ugly stick? She fell out of the ugly tree and hit every branch on the way down.

YUP. She sure looks like a socialist to me.

Me thinks she is also the "diesel" persuasion. A good many of them are forced to join those ranks because men avoid them like the plague.

I was embarrassed and hurt and ashamed, the roughed-up victim of electronic assault. I had to try and ignore it and keep working, keep trying to knock down what the blogs were saying when they weren't criticizing my hair or my looks or whatever it was about my life that they so resented.

Friday afternoon, as I was preparing that night's *Evening News* story rebutting the criticism, I got a phone call from Pete Slover, a reporter who worked at *The Dallas Morning News*, the newspaper where my husband had been a reporter for years. Slover worked in Austin and we had spoken from time to time, comparing notes about the Bush-Guard story and how difficult it had been for both of us to get good information out of the old records or the old men who knew most about the Guard units.

This time, Slover called me to tell me that he had discovered that Gen. Buck Staudt, the cranky and foulmouthed onetime chief of staff of the Texas Air National Guard, had retired on March 1, 1972, almost a year and a half before the August 18, 1973, Killian memo that mentions Staudt as putting on the pressure to "sugarcoat" Bush's evaluation.

I told Slover that I had discovered that myself, *before* running the documents, but felt that the memo wasn't contradictory in the least. The memo made it clear that Staudt was no longer working in TANG Headquarters in Austin because the memo concluded that "Austin is not happy today either." Staudt and Austin were treated as separate entities, showing that Staudt was *not* in Austin.

Slover had noticed that himself and said that the Austin reference was certainly a strong sign that the memo acknowledged that Staudt had resigned.

We also talked about how Staudt had gone to work at Conoco—the Houston oil giant—and secured a membership on the board of the Houston Air Commerce Committee, which oversaw the operations of Ellington Field. The airfield was wholly owned by the city of Houston and leased for use by the National Guard at the city's pleasure. With Staudt remaining a constant at Ellington after his retirement and in two influential positions of power, he was in some ways in an even better arm-twisting position for wielding influence on the base in 1973 than he had been in 1972. Staudt had maintained his close relationships with the Guard brass and no one had denied that he remained a familiar presence on the base. Slover took all this in and agreed with me on the phone. Then he hung up and spent the evening writing a news story that attacked my work with complete disregard for the information we had discussed and which he had acknowledged as being true.

Slover's story, which came out Saturday morning, September 11, was used as a club to beat me over the head all weekend and into the weeks ahead, even though he knew the facts were not as simple and straightforward as he had presented them in his one-dimensional story.

Worse, the story had only one source for Staudt's lack of clout outside the Guard—a fellow by the name of Earl Lively, a Dallas real-estate businessman and active Republican, who as always was eager to do whatever he could to knock down an unfavorable Bush story. The report completely ignored Staudt's well-known influence at Ellington after his retirement.

This type of event fit into a larger pattern of Slover's reporting. He had long ago established himself—to himself anyway—as a self-proclaimed "debunker," a reporter who particularly enjoyed taking apart the work of others. Hey, it beats doing your own work.

One dark chapter in Slover's reporting past involved the destruction and subsequent suicide of Jim Hatfield, a tragicomic figure who in 1999 had written a shabby and pasted-together biography of then-candidate George W. Bush called *Fortunate Son*. Hatfield claimed to have met with someone high up in the Bush camp who shared with him details of Bush's cocaine addiction and early drug arrests. The problem was that there was never any real evidence. All of Hatfield's sources were anonymous. All of his attributed quotes seemed to have been taken from other articles written by other people. He was not a good reporter—in fact, he wasn't a reporter at all. He was an easy person to debunk and destroy.

Slover stuck a fork in the book and in Hatfield's shaky psyche when he revealed that Hatfield had spent five years in prison for solicitation of capital murder. It was a good story that had tragic consequences for Jim Hatfield, who was found dead in a hotel room, an apparent suicide. After that story, many news types whispered that Slover had the story handed to him by the Bush camp, something he vigorously denied.

In 1997, Oklahoma City bomber Tim McVeigh's attorney demanded, in court papers, an investigation of whether Pete Slover stole computer files from a laptop belonging to the McVeigh legal team, then published a supposed confession that McVeigh made to his lawyers. *The Dallas Morning News* denied the charges. Early in his career, Slover had also been charged with trespassing for being in a Texas county clerk's office for nearly two hours after the office was closed and locked for the night. Slover pleaded no contest, received six months probation, and was fined one thousand dollars. Pete has always gotten an "A" for effort. He has occasionally gotten an "F" for fairness. Now I felt I had been "Slovered" as well.

Shortly after his unfair little story came out, I got an e-mail from Robert Strong, who had worked as a clerk and personnel staffer at the Austin headquarters with Staudt. "The fact that Staudt was no longer on active service would NOT have kept him from being brought in to influence people at the 147th," Strong said. "Staudt became an executive at Conoco in Houston and was still in 'the game.'" Strong wrote that he found it "a hoot" to see Earl Lively sticking up for Staudt because the two men had always loathed each other. "Politics does make for very strange bedfellows," Strong said.

How you felt about President Bush determined how you felt about the memos. How you felt about the media determined how you felt about the memos.

And then there was Marian Carr Knox, an eighty-six-year-old former secretary to Jerry Killian who was alternately my best friend and my worst nightmare on the continuing story. No matter where she stood on the facts of the story, I thought she was a simply delightful woman. Bright as a button, Knox had retired from her job at Ellington Air Base in the late 1970s and could still remember all kinds of details of life on the base. But her memory was very selective and prone to the kind of unwavering black or white pronouncements that I plan to issue myself when I am eighty-six years old. She helped us and hurt us in equal measure, but I found her a wonder to be around.

A fan of Dan Rather's, Mrs. Knox did not want the attacks on her favorite Texas reporter to go unanswered. Besides, she knew firsthand that the content of the memos was totally true. She said she had been there to see how then-lieutenant Bush got favorable treatment and how he had avoided taking his physical, angering Colonel Killian and creating discord among the other pilots.

The only problem was that she said she also thought the memos were fakes simply because she hadn't typed them. They were far too sloppy to have come from her desk, she said. She was incredibly self-righteous about her typing ability, and anyone who suggested she had anything to do with these sloppy messes was in for a fight. Further, Mrs. Knox didn't believe anyone else at Ellington could have typed them for Killian. She believed that she alone, despite evidence to the contrary, was the typist for all of Killian's work. In fact, she seemed to think that Jerry Killian himself—like many men at the time—was physically incapable of typing even the simplest passages onto paper. Ultimately, Knox thought the typing on the documents was so inexcusably poor that she had to declare them to be forgeries.

Then why was the information in them accurate? Knox wasn't sure. But she was full of stories about how Lieutenant Bush had behaved on base. "It seems to me that Bush felt he was above reproach," she told us on-camera. Dan asked if Bush had gotten into the Guard on the basis of preferential treatment. Mrs. Knox—who had spent decades in the organization—said, "I'm gonna say that he did. I feel that he did, because there was a lot of other boys in there that same way. . . . Now Bush seemed to be having a good time. He didn't seem to be having any problem with the other pilots. But in his time there, others seemed to be resentful of him because of his attitude. . . . 'I didn't have to go by the rules.' It seemed that way to me."

Mrs. Knox said that Killian had written memos very much like the ones we had, that he kept them as sort of a personal journal. "Jerry Killian gave [Bush] a direct order to take the physical and George did not take it," she said. "After that, he disappeared. Killian was not frustrated, just upset that George did not follow orders. You're taught to follow orders in the military." Knox said Killian kept the memos because "he just wanted to protect himself."

For me, the headline out of our interview with Marian Carr Knox was that someone who worked in the office of Bush's National Guard commander was confirming all the rumors about Bush's slacking off on flying, about receiving preferential treatment in getting into the Guard and preferential treatment once he was there. Other news organizations simply picked up Knox's disavowal of the documents, burying her account that the information in the memos was completely accurate.

In order to get Marian Carr Knox's interview on the air on Wednesday night, September 15, we had to fly her in from Houston on a private jet. Lucy Scott and I rode along. Knox regaled us from Texas to New York with bits of hard-won wisdom on the difficulties of being a working woman, raising sons, the importance of rocking the boat, gardening, how to cook a good rib roast, and the need to stay active as you grew older. She was wonderful company.

Once again, our story that Wednesday was a crash. This time, Josh was particularly worried. I remember him running into the office and yelling at me to just slam something together in the editing room. I felt under control on the Knox story, much better than I had felt the week before. I sat at Dana's desk with my yellow highlighter, methodically going through the transcripts I'd patched together from our interview, carefully choosing statements and pieces of Knox's conversation to use in the story. For the first time in a week, I almost felt normal again. It was great to be focused on something, head down, working.

Normalcy didn't last long. Knox's account hurt us as much as it helped. The morning after the story ran, Andrew called me and tersely asked me to set up a conference call with Bill Burkett for later that day. I arranged the phone call and at the appointed time Betsy, Dan, and I were shown into Andrew's office. I don't know why Josh was left out. Just lucky, I guess.

In typical Bill Burkett fashion, maintaining high drama at all times, he asked that Betsy and I leave the room for a moment so he could talk

directly to Dan and Andrew. I didn't have a clue what Burkett was saying as we stood outside, but I later learned that he had told Andrew that
I had done a good job and that I shouldn't be judged too harshly for
what was happening. It was a nice thought, but I can't imagine that Andrew gave it more than a passing listen. He was in *Survivor* mode and I
had rather publicly failed a tribal challenge.

Betsy and I chatted nervously outside Andrew's office while we
waited to be summoned back in. She asked me what I was most worried
about, perhaps thinking I might say that Bill Burkett would confess to
something I hadn't thought of or that the documents would somehow
clearly turn out to be forged. I remember telling her that I was most
afraid of losing my job over this. Betsy pointedly did not answer. She
looked down quickly without making eye contact and I realized freshly
how deep and how profound my professional troubles were. I don't
think for a moment Betsy dreamed that she would be out as well.

Within a few minutes, we were allowed back in for the coed portion
of the program. It soon became clear that Andrew wanted some kind of
personal accounting from Burkett, asking the same kinds of questions I
had either asked Burkett long ago or in the past few days: where had
these memos come from, what did he know about them, and what
could we at CBS do now? Were there more documents? Would he go
public as the source? Where should we go from here?

Andrew got more than he bargained for with Burkett. The wide-
ranging conversation went on for more than an hour and a half, veering
between Burkett's rage at being denied medical benefits to his thorough
grasp of the personnel and staffing problems that had plagued the Texas
National Guard for years. He told Andrew about the thick and convoluted background of infighting, grandstanding, and payback that had
been part of the Guard. He told Andrew about his stumbling onto the
shredding of documents in 1997 and how he saw Bush records and
those of other Guardsmen stacked in wastebaskets on the way to be
destroyed.

But in this phone call Burkett told Andrew a different story than he
had told me about where the Killian documents had come from. A
couple of days after I got the papers from Burkett, I had begun hound-
ing him about where he had received them, whom he had gotten them

from, what he knew about their provenance. After both Mike and I badgered him in a series of nonstop phone calls, Burkett broke down and grumbled that he had gotten the papers from George Conn, an on-again, off-again National Guard friend of Burkett's who split his life between Dallas and Germany. Burkett told me that Conn would never confirm his story, but I began trying to reach Conn through his Dallas phone number anyway. I got no answer, but I frantically hoped to be able to reach him as soon as he got the message. I also called a mutual acquaintance of Burkett's and Conn's and begged for the phone number in Germany, but to no avail.

In the call with Andrew, Burkett said that he had only told me about Conn because I had kept after him so endlessly that he had created a story to get me to back off, go away, and stop asking about it. Burkett said that he had promised his real source to keep the truth a secret.

Now Burkett poured it out on the speakerphone to our shell-shocked group. Dan was across the room, slouched in an easy chair, wearing a baseball hat. Betsy was twisted into a pretzel on the couch, taking notes as quickly as she could. Andrew was hunched over his speakerphone, stroking his mustache and asking rapid-fire questions. I was folded stiffly into a chair beside Andrew's desk, taking notes and deep breaths, watching the others in the room as they listened to the booming and demanding voice that had so dominated and nearly destroyed my life in the past few weeks.

Burkett told us that he had received a phone call in early March of 2004 from an unidentified man, who said that a woman named Lucy Ramirez wanted to speak with him. Burkett said he was told to call her at a Houston Holiday Inn that night between 7:00 and 10:00 P.M. and that he was given a specific room number to ask for. Burkett said that Ramirez told him she was a go-between, a person who was supposed to deliver a package of documents to him.

Burkett told us that Ramirez made him promise that he would handle the package he received from her very specifically. He agreed to copy the documents inside, then burn the original papers he had received, which were also copies, not originals. He was also to burn the envelope they had come in. Burkett said that he agreed to this, assuming that Lucy or whoever she was wanted to destroy any DNA evidence that might be gleaned from the papers or the package they had come in.

Burkett said that Ramirez asked him if and when he would be in Houston and he told her he would be at the Houston Livestock Show within a couple of weeks, where he and his wife, Nicki, showed and sold Simmenthal cattle. It was an annual showcase for the breed and a good way to advertise the bull semen (yes, you read that right) they and other ranchers sold to make a living. Burkett told Ramirez what day he would be working the front information booth at the show, which was held in a large arena.

Burkett said that on his first day working the booth he was handed the papers by a dark-skinned man. He said the man approached him, asked his name, and handed him a legal envelope. We were able to confirm with the cattle association that Burkett had indeed worked the front booth on that date. A coworker of his at the cattle show said that, as Burkett told us, he had asked her to hold a legal envelope for him while a man handed him the papers.

As a fittingly bizarre last touch, Burkett told our group that he had hidden the papers in his venison locker, close to one hundred miles from his home. He boasted that he'd driven so fast to get to our meeting that the papers were still cold from his freezer when he handed them to me.

While Burkett's tale of bovine intrigue and Miss Marple mystery unwound in Andrew's office, I looked around the room and saw that Betsy and Andrew were sitting silently, openmouthed, blinking, blinded by their sudden exposure to the weirdness that is and always will be Texas. Dan, having been born and raised in Texas, took the colorful story more in stride.

If this had been a story about an action by the New Jersey mob, it would have played out at the Bada Bing club. If this had been a Las Vegas handoff, the documents would have been passed at a casino. Because this happened in George W. Bush's chosen homeland, the natural setting for the big scene was a cattle show, complete with bull semen, cowboy hats, mysterious phone calls from a Hispanic woman, and a document handoff. The scene sounded like a marriage of *The Manchurian Candidate* and *Hee Haw*.

As I sat listening to Burkett's scenario spill out, I realized how truly ridiculous this sounded from our vantage in New York. But in Texas, one of the world capitals of "shit happens," a place where bull semen is worth its weight in gold (and the bizarre long ago became the mundane), I believed it was quite possible that Bill Burkett was finally telling the truth, the whole weird truth, and nothing but the truth. By God, in Texas, anything could happen.

CHAPTER 13

We sat in Andrew Heyward's office for a few long moments, recovering from the convoluted saga we had just heard. Before hanging up with Bill Burkett, Andrew asked if he would be willing to go public and do an interview laying out his whole story. Burkett agreed. We settled on doing the shoot in Dallas that Saturday, September 18, and we started knocking around the details of where, when, and what we needed to get on-camera.

When the speakerphone clicked off, we sat slumped in our chairs, stunned. Betsy shrieked with amazement that she had never heard anything so outrageous in her life, that she had always thought of Texas as a colorful western outpost of cowboys and open spaces. But this strange brew of long-hidden documents and political plotting? Come on.

Betsy, God bless her, like so many people who spend their lives in the Capital of the World, saw Texas and much of the rest of the country as nothing more than a background location for video post-cards. Texas was viewed as a kind of remote theme park where confused and clueless people chose to live despite the tornadoes, the heat, and the dearth of yellow taxis. Betsy said she had actually been to Texas several times, but the Texas she saw apparently did not include the partisan intrigue, boiling hatreds, old grudges, and angry men in cowboy hats who were handed political hot stuff at cattle shows and hid their booty in bloody deer lockers before handing it off to reporters. Well, I sure was aware of the machinations and mania of my adopted home state. After fifteen years there, I was getting a little sick of it. Although professionally, I knew I could always count on Texas's daffy dark side to provide colorful news stories and lessons in human nature not taught in most of civilized society.

Where else would the mother of a girl who yearned to be a high school cheerleader plot to kill off the competition? In what other state would a candidate for governor tell reporters that bad weather was like rape: It's best to "just lie back and enjoy it"? And in what other society on the planet would God speak directly to twenty Pentecostals, from elders to infants, convince them to take off their clothes, pile into a 1990 Grand Am, and drive to Louisiana as fast as they could in order to avoid Armageddon? Those particular Texans had lost control of their speeding car just across the state border, hitting a tree and ending their naked odyssey without injury, possibly putting the Second Coming on hold.

Texas is, as my mother used to say about many things, "just a little bit that way." And Lone Star politics are a little bit that way, as well.

Chicago's political chicanery, Louisiana's Cajun-flavored voter fraud, New York's Tammany Hall election tampering, and Florida's hanging chads have little on Texas, where deep-seated political struggles last for generations, where candidates are often quickly elevated to the national level partly because of their proven ability to survive the trial-by-deep-fryer that is Texas politics. Texas offers a unique American voting and campaign experience: outrageous, inelegant, hilarious, harrowing, and completely without written rules. Wild and woolly and no-holds-barred. That's Texas and its sprawling, brawling political stage. Not to mention that the proceedings unfold in some of the country's hottest weather, lending them a special sweaty-faced intensity.

Since the Bush-Guard story had aired, CBS had come under increasing pressure to reveal the source of the documents. In *The Washington Post*, *The New York Times*, *USA Today*, *Newsweek*, and other places, there was open speculation that Burkett had been the source. We at CBS did nothing to fuel or fend off the guessing. We refused to comment.

But Burkett's history as a whistle-blower within the Texas National Guard, his publicity-seeking persona when it came to criticizing the president, his blunt dismissal of Bush's military career, made Burkett an obvious choice for reporters trying to ferret out our source. There was also a much bigger clue that eliminated the guesswork for many of our news rivals. Reporters from several news organizations knew about Burkett's involvement because they had actually been chasing the same documents that we ended up getting. Those reporters had been talking with Burkett and some of his friends about documents he claimed to know about, so there wasn't much mystery over how his name made it into the papers.

But Burkett blamed CBS for the speculation that he was the source and he was *very* angry at us. He held us responsible for the reporters and photographers who were gathering outside the metal gate marking the entrance to his small West Texas cattle ranch. Camera carriers and notebook toters had been milling around near his mailbox for days, trying to get some comment on the memos' controversy or at least a glimpse of Burkett or his wife, Nicki.

Burkett's anger and suspicions about CBS may have been over-the-top, but his feelings weren't completely off base. We had made a spectacularly stupid mistake. *The New York Times* and others reported that copies of the memos CBS showed to some interview subjects included notations indicating they were faxed from a Kinko's outlet in Abilene, a comparatively short drive from Burkett's ranch. Mike and I had faxed the first two documents to New York from the Kinko's shortly after we got them from Burkett. If our New York staff had had the sense to cut off the telltale fax marking, that link couldn't have been made. But they hadn't. It didn't help, but that was certainly not the only reason that reporters focused on Burkett as the source. The faxing was foolish and I regret it and have to take responsibility for my role in exposing Burkett.

Michael Isikoff from *Newsweek* had called me in New York just two days after our story ran on *60 Minutes II*. He asked if I wanted Burkett to come forward. That's the old reporter's trick of hiding a question within a question. Jeez, Mike, you know I'm not going to talk about anything like that. I told him I was worn out and I was heading home to Texas. In the next week's *Newsweek*, Isikoff described me as being so serious about seeing Burkett that I decided to fly to Texas to meet with him. The truth wasn't quite so dramatic; I was just going home to Dallas. Like much reporting that's done on the fly, some of what was written about the memos controversy was just plain wrong.

Some news organizations tried using open accusations to get Burkett to admit that he had something to do with acquiring and handing over the documents. Others tried reverse psychology. Still others, like *The Washington Post*, tried honey, running a story on Burkett with the stroking headline, SUSPECTED CBS SOURCE IS WELL-REGARDED TEXAN. The article was an accurate account of how Burkett was viewed as eccentric in his hometown primarily because he tended to vote Democrat in a Republican stronghold. I was surprised at how measured and reasoned the story was, compared with the accusatory mischaracterizations in most of the media coverage.

Burkett was unmoved by the prodding, still refusing to fess up to anyone about anything. Despite his disgust with us for messing up in faxing the memos, I believe he felt responsible and loyal to CBS and to Dan Rather. Burkett told us constantly that we had disappointed him deeply and profoundly. But he could see that as bad as things were for him at his isolated ranch, Dan was being eaten alive in newspapers and on Web sites from New Mexico to New York City for supposedly using fake documents to attack the president. Burkett wanted to help. Although I didn't realize it at the time, I now believe CBS executives were planning to use Burkett's sentiment to deflect as much damage as they could away from the network and onto him.

When Andrew asked Burkett to speak out publicly, I thought the aim of the interview would be to make clear where the documents came from, where Burkett had gotten them, and how he had misrepresented to me where and how they'd come into his possession. I thought it was possible that his stepping forward and his presence would actually help the story when viewers saw that Burkett was sincere and plainspoken, that he wasn't a slick political operative or a fire-breathing three-headed idealogue.

Andrew Heyward sent an e-mail to me, Betsy, and Josh on Friday afternoon as I prepared to go home and get everything ready for the Burkett interview Saturday morning at a Dallas hotel.

His message was composed in typical Andrew fashion. Long sentences with minimal capitals and punctuation, meant to be read the way Andrew spoke—without taking a breath:

> In the interest of "transparency" and re-creating our amazing phone call, which we all agree is the goal, there should be a line of questioning about his motives for giving us the docs, which at

least touches on his Democratic leanings and his views of the Prez. put another way, we need to inoculate ourselves against the wave of stories that will FOLLOW our interview and attempt to discredit Bill. . . . just urging you to cover all bases, even if Dan needs some encouragement. Mary: you'll be most effective on that score, rather than the "front office" "pressuring" him into turning over every rock. pls let me know if you disagree. thx ajh

Andrew was letting me know that he wanted Dan to be particularly tough in questioning Burkett about his views of President Bush, as though that in itself would hurt Burkett's credibility. When I read his e-mail, I felt that Andrew probably wanted us to be harder on Burkett than I thought was fair. It was not illegal to have a lack of support for the president, nor was that any indication that the documents were forgeries. Who the hell was going to come forward with materials that were incriminating to Bush anyway? Certainly not a Bush fan. I knew that Andrew was under growing pressure in the midst of the criticism that was battering CBS News, and I had to assume that the head of the news division also was feeling tremendous corporate pressure pushing down on him from above.

I wrote back to reassure Andrew. Privately, I was starting to get worried. Too many agendas and elements were converging to put pressure on this interview. We were all obsessively concerned with straightening out questions about our story. The reputation of the top franchise of a legendary news division was suddenly at stake. The corporation was afraid of appearing biased against a hard-nosed administration. Dan worried about his legacy. Andrew worried about his own future. Some of us were worried about our jobs. I was worried about everything.

We were about to go into what had become known as "a full CBS," a situation so completely out of control and overwrought, so achingly self-interested and paralyzingly self-conscious, that it could only be a production of CBS News. The news division usually reserved such crosscurrents of angst for tributes honoring ancient reporters or producers who steadfastly refused to retire. Those occasions often degenerated into corporate family fights between crotchety old newshounds. CBS News has a geriatric ward unmatched by any other news organization. At any gathering, they argued about who got to sit where, bellyached about the company that had made many of them wealthy, and bitterly recounted how much better things had been when they were making all the decisions.

But this fight over the Killian memos, this battle between the bloggers and the new version of CBS corporate news, was going to be one for the ages. The Burkett interview was sizing up as a crucial round. Already there was raw fear, anger, and worry that we at CBS News were losing everything. It didn't take much to visualize a complete shrieking, stomping, hair-pulling pig pile of a meltdown in the making. And I'm just talking about myself.

Our guest list at the hotel for the big interview with our source was eclectic, to say the least. Betsy West would be there, representing a terrified, angry, and desperate corporate CBS. Andrew Heyward, of course, would not be able to make it. I believed he preferred to send Betsy anyway, so he could blame her for whatever went wrong.

Dan was flying in—as always without rest—to do the interview. I knew he was getting on the plane already pissed off at the shallow, adversarial nature of the media coverage of this whole story and the controversy it sparked. He was sick to death that, once again, he was on the hot seat for asking the kinds of questions that other reporters should have been asking for years.

Bill Burkett's attorney, David Van Os, who was running for the Texas Supreme Court as an extreme long shot and had an accent so thick it nearly took solid form in the air, would come in from San Antonio for the interview, to represent Burkett's interests. Van Os naturally would also be representing his own personal, political, and financial ambitions. From what I had seen, those appeared to be bound by neither limit nor logic.

We were also expecting Mike Smith, Lucy Scott, and Roger Charles from our producing team, as well as a hairdresser, a makeup person, and two camera crews, including soundmen and a lighting director. I also arranged for a dog handler in case Burkett brought along his dog, Julie, who was trained to help him predict when he would suffer a neurological seizure. I feared for Julie the dog's own health if she was allowed near me. My subconscious neural readings felt so ferocious that they might have made the internal fears of someone at the Alamo seem like child's play. My building anxiety might put poor Julie in a coma.

The Crescent Court hotel staff, unaware that our well-attended and potentially high-priced soiree was not exactly a celebratory get-together, had done its best to pull out the stops to please us. When I got there, camera crews were setting up in the massive conference room, creating a scene that looked like a lavish wedding interrupted by a space launch. There were large sprays of flowers and groaning banquet tables of food. Platters of tiny crustless sandwiches weren't wasted around our hardworking, cable-pulling television crews. They ate the sandwiches by the handfuls. Stiff and starched hotel linens were arrayed everywhere in an attempt to make a cavernous space crammed with technical hardware look pretty. Waiters draped them on tables and chairs and anything else that didn't move, including camera boxes and equipment. The sea of white linen was a nice foil for the thick black coils of cables piled all over the floor, spreading out in every direction, snaking underfoot, and tripping the unwary.

Indecipherable monitors and audio equipment throbbed and squealed irregularly as technicians tweaked and toggled their way through equipment checks. I paced the room nervously, terrified as I thought about what had happened in the past few weeks, even more afraid of what might happen in the days ahead.

Bill and Nicki Burkett and David Van Os had arrived at the hotel and were in their rooms, freshening up and talking over what tone they wanted Burkett to use in the interview.

We were still waiting for Dan and Betsy to land from New York when my cell phone rang. It was Betsy saying they were on the ground, but it wasn't going well. They were being pursued by a local FOX television crew that had shown up at Dallas–Fort Worth International Airport. I couldn't understand everything Betsy was saying breathlessly into the phone, but it sounded as if there had been a face-off of sorts outside baggage claim, where the young FOX reporter with good hair had asked the older CBS anchorman in a bad mood something foolish. The exchange went about like this. Question: "Dan, you broadcast those fake memos. Do you feel duped?" Reply: "Well, you work for FOX News. Do you feel duped?"

I giggled in relief at Dan's cranky comeback. It let me know that he was feeling feisty. I needed him to be on his game that day, to be strong, to be himself. He had never let me down. Hearing what he'd barked in response to a smart-aleck question let me know he was doing just fine.

Betsy called with updates as they drove to the hotel, telling me that the FOX car was still following them into the city. Damn. I did not want some kind of rinky-dink run-in at the hotel before the interview started and I didn't want any mention of our Burkett interview on television or elsewhere until we had shot and aired our story. Lucy Scott and I began making arrangements to have the hotel open its rear delivery entrance so that Dan's car could get into the building and lose the pursuit car.

It was always something like this with Dan, although it certainly wasn't his fault. I had traveled with him enough to know that he was quiet and unobtrusive and unfailingly pleasant to people who recognized him, whether they wanted their picture taken, their hand shaken, or a chance to talk about current events.

But, God love him, poor Dan could attract a certain element that sometimes seemed drawn to him like metal to a magnet. On occasion, they were the type of people who received radio signals through their fillings, lost souls who thought they had a special friendship with him, angry viewers who wanted him to stop sending them secret messages. You know, the usual.

After years in local and national television news, I can tell you that this happens on some level to most everyone who is on television. Perhaps because Dan has been on the air for decades, covering events of great national drama with his trademark intensity, he seems to draw a higher level of interest from people.

Dan's celebrity has had a strange price. His critics have made him pay, quite personally and in spades, for the unusual incidents that others have caused. Somehow, he has been blamed because people attacked him. Talk about not being able to win for losing.

Years ago, a man mugged him, chanting "what's the frequency, Kenneth?" When the man later killed a person in another attack, people still talked about *Dan's* problem. Ridiculous.

As someone who has been with him through a few of these episodes, I want to set the record straight. Dan does not have a problem. But a lot of other people do. One small incident left a particular impact on me because it could have been prevented if CBS had provided the most basic assistance that other companies routinely offer.

One day, Dan and I were crossing West Fifty-seventh Street from one CBS building to another. Rushing toward us came an elderly woman, and by that I mean someone well past the age of on-camera employment at *60 Minutes.* She was dressed shabbily and reached out to Dan, calling him in a voice that was plaintive, angry, and very troubled. She was clearly having mental difficulty. I was the only person with Dan and I didn't know what to do. We kept making our way across the street as he talked soothingly to her and gently tried to disentangle himself. She kept screaming about stories in the news, events in her life, problems in the world.

What if she's armed? I thought. *What should I do?* Eventually, I was practically pulling her off of Dan as we went up the stairs and into the building. The crack CBS security team continued to make small talk among themselves as we shoved and stumbled our way past them. They didn't seem to notice that the man counted on as the face of the network was being manhandled by two women, only one of them friendly.

Our mangled ménage à trois pushed toward the elevators and, mercifully, amazingly, a set of doors opened when we hit the button. I shoved Dan inside the elevator as, ever the gentleman, he continued trying to politely extract himself from the deteriorated conversation. As the doors closed onto the woman's arms, security guards finally arrived, grabbing her by the legs and lifting her into the air. Her full-throated wail faded as our elevator car ascended. I tried to lighten the moment. "Old girlfriend?" I asked. Dan laughed ruefully. I felt bad that someone I liked so much risked the possibility of a scene like that whenever he went out in public.

One of the other difficulties of being Dan Rather was that people often tried to do things in an extra-special way for you. Sometimes that helped, and sometimes that created all kinds of problems.

The Dallas hotel, in trying to do its best for us, had thoughtfully put our rooms in close proximity, a fabulous idea if we had been part of a wedding party. It was a terrible idea in this case, when half the people involved in the shoot weren't really speaking to one another or were deeply suspicious of one another, while others believed that someone in our group was destroying their livelihood and any further damage would seal their doom. It was a tense, almost comedic scene. We went in and out of rooms, slamming doors and speaking in exaggerated whispers. We passed one another in the narrow hallway, carrying everything from suit coats to corporate secrets, from political baggage to personal hygiene products. We looked like a modern version of the Marx Brothers in *A Night at the Opera*. We were a mess.

Betsy and Dan finally arrived, both of them looking tired and like they were carrying a heavy burden of duties for the day. Dan sat down, took off his coat, put his feet up, and asked me how the Burketts were doing. He had never met them face-to-face, although he had spoken with Burkett on the phone a couple of times. I decided to check on them and then take Dan in to say hello.

I took Betsy to the Burketts' room first. Their meeting did not go particularly well. The Burketts saw themselves as honest, down-to-earth ranchers, people accustomed to living in splendid rural isolation with only their cattle, their kin, and their principles for company. They told Betsy how this story could end up costing them everything. The economic fallout from angry Republicans could ruin the Burketts' reputations and end up taking their ranch, costing them the respect and support of their children, and destroying their plans for retirement.

Nicki, an eloquent speaker with an uncanny ability to cut to the heart of an argument or make a searing point, stood in her hotel room in a shapeless cotton shift and told Betsy, "Here I stand dressed like a little peasant, hoping and praying that you're going to treat us fairly." I now believe Nicki instinctively knew something that day that I did not—Nicki felt that Betsy had been given the corporate responsibility to make sure that Burkett took the blame for everything in this interview, to ensure that he presented himself as the one who didn't tell the truth, that he had been brought there to be the fall guy for this whole story. Nicki knew that her husband would probably do exactly that out of a sense of his own martyrdom, out of the belief that he owed it to us because he had indeed misled CBS about where he had gotten the documents.

Betsy and Nicki could not have come from more different worlds. Betsy had graduated from some hallowed East Coast college. She was well dressed and well read. To a West Texan, she was a visitor from a distant planet where women talked about trust funds instead of tractors, where they shopped for shoes with "toe cleavage," where their children were born with more money than the Burketts' children would die with.

The room was quiet by the time Dan came in to greet the Burketts. He walked in, as he often did just before a shoot, with a large white paper square tucked into his shirt collar, a protector for the makeup he was going to have sponged, sprayed, and patted on before the cameras started rolling. I was relieved that Dan was there to take over the small talk and put some distance between Betsy and the Burketts. Dan knew people like Bill and Nicki, had known them all of his life.

They talked briefly about the conference call with CBS and Dan told Burkett that he wanted the taped interview to hit the highlights of what he had told us then, how he had heard about the documents, how he had obtained them, the way he was told to copy and then destroy them, the works. Dan told Burkett that he was going to ask him why he had misled us about where the memos had come from. Burkett said he knew that, he expected that, and he very much wanted to set matters straight.

Dan told the Burketts that he had to go get his "war paint" on, and I went with him across the hall to his room. Once inside, he said, "You know, Mary, I think he is a truth teller." I thought so, too. But Bill Burkett's version of the truth could get pretty convoluted. It could be hard to see clearly. It could be self-serving. However, at the end of the day, I didn't think for a moment that Burkett was any of the things that the conservative blogs had called him. I didn't believe he was a con man, a political operative, or a person capable of doing anything like forging documents, faking old memos, or giving anyone in the media something that he knew had been faked. Bill Burkett could be accused of making foolish choices, but he was no forger.

As we talked, Dan's door burst open and Betsy flew in, visibly upset about what she had heard Burkett and David Van Os discussing in front of her in the next room. It seemed that Van Os was telling Burkett he shouldn't do the interview unless there was some kind of agreement in place with CBS. Burkett said we did have a verbal agreement. Van

Os said Burkett should never have given us the documents without an agreement. Betsy was so upset at the loose talk about contracts and agreements that her corporate sensors went on red alert. She started frantically looking room to room for a tape recorder on which this conversation could be captured for the ages and possibly used later in court to protect CBS. Lucy Scott told me in an aside that she would take care of it and pretend to look for a tape recorder to calm Betsy.

We had entered the seventh circle of CBS hell, or at least I thought we had. Within moments, Betsy burst back into the room, declaring, "Something very odd is happening in there." She nodded toward the Burketts' room across the hall. She said that when she opened the door to their room, she saw that they were "on the ground, on their knees, at the side of the bed," mumbling. "For God's sake, Betsy, this is Texas," I told her. "They're praying."

Finally, after the lifting up of prayers, the application of pancake makeup, the ritualistic pressing of wrinkled clothes, the big talk of the Texas lawyer, the Technicolor fears of the corporate vice president, after all of it had been played out and put aside, our little group formed a grim processional and headed down to the massive conference room to do the interview.

Burkett and Dan took their seats under the great arc of lights at the front of the big room. Betsy and the rest of the group and I sat in chairs perched by a long banquet table off to the side. I worked with the cameramen for several minutes, fussing with the way the lighting looked for both Dan and Burkett, holding true to my unwavering objective of getting an interview setting just right. I always wanted to be fair to everyone, no matter who they were, no matter whether I liked them or loathed them, respected them or really wished I didn't have to be in the same room with them. I wanted them to look handsome and smart. I wanted them to have their best shot to tell their best story, to make their best sale. On this day, I wanted this for Bill Burkett.

I listened on my headset as Dan and Burkett chatted. Out of the blue, Burkett asked Dan if he would come to his funeral. Dan said he would. I didn't know if this was a play for sympathy, a sincere request from a man whose health was not stable, or an allusion to what this interview might turn out to be. I didn't know what he meant, but starting a long, potentially life-altering conversation with a reference to your own death did not strike me as upbeat. I squirmed in my chair and listened to my heart pounding in my ears.

As usual, just before the interview started, the cameramen counted down and synchronized their time codes for the audio transcripts. This time, my heart boomed with each number they spoke. Finally, it came. "And we're rolling."

Dan generally began interviews the same way, no matter whom he was talking with: "First of all, thank you for doing this." He began that way again, a nice normal touch for a conversation that had gotten a far bigger buildup than it should have.

For two and a half hours, Dan and Burkett talked. We listened as he gave details on how and where he had gotten the memos, why he had given them to us, what his motivations were, and how he felt about it now that the whole story had become such a mess. We stopped to change tapes, to take a drink, to take a break, to hand Dan a new question, or to give Nicki a chance to check in with Bill.

Betsy was doing exactly what I thought Andrew wanted her to do. She stayed focused on trying to get the most self-incriminating comments possible out of Burkett. In her defense, I strongly believe that's what she had been ordered to do to protect the company and separate CBS News from Bill Burkett as much as possible. I had mixed feelings. I felt sorry for Nicki and Bill, who were really just small individuals in a political and corporate clash of the titans. On the other hand, I was furious at Burkett for misleading us, lying about the provenance of the documents, and playing so many games when it came to answering straight questions. He told us half-truths when he could have told us the whole truth. He said he did it to protect people, but I had to take his word for it and my trust tank was running extremely low.

Again and again, Betsy handed me notes that I would read and take to Dan during a break. The notes hit over and over on one thing. Ask him why he *lied* about where the documents came from. Ask him why he *didn't tell the truth* when he gave us the memos.

Burkett, after putting the best face he could on his imperfections, said flat out that he had not told the entire truth in order to protect others, that he regretted it, and that he wished he had done otherwise. When Betsy wanted the interview to keep going over this same ground,

I started to feel uncomfortable. Dan and I thought we were shooting this for a story that would run on *60 Minutes* the next Wednesday, but even for a story of that length, we had what we needed. Let's wrap this up.

Betsy wanted more. I think she wanted some kind of an apology. It was humiliating to see Burkett asked again and again why he had lied. I could see Nicki pacing off to the side and growing angrier and angrier. Dan was unhappy and, eventually, he cut off the questioning.

We went back to our rooms. No one felt good. Dan packed up quickly and headed for the airport to catch a plane to Austin so he could visit his daughter, Robin, and her family. Her young son's presence was like music to Dan. I wanted him to hurry up, to get to the airport and get to his grandson, so he could start decompressing from what had been a crummy day.

Betsy, Roger Charles, Mike Smith, Lucy Scott, and I were sitting in Dan's abandoned room when there was a small knock on the door. "Come in," we called out, thinking it was a cameraman or a sound guy who wanted to ask us about the tape or the teardown of gear in the conference room.

Instead, Nicki stood there, a small figure in that plain dress, her eyes glistening and her lips pursed. Betsy made the mistake of asking in a sympathetic voice, "How is Bill doing?"

Nicki exploded, opening her mouth and shooting a stream of fire at what she saw as the well-heeled, carefully turned out, soulless corporate hack on the other side of the room. "Don't you dare ask me how Bill is!" Nicki shrieked. "Bill is sick. He is a sick man. And you don't give a damn about him. You just spent two hours trying to destroy him. You made him crawl on-camera. You made him say, again and again, that he lied and it still wasn't enough for you. You wanted more. You want to put all the blame on him for all the things that you have done wrong in putting this story together. You want to wrap it all up in a neat little package and say, 'It's all Bill Burkett's fault.' Well, it's not, and you know it. And you promised that when we came here to do this interview, we would get a fair shake, and we got nothing from you but lies." Nicki was quivering. So were the rest of us.

But Nicki stood her ground and glared at Betsy as she went on. "You may think I am nothing but a stupid little hick who doesn't know a damn thing about a damn thing. And you are so smart and such a big shot. But I keep my promises and I don't destroy people just to protect myself. I don't destroy people and humiliate them and then pretend I give a goddamn about how they are. To answer your question, Bill is not good. But then you knew that already."

Nicki turned with a *whoosh* and marched out the door, slamming it behind her. Oh God, this was going badly.

I went to the Burketts' room and they told me they didn't want to stay at this hotel. There were too many bad memories there. Okay, no problem. Out of guilt and my own desire to make myself feel better about this rotten, exploitive day, I got them a room at the Mansion on Turtle Creek, the toniest hotel in town. Of course, David Van Os told me he needed a room there as well. And he reminded me that CBS really should pay for dinner for the three of them. That was the least we could do.

Sure. I was so tired and depressed I probably would have sent them a limousine so they could get a tour of the city. I wanted to go home. The sooner I got there, the more time I would have with my husband and son. I knew I was heading back for New York very early in the morning and I needed some love and attention myself.

On Sunday, Betsy and I met at the airport at about 8:00 A.M. We were going to fly back together, something I didn't mind at all. Betsy could be very East Coast and corporate, but she had a disarmingly zany side as well. On this morning we laughed ourselves silly when Betsy was pulled out of the boarding line for a special security check and somehow managed to spill dozens of doggy treats she had stuffed into her jacket pockets. The passengers behind us crunched and crackled their way onto the plane, crushing kibble with each step.

On the flight to New York, we joked that at the end of the day it was very often CBS women who had to get on the plane, do the dirty work of confronting people, and carry out the orders issued by men in the corporate offices. As in so many corporations, when it comes to "nut-cuttin' time," as they say in Texas, many of the men head for the hills. They are just not available. Not that I blame them.

On the flight, Betsy and I talked mostly about being mothers. What kind of mothers we were, what kind of mothers we'd had, what kind of mothers we wanted to be. It was a wonderful break from the *Sturm und Drang* of the previous days, from the feeling that every decision we made, every choice we made, might be our last. I don't know if Betsy felt that bleak, but I certainly did.

I said good-bye to Betsy and had barely made it to baggage claim at New York's LaGuardia Airport when my cell phone went off. It was Dan calling from Austin. Even through the gate announcements, the buzzers, and the bustle of the crowd, I could recognize that dark timbre in his voice that let me know when something was terribly, terribly wrong.

"Mary," he said. "Andrew has decided to make an announcement tomorrow, apologizing for the story and saying that we cannot authenticate the documents." He let that sink in, then went on: "Furthermore, he tells me that he is going to appoint an independent panel to investigate the way the story was put together. Andrew thinks, he is not sure, but he thinks the panel is going to be headed up by Dick Thornburgh, the former attorney general."

I was reeling. I leaned against a wall and listened, my heart in my throat. "Now, Mary, this is very bad and this is going to be very hard. And I am calling to tell you this, not just to give you a heads-up that this is what's coming, but because I want you to get yourself a lawyer as fast as you can." He took a deep breath. "You need to start protecting yourself. We all do."

I told Dan that I appreciated his tip. I told him that I loved him. I told him good-bye. And I went to the ladies' room at LaGuardia and cried my eyes out. Jesus Christ, I was finished.

CHAPTER 14

I staggered around the steel and stone restroom, groping for something soft to lean on while I sobbed. There was nothing but hard, cold marble. So I cradled my pounding head in my hands as big, fat tears blurred my vision. I watched them drip, drip, drip slowly and steadily onto the freshly mopped dark tile floor. Once again, I was creating extra work for someone.

I looked at my watch and realized that Dan might not yet be on board his flight out of Austin. I was so taken aback at what he'd told me that I'd forgotten to ask him something important about our schedule for the following day. When I tried his number, his daughter Robin answered. Dan must have forgotten his cell phone again. Some things never changed.

Robin told me that her father was already on the plane. She sounded as though she was terribly upset, too. I didn't know Robin other than as a voice on the phone or as a lead character in one of Dan's many stories about his talented and headstrong family. I'd never met her, but that didn't stop me from pouring out my feelings. I told her how incredibly sorry I was, how awful I felt, how her father had been great to me and how—at least right then—I strongly felt I had let him down. I didn't deserve his loyalty.

Robin's response summed up her dad in a few lines better than all the ink that has been spilled about Dan in decades. "This is going to get really bad," she told me. "This is going to be a rough time, but you should know this above all else. My father is loyal, period. Despite any-

thing else, despite everything else. He will never walk away from someone he considers a friend. And he considers you a friend."

Through all the problems, all the embarrassments and the insults,
my awful firing and public rebuke, the supreme unfairness of Dan's
stepping down from the *Evening News*, through all of it, he has never
blamed me. Never turned on me. Never failed to call to say hello or
drop me a note to make sure I was doing all right. He has checked in
with my husband and sent kisses to my son and behaved as a good
friend from beginning to end and back again. That is something I will
never forget and I will never stop feeling grateful for.

When Dan and I met the next day, September 20, we gave each
other a quick hug, the way we have for years. We didn't dwell on what
we had to do that Monday. We just went to work, sad and sorry and angry, but still doing our jobs, trying to craft a few concise sections of the
long Burkett interview into a piece for that night's *CBS Evening News*.
There would not be another *60 Minutes* story, no further explainers, no
continued investigations of the documents, no more efforts to show
that our work had been valid. It was over. Andrew and whoever was
calling the shots above him had spoken.

CBS News soon issued a statement that it could no longer stand by
the Bush-Guard story and announced that it would select an independent panel to investigate what had gone wrong on the story. Despite
my highest hopes for a full and fair investigation, CBS's strategy would
prove the corporate equivalent of declaring yourself guilty and then setting up a trial.

Dan's office released a statement later that day:

> Last week, amid increasing questions about the authenticity of
> documents used in support of a *60 Minutes Wednesday* story
> about President Bush's time in the Texas Air National Guard,
> CBS News vowed to re-examine the documents in question—and
> their source—vigorously. And we promised that we would let the
> American public know whatever the outcome. . . .
>
> Now, after extensive additional interviews, I no longer have the
> confidence in these documents that would allow us to continue
> vouching for them journalistically. I find we have been misled on
> the key question of how our source for the documents came into

possession of these papers. That, combined with some of the
questions that have been raised in the public and in the press,
leads me to a point where—if I knew then what I know now—I
would not have gone ahead with the story as it aired and I certainly would not have used the documents in question . . . We
made a mistake in judgment and for that I am sorry.

There was no indication that the memos weren't real. But it was a
white flag. CBS News had given in and given up. The executives who
made the decision to surrender had never understood our story or its
foundation. They had never even tried to. Far from standing unequivocally by journalistic principle, the bold leaders of CBS and Viacom reacted only in fear, motivated by corporate and political interest.

Burkett's confession as to misleading us about where he had gotten
the documents gave Andrew Heyward and corporate CBS the cover
they needed. They were looking for a way out, and Burkett's changing
his story must have seemed heaven-sent. I don't know what would have
happened if Burkett had stuck to the original story he told me.

What this apology was intended to accomplish for CBS was to stop
the blogging, stop the attacks, stop the editorials, stop the bleeding.
Naming an independent panel also sounded appropriately severe, almost as though they would be investigating before bringing criminal
charges, something that the bloggers already were baying for and that
some Republican politicians such as Tom Delay had already thrown
their weight behind. CBS thought that prostrating itself was a good way
for a news department that had been hit by a meteor to crawl out of the
crater and get back to higher ground. At least that is how the company's
decision makers must have viewed it.

This approach also provided something the suits at CBS News and
the men at Viacom had desired for a long, long time. They now had
the chance to remake the news division into a leaner, meaner—less uppity, more malleable—machine.

I can't believe that in the bowels of the CBS building and up in the
clouds at Viacom's corporate headquarters there weren't some wicked,
self-serving conversations about how this could turn out to be "for the
best" for the corporation. Cynical executives knew that the company
could make this bad news work for them. The Bush-Guard scandal

would weaken Dan and allow them to remove him from the helm of the *Evening News*, which they had wanted to do for years as the newscast's demographics sagged, its ratings declined, and the nation's press backed away from aggressive coverage of a combative administration. It was much easier to blame Dan for the image problems than address the combination of forces that were eroding the *Evening News* audience. There had been large shifts in viewers' work habits and television viewing patterns, of course, but CBS was also saddled with a notoriously weak string of affiliates in large cities. Topping the rise of the Internet and the change in public interest toward current events, the clincher in most every market was "Who airs Oprah?" The queen of talk could make or break a station's ratings with her huge audience leading into the local news, followed by the network's evening newscast.

I never figured out how the network brass could boost the ratings, no matter what they did, without confronting another bottom-line problem for every evening newscast. Who the hell was home at airtime anymore? The *Evening News* comes on at 5:30 or 6:30 P.M., depending where you live. I was never home from work then and almost no one I knew was, either. I might be on the way there with my son, but if I got home in time from work or going to the store, I sure wasn't immediately glued to the television set when I walked in the door.

People who *were* home—especially the all-important eighteen-to-forty-nine-year-old crowd—were not watching the news, either. They were busy feeding the kids, doing homework, cooking, exercising, or watching one of the other ninety-six channels on cable. Few of us rush home for a network news "appointment" assigned to its scheduled time in a bygone era when watching television meant choosing among three or four channels. Through the generations, that schedule has been virtually unmovable, in complete disregard for anyone's needs other than the networks' own. The networks did not want to give up any lucrative prime time for news.

The Bush-Guard controversy had done in a few weeks what endless infighting at CBS hadn't begun to accomplish. It embarrassed the news division and softened it up for personnel and airtime cuts. It scared the crap out of anyone and everyone working at CBS News and made them much more amenable to the kind of slick changes that Les Moonves and the Hollywood crowd had wanted to make for years.

236 | MARY MAPES

This supposed scandal had more than a touch of the perverse logic behind the scheme in *The Producers*. For Viacom, struggling to remold CBS News into a twenty-first-century infotainment machine, a failure like this ultimately could mean great things. A chance to make nice with an administration that has a lot to say about legislation that a big corporation badly needs—an administration that wouldn't exactly protest seeing an old nemesis like Dan Rather knocked down a peg or two, either.

For me, getting through the hours of September 20 until the *Evening News* was like waiting for a death. Maybe an *execution* is more like it. The office was quiet. There was no laughter, no joking, none of our typical black humor. Reality was dark enough.

I spent hours—much longer than I needed, really—editing the few pieces of the Burkett interview that Andrew had personally selected and determined we should run. Not surprisingly, they were the ones that told the story in the broadest and crudest possible brush strokes: Burkett acknowledging that he had lied to us, Dan saying that since Burkett had lied we couldn't trust the documents. Cue the apology, fade to black.

I couldn't watch the broadcast. I didn't want to see Dan say those things. I knew how proud he was and how hard this was for him. I was so sad, so ashamed, so very sorry. It was the worst night of my life professionally. I'd hit bottom, or so I thought.

Whenever I thought I'd found the floor, gone as low as I could go, when I believed the worst had already happened and there was nowhere to go but up, something would rumble along to make my previous fear, unhappiness, and failure feel like a warm-up. This was like living in a goddamn horror movie. Every time I thought the monster had been killed, I found out—the hard way—that it had just been hiding.

On this night, the monster was still very much alive even after Dan's apology.

I was sitting in Dana's office talking with Josh. He was on the couch telling me about the kinds of stories he had always liked to do. He called them victim stories. Anyone who watches television news knows them well: tales about victims of some disease or some kind of societal shortcoming, stories that make you identify and empathize with someone you might have little in common with. I had certainly done my share. Those kinds of stories have been staples of television news coverage since the dawn of the cathode ray tube. They can be affecting.

They can make a difference. But they are not investigative pieces, and victim stories did not require the inner steel and stamina that tough investigations often called for. Josh seemed like a nice guy, but I recall thinking at that moment that he wasn't tough enough to do or to defend hard-edged journalistic investigative work.

Betsy walked in. From the look on her face, I could tell something was wrong. Something new. "Mary, *USA Today* has called and asked if you called the Kerry campaign and put them in touch with Bill Burkett in exchange for the documents," she said. I asked who the reporter was. She said it was someone named Dave Moniz.

I knew right away what was happening. Bill Burkett had been a longtime source for Moniz. The two had collaborated on a series of stories about ghost soldiers and Burkett had given Moniz his own copies of the Bush-Guard memos on the night our story ran. Burkett had boasted to me that he helped Moniz to such an extent in writing his next-day article that Burkett should have demanded a byline.

Now it sounded as though Moniz and Burkett had talked again and that Burkett's loose lips and careless characterizations would once again cause problems. I wasn't too concerned, though. My contacts with the Kerry campaign had been very limited, and I had done it all with Josh's permission.

"I know what this is about," I said, turning toward Josh. "Do you remember when I told you that Burkett wanted to give the Kerry campaign advice on the Swift Boat attacks and he wanted me to pass on his phone number?"

This is how I remember the rest of the conversation.

Josh stared at me blankly.

"Josh, you told me that producers and reporters talk to people all the time, that it was no big deal," I insisted.

Josh didn't say anything. Betsy was starting to look alarmed.

I tried again. "Josh," I pleaded, "do you remember when I said that I also needed to do a bullshit check on Burkett after he told me he had spoken with Max Cleland and Howard Dean? I didn't believe him, so I said I could use the contact with the Kerry people to check on that. And you told me I could give them Burkett's phone number. That's what I did. That's *all* I did. Do you remember any of this?"

Josh was very quiet. Then he said, "I must not have made myself as clear as I might have. You must have misunderstood what I said you could do." It felt like the end of the world, all over again.

Betsy exploded. "Jesus Christ! What else is going to happen here? This is absolutely unbelievable." She turned on her heel and marched out. Josh excused himself and slipped out of the room. Months later I would come across a tidbit in a book that made me laugh out loud, albeit bitterly, about Josh's selective memory.

Kristina Borjesson, a former CBS producer, edited a book called *Into the Buzzsaw*, which examined the censorship that has killed controversial stories. I've never met or spoken with her. Maybe someday we'll compare notes. In the book, Borjesson recounted her own brush with censorship at CBS when she was covering the crash of TWA 800 and working with a source named Sanders, who had a contact inside the investigation. Sanders had obtained a sample of an unidentified residue from a seat on the doomed plane. Borjesson wanted to have it tested and report the findings. Good story.

In the book, she says she went to see Josh Howard, then the senior producer at *60 Minutes*.

> I warned him that a federal grand jury had been convened to deal with legal transgressions connected to the TWA 800 investigation, including evidence being "stolen" (which is how the feds viewed the residue samples sent to Sanders) from the hangar. Howard wasn't fazed. "We've dealt with grand juries before," he said. I was elated. In the world of news, *60 Minutes*, I told him, was the "last broadcast with balls."
>
> With Howard's permission (which he more recently told me didn't recall giving to me, although he does recall getting the sample) in hand, I called Sanders, and he FedExed the sample to me.

The story goes on to recount how CBS backed away from the story and gave Borjesson her "walking papers." But what fascinated me was the nearly identical situation she had encountered with Josh Howard. First he declared her request to be essentially no problem, something that he had experience with. Then, when the story hit the fan, he couldn't remember ever saying that.

What are the odds of two producers who have never met recounting nearly identical experiences years apart? To me, it seems obvious that Josh had sandbagged us both, using that old standby, "I don't recall."

That day, before Josh denied giving me permission and vanished, I had been sitting there vanquished but convinced that the worst was over. Now without even two minutes to rest and regroup, I was being summoned to explain myself again. This time, though, I knew there would be no battle, no defense, no defiance. This time, I was alone. Betsy was not going to work to help me. Josh was trying to pretend he'd never met me. I was not going to ask Dan for anything more. Andrew would have been happy to run me down with a cab, given half a chance.

I stood up and unplugged my computer, packed it into my bulging briefcase, and started the trek down the hall. I left the door to Dana's office open and passed Yvonne's doorway, dark and empty and quiet. I walked alone down the hall to the ladies' room, pushed the door open, and saw that, for once, it was empty.

The big mirror that hung over the counter had been a fixture in the lives of 60 Minutes's many women producers over the years. The mirror itself was an old friend, even if we didn't always like what we saw in there. But the old mirror, wide enough to service a sorority full of faces, had reflected back to us countless good conversations with beloved friends. We had peered into it, putting on lipstick, joking about our jobs, or combing our hair before we went out to dinner, attended an award ceremony, celebrated a triumph, or worked wildly to make a deadline. I recalled talking with a pregnant friend as the mirror reflected our images and she described how she felt her body changing, her heart expanding. The old mirror had caught glimpses of all of us laughing, crying, celebrating, commiserating—sometimes saddened but always engaged.

A moment later, I stood in the lobby and waited one last time for an elevator. I didn't know that I would never be in the building again, but I was certain that this place and this life at CBS that had once been so important would never be the same for me again.

I said good-bye to the nearly sleeping security guard, pushed out into the night, and made my way again to the hotel, out to the airport, and back home to Texas. From then on, all my battles would be fought from there. My days of fighting for CBS, from inside CBS, were over.

The next morning's USA Today had an article about my contact with the Kerry campaign, paraphrasing Burkett as saying that he had asked me to get him in contact with the campaign in exchange for giving me the documents.

That was absolutely false and I knew I could knock it down if anyone cared enough to listen. I already had been told by CBS News not to talk to any reporter, so I didn't make the phone calls I probably should have. I couldn't fathom how Burkett could so blatantly misrepresent a small part of our conversations. I sent Betsy an e-mail, reminding her that we had taped Burkett twice, once in an on-camera interview and once when he spoke to us by speakerphone, while he outlined the conditions for getting the documents. He had never said a word about requiring a chance to speak with the Kerry campaign.

I also reminded her that I had gone to Josh, aking for advice on what to do when Burkett first brought up the subject of giving the Kerry campaign his phone number. Then I had limited myself to exactly what Josh had told me I could do: give Burkett's phone number to the campaign. That's all I had done. I didn't even know anyone with the Kerry campaign, so I had called the campaign press office and talked with a spokesman who handled calls from reporters around the clock. I told him who I was and that a guy named Bill Burkett wanted to talk about the Swift Boat attacks and how the campaign should respond. That's pretty mundane stuff for any campaign.

Burkett thought he had some advice for the Kerry people. They, of course, didn't call Burkett because they apparently didn't believe they needed the campaign insights of a West Texas rancher. Their failure to call did not surprise me one bit, but I had done what Burkett asked and not one whit more.

Chad Clanton, the campaign spokesman I talked to, had given me the number for Joe Lockhart, one of Kerry's advisers, but I didn't call him or give his number to Burkett. I had no reason to talk to Lockhart. I had told Burkett that I would pass along his phone number so that the Kerry people could call him if they chose. Given all of the daily interplay between reporters and politicians and their campaign people who routinely share ideas and form close relationships, my contact with Kerry's office was awfully boring.

As we had worked maniacally on Labor Day to get our original story put together, Lockhart called my cell phone and asked what this Burkett guy wanted to talk about. In about a two-minute conversation, I was fairly dismissive of Burkett but told Lockhart that he thought he had some insight into how to handle the Swift Boat veterans' issues. I didn't ask that he call Burkett. I didn't even give him the number again. Lockhart had it, called Burkett, and apparently talked for three or four minutes about the Swift Boat attacks, according to later news reports. Lockhart and Burkett both said they never discussed the Guard documents.

During the panel investigation, I came across some e-mails that Burkett had sent to me on Labor Day as I worked to get our story ready in New York. Burkett had already given us the documents even though he had not gotten his hoped-for call from the Kerry campaign, further evidence that we had no horse-trading agreement. Burkett was getting frustrated, though, which is a fairly perpetual state for him. He asked again by e-mail that I put him in touch with the Kerry campaign so he could advise them on how to fight the Swift Boat charges.

"Have them call and give me a secure number," Burkett wrote about 9:00 A.M. "All they have to say is call your broker and give a number and I'll call right back. Or you can get me a number that I can call."

I remembered laughing when I read it. "All they have to say is call your broker"? This was getting way too cloak-and-dagger for me. I had given Burkett's phone number to Clanton, told him that Burkett wanted to talk about Swift Boats, and left it at that. I doubted very much that anyone would call Burkett and, frankly, I didn't care whether anyone called. That may sound terrible, but I wasn't fighting a political battle. I wasn't working for a campaign. I was trying to get a story on the air. Period. I told Mike Smith to call Burkett and hold his hand.

Burkett's hopes and dreams were not mine. Kerry's success or failure was not my business. Nailing down this story, getting it confirmed, getting it on the air, and getting home to Texas was all I cared about, all I was interested in, all I was focused on.

Burkett sent me one other e-mail mentioning the Kerry campaign that day. At about one-thirty in the afternoon, he asked that I "expedite the Friday event with a serious call contact today and as early as possible." I'm still not sure, but I believe that was a reference to Burkett's desire to meet with someone from the campaign on Friday. He had mentioned wanting a meeting. I had listened to him, but I certainly had no control over anything like that and, again, no interest in it. I wasn't even sure where Burkett was. He had left West Texas and gone to a cattle show in Montana or Idaho or maybe Wyoming. I do think that, in a fit of egotism, he had grand visions of being visited by high-level Kerry staffers as if he were a political consultant with powerful and unique ideas for combating some of the campaign's public relations troubles.

Burkett had rambled on about the Democrats responding to the Swift Boat attacks, ideas that sounded reasonable enough. But I didn't believe for an instant that the Kerry campaign didn't have its own PR whizzes working on the issue, and I couldn't imagine that they would seek Burkett out.

Burkett was clearly frustrated at my lack of clout with the campaign and my failure to get him connected with the Kerry people. "If your inside contact won't call me, at least maybe they can give me an e-mail address," Burkett wrote. I had given him no way to contact anyone with the campaign.

I wrote back and asked him again for a phone number where someone could call, although I had no intention of passing it on. If I were trying to put him in touch with people, I suppose I could have. But I didn't want to, I didn't need to, and I didn't promise to do it in exchange for the documents. I promised not to reveal his name, nothing more.

There is an old saying in television news—a joke about how shallow we are—that I have used when swearing to do something, meet a commitment, or otherwise fulfill a promise. It applied to this situation perfectly. The line is always said with tongue in cheek. "You have my word as a television producer." That means you have my worthless word as a conniving television producer who will say almost anything to get what she wants and then leave you in the lurch once she has what she needs. That's what I did with Burkett and his imagined work as a political consultant. I gave him my word as a television producer and then proceeded to ignore his demands because they fell outside what I could do or would do for him.

I paid dearly and publicly, however, for my too-cute-by-half behavior. I shouldn't have let Burkett think I might have some kind of sway with the Kerry campaign when I didn't. I shouldn't have told Burkett I was going to pass on his phone number and then done it, not caring whether the campaign threw it in the trash. I should have told Burkett no when he asked me to hand off his phone number. And once the shit

hit the fan, I shouldn't have expected Josh Howard to sacrifice himself for me and be forthcoming about his approval to call the Kerry campaign. After all, I only had *his* word as a television producer. It wasn't fair, but in a way it served me right.

Throughout the debacle at CBS, as story after story was ground out about my work, my failings, my faults, and my dismal future, I was told by my CBS supervisors not to talk to any reporters and, like a fool, I did what I was told. Not one article ever got the details correct, and news coverage invariably mischaracterized key elements. It was frightening and chilling to see how inaccurate the nation's best newspapers were, how much they speculated and twisted what they reported, either ignorantly or deliberately. Now, as the tale of my supposed contact with the Kerry campaign grew, I started to get very worried.

Reporters were calling my house at all hours of the day and night. I felt that I couldn't trust any of them, even the people I had known for years. Everything was different now. The speeding media train that I had ridden for so long, so blithely, was now aimed at me, and I was tied to the tracks. When journalists were getting so many things wrong, who could I trust to get anything right? Per CBS's orders, I once again declined to answer questions from Jim Rutenberg, a *New York Times* reporter, on September 21. The next day when I retrieved the blue-bagged *Times* from my Texas lawn, I saw a story that made me wish I had not followed CBS's toxic advice so religiously.

The article said that the network had issued a "rebuke" of Mary Mapes that served to "underscore the change in Ms. Mapes' status in the last week" because of revelations about the supposed contact with the Kerry campaign.

"It is obviously against CBS News standards and those of every other reputable news organization to be associated with any political agenda," the network said in a statement, clearly beginning to treat me as though I had contracted a contagious, fast-moving, and disfiguring disease. The corporate statement, in itself, was straightforward. Journalists obviously shouldn't be associated with a political agenda. But the *Times* article concluded without doubt or attribution that I had violated that standard. I had done no such thing, but the *Times* had put one and one together and come up with something more than two. The only bright spot in the article was a comment from Jeff Fager. I had "always been a first-class producer with an impressive body of work," he said. "I hope we all find out soon how this could have gone so horribly wrong."

I wrote Betsy what would be my last e-mail before I was pulled under the waves. I was starting still another day with a migraine, figuratively and literally. I was frustrated, afraid, and deeply hurt. I wasn't sure how much longer I could go on. And it wasn't even 9:00 A.M. I wrote:

> Betsy, I am extremely disappointed in the direction of the coverage this morning re my going off the reservation in terms of CBS policy. As you know, I specifically asked for Josh's permission before making an initial call and was given a go-ahead. The characterization that I was rebuked by CBS either comes from the starkness of the statement yesterday or the fact that in delivering it, someone also implied that I had violated policy.

I finally began to show some of my frustration with the way the news department had hung me out to dry. I'd been a good soldier. Now I was finding out the hard way that I hadn't been good enough, that I was as expendable as a piece of tissue.

At least and at last, I wanted Betsy to know how I felt. "I am really getting weary with this. I did not lie, plagiarize, make up anything, work for the Kerry team or torture puppies. I worked hard, checked constantly with my superiors and played by the rules," I wrote. "I am grateful to Jeff for finally speaking out, but feeling really blue about everyone else."

I don't remember if I got a response other than another warning that I should not talk to any reporters.

I was given the mind-numbing directive from Andrew that I should stop working on the story completely. I was not to make any phone calls, not to contact sources, not to do any interviews, not to ask any questions, or dig for any information whatsoever.

Then came an even more stunning development. Andrew Heyward called me at home and told me that he was hiring a private investigator to take over the story, travel to Texas, and pick up our work where we left off. I was to stop in my tracks and cooperate fully with the PI, hired by supposed journalists to do the job of journalists.

The investigator's name was Erik Rigler and his work for CBS turned out to be done more for show than for tell. None of the many interviews he did or the substantial evidence he uncovered that our Bush-Guard story was true were ever made public.

Once again, like a trusting fool, I did what the president of CBS News asked, even though this strategy wasn't merely unorthodox but unprecedented in the annals of journalism as far as I could tell. Andrew was the boss. Or at least his bosses were. I worked to get my massive amount of information together for Rigler, making long lists of interview subjects, names, addresses, and writing out characterizations. I would hand over all the details and potential trails that I hoped he could use to push the story forward. I had to pray that he could.

That week, I sat at home with my husband. Our boy was in bed and the dogs were sprawled on the floor, passed out in contentment as I regaled poor Mark for the umpteenth time with the details of my despair. Every night I went on about my hopeful desperation at needing to move the story ahead, my frustration with the unfairness of the situation, my impatience at waiting for a private investigator to do the work that I knew best and that I knew should belong to journalists.

The phone rang. Mark answered it, as he did most of the time now. For a while, I didn't want to answer without knowing who it was. I might get trapped into a conversation with a reporter or, worse, end up getting blasted by bloggers who had found my phone number and wanted to attack me because they thought they knew everything there was to know about me, my story, and my assumed bias.

This time, the phone call was from Mike Smith. He didn't have much to say; he just wanted to express his support, share a little of the misery, and maybe a couple of laughs. We were all in desperate need of a few chuckles these days. Mike had told me months earlier that some in his family were very conservative politically. Now Mike said a relative had called and told him in no uncertain terms, "Mike, you have really screwed up this time. You really blew it on this story."

I laughed and said, "Hey, I'm just waiting for my alcoholic father to call up some conservative radio station and attack me publicly." I was kidding, but like many jokes, this one had some truth to it. My father and his propensity for cruelty was a shared secret in the lives of his five daughters, and it had crossed my mind that he might seize this opportunity to draw attention to himself.

Don Mapes was a man who had not been a real part of our lives for

246 | MARY MAPES

years, but he was someone we hauled out occasionally to serve as an emotional bogeyman. He was never a strong or comforting figure in our lives, never someone we counted on for love or support or paternal advice. He was someone we knew we could count on to keep being abusive, at least emotionally.

My husband of eighteen years knew about my father, all too well. Many of my friends knew about his sad history, too. My sisters and I talked about him once in a while. But people I dealt with professionally didn't know that my father was an angry alcoholic from whom I had been estranged for most of two decades after my parents divorced. There was no reason for them to know, of course. Even my son didn't know my father. Robert was only seven and I didn't want him to have anything but love and stability in his life. I wasn't going to trust his tender little heart to someone who had proved to be unworthy, who had abandoned his family, abused his wife and daughters, physically and emotionally, and failed to learn anything from his shattered relationships. My father had basically lost his right to be part of our lives.

After I made my joke about half-expecting my father to speak out against me, Mike grew quiet and then said something that rocked me. "Well, then, you know."

What?? I shot straight up like I had an explosive charge under my chair. *Then I know what?* Suddenly I was peppering Mike with questions, barking at him. Even someone as laid back as Mike knew he had said something wrong, let something slip, blown it big-time. The poor guy assumed I knew that my father had struck again, that he had spouted off in his characteristic thoroughly uninformed way about me and my Bush-Guard story. I didn't know about it until Mike mistakenly broke the bad news.

He hung up quickly, telling me that maybe I ought to talk to my husband. Mark sat next to me and said, "Mary, I am so sorry. I am so, so sorry," apologizing for my father's latest, but hardly greatest, misbehavior. Mark gave me a hug and kissed me. He told me that Peggy and Diane, my two sisters in Seattle, had called the day before and told him in disgust that my father had once again reappeared to spread hurt in our lives. Mike knew about it, too. My sisters didn't know whether to tell me right away, and they decided with Mark that this newest disappointment could wait a day or two. They thought I already had about as much heartache as I needed for the moment. They were right.

With the tempest over the Bush-Guard story raging on talk radio just a couple of days after our story aired, my father had called a conservative station in Seattle that was chomping on the red meat. When he identified himself to the call screener as Mary Mapes's father, it got him onto the air immediately. The talk-show host might have thought he was going to get an earful from an angry old man defending his beloved daughter. Instead, the caller gleefully joined in the attack against me and CBS.

My seventy-six-year-old father, who drank and punched and tormented his way through our childhoods and hadn't spoken with me for more than fifteen years, talked about me on the radio as though he knew me well. "I'm really ashamed of what my daughter has become," Don Mapes said in comments that were welcomed and repeated endlessly on conservative Web sites and chewed up and spit out by Neanderthal bloggers. "She's a typical liberal. She went into journalism with an ax to grind and that was to promote radical feminism."

Of course to my father, radical feminism meant refusing to accept that a man has the right to smack his wife around every time he goes on a toot. Radical feminism meant believing that women should get an education. He did not feel that way. He had refused to sign financial aid forms when his daughters wanted to attend college, leaving our mother to forge his signature and hope that no one found out. To my father, radical feminism meant women actually having the chance to make their own choices in life.

"When I heard about *60 Minutes*, I suspected she would be the producer of the show," he was quoted as telling the host, one of the countless aspiring blowhards on conservative radio. "Dan Rather and she have been working on this ever since Bush was elected."

Considering that I hadn't had contact with my father since George H. W. Bush was elected, I didn't know how he felt he could possibly know this, but clearly that wasn't the point. He just didn't want anybody out there beating up his daughter without him having a chance to get his own licks in.

For the first time since my mother died in 2001, I remember thinking that I was glad she wasn't alive. Seeing this would have broken her heart.

The mainstream media again faithfully followed the bloggers' lead, turning to my father for learned comments about his media daughter and her motives. Reporters gave him automatic credibility because he was a parent. Sadly, he deserved no such respect or authority.

Mark and I called my father and asked him to stop talking, stop pretending, and stop beating me up in public. He told me he had every right to say those things, but he agreed to stop when I literally begged him to shut up. That's what he had wanted all along, one more chance to be the bully, one more chance to belittle someone who had gotten out of his grasp.

I did find it funny that my foolish father apparently did a long interview with Jeff Gannon of Talon News, a Republican organization's "news" arm. Gannon was later exposed as a male escort. In trying to hurt me, my father once again made an ass of himself.

I don't hate my father. I feel terribly sorry for him. I wish I had a father I could be proud of, but that is a pain that many hearts know. Once, a long time ago, he was handsome and funny, a talented pianist with five little girls who loved him. Alcoholism, anger, untreated emotional problems, and a lifetime of bad choices later, he is an isolated old man who has grandchildren he doesn't know and daughters he never sees.

The problems that divide my family are not that unusual, unfortunately. What was different for me was that they were declared fair game by the "family values" crowd. "Even her *father* says she is a liberal!" Rush Limbaugh bellowed into his microphone. Time and again, my father's comments were referenced as clear evidence that I was a feminist fool and a liberal tool.

This time, I had really hit bottom. I had no more secrets, it seemed, no more privacy. But I still had a chance to defend myself before the panel that would determine whether I lived or died professionally. It became my sole focus.

Growing up with a father like mine burdened everyone in our family. But the emotional roller coaster, the constant disappointments, and the early disillusionment ended up offering blessings, as well. Fire tempers steel. I was tougher than I would have been if I'd had a better father. I was stronger, faster on my feet, able to bounce back and run farther. I had to be. I'd been doing it all my life.

With the help of my attorneys—there's a phrase that a journalist never wants to have to use—I threw myself into building a strong defense to present to the panel. I was not going to go down without a fight.

CHAPTER 15

It was late October and New York's weather had become chilly. Dick Hibey, law associate Dan Lewis, and I turned up our collars as we walked through the wind toward Black Rock, CBS's famously imposing corporate headquarters. Dan struggled to pull along his spindly metal cart stacked high with boxes and black notebooks, each containing a reporter's treasure: copies of my notes on phone calls and conversations with sources, my e-mails, some of my phone records, my journalistic secrets. They all had been requested by the panel and my bosses told me I had to comply. CBS had already obligingly downloaded all my e-mails from the past who-knew-how-many months and given them to the panel in advance.

I brought along a statement I planned to read to the panel and what I called a meshing document I'd meticulously put together, the crux of which I had worked out prior to airing the Bush National Guard report. The meshing analysis showed how the new documents fit perfectly with Bush's known records and was just one of the elements that helped give me the confidence to go to air.

Together, these notebooks and boxes, records and ruminations, constituted the skeleton of my dead story, a report that the press had already determined to be dead wrong. Now, the corpse and I were headed in for the autopsy.

Black Rock is every bit as inviting as its nickname implies; a tall, coal black tower of glass and steel, a place that no CBS News employee, past or present, walks past without a shiver. This massive metal phallus (a coincidence, I'm sure) was home base for all the decisions over the decades that had curtailed and weakened the news division. Out of this dark and gleaming building had come the dreaded phone calls and deep cutbacks, the corrosive corporate decisions that threw employees' lives into upheaval, the choices that gradually and inevitably meant less airtime, less money, and more layoffs.

I had slept very little the night before my first session with the panel. Dick Hibey had worked with me on the train from Washington the previous evening on my demeanor before the panel. Helpful, but not blabby. Personable, but not frivolous. Myself, only not really.

Friends who had already testified had given me the drift of what I could expect. The panel had asked everyone not to share their experiences inside the hearings with others, particularly not with people who would be called to the panel later. But in a few cases, friendship and concern about me had proved stronger than the fear of losing a job and I had been told the bare outlines of the panel makeup and the nature of the questioning.

I would be meeting panel members and answering their questions in one of the CBS conference rooms. I knew who the questioners would be. All of them, like Dick Thornburgh, were from the massive law firm of Kirkpatrick & Lockhart Nicholson Graham, a Washington powerhouse. The lone exception to the all-lawyer panel was former Associated Press CEO Lou Boccardi, a career manager who hadn't worked in daily news for decades.

I knew that the panel had asked other CBS employees whether I had been obsessed by the story or by President Bush himself. I knew they had asked some of my colleagues if I was a liberal, a Bush basher, or maybe a hothead. At least one person had been asked whether I had tried to physically intimidate people. Had I thrown things, screamed at people, attacked anyone? Good Lord. I didn't know whether to laugh or cry at such a twisted line of inquiry.

I did not know what the panel's attitude toward me would be. But deep inside, I felt this whole process was turning into a witch hunt and, as the only woman in the middle of the story, I felt my DNA and my female intuition telling me that this could be bad. Very bad.

When we got inside the Black Rock lobby, we found that we had not been cleared by security to go up, so there was a brief delay as the guards called upstairs and gave our names. I remember thinking: *We ought to just make a run for it.* At least that's what the cornered little kid in me wanted to do. Race into the street, commandeer the first taxi, bus, or pedicab that came along, careen off, and just keep going.

I was nervous—not hyperventilating at this point, but definitely not happy. Dick tried to cheer me up by taking my mind off the subject. He talked to me in the distracting way of a parent trying to calm a child about to get a shot. I remember his regaling me that day with a story about his late mother's propensity for finding the most incredible things in her huge, tightly packed purse. He recounted how he had always marveled at the mystery of her purse, wondering what she kept in there, how she held it so close everywhere she went. His fascination with her purse peaked in her later years, when he and his brothers were discussing a couple of long-retired baseball stars. Out of the blue, Mom had pulled two forty-year-old baseball cards of those two very players out of her purse. Her sons were amazed. With regret, I silently acknowledged that I was going to have to pull something equally unexpected out of my bag to get through this day intact.

Dick, Dan, and I got in the elevator and headed for the high altitudes while I told myself again that I had done nothing wrong, that I had nothing to fear, that I was going to treat the panel the way I wanted them to treat me—with openness, candor, and goodwill. And I really did believe at the time that full participation in the panel's inquiry was the only way to save my job, that I would be able to convince them of my good work and good record, that they would be fair.

I was a fool.

We reached our floor and stepped out, where attorney Mike Missal was waiting for us, oozing the kind of false, soft-voiced solicitousness of a funeral home director. "Do you need to hang your coats? Do you need to use the restroom? Would you like something to drink?"

Missal had that flat-eyed, impersonal corporate attorney behavior down to an art form. He was pleasant but offered no information, no encouragement, no unnecessary bonding, as he guided our group through the foyer of the network offices, past pictures of CBS luminaries like Lucille Ball, Ed Sullivan, and Candice Bergen and the rest of the cast of the *Murphy Brown* show. I didn't have much of Murphy Brown's fight in me at that point. I was too worried.

I felt like I had arrived at the oncologist's office and was about to hear terrible test results. Missal made me anxious by being so unctuous, fluttering around me with what seemed like a stream of insincere chatter about my comfort, my flight to New York, my stay at the hotel the night before, how I was feeling now.

How the heck do you *think* I feel, Mike? I feel like the pig that just arrived at the luau: I don't care how polite the host is; I am not entirely pleased with the way the day is shaping up.

I half-wondered if Missal was being overly gracious because he was concerned about that bogus physical intimidation issue. Did he think I might fly off the handle and attack him? Drop my briefcase, wrestle him to the ground, and bend his arms behind his back?

I had to laugh to myself. I had never had anyone view me as a physical threat before. This was new and exciting. Perhaps there was some small measure of fun to be had here, after all.

Dick, Dan, and I went into a small conference room to prepare our notebooks to be handed out to the panel. Dick patted me on the back and told me, "Be yourself." Most important, he wanted me to pay attention to him for signals that I should pipe down. I knew he was worried that I would get wound up, start talking, and just keep talking, an absolutely legitimate concern given the fact that I was desperate, hurt, scared, and extremely pissed off. In other words, I was a typical witness.

Dick spoke to me in practiced, soothing tones, telling me repeatedly, "Just answer the question. Tell them what time it is," he instructed. "Don't tell them how to build a clock."

Finally, we entered a large boardroom, where I met the panel. They were very mannerly and proper, again very corporate. Dick Thornburgh was quite tall. Lou Boccardi, quite short. In fact, he was tiny. I wondered if he, too, was afraid I might turn over the table and put up my dukes.

Missal was still there, asking if I needed anything. Now he was joined by another attorney, Larry Lanpher, who had curly reddish hair and round horn-rimmed glasses. There were two women, associates at the Kirkpatrick & Lockhart law firm, sitting ready to take notes on everything I said.

The panel and the two lead attorneys, Missal and Lanpher, were bunched at one end of the large conference table. The legal associates were settled at the midpoint of the table. There was a wall of windows on one side of the room, but I felt I didn't dare look away from the action.

There were no tape recorders in the room. No cameras. No real record. It seemed odd, upon reflection, that a company such as Viacom, which could certainly provide the technology to record this series of hearings, chose not to. Later I thought I knew why. Not only did corporate officials not want tapes that could be leaked to the public, but the company wanted the panel to be the final keeper of the truth, the only entity with a complete record. That way, whatever they said would become the reality. There would be no videotape to go to, no audio recording that would settle a dispute about what was said or by whom.

We took our seats and water was passed around. I sat at the head of the glossy wooden conference table. Dick told them that I had an opening statement. I opened my notebook to my long-winded sixty-five-page statement and tried to warm them up by asking for their patience and saying that I was about to demonstrate why I had become a producer, that I had no real voice for recording or reading aloud, and that I had no screen presence. I meant it as a self-effacing joke. Everyone stared at me. Gee, tough crowd.

I took a deep breath and began.

I told them about my background, my twenty-five years in television news, the stories I had done, my preference for living in Texas rather than New York or Washington, and how that choice had more or less dictated that I would offer 60 Minutes whatever investigative coverage I could of George W. Bush's stint in the Texas Guard when he seized the national stage so many years later.

I told them how frustrating it had been to remain silent at CBS's request for the previous weeks while my media compatriots raced forward with mischaracterizations and pundits came out with sweeping conclusions. I told them I had been tormented watching incorrect information being taken as fact as I sat quietly by, unable to correct or question or criticize what was being said and written.

And—ever the optimist—I told them that I was "very eager to use this review process to set the record straight."

Using my notes from 1999 and 2000, I recounted how I had begun working on the story only to drop it twice and then pick it up again in the summer of 2004. I offered them many quotes from people who'd known Bush in the Guard and I told them all of this background had informed my work on the story this last time around. I reminded them that they had copies of all my notes that they could refer to if they wanted to see what I had recorded at the time of those conversations.

They listened and wrote, their pens scribbling rapidly. As I talked, I referred them now and then to various sections of my notes or documents in the almost-one-thousand-page black file my attorneys and I had prepared and brought along for the members of the panel. No one they had previously spoken with could possibly have been so specific about the information behind this story. No one grasped the facts, the nuances, the totality of the story as I did.

The dates and details, the ins and outs, the innards of any story were always the responsibility of the producer. The panel had saved me for late in their inquiry and now they were finally hearing most of what they said they wanted to know: how we had gotten from the first phone call in 1999 to airtime on September 8, 2004.

I carried on for most of the morning, leading them step-by-step from my search for the documents to my request for permission to call the Kerry campaign, through the absence of my bosses during a large portion of the producing work to the chaotic editing of the story, past the compliments I got from my supervisors the morning after air, all the way through the bloggers to the catastrophe that ensued.

I finished by saying something that would turn out to be prescient. I said that I feared that this investigation might, in some form, conclude that the absence of CBS executives as active participants in the process leading up to the airing of the story was evidence of the system failing to stop a story that should not have aired.

I told them I strongly disagreed with that. I believed then—as I still do—that "it is more accurate to say that their absence prevented them from having a greater level of connectedness to the story and the huge amount of reporting that supported and confirmed our work, which would have emboldened them to insist later that CBS stand by the work rather than capitulate to unrelenting pressure from politically or competitively motivated critics."

There had been a "systemic breakdown," I told them, "but it was in the network's failure to appreciate the totality of the evidence we had compiled over several years. This lack of understanding led CBS to back away from a story that needed no apology on September 20 and, respectfully, needs none now."

When I finished my long speech, there was no applause, to say the least. The panel members looked at me silently. Finally, the ever-solicitous Mike Missal asked if I needed a break, maybe some more water, perhaps a trip to the ladies' room? Gosh, I wasn't that delicate. I told them they could go ahead and start their questioning. Let's get this witch hunt on the road.

Out of the gate, Missal's questions were about politics, not just electoral but personal and professional. He was on my right at the table. Boy, was he. Why did I choose to talk to certain people? Why did I choose to work with certain people? Why did I word my e-mails the way I did? Did I think this person or that person had a political bias against President Bush? Why? Why not?

As the lead counsel on the review, Missal asked the most questions and telegraphed the most clearly how the panel approached its job. He asked questions politely, but with the unrelenting air of the smartest boy in the fifth grade, the kid nobody else wanted to play with, the kid who had a mean streak beneath his glasses and carefully combed hair.

Missal wanted to know all about my work with independent researcher Mike Smith, how we had met, what we had worked on, and why I trusted him. He read aloud from e-mails where Smith and I had teased back and forth and jokingly tried to gather information on each other's projects. Missal made it clear he viewed the e-mails as inappropriate, in some vague but very important way.

That summer, Mike Smith had been working with ARD, a German public television network, which had done a number of interviews and gathered information for a documentary on George W. Bush. The documentary included a segment on the president's controversial stint in the National Guard. Mike felt that he and the ARD people had come across some good, new information that I might eventually be able to build into something. Because of his loyalty to ARD, he wouldn't tell me what it was, but in typical Mike fashion, he teased me, sending an e-mail saying he had come across some "tasty brisket."

Missal harrumphed and questioned me as if these exchanges constituted some kind of moral shortcoming, this tasteless joking about stories we were working on. Was this kind of thing typical in journalism? Missal did everything but sigh and shake his head in disgust.

There was no acknowlegment that irreverence and skepticism—even sometimes downright tasteless joking—are part of every news operation. That is a fact of life in the newsroom. Sometimes on the hardest stories, approaching your work with a sense of humor is almost as important as bringing respect, fairness, and an open mind to the process. Laughter can relieve the tension, the heartache, the heavy responsibilities in gathering news.

Missal questioned me about Mike's background as an assistant and researcher for liberal political columnist Molly Ivins. Her name on Mike's résumé must have been a red flag, literally. Missal wanted to know whether Mike was a "liberal," someone who disliked Bush, someone with a political agenda that drove him. I knew Mike as a borderline starving freelancer whose duel agendas were a paycheck and an unrelenting drive to uncover whatever someone else wanted to hide. I could sense from their demeanor that my answers were not good enough for the panel.

I don't know that I expected anything else, considering Missal's regular areas of interest. The Kirkpatrick & Lockhart Web site listed Missal's legal specialty as "security enforcement, arbitration, and security litigation." I can assure you that Missal brought to the panel all of the rollicking good humor and personal flexibility his professional background implies. Zippo.

I fielded questions on everything from Bill Burkett and how I met him to how often I talked with Dan Rather about stories. Missal and Lanpher asked most of the questions, with Lou Boccardi chiming in on occasion and Dick Thornburgh raising his finger at the other end of the table every now and then.

I was as forthright as I could be, sharing the kind of information with them that I had fought not to reveal in 1999 when I faced jail over journalistic freedoms and protecting sources. For a journalist, the panel's interrogation felt extremely odd, as though I were betraying my principles by blabbing this way even though I was giving information to someone hired by CBS. But what else could I do? I loved my job and wanted to keep it. This is what CBS wanted me to do. I didn't think at that time that CBS would turn on me and fire me, even if the panel report was not as positive as I thought it should be. I was candid and trusting, forced to plunge ahead with a kind of uneasy faith that this corporately conceived process would work. Perhaps the panel would itself uphold the best principles of journalism and be fair, thorough, and accurate. I had no choice but to hope that they would.

We broke for lunch and went into an adjoining room, where bread and lunch meats, chips, and cookies were laid out. I was famished. Mike Missal, once again playing the thoughtful host, told us that we could fill our plates and adjourn to yet another conference room for privacy. I couldn't wait to ask Dick how he thought it was going for me and I was grateful for the time alone with my team. I figured the panel would probably spend its lunch talking about us.

Dan Lewis, the whippet-thin on-again, off-again vegetarian, rummaged through the trays of food, carefully gathering up all the chips, bread, cheese, and cookies. Dick ate everything he could get his hands on. I filled my plate to overflowing, then proceeded to talk my way through the lunch break without eating much.

Dick was exuberant at the way the morning had gone. He thought I had done well, that the panel was not coming up with any evidence of incompetence or ideologically driven work, which they were supposedly looking for. Dick thought I had handled all of the questions well, that I hadn't gotten angry, that I hadn't come up short on any of my answers, and that I had been pleasant. I, too, felt I was on track.

I was eager to get back to the hearing room and get it over with. Like Dick, I felt that I had done a good job of answering questions. Maybe this was not going to be so bad, after all.

When we went back in after the lunch break, the questioning got tougher. Lanpher and Missal, Thornburgh and Boccardi grilled me on whether Bill Burkett had been offered any deal for handing over the documents, any money, any protection.

I answered honestly that he had not. I knew that Burkett wanted and received a promise that we would not "out" him publicly, that we would protect him in that way, but that was as far as our promises went. I couldn't and didn't offer him anything more.

I told them Burkett hadn't asked for money—that actually doesn't come up often, most sources don't ask for money—and that he hadn't demanded much of anything. They wanted to know if I had questioned Burkett that day in Clyde, Texas, on the "provenance" of the documents—where they came from and where they had been—where Burkett had gotten them, and the political views of the people who had handed them off. I hadn't done that. I just wanted to get the papers and get out of there and start working to see if the documents were real. For the panel, that seemed an inadequate answer, too.

It was clear that they felt I should have single-handedly put Burkett under oath and then grilled him on the details of his story. As a reporter, I knew that wouldn't have worked, particularly with a person who saw himself as a whistle-blower of sorts. My first obligation was to get what he had. I felt the other answers would come later if I could get the information out of him, but I wasn't going to take the time or the risk at our very first meeting.

I had to laugh to myself at some of the panel's rigid, legalistic ideas of how reporting should work. If these men and this panel did investigative stories, nothing would ever get on the air. Abu Ghraib would have remained a dirty little secret because, by their standards, I didn't know exactly who else had the photos, and that was enough to kill the story. The panel members undoubtedly would have found that I couldn't "prove" the photos were real.

With these guys running the newsroom, the details of Watergate would have stayed with Deep Throat in the parking garage. Based on their questioning, I'm convinced that Dick Thornburgh, who worked for Richard Nixon, would have found Mark Felt an inadequate source, clearly a person with an agenda or political and personal motivations, something he and the panel thought was inappropriate. The panel would have wanted to wait for someone who handed things over with no motivation and freely shared every detail of their pure-as-the-driven-snow life and nonexistent political background.

I tried to tell these blank-faced men and their scribbling legal associates that in my twenty-five years in news I'd learned that their kind of "dream" source just doesn't exist—at least I'd never met such a person. Whistle-blowers have motivations. Informants have agendas. Sources have reasons to talk.

It was clear that these legal eagles were unsatisfied. They seemed convinced that they knew a better way, which, frankly, would have resulted in shooting down every story, offending every source, and blowing up every lead that came their way. They had as much business in a newsroom as I did in court, arguing a complex securities case, which is to say none, nada, nil.

We wrangled for hours about paying for story materials like pictures or videotape, something that happens occasionally but didn't in this case. CBS had never paid for information in any of my stories. The panel showed me e-mails from Roger Charles, to whom we had faxed the documents shortly after we got them. He had written back: "I feel better now," that the references and formats and the contents were looking good to him.

The panel insisted that Roger must have felt the documents were fake at one time. Otherwise, why would he have written that he felt "better *now*"? There was no budging them on this tiny, but to them, absolutely vital point about a short message that had been dashed off to me by someone who never could have imagined that his words would later be dissected by what was essentially a roomful of attorneys. And the dissectors may have had partisan motives, as well as their own biases in favor of the corporation that was likely paying them millions of dollars to make mincemeat of my e-mails, my notes, and my career. On this point and others, the panel was immovable and their interpretation was absurd.

During a break in the questioning, I made small talk with members of the panel, in what was obviously a failing attempt to get them to see me as a whole person, someone who worked hard but had a full and rewarding life.

I think I made a fatal mistake with Lou Boccardi when we talked about the upcoming Halloween fun and how I was anxious to get home. My seven-year-old son loved dressing up and, as I told Boccardi, our street celebrated the holiday with literally thousands of kids pouring into our neighborhood to trick-or-treat.

In retrospect, I believe he must have thought I was lying. He quickly began to press me for details. "Really?" he asked. *"Thousands?"* I told him it was hard to believe but true, and it was. It's a once-a-year phenomenon in our urban neighborhood. We regularly get two to three thousand or more trick-or-treaters arriving in costume in the front yard, as did all of our neighbors. We live in an old historic area that has become a haven for trick-or-treating. Church buses, pickups, vans, and cars flood in by nightfall, each vehicle packed with kids whose parents want a safe place for them to go door-to-door. We always have friends over to hand out candy because we simply can't handle the volume ourselves. Homes on our street decorate for the holiday: One neighbor sets up a false pipe organ on the balcony and puts on a *Phantom of the Opera* show complete with shooting flames. As I chatted, I felt that Boccardi was looking at me as though I must be a compulsive liar who needed medical help.

In fact, when I returned for another session with the panel in early December, the first thing Boccardi asked me was how many trick-or-treaters we had that year. When I told him we'd had a big year, more than two thousand, he'd nodded knowingly, apparently convinced that I was one sick puppy who had no business being anywhere near the public airwaves.

As we were breaking after the first full day, Larry Lanpher called my attorney, Dick Hibey, over to a quiet corner and whispered something to him. I asked Dick about it before we left and was told that the panel planned to bring forward the private detective's report on me the next day.

"The what? What report was that?" I was incredulous. Dick told me that Erik Rigler had prepared a report on me for the panel and that they wanted to discuss it. I reeled. In a heartbeat, I realized that the investigator Andrew Heyward had supposedly sent to continue the work on my story, the man I thought might be my salvation, was actually turning in information on me. I had welcomed him into my home and freely shared all my information with him, and I was one of the subjects of his investigation.

My God. That's how bad it was. It had never occurred to me that such a betrayal could be possible.

I told Dick to have the report faxed to my hotel that night if they wanted to include it in the next day's hearing. I was spitting mad on my way back to the hotel that evening to wait for the fax.

When I saw the tepid report, a bland recounting of what my husband and I had told Rigler and his wife, I was livid. Not only did the write-up include errors in its details, it was really poorly done. Poorly reported. Poorly written.

As I fumed, Dick insisted that there was nothing to worry about, that the report couldn't hurt me at all. I knew that. It was the existence of the report and what it told me about who I worked for that hurt.

Such a massive signpost was unmistakable even to a naïve fool like me. My position in the company had changed, drastically. Andrew Heyward hadn't sent Rigler down to work solely on the story. The private investigator was looking at me as well. Despite what I'd been told, CBS didn't give a damn about me or my story or my life. They wanted to be rid of the whole mess. After fifteen years of accomplishment, I had become a huge corporate and political liability. They had had enough and wanted me gone. They seemed willing to do anything, even investigate me, to make that happen.

My anger kept me warm all the way to the hearing the next day, where once again the panel had a grand old time picking apart countless e-mails that had been dashed off months earlier without a second thought. Why had I made that joke? What was the meaning behind that wisecrack?

At one point, Dick Thornburgh motioned that he had something to say.

"Yes, Dick," I called to him.

"You'll have to pardon my language here," he droned.

"You mean *my* language, right?" I answered, trying to make light of whatever was to come.

God only knows, I thought to myself. I was sure I had used the "f" word in my e-mails. Was I actually going to have to sit there and listen to *Dick Thornburgh* read aloud some bawdy line I'd written?

"Yes, it is your language," he said flatly, making it clear that he disapproved. Oh, shit. What had I said?

"You've written here, 'I am so sick of all of this horseshit.' What did you mean by that?" he asked. I looked at the offending e-mail and saw that it had been sent to Betsy West back in September in the context of complaining about the bloggers and their attacks. I told him I had been talking about bloggers and the bad information they were putting out.

"No, that's not what I mean," he went on. "Why did you use *that* word?"

"You mean 'horseshit'?"

"Yes." He stared at me sternly, waiting for an answer.

My God, this was like being called to the front of the class in fourth grade and scolded for saying a naughty word. I sputtered on about the bloggers and how I was annoyed at their one-sidedness, their lack of fact-checking, and their ugly, juvenile name-calling.

As I answered, he kept pressing and eventually it became clear that Thornburgh didn't care what I was talking about in the offending e-mail, just the word I had used. It wasn't context he was looking for but contrition. He wanted me to admit that I had used a bad word gratuitously. This was bizarre. I could feel myself fighting a grin.

"Why did you have to use *that* word?" he continued, going in for the kill. "Wasn't there another word you could have used? What did you mean by 'horseshit'?"

What could I say? That "bullshit" is overused and "chickenshit" has an entirely different connotation? I was dumbfounded and finally stammered my way to a conclusion, confessing that I had used the word "horseshit" because I had a horse as a kid and it seemed to suit the situation.

Thornburgh leaned back, satisfied that he had scored a victory in his clever line of questioning, and exposed me as a craven individual who not only didn't choose her words carefully but also had a serious case of potty mouth. He looked triumphantly around the table, then finished with, "I'm okay. Who's next?"

I thought back to how Thornburgh had been described to me by a mutual friend as an "empty suit," the perfect person for politics, a blank slate ready to carry out whatever orders he got from headquarters. Now I knew differently. He wasn't an empty suit at all. He was completely full of it. Horseshit, that is.

CHAPTER 16

The house was suddenly so quiet. Robert was in school. Mark was at work. I was locked inside, with only our dogs as companions. I was literally the one in the doghouse, though, trapped in some kind of journalistic home detention program. I couldn't work. I couldn't even show up at the office. I would terrify everyone.

I was a newswoman who had become bad news. I told my husband I had "news Ebola," that I could have cleared an entire floor at CBS just by getting off the elevator. This was a strange new circumstance for me. Work had always been about laughter and achievement, excitement and intrigue. My friends were there. I had fun at work. Now I imagined that my very presence could frighten people into stampeding the other way. It made me sad beyond words.

As October stretched into November, buddies from work called regularly to chat or to bring me into the loop on the current gossip. They told me they thought this was all so unfair. As time went on, without a verdict from the panel and with criticism of CBS continuing to echo through the mainstream press, the phone calls began to change. People began to say that they were praying for me. Being a keen observer of human behavior, I realized this was not a good development.

My coworkers believed I was dying professionally. They believed I would not be back. I began to believe it, too.

The realization of what a jam I was in was almost overwhelming. It colored every day, every conversation, every moment of my life. I thought constantly about what I could say to the panel that would be of help, and I found myself swinging back and forth between the extremes of hope and fear: the hope that the panel might truly be independent and fair enough to see that we had conscientiously corroborated the documents under brutal deadline pressure, and the fear that the carefully selected panel was a political setup, designed to deliver a predetermined outcome and justify a journalistic firing squad.

It was becoming obvious that the panel and its phalanx of attorneys were carrying out a corporate housecleaning, not conducting a journalistic investigation. They weren't journalists and they didn't know journalism from gerbils. They were lawyers, every last one of them, except for Lou Boccardi—and he hadn't been a working newsman for decades. At least one reporter who worked for him at Associated Press told me that Boccardi had a reputation for disliking and discouraging investigative journalism during his long service as head of A.P. I wondered how other professionals would stand up to this kind of scrutiny sanctioned by their corporate bosses. How would a group of airline pilots or accountants or architects like having their work picked apart not by a panel of peers, but by a panel of people who had never done that particular kind of work? These "independent" judges were not investigating the substance or the substantiation of our story. Their charge as laid out by CBS/Viacom was to figure out how the story had gone wrong. There seemed to be absolutely no consideration given to the possibility that we were right about the content of the story and right to have reported it. I felt they were not going to clear me or determine that I had done my best or done nothing wrong. I felt they were going to stick a fork in me.

I couldn't work on the Bush-Guard story anymore, of course. We'd been forced to abandon all efforts to keep digging and come up with new information that might exonerate ourselves and our story. I soon found out I couldn't work on anything else, either. I remember stumbling across a news nugget that I thought would make a great jumping-off point for a 60 Minutes piece. I always had a lot of ideas for stories; many more than I had time to produce myself. Normally, I would have fired off a note or written a story proposal, started making phone calls and gathering information. This time, I agonized. What should I do?

What could I do? Should I just let it pass? Maybe I could test the waters to see if they might let me do some work.

I finally sent Josh Howard a friendly e-mail asking whether I could work on a story completely unrelated to Bush, the Guard, or politics. I was withering while I waited. I wanted to go back to work.

He sent back a chatty message saying that it was great to hear from me, that he missed me, "but not those last minute crashes!" He added that he thought it best if I didn't try to do another story right away.

That was it. I believed that Josh thought—and maybe even hoped—that I was going to be fired, too. The distance between New York and Dallas had never seemed greater.

I felt like I was being suffocated. I was slowly, publicly, professionally, being snuffed out. All I could do was wait for that last gasp, the moment when it would finally be over. The life I knew was fading away. If was more than a little depressing.

At CBS, on the Internet, and in public opinion, it seemed the verdict was in before the jury got back from lunch. I had been found to be a fool and a failure, a pariah, a sham. The documents I had used in my story were not authentic and neither was I. All my insecurities, my inner fears about self-worth and self-respect, came roaring out. My worst childhood worries about whether I deserved success or love were being realized.

One day, I curled up on the couch with a cozy throw. I lay there watching the fire dance in the fireplace, my ever-present dogs passed out on the floor close by. I could hear their steady breathing. They were peaceful. I was at war. With myself, with the bloggers, with the panel, with the world.

There was no real reason to have a fire. It was about seventy degrees outside, one of Dallas's warm winter days. Joggers were running past my house shirtless. I was indoors, jobless, friendless, worthless. I was freezing to death on the inside.

I was in limbo, lost between wanting to work and mourning my old job. Adrift from my pals at CBS, left alone to ponder my bleak future, I tried to stay busy, but much of the time I succumbed to an ever-present, aching fatigue. I slept for hours some days: It was the one way to escape the clock, the calendar, the catastrophe that I had wrought in my career.

There were bright moments. A neighbor pulled up when I was sitting on the front porch staring into space. "Mary, you're right and they're wrong," he shouted. "Hang in there." It meant the world to me. But it didn't change a thing.

Much of the time, I felt like no one believed me. I had gone from being a person who could be counted on to someone whose version of reality was highly suspect. I couldn't be sure of anything anymore. I was starring in a new-millennium remake of the old movie *Gaslight*. Only I wasn't Ingrid Bergman and this wasn't a tale of one woman's private descent into apparent madness. This was playing out in front of anyone who read the papers or believed the blogs.

I constantly asked my husband what he would have done, how he would have handled the story. He was the only person I could badger with these kinds of questions. The poor guy was married to me. He had no escape. Patiently, he sat with me as I went over in excruciating detail the time line and the choices I had made. He assured and reassured me that I had done exactly the right thing at every point along the way. It was an exercise in futility, but I was relentless in second-guessing my choices, questioning my decisions, and judging my professionalism.

Friends dropped by with food and treats. A wonderful basket of spa treatments appeared at my door, packed with lotions that smelled like lavender, gooey masks guaranteed to drop years from my face, and buffers that promised fresh new beginnings if I would just take a moment to exfoliate. I *did* want to shed my old skin. I wanted out of what my life had become.

My doctor suggested that I try a low dose of medication to help me get past this period of angst, anger, and uncertainty. This was completely new for me. I went from not knowing what a Xanax was to a desperate housewife who sometimes felt she was popping antianxiety pills like Tic-Tacs. Actually, I used them exactly as prescribed, but they didn't seem to have as much of a calming effect as I had hoped. My heart was still racing. I still couldn't sleep at night. I was sleepwalking through each day, each disaster, in a somewhat deadened emotional condition.

At one point, Dan Rather called and asked how I was feeling. He knew the finger-pointing, the embarrassment, and the isolation were hard on me. I told Dan I was doing fine, that I was "medicated and dedicated." That was only half-true. Mostly I was feeling a dedication to my medication. Nothing else could be counted on; nothing else was breaking my way. And with the medication, it was as if each fresh crisis, each new indignity, each wretched new development washed over me without really getting me wet. Nothing seemed to have any real impact on me anymore. I just kept watching the clock. Is it time for another pill yet?

I had been beaten into a kind of psychologically numb, emotionally empty, physically fatigued submission. "Gosh, it looks like I'm going to be publicly destroyed and then lose my job. My family and I will be financially wiped out. I'll never work again and my name will be synonymous with failure and shame. Oh well. I think I feel a nap coming on."

Some of my friends called it my Judy Garland period. One glass of wine and I sounded like a cross between Foster Brooks and Seymour Hersh: a lush obsessed with investigative reporting.

After a few weeks, I realized I couldn't go the medication route. A person should only wake up drooling on the couch in the middle of the day so many times without considering some other strategy.

Even the low-dose approach gave me more separation from life than I could handle. Although I wanted to disconnect from some of my feelings, I found I had even less tolerance for living without any feelings at all.

So I went back to getting by the old-fashioned way. I talked with friends and took their counsel. One told me to exercise every day, which turned out to be excellent advice. I ignored it scrupulously.

To entertain and occupy myself, I starting knitting, something I had picked up a few years earlier.

Now it became an obsession. I regularly drove half an hour to my favorite yarn store and staggered in like a crack addict, moving from counter to counter, fondling yarns. The saturated colors, the fantastic textures, the richness of the strands, the yarns, were everything my existence then was not.

I bought new needles and fantasized about what this or that yarn would look like woven into small, even stitches, a metaphor for what I wanted to do with my life: put it back together, knit it into what it used to be. I had become unraveled.

I did not find total serenity with my knitting, though. I knitted as if I were being pursued, like the house was on fire and I couldn't get out until I finished the project. I sat with an ever-growing pile of fantastically hued and textured scarves and an unfinished project or two or five. Anybody want a yellow and white cardigan with ducky buttons for a six-month-old with one arm slightly longer than the other? How about a hand-knit teddy bear with an unusually angry look on its face?

I spent weeks working endlessly, day after day, on a cream-colored throw made of tiny squares, each of them in alternating stitches, the creation of a frenzied knitting monk. I collected beautifully photographed knitting books and spent hours looking at them longingly, lustfully. It was knitting pornography and I treated it that way, sneaking my stash out in the evenings after Robert had gone to bed and I was sure that Mark was busy with something other than comforting me. Those volumes were my secret vice. Their photographs spoke to me in soothing close-ups of perfect stitches. The order, the predictability of the work, the evenness of the yarn were like tranquilizers to a troubled soul. I embraced it like a new kind of medication. Valium in full-color hardcover.

I began knitting Christmas presents for everyone in my extended family. Scarves and baby sweaters, shawls and purses, throws and pillows. I was Johnny Cochran with a set of bamboo size 10 needles, a mountain of yarn, and a long holiday list. If I can't knit it, you're not going to get it.

A friend told me she had tried knitting to keep her hands busy when she quit smoking. Fueled by stress, she knit so much, so fast, that she developed carpal tunnel syndrome. She warned me against "overknitting." My hands were okay, but I developed a serious case of "knitter's ass." I needed to get off mine and get moving again, but going outside to exercise, even to walk on our street, meant seeing people, and that meant answering questions or accepting condolences. I just didn't want to deal with any of it.

We kept Robert in the dark, but he knew something was wrong. He wasn't used to seeing Mama sitting in the same place when he came home that she had been in when he left. He wasn't even used to seeing me *sitting*. Robert tried in his seven-year-old way to cheer me up by dragging me to department stores where he made me try on glamorous evening gowns. He calls them prom dresses. I remember looking into the dressing-room mirror as I slithered into a wild and colorful sequined number at Neiman Marcus, thinking I was absolutely in limbo, too old for the prom and too young to be put out to pasture. To complement my glittery gown, I had chosen to wear no makeup, and my unkempt hair looked like an abandoned grass hut. But little Robert loved me no matter what. I remember seeing his tennis shoes peeking under my dressing-room door as he waited expectantly for his mess of a mother to model the latest gown, ready to say what he always said when I emerged in a dress he had carefully chosen for me to try. "Oh, Mama, ooo la la," he would say. I would have been lost without him.

Maybe our shopping trips were Robert's way of letting me know he wanted to see his mother looking halfway presentable again. He may have been telling me I needed to stop wearing sweatpants every day, all day.

I tried listening to inspirational music. At least I thought it was inspirational. I had a Johnny Cash CD of old hymns going constantly each day while I knitted and felt sorry for myself. Our house sounded like a Pentecostal funeral home without the fainting and yelling. Johnny was the minister. The dogs were the mourners. I was the dead body.

Basically, I was pathetic. Hilariously so. In the end, I could not take myself seriously enough to continue my pity party.

Besides, as I mourned my life, I had time to think about the long line of strong women that I came from. They wouldn't act this way and I couldn't, either. I remembered some of my mother's advice. "Don't give in to yourself." She knew what she was talking about.

My great-grandmother was a strong and strong-willed woman who farmed all her life, yet had an innate appreciation for fine linens and good food. Nora Mapes lived through more than her share of tragedy. She didn't just lose a job or something meaningless like that. She lost three of her children early in their lives to the kinds of ailments that are now easily treated with antibiotics. But she went on, without giving in, without giving up, without letting self-pity paralyze her or limit her life.

Her name was Nora, but we always called her Nunna. She taught generations in our family and an entire community lessons about strength and steadiness, loyalty, and having the right priorities, particularly during the difficult days of World War II. Back then, my great-grandparents raised strawberries in Skagit Valley, a fertile pocket of flatlands north of Seattle near Puget Sound.

Strawberries were a primary crop in the valley, and among the many farming families were a number of Japanese heritage. When the order came for Japanese immigrants and descendants on the West Coast to be sent away to internment camps, these farmers had few options. It wasn't like closing up a store. For farming families, putting their lives on hold would cost them their crops and, ultimately, their farms.

My great-grandparents were close to one Japanese family in particular, the Sakumas. Rather than letting their friends lose everything to an unfair order by the federal government, Nora and Oscar Mapes and their son James—my beloved grandpa—took matters into their own hands. They promised the Sakumas to care for their farm as though it were their own. They would protect the land, harvest the crops, till the soil, and keep anyone else from taking advantage of the Sakumas' absence. Many Japanese families were losing their farms to people who came and took the land while the owners were gone. My family promised the Sakumas that wouldn't happen to them. They promised that when the U.S. government said they could come home, the Sakuma farm and their friends would be waiting for them.

It wasn't easy to fulfill that commitment, but my great-grandparents viewed it as their duty. Many residents of the small town turned against the Sakumas and the other Japanese families, but my family held firm. They accompanied their friends to the downtown train station to publicly embrace and say good-bye on the day the Sakumas were forced to leave. Then Nunna and Grandpa went to work making sure that the Sakuma farm would survive.

When others in town whispered about my great-grandparents and their inappropriate friendship with the banished Japanese, Nunna held her head up. When my family was gossiped about for being traitors, they ignored it. And when the Sakumas came home, my family was there to welcome them. Today the Sakuma farm continues to thrive and whenever we go back to the Skagit Valley we make a point to stop by, sit a spell, and enjoy the sweetest berries on earth. It is the fruit of one fine family's labor and the legacy of a promise made and kept by my own family generations ago.

Later in life, when Nunna would recount this story at the urgings of her great-granddaughters, she would always end with the same sentiment. "There is nothing harder than doing the right thing," a statement she didn't deliver in a self-pitying way, but as a kind of call to arms for living a good life. My sisters and I grew up wanting to do the right thing, no matter how hard.

I distinctly remember talking with her about how she and Grandpa had chosen to act during World War II. We were in Nunna's living room, watching a news broadcast on her old green television set. It must have been the mid-1960s and I listened carefully as Nunna explained to me that there were always going to be people who didn't like others for superficial reasons. She saw parallels between the civil rights movement, the disenfranchisement of Native Americans, the internment of the Japanese, and the need for all of us to be ready to do the right thing when history called on us.

Facing my own desperate hour, I clung to Nunna's strength, to the certainty that although I was having my own rough ride with history, I was made of the same stuff as my great-grandmother. Like her and the friends she helped long ago, I would survive and thrive and live to regale my own great-granddaughters with the story of how strong I was when I needed to be.

However, I know that Robert would have to become a father no later than age twelve if I am going to live to see my own great-grandchildren. Shoot. Well, I'll find *someone* who won't mind listening to an old lady.

In late November, CBS/Viacom's panel contacted me again through my attorney. They wanted me to return for another session of questioning. My attorneys and I started to prepare for our next go-round with the panel, which was set for December 8. How festive, a holiday visit with my new friends.

A few weeks earlier, I had worked with Dick Hibey and Dan Lewis on a written version of what I called my meshing document, combining the new Killian memos with the president's previously released military records. I had gone over the detailed information verbally during my first two days with the panel, and then we sent the Thornburgh-Boccardi group a written version of the meshing document, which is extensive and complex. In return, the panel members said that my entire December session with them would focus on the way I put the old and new documents together, how I interpreted areas of agreement, and why I believed the meshing provided strong evidence that the memos were real.

I knew this meeting was likely to be the most adversarial, the most prosecutorial. If my previous sessions had been contentious, sparring with the lawyers over what happened when and who said what, this round of questions would likely go to the heart of the whole series of hearings. Was I completely misguided in concluding that there were ample reasons to believe in the memos? I had done my homework and thoroughly researched the topic and the material. I knew my stuff even if others didn't. Despite what conservative critics or media competitors were willing to believe, I hadn't simply grabbed some dubious documents, asked no questions, and rushed them onto the air.

I knew I was going to have to defend every word in my meshing document. I knew the lawyers were going to try to take it apart, piece by piece, line by line, point by point. The panel had long since abandoned asking general questions and gathering information about the story. I felt that they were just searching for someone to blame. And once again, there I would sit, holding my documents and my notes and my ground. Every time I was around these guys, I felt like I had a big colorful bull's-eye stuck to my shirt.

I was not anxious to go before the panel again, but I wanted this to be over more than I wanted to avoid another meeting. And ever the optimist, I still hoped that they were actually listening to the evidence I was presenting to them. I flew to Washington, where the panel and I were to hold our last tango.

A day or so before the session with the panel, I agreed to have lunch with Wyatt Andrews, a longtime CBS reporter assigned to cover this debacle for the *Evening News*.

I told him I wouldn't mind talking as long as it was off-the-record and, frankly, I wanted to show him my meshing document and let him see that there were ways beyond typeface and font style that the memos could be analyzed. No mainstream media people had bothered to do that, but I was hopeful that Wyatt with his years at CBS would give me a listen.

We met at a fine Washington restaurant and I soon found out that I was going to be doing most of the listening at this lunch. Wyatt proceeded to tell me that he knew he was more conservative than I was, an interesting point, since I had never come close to talking politics with him. He went on to say that he frankly thought the memos were fakes, based on what he "knew" about the fonts and the other questions the blogs had raised about the typeface. As far as I know, Wyatt had never made a single phone call about the Bush-Guard story, never examined a single official record, never made any effort to understand or break ground on this story. He and his producer had actually asked me for help with the official documents and in understanding the time line of Bush's service as they prepared to do stories on the panel and its investigation of my story.

Amazingly, Wyatt thought he knew everything about it anyway. That made him no different from scores of other mainstream reporters who covered and characterized the CBS controversy.

I asked Wyatt to read my meshing document and look at some of the ways I had tried to gauge the truth of the memos, based on comparisons with other documents from Bush's records that we knew to be real. It wasn't simply that there was no disagreement between the new memos and the official records. It was an indicator to me that if anyone had forged the Killian memos, they would have had to be privy to a tremendous amount of information—information that wasn't in the public sphere, information that no one outside of the unit would have had, information that I didn't believe any forger could possibly have figured out, or would have bothered to try. Reporters, after all, didn't bother with the substance of the story, either.

Wyatt listened to me with great skepticism. He didn't seem to be thinking about what I was saying. It was as though I was having lunch with the personification of "conventional wisdom," the group-think that has taken over press coverage in Washington. Conventional wisdom—or the CW, as *Newsweek* magazine's self-aware column calls it—doesn't consider anything outside of what "everybody knows" or "believes." It doesn't question authority too aggressively or step out of line. CW is complacent and self-satisfied. It doesn't break stories like Abu Ghraib or get people like Essie Mae Washington-Williams, Strom Thurmond's daughter, to come forward. CW thinks it already knows everything and it never admits that it doesn't have the answer. CW runs in packs, travels in herds, and never goes out on a story alone. Washington is as full of conventional wisdom as Wyatt was full of himself that day.

There are many great reporters and commentators who buck the CW. People like John Burns, who writes beautifully for *The New York Times* from inside Iraq; Michael Isikoff, who investigates for *Newsweek*; Sy Hersh, who has sources in every dark place on the planet; Helen Thomas, who still gets a kick out of asking hostile questions at the White House. I love reading Maureen Dowd and P. J. O'Rourke, two great writers who agree on absolutely nothing.

Woodward and Bernstein bucked the CW and I wish more reporters, particularly in Washington, D.C., would throw out their ideas about what "everyone thinks" and "everyone knows" and go after the stories that no one else is chasing, ask the questions no one else is asking, and dare to look at the world in ways that few people do.

Wyatt took a copy of my meshing document home with him and must have given it a quick dismissive read. The next day he sent me an e-mail saying the meshing was "interesting," but "I still have a problem with the proportional spacing" issue. That's the variable letter-spacing feature that any reliable typewriter authority will tell you was available on many machines before the early 1970s. Despite all of the substantive material laid before him, Wyatt was still riveted by a non-issue that had no validity in the first place. The truth was that you could put everything Wyatt knew about proportional spacing on the head of a pin. And Wyatt, like most of the Washington Press Corps, didn't give a damn about Bush's time in the Texas Air National Guard. Working that story would have required leaving town, looking for answers somewhere other than press conferences, and actually running the risk of coming in contact with real Americans. In other words: *We'd really rather not bother.* Or, as we journalists like to say, "There's no story there."

I came away from my lunch with Wyatt as disillusioned about reporting as I have ever been. How did we get from Watergate to this? When did reporting go from being part of the public's right to know to being an arm of the administration?

While I fussed over what had become of my profession, I had to prepare to defend what had become of my job. Once again, the panel was waiting.

I had dressed carefully for my first two visits with the group, trying to find outfits that didn't seem "angry." I chose clothes in lighter colors and textures, a feeble attempt on my part to look like a nice girl caught in a bad situation. By the time our last meeting rolled around, I no longer cared what they thought of me. Actually, it was worse than that. I *knew* what they thought of me.

So this time I dressed like I felt, like Johnny Cash on his way to a funeral when he was in a bad mood. Black pants, black jacket, black shoes, black purse. Oh, wait, I think I'll add a black sweater. And that perfect last touch, a black scarf. Now, I was set, ready to go, as dark and dour on the outside as I was on the inside.

On December 8, in Washington, we went straight to the offices of Kirkpatrick & Lockhart, Thornburgh's high-dollar firm. This building's designers also seemed to have fallen in love with black marble, tinted glass, and bronze. Everything inside the place was smooth and cool and dark, a study in money and masculinity.

After a warm round of faux-friendly greetings, we once again sat down at a big conference table. I had my notes, my meshing document, and my pie-in-the-sky beliefs about journalism and professional duty. Thornburgh, Boccardi, and company had their obligations as well. Their questions seemed designed to shake me, show me up, get me to make a mistake, or reveal that I had made one along the way. This was like the world's most serious game of Trivial Pursuit. If I could just answer every picky question, keep going, avoid coming up empty when asked something obscure, and stay out of the sticky spots, I would make it to the end with my dignity—if not my job—intact. If I made one misstep, blew up in anger, or did not have the answers to every single question, then I would be shamed and shunned—not to mention fired.

All of us were on edge. My attorney, Dick Hibey, and Larry Lanpher, one of the lawyers on the panel, started arguing almost immediately. Dick can yell louder than anyone I know, and he proved it this morning, right off the bat. I wondered if that was Dick's way of telling the group he was not going to put up with any mistreatment of me. Once again, I sat there watching the set-to as though I were attending someone else's trial. Part of me still couldn't believe that this was what my work and my life had come to.

The day deteriorated, as I knew it would, into one long game of Stump the Witness, where the lawyers took turns trying to ask questions that I couldn't answer. Time and again, they swung and missed. They parsed the memos and tried to get me to admit, for example, that the abbreviation "Grp," used for "Group," wasn't in any other official documents that way. But it was. Luckily, Dick and Dan and I had set aside a stack of official records with various abbreviations, spellings, formats, and signature block styles. Military records aren't so strictly constructed and carefully typed that they unvaryingly use the same jargon and references. We could easily point out examples of variations in style whenever the panel's lawyers tried to use a specific physical element in the memos to debunk the entire group.

They seemed intent on declaring that bad typing technique, poor layout, and incorrect abbreviation were proof that the memos were false. I thought those characteristics were simple proof that the Killian memos were badly typed. Or, as Dick bellowed at one point in the proceedings: "I know who typed these. It was some idiot like me. I was an E-5 and a typist and I didn't know what the hell I was doing." The panel seemed unmoved by Dick's humility.

Larry Lanpher did a lot of the questioning this last day and he had an annoying way of starting most of his questions, "Mary, not to nitpick, but . . ." Oh, come *on*. I didn't mind the nitpicking, but I was annoyed by the pretense that they *weren't* nitpicking, that they weren't trying to destroy my work. They were. As the day went on, the panel became more prosecutorial, more challenging, and less patient with my explanations. To me, it seemed they didn't want to listen and, more important, they just plain didn't get it—whether that was intentional or not, I can't say. They didn't seem to understand what I had done to demonstrate that the Killian memos were most likely real and deserved to be reported. The panel's lawyers may have been high-powered legal minds, but as journalists they were a bust. I wondered to myself how Dan Rather had felt when he sat in the same hot seat for his two rounds of questioning. I wondered how he would have felt if these same attorneys with no journalistic background were to question and lecture him on how to do his job?

I don't want to seem immodest or brag about how well I did in front of the panel, believe me. I was just trying to survive. But I think my information held up extremely well and Dick, who has been through the wringer with many clients, said he thought they didn't lay a glove on me.

Despite their months of study and the money that CBS paid them for their keen judgment, the panel members were not as prepared or analytical as they might have been. Thornburgh and Boccardi, the two named panelists, couldn't be bothered to attend all of the interview sessions. The lawyers' attempts at nitpicking were sometimes laughable.

One time, Larry Lanpher pointed out the abbreviation "O.E.T.R." on one of the Killian memos. I explained to him that this was shorthand for the Officer Effectiveness Training Report. He came back at me like Perry Mason trying to wrap up a case with just a few minutes remaining in the show. I could almost hear the music crescendo. "Isn't it true, Mary, that the phrase 'Officer Effectiveness Training Report' doesn't actually appear *anywhere* on *any* of the official documents? That the phrase is something that you have created to explain this incorrect abbreviation in your memos?" He thought he had tripped me up, at last.

I was taken aback. That was such a simple question to answer. Off the top of my head, I gave him a page number for one of the old official documents that I had used in my meshing study. I asked him to look at the top of the document where it said: "Officer Effectiveness Training Report."

"Oh," Lanpher allowed. "I see that. I'm sorry. That was a foolish question. My mistake." And then we just kept going on to the next one and the next one and the next one.

As the day dragged on, I grew more and more tired. Tired of this exercise, tired of this government-document, official-memo attempt at a game of "Gotcha!" But I was eager for what I knew was going to come before the end of the day. They were going to ask about my politics. I knew they had asked everyone else about my politics and I couldn't believe that they wouldn't hit me up for what kind of card I carried, too.

When it appeared we were wrapping up for the day and the topic still hadn't come up, I finally said something. "Aren't you guys going to ask about my politics? I know you have asked other people about what I believe. Aren't you going to ask me?"

I could see Dick Hibey glaring at me as though I had gone mad. But Lou Boccardi jumped at the chance. "Well," he said, "wouldn't you say it's true that most of the people that you work with think you are a liberal?"

There it was, the "l" word. I asked him whether he thought most of the people he worked with thought they knew his politics. He didn't answer. Instead, he asked whether I would describe myself as a liberal.

"You mean, are you asking me, 'Am I now or have I ever been a liberal?'" I said, a joking reference to the Army-McCarthy U.S. Senate hearings of 1954, where people were grilled as to whether they had ever been members of the Communist Party.

Lou pressed on. "*Wouldn't* you describe yourself as a liberal?"

I began talking about my beliefs, about how life is complicated and how labels are not one-size-fits-all. I told them I didn't support the death penalty. I told them that as an adoptive mother, I had very complicated feelings about abortion. Dick was giving me the "shut up, you idiot" look.

Finally, to Dick's delight, I did shut up, but only after the panel made it clear that they thought I was a liberal and that, moreover, they felt they had strong *proof* I was a liberal. They ought to be ashamed of themselves for asking those questions of a journalist with an outstanding twenty-five-year record, and then pouncing on my answers. Why were they even considering my politics when they were supposedly just trying to get to the truth of a story? We have been down that road before in this country.

The panel and I kept talking about other issues: the Vietnam War, the National Guard, and the lingering questions that Americans still struggled with because of the unfairness of the draft system during Vietnam.

Dick Thornburgh said that we at CBS hadn't "proved" that Ben Barnes had helped George W. Bush get into the National Guard and that because we hadn't "proved" it, we shouldn't have aired the Barnes interview. This was unbelievable.

Once again, for Thornburgh and the whole panel, I went through the list of young men who somehow had had the good fortune to find their way into the protection of the 147th Fighter Interceptor group in Houston, under the command of the powerful and highly political Gen. Buck Staudt at a time when their peers were being sent to Vietnam and dying there. It wasn't just George W. Bush. Lloyd Bentsen's son was in the Texas Air National Guard. John Connally's boy had made the cut. H. L. Hunt's grandson was safe inside the 147th. Members of the Dallas Cowboys football team, movers and shakers at the Houston Country Club, the wealthy, the well-to-do, the connected, the up-and-coming, and the children of the old and conniving. All of them were well represented in the Texas Guard. They were particularly populous in the 147th, a unit so highbrow, so hoity-toity, it was called the Champagne Unit.

Dick Thornburgh was sitting at the side of the oversize table, making a big frowny face as I went through my list of names and my litany of reasons that I thought these men had taken advantage of a system that was rigged to favor the rich and privileged. I asked Dick what was wrong.

His response summed up everything that was wrong with the panel, everything that was wrong with his being on the panel. "Mary," he said, "don't you for a moment think that it is at all possible that all these fine young men got in on their own merit?"

I nearly fell off my chair. What a sanctimonious, country club attitude. How many people in America would dare to express such bias—in contradiction to all reason? Who could brazenly assert that no one ducked into National Guard units during Vietnam to avoid combat? Well, one of those freethinkers—chosen by my employer, no less—was sitting there in judgment of my work as a journalist. Can you spell "screwed"?

"No," I told Thornburgh. "No, I do not think that's possible. Not for a moment do I think it is possible that all these fine young men got in on their own merit." I told him that to believe that was to disbelieve American history, to disbelieve what the rest of the country had long ago accepted about Vietnam. It was an unfair war, fought by the poor, while many of the wealthy and well-off pretended to drill and practice and put in time in Guard units here at home, many after their college deferments had run out.

"Please don't tell me you're going there," I said to Thornburgh. "Please don't tell me you are even considering that."

Thornburgh's only response was to look down at his papers and make a few notes. I would love to have seen what he was writing, if he actually wrote anything. For all the insight he and the others brought to the panel hearings, his scribblings may as well have been a grocery list.

I gathered my things and looked back as I left the room. The lawyers were standing around the table, talking among themselves and devouring the last of the mixed nuts, raisins, and M&Ms that had been sitting in the middle of the table throughout my grilling that day. They said their good-byes and thank-yous to me and kept eating.

I couldn't help but reflect sadly on what had become of CBS News. The once proud network whose anchorman bravely called out Joseph McCarthy and denounced his 1950s witch hunts in Washington now had returned its agents to the capital with a different agenda. This time, the network hired high-powered lawyers to do some hunting of their own among the news division's journalists. Suspected "liberals" had become the new communists. People who'd had long and successful careers at CBS, whose work had never before been questioned or criticized, were suddenly grilled as though they were strangers under investigation for committing unspeakable crimes. The network had eagerly handed over to the panel our notes, phone records, and e-mails to be used against us, material that otherwise would have been privileged. What in the world would Edward R. Murrow think of his network now?

This time, however, politics was only part of the equation. Money was at the center of this inquisition. I am convinced that CBS and Viacom did not want an angry administration making vindictive decisions that would cost them a single dollar. So corporate executives decided to stage this upside-down, inside-out reenactment of the legendary face-off between Murrow and McCarthy. At this new CBS, the journalists were the bad guys. The corporate fat cats would cloak themselves as seekers of truth. And the American public and its right to be informed? Well, who gave a damn about that? It never even came up.

All of this didn't just break my heart. It was breaking CBS.

CHAPTER 17

It was starting to look a lot like Christmas around our house, but it sure didn't feel that way to me. The tree was up, the presents were wrapped, but the holiday-cheer-o-meter was running a little low this year. Every morning, I woke up worried that the panel report would be coming out that day. Rumors about its impending release were rampant. There were constant calls from reporters saying they had heard it would be out this week. Scratch that. Next week. No, wait. It'll come out as soon as Les Moonves returns from his honeymoon with Julie Chen.

There was even speculation that the report would be released on Christmas Eve. What a special gift that would have been.

Two days before Thanksgiving, Dan Rather announced he would step down from the *CBS Evening News*. He had called me a few days before making it public, telling me that he though it was time. I didn't. I thought it was the result of Les Moonves's taking advantage of an unfair situation to do something he had wanted for years, make the *Evening News* feel a little bit more like *Entertainment Tonight*. I beat myself up mercilessly for what I had done to Dan, someone I truly cared about. I beat myself up for unleashing this monster on everyone at CBS News.

We didn't carry out our Thanksgiving tradition of hosting friends and family for the holiday. I was just too blue. But we vowed to make it up in December. I prepared Christmas dinner for a large group and served the food with half an expectation that the meal might be broken up at any moment by news that I was being publicly fired. I felt hunted as the calendar counted down the days toward the end of 2004. I knew that each night and each morning brought me closer to what was probably going to be a humiliating and harrowing experience. I did not hold out much hope that the panel would find in my favor, but I felt as though I had presented such an extensive and detailed account of our work on the story and the foundation supporting it that part of me remained optimistic. My attorneys, Dick and Dan, who'd been with me through every moment of the questioning, told me that I'd done marvelously before the panel, that the lawyers had never been able to score a point against me, let alone a knockdown. And I knew that Dick and Dan weren't just trying to make me feel good.

The circumstances had been extremely difficult for someone who believes as strongly in journalism as I do. To have not only my fairness and integrity, my journalistic principles, questioned, but then to be accused of promoting just the opposite was almost unbearable. The panel's prosecution of our competence and fairness had been any professional's nightmare: being asked about everything from the broadest philosophical issue to the minutiae of word selection in e-mails and notes that should have been protected and every tangent in between. Then, adding insult to injury, to be questioned about bias by a group of lawyers led by a politician whose own political bias was a matter of public record. It was too much. The only restraint they showed was in refraining from asking how I had voted in the presidential election. I didn't need to ask Dick Thornburgh how he voted.

I was convinced that Thornburgh and his law firm weren't really interested in giving these already-convicted journalists a fair shake. This unshakable Republican had never demonstrated that he could be impartial on any issue going back to the Nixon administration, as far as I knew. What message had CBS sent to the current administration with the makeup of its supposedly independent panel? Lou Boccardi I wasn't as sure about. He seemed like he might have some sense of fairness in those brittle bones of his. For decades in the glass offices of the A.P., he had managed the managers who manage journalists, but I prayed he would recall what it was to *be* a journalist. Maybe we wouldn't all turn out to be peons in his eyes.

I didn't make up the rules, but I had to play the game. And I'd gone at it as hard and as well as I could. I had answered every single one of the panel's questions, fully and absolutely honestly. I had done my very best to try to give them a full picture of the events and the choices we had made and tried to put everything in context for the panel.

"There's no way they can say I didn't do my job," I must have said a hundred times to my husband as 2004 was giving way to 2005. It was really more of a question than a statement. I was seeking reassurance, trying to talk myself into believing that the panel had believed me. "I wish we'd had more time to put our story together and I wish I'd been able to put more background in the story, like Hodges's confirmation and the way the new documents meshed with the old ones," I kept on. "But those weren't all my decisions! I didn't choose the airdate. I didn't take that validation out of the story." I couldn't stop. I was practically sputtering.

"There's no way they can say I didn't do my job," I repeated. "Is there?"

"Not if they've listened to you, not if they've paid attention," replied my patient husband, who had lived virtually every detail of the story along with me as it unfolded and then had to listen to my endless replays of the events. "If those guys have any sense of justice, any sense of fairness, you'll be fine," Mark said. My husband, a broadcast and print journalist for nearly thirty years, was particularly disgusted with the media's coverage of the Bush-Guard controversy. Mark was incensed at how other reporters had jumped to conclusions, mischaracterized and twisted information.

What if there's some kind of split verdict, Mark and I speculated, where Boccardi and Thornburgh don't agree? We should have known better.

By the holidays, the radical right's Web sites had spent weeks calling for our blood, angry that the report still wasn't finished. C'mon. The bloggers had found us guilty in a matter of hours. What was taking these slowpokes so long? There were charges from the right that the panel was going to issue a whitewash. I had no such expectation. I was just hoping and praying for a little fairness.

What I did know was that the process of the investigation had been incredibly damaging to CBS News and the already fragile psyche of its newspeople. This was a company with a large contingent of "lifers," people who had come up through the ranks, worked their way into important positions, and stayed there for decades. As the years passed, all of us had watched helplessly as our beloved news organization was gutted by round after round of corporate abuse. Larry Tisch had once been the nemesis of the news division, back in the eighties, and that already seemed like aeons ago. Then Westinghouse came along with its attempt to run CBS News as though it were a household appliance company. Now, Viacom and its ancient chairman, Sumner Redstone, were having their way with the news operation. The constant change was debilitating. The lack of stability and real respect or protection for the news division, along with the continuing demand that newspeople do more with less, was brutal.

The in-house investigation was only the latest ordeal for CBS News, but it cut deep into the one aspect of the operation that had once seemed unassailable: the trust that employees had for one another, the respect they had for one another's work.

The panel investigation terrified people and turned them against one another. People who had been friends regularly ratted each other out to the panel. "I saw so-and-so do this," one would report. "I saw that she didn't do *this*," another would counter.

Spending hours in the hot seat under the panel's questioning did not lead to insight as much as intimidation. People were scared. Scared of what was going to happen to *60 Minutes II*, scared of what was going to happen to them, scared that if they didn't cooperate they could be blamed.

That insidious damage to an institution I loved and revered hurt me more than anything else. And, believe me, everything else hurt *a lot*. I had been mortified by the cruel blogs and raked through the coals by the shallow and competitive coverage of other mainstream media outlets, which were practically smacking their lips at the trouble Dan and CBS suddenly found themselves in. I had been humiliated by the panel's questioning and its casual and callous use of our e-mails, phone records, and notes. But most of all I hated the way this process had changed my colleagues inside CBS News. The trust that once bound us together had disappeared. The belief that we stood by one another through thick and thin had vanished. The sense that we were special, that we were the best, was gone. "We went into this together and we are all going to come out of this together," Dan had told me at the beginning of the panel investigation. Now I believed he was half-right. We started together, but that was it.

Somebody had to be thrown into the volcano to please the angry gods. In the movies, that somebody was always the girl. I had a feeling I would be led to the mountaintop soon for the big closing scene.

The new year found all of us who were still part of CBS standing by, milling around the lobby, making small talk until it was time for the final act, the fat lady's entrance, the swan song.

Finally, on the morning of January 10, after weeks and weeks of excruciating delay, I got an early call from a friend inside CBS in New York saying the report was coming out that day. This was it.

By 9:00 A.M., my wait was over. The phone rang. It was Andrew Heyward. He spoke quickly and without emotion. "Mary," he said, "the report is out and it's very bad. I'm going to put Jonathan Anchultz on the line. Jon, get on." I knew instantly what would happen next. The guillotine blade glinted in the sun. Andrew was going to fire me. CBS policy requires a witness to any firing, even on the phone. I suppose this is protection for the executioner executives, but Andrew had little to fear from me. I had been neutralized publicly, professionally, personally. Now I was on the way to nonexistence.

"Mary? Jonathan? Can you hear me?" Andrew's voice had gotten more hollow, more distant. I was going to be fired on a freaking speakerphone. Nice touch. Couldn't they each have picked up a handset? Andrew must have needed his hands free for something else. Neither I nor my years of dedication and accomplishment could command Andrew's entire attention even at this pivotal last moment. This had been a large part of the problem all along.

"Mary, as I said, the report is out. It's very bad. You're being terminated."

Wow, that seemed a little extreme. I thought I was only gonna be fired. A few smart-aleck retorts occurred to me, but I let it go, settled on being a big girl, and said nothing.

Terminated. I felt like he was going to unplug me from life support or send Arnold Schwarzenegger over for a visit. I had never been terminated, much less fired. My face felt hot at this newest embarrassment.

I don't remember Andrew saying he was sorry, probably because he didn't. I do remember telling Andrew I would be in touch with the office. And then it was over. The job and the life I had worked so hard to get and so hard to keep were gone.

Mark had listened to my end of the conversation and could tell what had happened. He came over and sat down and told me everything would be all right. We had each other. We had our boy. We had our friends and our family. We had our house, although who knew for how long? At least we could still laugh. We've always been able to do that, even between the tears. Robert was already in school, so my husband and I had a few quiet moments. What now? Who knew?

Soon the phone calls started pouring in from friends and colleagues—well, ex-colleagues—and, surprise, from reporters and producers. Mark took some time off and helped me avoid the calls and front-porch visits from the media. Now that I didn't have CBS telling me not talk, I had plenty to say, but I wasn't sure exactly what it should be or when or to whom. Right now, I needed to talk with my friends and my sisters and the people who called to tell me they loved me, the men and women who hadn't abandoned me when the going got tough.

Before saying anything publicly, I had to read the panel's report, talk with Dick Hibey and a lot of other people, and then decide a few things like, oh, what I was going to do with the rest of my life. Mostly I wanted to be alone, to hole up and hide and nurse my wounds in private.

I felt like someone who had been excommunicated from the church where she had worshipped since childhood, a place that had given me an identity, where I had marked my greatest triumphs.

For fifteen years, CBS had been like a family to me in every sense of the word. In so many ways, CBS was just like my family: wildly dysfunctional but funny, full of colorful and flawed characters who were capable of brilliant work and whom I enjoyed being with beyond description. I loved the place and I loved so many people there. CBS News had made me feel valuable and proud of myself and, in the process, had filled my life with wonderful experiences. Now that I had been found unworthy, I felt profoundly ashamed. I ached all over.

Dick called and told me he was sorry. Like me, he had hoped and prayed for something better and believed that it could possibly happen. He gave me some information that Andrew hadn't bothered sharing. Josh Howard, Mary Murphy, and Betsy West were being asked to resign. I had been fired. I was the clear villain. They were being asked to step down. They must have been sort of subvillains. Frankly, I was shocked at this.

I was told by some CBS employees that Josh in particular had worked very hard to vilify me both at the office with my coworkers and at the panel hearings, where he denied that he had given me permission to call the Kerry campaign and characterized me as some kind of hotheaded diva who didn't take direction. I thought that inventive backbiting alone would ensure Josh's survival. I'm sure he thought that, too. But he was gone, just like me. What could be worse than betraying and misrepresenting someone in order to save yourself and then finding out you hadn't saved yourself at all? How embarrassing.

I wasn't sure how Betsy and Mary had portrayed me to the panel and, to a great extent, I didn't care. I felt terrible for both of them. I even felt bad for Josh. None of us deserved the death penalty. In my opinion, this firing squad was not being carried out to better CBS but to better Viacom's relations with an angry administration, to soothe conservatives who had long loved to castigate CBS News as a liberal oasis.

The reasons behind this public flogging became clear as the day went on. Les Moonves appeared on television repeatedly in what became his greatest role—at least since his supporting appearance on the 1970s action-drama *The Six Million Dollar Man*. Now he was starring as the avenging corporate executive rising up to restore journalistic purity and accountability where the immoral and ethically bankrupt had concocted their journalistic conspiracies. But good Lord, watching Les Moonves talk about sources, investigative techniques, and journalism in general was like listening to Jessica Simpson discuss heart transplant surgery after she'd watched an episode of *Chicago Hope*. The words may have sounded right, but they were certainly coming out of the wrong mouth.

Thornburgh and Boccardi, a retired Republican and a retired newspaper executive who had absurdly come to represent the new face of journalistic excellence, were preening on the morning news programs over the tough verdict they had worked so hard to reach. Of course, they were on CBS's *The Early Show* first. It was the only time I had ever seen that broadcast scoop anyone. Their beleaguered and weary demeanor, as though they hated to be the bearers of such bad tidings and sad conclusions, belied the venom in the report that one of Thornburgh's underlings had primarily written and edited.

Online, I began reading some coverage of the panel's report. It was hard to fight through the legal verbiage of the report itself, but it was easy to see the verdict was not good. Conservative blogs were crowing, of course—except for the far-righters who blasted the panel for not concluding that the documents were forged and for not blaming our story on liberalism run wild. Coverage in the mainstream media was blistering, as well. *The New York Times* reported that "an independent panel" concluded that "the network's news division rushed the report onto the air in September in a frenetic dash to beat its competitors."

The article went on to say that the "independent panelists presented evidence they contend shows that Ms. Mapes misled—or at the very least was not forthcoming with—her superiors about the origin of the documents or of the results of efforts to verify them."

Les Moonves was quoted again and again in stories about the panel result saying that "the bottom line is that much of the September 8 broadcast was wrong, incomplete, or unfair." Hey, over here, Les. I knew precisely what it was like to be on the receiving end of that kind of reporting. I had lived it since my story ran and came under attack. I was living it right now, watching the panel members wringing their hands over my supposed shortcomings, not to mention the network's big cheese denouncing a producer who had strived each and every day to make Moonves's network news operation a little better.

One of the truly strange things about virtually all the coverage of the panel report was how unquestioning the media were of the notion that this panel had actually operated independently and reached a fair outcome. It wasn't their ox being gored, I guess. In fact, it was a cloven-hoofed competitor. What was there to question? But it amazed me that, almost without exception, reporters docilely accepted the idea that a panel made up of attorneys, with the sole exception of one retired publishing executive, was the appropriate tribunal to judge the work, the ethics, and the internal decisions of journalists. Rarely can you see so many media outlets agree, unless it's that a disaster was "tragic," a murder was "brutal," or some not-so-unusual event was "bizarre."

The coverage of my story had entered that unique category. I had become something everyone agreed on. Bringing up my name could halt the shouting on *Crossfire*. Everyone agreed. All the faces in all the little boxes on cable television clucked and quacked about what I had done. For once, they were on the same page. Liberal or conservative, political hothead or pointy-headed professor, most thought I was a dupe, at best, and a plotting traitor, at worst.

It seemed that from Dr. Laura to Larry King, television and radio hosts tsk-tsked and shook their heads over my story. "So sad." "So unnecessary." "Such a squandering of the once-proud legacy of CBS News." "Such a terrible thing she has done to Dan Rather." "Such a shame."

As I watched my dissection by the pundits, I wondered if I should consider making appearances in the Middle East as part of the road map to peace. The two sides could certainly agree on the enormity of my failure and then begin building from there toward real progress. Perhaps my power could be used for good instead of evil.

I have never experienced anything so devastating as watching what felt like the whole world turn on me and agree that I had been found terribly lacking in every way. I envied Betsy, Josh, and Mary for being asked to resign. As painful and unfair as that was for them, it seemed so much more civilized than being thrown out the door with boot marks on my butt. The ho got the old heave-ho.

Hurt and angry, I knew there was no one out there defending me or even raising the possibility that the panel might have issued a report that was anything less than fair, impartial, and perfectly appropriate. Predictably, there were a number of wing nuts who were disappointed at the panel's failure to call for a public beheading, who complained that Dan Rather should have been forced to wear a sandwich board with an apology on it in front of the White House, or who wanted the CBS building burned to the ground and the earth beneath it salted. But those people had nursed their grievances since long before George W. Bush went to Washington.

In a new age of corporate media self-flagellation and supposed "greater accountability," there was no one to hold the corporations accountable for their own investigations. Few gave a thought to the possibility that journalists might sometimes be worthy of defending in these internal investigations, even in a case like ours, where the instigation for the investigation had such an obvious political impetus.

On January 10 and the days that followed, I heard the CBS "scandal" repeatedly compared to the atrocities of Jayson Blair, Stephen Glass, Janet Cooke, Jack Kelley, the short list of discredited reporters who confessed to committing journalistic crimes ranging from plagiarism to fabrication. Stealing other writers' work or filing pure fiction as news accounts! In short, *lying.* I had done nothing like that.

At worst, I had been overly competitive, a fast worker, confident, and aggressive. Those used to be considered my good points. Now I had been fired, in part, for the very things that had won me a position of trust and favor within *60 Minutes.*

I downloaded the report and began to read the damned thing. At over two hundred pages, the report was bloated and flatulent, full of hot air, with long sections that amounted to little more than lists of exhibits. It came complete with an impressive index and nice typing. At first glance—and that is about as far as most appraisers got—it seemed that CBS had gotten its money's worth. Les Moonves must have been very pleased. This report looked like it had been put together by really smart people who had figured out a whole bunch of important stuff.

As I read through it, I saw two substantial saving graces to the report. One was that the panel, whether I accepted its authority or not, had decided that there was no political bias in the way Dan and I had done our jobs. Lucky me. I guess I had passed their not-too-liberal litmus test. In the report, they cited the fact that I had told them "proximity, not politics," motivated me to work on the story. That was true. I'm shocked that they believed me. I think it helped that so many of the people I worked with over the years were brave enough to tell the panel what it probably didn't want to hear about me: that I had a history of being fair and honest and a decent reporter who put whatever personal beliefs I had aside when I sat down at the keyboard to work on *any* story.

This is how the Boccardi-Thornburgh group put it: "The Panel was told by many at *60 Minutes Wednesday* and CBS News who worked with Mapes that she was motivated by reporting on a significant story and that they did not believe that political ideology became a part of her stories." What a disappointment that must have been for them.

The panel also came to this key conclusion: It was "making no find-ing as to the authenticity of the Killian documents." That was signifi-cant and fascinating to me for a couple of reasons. First of all, I was being fired for producing a story that supposedly was completely and totally wrong. Yet the centerpiece of our story, the Killian documents themselves, could not be found to be false.

The panel pointed out that "the review of military records is a highly technical exercise, which is fraught with difficulties even with the help of knowledgeable Guardsmen." It's the height of irony that the panel, with a mountain of money at its disposal, months of time to work on the case, and the professional fates of many respected journalists hang-ing in the balance, could not determine whether the documents were true or false *and never really tried*. They came to a sort of unstated con-clusion that they believed these documents appeared to be false. The conventional ignorance that had gripped our story and torn at its un-derpinnings was good enough for these prosecutors.

Second, and here is where I believe the panel failed miserably, they completely left the documents behind in going after the people who reported on them.

With far less time and far fewer resources—but a much greater well of knowledge about the ins and outs of Bush's Guard service—I came to a well-grounded conclusion that these documents appeared to be true in every way. Neither I nor the panel had a smoking gun that de-termined one way or another with 100 percent certainty that we had made the correct deductions.

We each believed and reported what we saw as the preponderance of evidence. They felt comfortable publishing their conclusions. I felt comfortable going to air. I got fired for my work. They got paid lots of money. Go figure.

Fairly early the day I was fired, I decided I needed to make a state-ment. I knew that many of my former CBS colleagues would see it and I wanted especially to speak to them.

And after seeing Les Moonves wax on about the proper role of jour-nalists and journalism, I wanted people not only to think carefully about what he was saying but also to consider the impact his views and his ac-tions would have on investigative journalism at CBS and elsewhere.

"I am shocked by the vitriolic scape-goating in Les Moonves's state-

292 | MARY MAPES

ment. I am very concerned that his actions are motivated by corporate and political considerations, ratings rather than journalism," I said in my statement. "Mr. Moonves's response to the review panel's report and the panel's assessment of the evidence it developed in its investigation combine not only to condemn me, but to put all investigative reporting in the CBS tradition at risk."

Who at CBS would now be willing to put their necks out for a story, knowing that if they made a misstep, if they overstated or understated, if they came under attack, if they pissed anyone off, they, too, could be the focus of a gigantic, public, and humiliating investigation? Would I have pursued Abu Ghraib so aggressively if I had seen another CBS producer fired for chasing a similar story too hard?

I wanted people to understand that there were also limits on my responsibility in terms of when the story aired and in what form it aired. I did not have the ultimate authority at CBS News. And the man who did was the one who got away without reprimand, without being held responsible in any way.

"It is noteworthy that the panel did not conclude that those documents are false. Indeed, in the end, all that the panel did conclude was that there were many red flags that counseled against going to air quickly," I said. "I never had control of the timing of any airing of a 60 Minutes segment; that has always been a decision made by my superiors, including Andrew Heyward. If there was a journalistic crime committed here, it was not by me."

Indeed, Andrew had made the final call to broadcast the story, after viewing it less than an hour before airtime. Apparently, another story had been set to go in its place. There was no imperative to run the Bush-Guard story at that moment, other than competitive pressures.

I only wish that Andrew had been involved enough to understand everything we had done to validate the story, the context and the corroboration that we had. His leadership and unflagging support would have been invaluable when we were attacked.

Dan Rather and I had already made it clear that we were okay with delaying the piece. We had even asked if we could run the Barnes interview portion of it then and the documents portion on the following Sunday or Wednesday.

When the Abu Ghraib story was delayed twice before it aired in April 2004, I had cooperated fully with those decisions. I demonstrated that I didn't exactly lose my mind and tear apart the office when a story of mine was put off at the last minute. I was a grown-up. That Andrew could make the final judgment to air a story that drew heavy criticism and then oversee the firing of everyone else involved, while managing to avoid bearing any blame for his own role, is truly a testament to his powers of persuasion with Viacom's executives. Either that or he has the proverbial naked pictures of someone in his office drawer.

Actually, I think Andrew is a wonderful fit for what Viacom wants in a news division president. He is pliable; he is flexible; he is forward-thinking. I fear that, like many of my former colleagues, Andrew is thinking about his own survival more than he is thinking about what is best for the news division. That is a tragedy for a news operation that has suffered more than its share of bad breaks.

What I would like to do is use some of the skepticism, the skill, and the reporting ability I learned in my years at CBS News to look closely at the panel findings. I don't know about Lou Boccardi, but I know I'm someone who has done a heck of a lot more investigative reporting than Dick Thornburgh or the gang of securities fraud and employment attorneys they locked up in a room and paid to sort out this particular mess. Now, I would like to take a crack at doing my own critique of the report. First of all, I need to apologize in advance to Dick Thornburgh and Lou Boccardi. I know how hard it is to be second-guessed.

CHAPTER 18

There is no such thing as a perfect investigative report. Every experienced, meticulous reporter knows that. My best work usually had at least one or two small flaws in the presentation that continue to drive me crazy years later. I remember each boo-boo very well and replay them in my mind: *I shouldn't have chosen that word. I shouldn't have used that picture. I should have included this or that, or left another thing out.* I would remember for years how I should have held a shot a beat longer, left a person's voice up a bit longer, cut out of a quote a little bit earlier. I would replay these moments in my head again and again, reliving each flawed choice I had made.

Some stories are more imperfect than others. I have never done a story, though, that I felt was wrong, misguided, or unfair. That includes the Bush-Guard story.

I imagine that Dick Thornburgh, the attorneys at his firm, and Lou Boccardi have the same sorts of feelings about their own work not being perfect. They certainly should. Imperfection is part of the human condition. I wouldn't feel qualified to judge their legal work and I wish they had been more aware that they were not the best judges of my journalism—or anyone else's.

What the panel did in examining the Bush-Guard story was set up a big corporate internal investigation that was intended for public consumption rather than mount a real attempt to find out anything substantive. It was the kind of going-over a company might pay big money for if it suspected that someone was pilfering money, making off with intellectual property, or releasing stock information in order to make a nefarious profit. None of those scenarios fit the problem at CBS News in the fall of 2004.

The fact that the company sought a corporate solution rather than a journalistic one reveals Viacom's belief that it needed a brass-knuckled investigation.

When *The New York Times* learned about Jayson Blair and the plagiarism and fantasy that marked his work, they didn't call in a former Republican attorney general and his fellow lawyers to look into what happened. They called in journalists. Ironically, one of them was Lou Boccardi, but the panel's work was driven by reporters and editors who could run down facts and separate fiction from reality, and who automatically understood the demands and inner workings of a news operation. The same thing happened at *USA Today* when Jack Kelley got into trouble for inventing much of his reporting.

CBS News and Viacom's corporate executives could have made a similar decision to have journalists run an investigation that closely examined the quality of our journalism. I would have welcomed an honest, straightforward discussion with other reporters and editors about what we had and when we had it, whether we should have run with the story, and whether the criticism mounted by the radical right blogs was legitimate grassroots outrage or political Astroturf, a partisan creation. I would have loved to have gotten definitive answers on whether the questions in the mainstream media were real or just a feeding frenzy that started with bloggers and was sustained by competitive media outlets.

I believe the difference for CBS was that Viacom executives immediately saw our situation as not just a reporting problem or even a PR problem, realizing that this flap had the potential to be a massive financial problem.

After spending fifteen years at CBS News, watching how corporate ownership dictated everything from financial decisions to content choices, I interpreted CBS's actions in my case this way:

Not only did Viacom cringe at alienating conservative viewers and consumers of its news division's programs as well as its theater chain and radio and entertainment-empire kingdom. The company could not afford to alienate the Bush administration. In Washington, Bush loyalists and appointees constantly make decisions in an alphabet soup of federal agencies that mean multimillion-dollar differences for the company. When the panel was investigating our story, the FCC was considering how big the fine should be for CBS over the Janet Jackson breast-baring at the Super Bowl. Another agency has long been considering exactly when the networks should completely make the jump to digital technology, a decision that would cost CBS a staggering amount of money in upgrades for programming as well as equipment at its owned and operated affiliates. An uncooperative administration could make trouble in a hundred ways and kick Sumner Redstone where it really counted: in the wallet. And Redstone, Viacom's chairman and big chief, knew that the Bush administration didn't shy away from playing favorites with corporations and businesses who went along with the program.

Viacom's billionaire boss chose to lay down his cards in the early going, declaring on September 24, 2004, that he was voting for President Bush because he saw Bush as being best for business. "I look at the election from what's good for Viacom," Redstone said. "I vote for what's good for Viacom."

The cynical interpretation would be that Redstone, an acknowledged lifelong "liberal Democrat" who once took a certain perverse pride in having appeared on Richard Nixon's enemies list, made his unsolicited endorsement purely for business reasons four days after CBS's surrender over the Killian documents. But I'm not a cynic. I believe it is quite possible that Redstone had a real political change of heart, deciding that the Bush-created deficit, the growing difficulties in Iraq, the questions about abuse of war detainees, and the soaring price of oil were some of the "good for Viacom" factors that pushed him into the Bush column.

At Viacom, money matters most. And the hubbub over the Guard story raised terrifying possibilities for corporate executives like Redstone, who must have had dark visions that Viacom's financial future could be clouded by the controversy.

As the corporate conflagration spread, I can only imagine the fiery e-mails that must have zipped back and forth between Redstone and Les Moonves, between Moonves and Andrew Heyward, between Redstone and his Washington lobbyists. They must have really been something to see. All I can do is imagine them, however, because none of those e-mails, none of the communication that passed between the corporate leaders and the news division leaders, made it to the "independent" investigation.

The panel did question Andrew Heyward for what he described to me as a few "embarassing hours," but I believe that is as high as the investigation went. Thornburgh and Boccardi investigated the network's decision to defend the story initially as well as the framing of CBS's apology. I believe that neither of those decisions was made in a vacuum and that Viacom executives probably had input in deciding how CBS News responded. But as far as I know, no one with a higher rank than Andrew Heyward was called in to be questioned. The buck stopped far short of the big brass.

As an investigative reporter, I can't imagine anything more important than determining whether the news division, its employees, and this "independent" investigation were compromised by corporate leaders out to save their own hides and their corporation's bottom line.

But in this case, at least in terms of what the panel report revealed, we are being asked to believe that the bigwigs at CBS News and Viacom had absolutely *no* discussion as right-wing criticism of the story exploded, the dispute over the documents became front-page news, and the executives groped for ways to stanch the bleeding.

And who are we to thank for this news blackout, for the complete absence of e-mails between CBS News executives and their corporate bosses who were hell-bent on stamping out the political flames sparked by that damn *60 Minutes II* story and threatening to engulf Viacom? Who made sure that a fire wall went up, tall and wide, separating CBS News from its corporate commanders?

CBS vice president Linda Mason, an old ally of Andrew Heyward and unofficial head of journalistic standards at CBS News, was assigned early on to go through thousands of CBS e-mails and cull those communications that touched on the Bush-Guard story for the panel.

Judging from the material that the panel made public in its report, Redstone, Moonves, Heyward, each Viacom board member, and every Viacom lobbyist were the absolute souls of discretion when it came to electronic communications. *Maybe* they didn't send *one single message* to one another about the *60 Minutes* Bush-Guard mess. *Maybe* they didn't discuss *anything* that might have been revealing or embarrassing, that might have shown an agenda beyond mere journalism, that might have raised serious questions about exactly what CBS was worried about in the hallowed halls of Washington.

That doesn't seem plausible, you say? You might be right. I think there probably were quite a few searing, explicit e-mails between corporate higher-ups that could have been lethal if they had become public. But I believe the big guys were lucky enough to have allies like Mason and perhaps the panel itself to protect them.

Now, I do not *know* whether Linda Mason withheld any relevant e-mails from the panel or whether the panel withheld any relevant e-mails from its public report. I do know how protective CBS News executives are of their superiors. They have to be.

Neither I nor anyone else at *60 Minutes* who worked on the Bush-Guard story had that protection. Our e-mails were eagerly turned over to the corporate prosecutors who were bought and paid for by Viacom. It was a unique way to allow outsiders to spy on those of us who had busted our butts and trusted our bosses and our company. The panel, of course, could read or misread those e-mails any way it chose. What could a calculating boss find in *your* e-mail? Anything that could be questioned, misinterpreted, or deemed inappropriate? Anything that could be used against you, especially if read in the worst possible light?

I used e-mail the way a lot of people use it—like air. I zipped off grocery lists, bad jokes, notes to my sisters, and ideas for stories. I felt a little foolish and frivolous—not to mention violated—when all my e-mails were revealed. I had to answer the panel's questions about my occasionally foul mouth and my irreverent humor, my bragging, my bitching, my life. God knows, my e-mails did show the real me.

Dan benefited from some low-tech protection. To understate things, he is less than proficient on a computer and doesn't really do e-mail. Looking for an e-mail from Dan is a truly hopeless task. Besides, Dan is old-school in the sense that he would rather get you on the phone or say something to your face. That is not a bad policy any way you look at it.

Any personal embarrassment at having our e-mails read isn't the issue, however. In order to judge what happened at the company, how the story came about, how CBS responded, how Viacom acted, *all* of the e-mails should have been turned over to the panel. We all should have been judged equally. It is astonishing that in the entire panel report there is not a single mention of an electronic communication involving the corporate brass at CBS News and those at Viacom. There should not have been a filter protecting the executives and letting others twist in the wind. That ensured an unfair investigation from the get-go, guaranteeing that peons like me would be the only ones who paid for their perceived failures with both public exposure and professional punishment.

Linda Mason had always viewed herself as something of a "conscience" at CBS News. I think she's absolutely right. In fact, her superiors were evidently so pleased with her performance, after the bloodletting Mason was promoted to senior vice president.

Mason was also intimately involved in trying to get Mike Smith, our Texas-based freelance researcher, to help lasso and deliver Bill Burkett to the panel for questioning. That didn't work out, but in the process of negotiating with Mike, Mason left behind a trail of e-mails and recorded phone calls that offer insight into the techniques she used to reassure the terrified people who were told to participate in the panel hearings.

Mike had worked for a variety of news outlets and was rightly worried about being questioned or having private information revealed about his employment with other projects or authors. Mason attempted to soothe him in this e-mail on October 16, 2004, saying that he had nothing to worry about:

> Mike—Let me assure you on several counts. First we definitely will protect your sources. For all the people participating in the review, the interviews and notes shared with the panel is part of the "work product" and as such any information will be "privileged" and will NOT ever be made public. . . . And you know that I feel, as you do, that confidentiality is one of the keystones of journalism.

By the time the report came out, the panel had made a mockery of that particular "keystone" of journalism. Luckily for Mike, he had the foresight not to turn over his personal notes and e-mails to the panel. E-mails within the CBS system about Mike's other employers were made public in the report. The names of sources that he talked to, the information he sent to me, and what I sent back were all cited by the panel, to our dismay and disgust. Time after time the panel used our cooperation and candor—our trust—to betray us.

Sources whose names were obtained during the panel's questioning of CBS employees were contacted and they were asked to testify or appear for questioning by the panel. Many of the sources were merely interviewed on the phone by a lawyer or lawyers from the panel.

In the final report, the panel relied on its questioning and the answers it received from various sources as the holy grail of information, not taking into account how differently a person might respond to a panel of corporate types than the quite possibly more subtle approach of a reporter.

I know that there were contradictions in what the panel gleaned from various sources of mine and what those sources told me. The panel members accounted for those differences in the darkest possible ways. In some cases, they openly assumed that my version of events was not true or was colored by my supposedly myopic zeal to get the story on the air. Realistically, I think that a phone call from a journalist who asks questions after building some trust with a source invariably yields more candid, truer off-the-cuff responses than a formal, speakerphone grilling done by lawyers.

The panel was never able to speak with Burkett, who finally said no to a meeting. He may have made the wisest choice of any of us. Of course, that left the panel free to plug pure conjecture about Burkett's motives, actions, and attitudes into its report. There is no way to know whether the panel would have been enlightened by speaking with the man who handed us the documents. But having no access to his thoughts and ideas didn't stop the panel. They wrote the report anyway, filling in the blanks in their investigation with supposition.

The same was true of the panel's dealings with Jim Pierce, a long-time document examiner whom we consulted prior to airing the story. Pierce was reluctant to talk to the panel because they would not promise him confidentiality. His refusal to participate was probably a good call for him as well. The panel handled the absence of this key examiner by basically ignoring that he existed and neglecting to include any of the valuable corroboration that his work provided. Instead, the panel focused on the examiners who had been hired by CBS and volunteered to participate in the investigation, particularly the two who claimed that they had doubts about the documents. The panel also misinterpreted—deliberately or inadvertently—the work of our primary analyst, Marcel Matley, despite Matley's protests to the panel. This did not lead to a fair understanding of how we at *60 Minutes* had tried to authenticate the documents or seek guidance on the typeface, font style, or format issues before air. That didn't matter to the panel. To paraphrase Secretary of Defense Donald Rumsfeld, the panel wrote the report with the information they had, not the information they might want. The report ignored missing information without comment.

This was a crucial call by the Thornburgh-Boccardi group, not just because the panel's choice made *60 Minutes* look bad but also because the information they might have been able to get from Jim Pierce—the information they blithely left out—was vital to understanding the important steps we had taken to validate the documents.

I talked with Pierce before and after the story aired, and he told me that he thought the font styles in our memos "have been around for a long time." That they were not "from a computer printer." He thought the font style was "from the late sixties." Pierce had told me that he had a friend and fellow document analyst look at the memos and that his friend told him: "Jim, these fonts have been around for ages, contrary to what the newspapers are saying."

When the panel investigation was underway, I didn't know who they were interviewing or not interviewing. I didn't have a chance to tell the panel which people I thought they should be talking to. The panel wouldn't tell those of us testifying much of anything. We were left to find out how the investigation had progressed after it was finished.

It didn't surprise me that Pierce declined to be interviewed by the panel without a promise of confidentiality. He had already suffered personally as a result of having his name linked with the Bush-Guard story. Pierce told us that the controversy over the story had brought television satellite trucks as well as conservative pranksters to the gated community in California where he lives. Pierce's neighbors were not amused, and he may have been worried about how fallout from the controversy would affect his business. Steering clear of the whole thing if the panel would not promise confidentiality was the safest thing to do. I almost wish I had done that. The result would have been the same, anyway. I would have been fired. But I would have saved time, avoided false hope, and probably been less hurt and embarassed by the outcome if I had told the panel to go fly a kite.

The panel could have learned a great deal about Pierce's opinion of the memos if they had bothered to read the transcript of an interview Pierce did with Dan Rather on September 14. I know they had the transcript because I provided it to them and it is listed as an exhibit without being mentioned in the voluminous panel report.

In the interview, Pierce went over his qualifications, including thirty-four years as an analyst and his training at the Los Angeles Police Academy and at the FBI Academy in Quantico, Virginia.

Pierce told Dan that based on his examination of the documents, he thought they were authentic and that the font used in them was a "thin Courier typeface."

Dan asked about other issues. "What about the issue of the superscript 'th'? Was that available during this period, late sixties, early 1970s?"

"Yes," Pierce responded. "In fact, I remember [it]. I can't give you specific dates, certainly before the date in question on these questioned documents, that I distinctly remember that 'th' combination."

"So it's your opinion that it was available at the time?"

"Yes, sir," Pierce answered, without qualification, without hesitation.

Pierce had told Dan that there was so much disagreement within the world of document examiners because "some people are not properly trained and not properly certified in the field of forensic document examination." He said there were people working as analysts whom he referred to as "charlatans."

"Based on what you know now," Dan asked him again "are these documents authentic?"

Pierce responded, "As it stands right now, there's a strong similarity. There's a strong probability that these documents are authentic."

"And tell me again why."

Once again, Pierce seemed unequivocal. "The typeface appearing on the typewritten materials on the questioned documents corresponds to the samples of typeface named thin Courier typeface, which was available going all the way back to 1955 and very prominent in the late sixties, prior to the date in question."

Then Dan asked a hypothetical question that had to have been among the most personal and most important in his career: "If you were a reporter who had these documents and had reported them as to the best of available knowledge, reported them authentic, should that reporter back off now or stick with it?"

Pierce came through again: "Oh, I think definitely that there is sufficient evidence at this time to say that the questioned documents are authentic."

It is a pity the panel could not have spoken with Pierce or used this transcript as a way of acknowledging his opinion. We had used Pierce on the air in an evening news story. Ignoring Pierce and relegating his role to just a tiny section of the report did not reflect the weight Dan and I gave his work and misrepresented the experience Pierce brought to his examination of the memos.

Another inexplicable element of the report is why the panel, with all that money and all that time, did not hire document analysts of its own to look at the memos.

James C. Goodale, the former vice chairman and general counsel of *The New York Times,* a man who was deeply involved in the newspaper's decision to publish the Pentagon Papers, wrote a scathing review of the panel report in March that appeared in *The New York Review of Books* and raised this criticism and a host of others. God bless his little heart, as we say in Texas. His willingness to question the mystifyingly blind approval that greeted the flawed panel report meant the world to me.

Goodale had a fascinating theory on why the panel may not have hired its own analysts: "One suspects that if the panel had done so, it would have ended up with some experts saying the documents were reliable, others not sure. And that would have put the panel back where CBS was." *Exactly.* And to get past that point in terms of deciding whether the documents were real or not, the panel would have had to do what I did: old-fashioned reporting and analysis of what we knew about Bush's career in the Guard, how that jibed with the new documents, seeking corroboration, doing extensive interviews, knocking on doors, making phone calls, and, in the end, making judgments based on the preponderance of evidence, not some obscure opinion about the shape of a single letter of the alphabet.

But using the same techniques and possibly reaching the same conclusions that we had was not an option for the panel. This panel had been hired to find out what went wrong, not what may have gone right. And that's what the panel did with "myopic zeal"—to use their damning phrase.

I shared with Jim Goodale what I called my meshing document. In his review of the panel report, he said he found my meshing "persuasive within the limits she set." He went on to criticize the way the panel used the testimony of Bush's fellow Guardsmen to attempt to disprove my conclusions. Goodale concludes that "in the end, even the panel, without saying so explicitly, has to concede the accuracy of Mapes's statement that 'there is nothing in the official Bush records that would rule out the authenticity of the Killian documents.'"

Goodale was hardest on the panel report—and made me laugh out loud—when he took on the panel's contention that Dan's interview with Ben Barnes was "misleading." Goodale wrote: "Why is this misleading? Because, the panel said, CBS has no proof that the person who received the call was influenced by it. Can the panel be serious about this? Should CBS not have reported the call?"

The panel members had another obvious option they could have pursued if they had wanted to actually trace the memos and make a solid determination about their authenticity. They could have hired a researcher—or, with their budget, as many as they wanted—to go to Camp Mabry and try to pull out more official documents from both Bush's record and those of other Guardsmen. Most of the panel's questioning was done by attorneys. They weren't journalists, and they didn't think like journalists. They weren't working on the story; I felt they were working on convicting us. As it was, the panel had what we had: a stack of Bush records and a few others I had gleaned from other Guardsmen. An influx of new records from the 1971–73 period could have provided a bonanza of material for the panel, information that could have been crucial in answering, once and for all, questions about format, typeface, abbreviation patterns, and other issues that the panel used to decide that CBS had probably erred in broadcasting its story.

But again, the panel seemed to have no real interest in the facts behind the story, only in analyzing in the harshest way possible how we had handled it. If, God forbid, the panel had determined with the help of new information that the story was true, Viacom would have been in a *real* pickle.

CBS had already apologized for the story. Dan had already announced he was stepping down from the *Evening News*. God knows what the lobbyists had told the powers-that-be in Washington. I think Viacom found itself in the strange position of actively working to disprove a story its news operation had reported, actively hoping the story would not turn out to be true.

With each question the panel examined, benefit of the doubt invariably went to the memos' critics. For example, Jerry Killian's son came forward after the story aired to say that his late father would not have written notes like this or kept files like this, contradicting what he had told CBS before the story aired. The panel accepted his beliefs as truth, without considering what he told CBS prior to the story, including, among other things, that Killian and his father had not been at all close. Gary Killian told Mike Smith and me that he knew virtually nothing about his father's Guard career. When the memos became public and the issue turned into a public political battle, I believe Killian's son and widow were recruited to rally the troops for the Republican argument. The panel believed them. I believe what they had said the first time we talked with them. I believe the truth is more complicated than the answers the panel accepted from the Killians and others.

Bobby Hodges was another example of someone whose questions about and criticisms of the documents' authenticity were largely accepted by panel members, at the same time Hodges's endorsement of the *content* of the documents was discounted.

General Hodges told *The New York Times* that network producers had "read them to him over the phone," but that "he had not authenticated the documents for CBS News but had confirmed that they reflected issues he and Lieutenant Colonel Killian had discussed — namely Mr. Bush's failure to appear for a physical, which, military records released previously by the White House show, led to a suspension from flying." Hodges had told me before our story aired that the memos, which I read to him in their entirety, reflected Killian's attitudes and actions when Bush failed to take his annual physical. The panel was unable to resolve the differences between my version of our conversation and Bobby Hodges's recounting of what had been said, leaving doubts about what had transpired in our September 6 phone call. I had no doubts and felt strongly that Hodges had confirmed the memos' content to me and, later, to others.

How could a forger have known that Killian had discussed these things with General Hodges? How could someone, whether working for one political party or another, have had that information and been able to incorporate it into a forgery? It simply didn't make sense.

Add to that the fact that secretary Marian Carr Knox later repeatedly confirmed that her boss, Lieutenant Colonel Killian, indeed felt angry and disappointed that Bush didn't take his physical, was leaving the Guard for Alabama, and had openly flouted the rules at Ellington Air Base, spreading resentment and a sense of disdain among his fellow pilots. Knox told reporters that she typed all of Killian's paperwork and that she typed memos similar to the newly discovered documents, which her boss kept in his locked desk drawer. She said she believed the new memos were fake, however. "These are not real," Ms. Knox said after viewing copies of the new memos. "The information in here was correct, but it was picked up from the real ones." She said she believed that the typewriters she used, a manual Olympia and an IBM Selectric, could not have produced the new documents.

In addition to Knox's recollections, add those of Richard Via, another retired Guard officer who had a desk next to Killian's. He also confirmed in September 2004, that Killian kept files in his locked drawer and that the documents' content accurately reflected questions about Bush's physical and other issues that were well known to officers at the time. Via said he and others "remember the physical and him going to Alabama was an issue," USA Today reported. Killian "was trying to cover his ass," Via said. "He was always worried something would come back on him." That seems perfectly consistent with a political climate in which Killian would keep "CYA" memos.

Killian's secretary "would type them up and he'd put it in his desk drawer and lock it," Via said. In a separate interview, Via said that Knox didn't do all of Killian's typing and that several others in the unit were competent typists and would type documents whenever they were asked. Via, however, also said he believed the new documents were fakes.

Nonetheless, three people in their own ways essentially confirmed all or part of the memos' content. Wouldn't a reasonable and impartial observer conclude that there is a pattern here?

How could these confirmations of the content be accounted for if the memos were flat-out forgeries? Would a forger somehow choose to forge—or accidentally stumble onto forging—the truth? Those questions were neither posed nor answered in the costly report, which found *60 Minutes* guilty of airing material the panel could *not* prove to be *in*accurate. People lost jobs they had earned over long careers of solid reporting because a mob of partisan bloggers out-shouted and out-attacked everyone else. CBS never knew what hit it. And the bloggers never had to prove anything. They threw anything they could think of at the wall in the hope that something would stick. To their glee, an awful lot of it stuck, at least long enough to topple Dan Rather, destroy the careers of some of his coworkers, and keep the Bush campaign on track through Election Day.

The panel did not look at the wildly partisan background of many of these bloggers. It did not identify "Buckhead," the first person to write a detailed, faulty, and suspiciously quick critique of the memos as anything more than a lifelong Republican operative. In an article for *Columbia Journalism Review*, Corey Pein was the first to raise important questions about the backgrounds of the bloggers who attacked CBS:

> One of the story's top blogs, Rathergate.com, is registered to a firm run by Richard Viguerie, the legendary conservative fundraiser. Some were fed by the conservative Media Research Center and by Creative Response Concepts, the same PR firm that promoted the Swift Boat Veterans for Truth. CRC's executives bragged to *PR Week* that they helped legitimize the documents-are-fake story by supplying quotes from document experts as early as the day after the report, September 9. The goal, said president Greg Mueller, was to create a buzz online while at the same time showing journalists "it isn't just Rush Limbaugh and Matt Drudge who are raising questions."

No, the "questions" were actually raised by Rush and Matt's behind-the-scenes conservative-cause moneymen and their radical-right adherents who ran vitriolic Web sites and had long histories of hardcore smear tactics.

Nor did the panel members look critically at some of the former pilots they chose to speak with in their investigation. Invariably, they talked with the men who had, for years, been known as Friends of Bush. These men—principally Maury Udell and Dean Roome—had never presented Bush as anything other than a first-class pilot and first-class person. The panel's consideration of their testimony about the specifics of the memos and their memories of Bush's performance did not take into account their lengthy loyalty to the president.

Actually, Roome did make a small detour from his strident praise for Bush in 2002, when he told *USA Today* a much less guarded version of what happened when Bush stopped flying. "Where George failed was to fulfill his obligation as a pilot," Roome said. "It was an irrational time in his life." He now says the comment was taken out of context.

Over the years, Roome had bragged to reporters that he was in regular contact with the White House. And there is evidence that he was telling the truth. On the wall of Roome's Texas antique store office hangs a signed picture of him with President Bush, and another that Roome says was taken in early 2004 at a get-together between the president and some of his friends from the Guard days.

Roome has told a number of reporters that whenever the media contacts him or requests an interview, he notifies through e-mail a long list of powerful and well-connected people, beginning with Krista Ritacco, an executive assistant to the White House communications director until 2004; Texas governor Rick Perry; Gen. Daniel James, the head of the whole country's National Guard; and Col. Lanny McNeely, the current 147th Fighter Wing Commander.

When Roome helped a media organization get permission in summer 2004 to shoot at Ellington Field, he sent one of the researchers an e-mail confirming that he had gained access for them. The e-mail also contained electronic links to the bigwigs listed above.

Do Bush confidants maintain close contact with people who know the most about Bush's Guard days and report to the White House when someone asks questions? Or do Bush supporters just like to stay in touch with old friends? Gen. Bobby Hodges, Maurice Udell, and Gary Killian are all on Dean Roome's group e-mail list.

Ultimately, the panel was highly critical in its judgments of journalists while abandoning critical thinking in its interpretations of information from other sources. The panel ended up endorsing the most benign interpretation of Bush's behavior, the history of how he got into the unit, and the cover story of how he got out. Their conclusions on a laundry list of issues portrayed a whitewash.

The panel believed the accounts given by Bush supporters and friends that there were openings in the Guard unit that young George W. Bush was accepted into. In doing that, the panel ignored countless confirmations of waiting lists from other people who served in the Texas National Guard at the time. In his book *First Son*, Bill Minutaglio wrote:

> Some Guard officials maintained that in fact there were no slots available and that there was a waiting list: "We were full," said General Thomas Bishop, who was the state's adjutant general in 1968. "There were definitely waiting lists. There wasn't any question about that," said another Guard official. "There was a 500-man waiting list prior to 1972, so there was not much recruiting."

In the end, the panel prepared a document that read more like a prosecutorial brief than an independent investigation. And I think no one was happier to receive this condemnation of its employees than the executives at Viacom. Now they could present themselves to the Bush administration as victims of irresponsible, out-of-control journalists, not as an operation that was actually doing some tough reporting. Gosh, it had all been a terrible accident.

In early January, before the panel's damning conclusions came out, *Broadcasting & Cable* magazine reported that CBS News president Andrew Heyward met with White House communications director Dan Bartlett "in part to repair chilly relations with the Bush administration." According to the story, "Heyward was 'working overtime to convince Bartlett that neither CBS News nor Rather had a vendetta against the White House,' our source says, 'and from here on out would do everything it could to be fair and balanced.' CBS declined to comment."

I had to laugh at the use of the FOX News slogan by the magazine's source in describing the kind of coverage CBS supposedly promised the White House. Was that a slip of the tongue or a change in CBS's approach to coverage?

The panel report was actually no more negligent than some of the poor reporting that ended up on the front pages of newspapers I had long relied on for fair and accurate reporting.

I honestly don't know what happened to lead so many news organizations to lower their standards, lose their skepticism, and let down their guard in accepting information from the radical right. Competition also creates strange bedfellows. And our elite media competitors and the suddenly empowered bloggers of the far right found oh-so-tasty targets in CBS, 60 *Minutes*, and Dan Rather. Those critics argued that CBS and Dan and I were the ones who lowered our standards and lost our skepticism, but we didn't accept the frayed, whole-cloth assessment of someone else, in many cases someone with their own heavily partisan agenda, as so many in the mainstream media did. We did our own digging and came to our own conclusions.

Many news outlets relied on so-called document experts who had no real credentials, but did have real political agendas. Other analysts were people drawn into the debate, making their best guesses without much background on either the story or the memos.

The Washington Post ran a two-page dissection of the disputed documents on September 19, not coincidentally the day before the official CBS apology. The story was rife with errors and mischaracterizations. Reading it still leaves me nearly speechless, not so much for what was in it, but for what was left out.

The story was coreported by Howard Kurtz, the *Post's* media reporter, who had been one of the leaders of the mainstream commentary corps denouncing the story from the beginning. What was Kurtz doing bylining what was supposed to be a straight story? He had already made his opinion on the documents clear.

A full-page graphic—and we all love graphics—compared four of the Killian documents to four official documents. There were obvious differences, but those four official documents did not constitute the entire universe of official documents, only samples that reporters happened to have on hand from Bush's limited released files, and which are filled with their own inexplicable oversights and unexplained gaps.

Even the official documents show a wide variety of abbreviation styles, typing skill levels, and differences in the sophistication of the equipment used. Even then, military clerks had more than just straight manual typewriters at their disposal. There were IBM Selectrics, IBM Selectric Composers, which could do everything from proportional spacing to superscript at the touch of a button. There were also crude versions of computers, which used magnetic tape to store and then spew out a stream of copy.

Every element the *Post* pulled out to prove that the memos were false could just as easily have been seen as proof that they were typed by an unskilled clerk or that they were done in an informal style for personal, rather than official, use.

In a Killian memo dated August 1, 1972, the *Post* pointed out that the number "147" had a "space between [the] number and [the] 'th' to prevent superscripting in Microsoft Word." The *Post* did not mention that in the document's very first line, where "111th" was typed, there was no space between the number and the "th," yet there was still no superscript. That's called a reporting oversight. Make it an abominable reporting oversight in an examination whose intent is to tear down the quality of a competitor's reporting.

The *Post* further emphasized that official documents did not use the abbreviation "Grp" for "Group," as a Killian memo did—another point that supposedly demonstrated that the Killian memos were fake. Yet in the official documents that we showed to the panel, we found other "Grp" abbreviations. Again, the newspaper's carefully cited claim was simply not true.

On and on went the *Post*'s misinformed examples, each of them easily refutable. But in print and filling entire pages like that, they sure seemed to add up to something. We proved that criticism after criticism of our story and the memos themselves was ill-founded, but it didn't seem to matter. Minds were made up. CBS News had no mechanism and no backbone for refuting bull-headed blogs or mistaken reporting, contributing to a tidal wave of conventional wisdom that CBS had been wrong, hoodwinked, or worse. Like bricks, these individual criticisms, though mistaken, were repeated and repeated, stacked one upon another until they gradually formed walls of perception—and eventually alleged proof—about our reporting, our documents, and our supposed errors. Our version, our truth, couldn't get through.

I was not allowed to speak. We were all reeling from ten days of nonstop professional and personal attacks. Unbeknownst to me, that September weekend Andrew Heyward was already preparing an apology to be delivered by CBS News. It would mark a fatal turning point for all our efforts, the equivalent of an unconditional surrender to public opinion about our story. The panel had been contacted and was in the process of gearing up to tear the story into little tiny pieces during the months of its agonizingly slow review.

Somehow, in just days, the bloggers' reality had taken hold, replacing critical reporting with rumor, personal attack, and outright lies. By the time Dan announced he was leaving the *Evening News* in late November, the bloggers' radical version of the truth had essentially *become* the truth. Whether it was right or wrong, the media was done and we were finished. They had wrapped up another scandal and set things right. The networks, the newspapers, even the blogs turned their attention elsewhere. The beast moved on. Those of us run over in the stampede to bad judgment were left alone to pick ourselves up, dust ourselves off, and try to defend ourselves to the panel, which had wholeheartedly accepted the conventional ignorance as fact.

We faced a coalition of bloodthirsty bloggers who wanted to prove their age-old theory about CBS—that the network was packed with liberals who approached every story with an agenda. We faced a mainstream press that was having way too much fun kicking us in the head to think about whether they were getting the story right or treating us as fairly as they might want to be treated. We also faced division within CBS News itself as all the old competitiveness, the old resentments and adversarial feelings that some within the organization had for Dan or for me or for *60 Minutes II*, came bubbling to the surface. There was attack from within and without.

And we faced a panel that I believed had an agenda. It had been hired to clean house and to send a message to conservatives. Viacom had to have been worried about negative fallout on everything from the fine over the exposure of Janet Jackson's breast to the possibility of being ordered to go digital overnight, from forced changes in ownership rules to new restrictions on billboards. I believe the company's executives were scrambling to keep the corporation from suffering financially for the supposed sins of its overzealous news employees.

We didn't have a chance.

CHAPTER 19

The report from the independent panel ended my career at CBS News on January 10, 2005. It did not end my work on the Bush-Guard story or on the memos that created such a ruckus when Dan Rather and I reported on them for *60 Minutes*.

Radical conservatives will bellow and bloviate all over again about what I've written here. Despite what they might say, I am *not* obsessed with the president's National Guard service. Never was. I can assure you that I can't wait to work on something else. Some days, I can't wait to work on *anything* else. By damaging CBS News, an organization full of people I care about, by hurting my friend and colleague Dan Rather, and by taking my job, the radical right and the bullying bloggers—through their blind and exploitive partisanship—pretty much assigned me to this story for the foreseeable future. No one regrets that more than I do. Unless it is George W. Bush. Because the president knows that what I and most Americans strongly suspect about his National Guard service is true.

Bush didn't keep his promise to his country. He swore he would fly military jets until May 1974 in return for being removed from the danger of being drafted. He didn't even come close, leaving the cockpit more than two years early. He didn't keep his word to the pilots who did fulfill their service, to the commanders who counted on him, or to the military, which spent more than a million dollars teaching him how to fly. He left without giving the National Guard or the country their money's worth. He walked away from his duty.

First Lieutenant Bush let down his commanding officer, Lt. Col. Jerry Killian, by choosing to transfer to Alabama and, after leaving his unit in Houston, dabble in the day-on, day-off lightweight work of his father's friend's Senate campaign. Bush was supposedly working as a kind of junior campaign manager for Winton Blount in the conservative Republican's race for the U.S. Senate. According to people who were with Bush in Alabama, including Linda Allison, the widow of late campaign manager Jimmy Allison, the future president came in late, left early, and didn't accomplish much other than impressing his coworkers with tales of his drinking derring-do.

Bush's transfer to a unit in Alabama meant he would no longer be able to fly. Far beyond that, every bit of evidence that has been pulled from the record and from witnesses indicates that young George W. Bush did not bother to show up at that Alabama unit at all.

Then, instead of returning to Houston when the campaign ended in November 1972, he stayed away from the National Guard, adrift in military paperwork—a young man seemingly content to fall through the cracks, to play the system and play around. Bush finally reappeared in late May 1973, returning at last to his old unit. This time he appears to have pushed paper and performed weekend duty for a few months, leaving the flying to the pilots who had taken their physicals, kept up their flight certifications, and kept their word about wanting to serve in the Guard. At the end of the summer in 1973, Bush sought and received an early out to attend Harvard Business School that fall. He also promised to join a reserve unit in the Boston area, but he again failed to live up to that agreement.

In the end, whether you believe the Killian memos or not, whether you believe in Bush's skill as a world leader or not, the record unequivocally proves these truths: President Bush did *not* do his duty, did *not* fulfill his obligations to his country, and he behaved in a manner that would *not* be tolerated for even one moment in today's overworked and battle-weary National Guard. The Guard troops serving now are making sacrifices each and every day that young George W. Bush never could have imagined when he, like so many other well-connected kids during the Vietnam era, was awarded a privileged spot in a thoroughly protected unit.

Worse yet, in the decades since, Bush and his advisers and protectors have equivocated, covered up, built a fire wall around the truth, and lied—at least by omission—to the American people about how he got into the Guard, when and why he left the Texas Air National Guard, and what he was doing when he should have been flying F-102s over the Gulf of Mexico in defense of America.

The tangled tale of Bush's National Guard service is one of those great presidential truths that hides in plain sight, that persists as close to the man as his shadow and is as impossible to shake—like Clinton's weakness for women, Carter's self-righteous streak, Nixon's obsession with secrecy, Reagan's ability to charm his way out of trouble, or Johnson's Texas-sized insecurities. President Bush's penchant for denying that he had any help as he grew up is too powerful for him to fess up to. He had help getting into the Guard, help getting out of the Guard, help getting into baseball, help getting into politics, and help getting out of trouble all of his life. As the Bush presidency moves toward its inevitable end, I believe that more Americans will finally be able to talk about this obvious truth without fear of being attacked by gangs of electronic marauders. It is a pity that a legendary American news organization was torn apart for finally reporting a story many in the country have long believed to be true.

What happened to us after we aired our original National Guard story in September 2004 should never happen to journalists who are simply doing their jobs. There is nothing wrong with raising legitimate questions, looking for answers, and bringing attention to issues of importance to Americans. People in public and political life often try to gloss over the gray areas in their backgrounds, to step away from their actions in the past, and keep everything simple and upbeat. That is human nature.

But it is the job of journalists to look for clues to a politician's character in his or her long-ago actions and ideas. We did that with Bill Clinton and *his* complex and sometimes disingenuous struggles to avoid Vietnam, with Ronald Reagan's propensity for using his movie roles to guide him in real-world situations, with George H. W. Bush in

examining how his World War II experiences were reflected in his in-
clusive approach to international issues.

These are the responsibilities of a free press. Our problem at 60
Minutes was that we tried to do these same jobs in the age of Karl Rove,
the creative force behind Bush's ascension to the presidency, as well as
a whole new style of political firefighting.

Whatever you think of Rove's politics, his ethics, or his personality,
the man's overwhelming will to win demands at least begrudging ad-
miration. Rove is relentless in pursuing his enemies, whom he defines
as anyone not actively working in his favor.

No one in modern politics can match Rove's success. You have to
look back in history to find anyone who comes close. That is what Rove
has done in shaping his political campaigns. He has studied long-ago
battlefield engagements and historical campaigns to pull out forgotten
and ethically questionable techniques that are now old enough to be
reused and made new again. And he has harnessed new technologies
to achieve his ends.

I have been asked repeatedly whether I thought Karl Rove was responsible for my getting the Killian memos—basically, for setting me
up. I do not. I never have believed that, although I have heard that theory over and over again from journalists and from Democrats, particularly in Texas, where Rove's opponents have spent years quaking in their
boots about this über-adviser they see as a real-life political bogeyman.

It's not that I believe Rove isn't capable of that kind of dirty trick. I
just think if he had done it, the resolution of the entire dispute would
have been more unequivocal. He would never have relied upon the
misleading and outright false charges of his political allies being believed and perpetuated by an inattentive press and a distracted public.
If Rove had somehow planted them, we would know with absolute certainty that the documents were not real. There would have been something definitive, something obvious, some final proof that they were
fake. The memos would have contained a wrong address, a bad date, a
mistaken air force manual paragraph or page number, an incorrect reference to a base or an individual's rank. Or someone might even have
come forward to admit that he or she had forged them. There would
have been no room for lingering questions. Instead, the documents included no such giveaway and the overwhelming evidence in any im-

partial appraisal of the Killian memos, based on both content and form, is that they are authentic.

I do believe, however, that Karl Rove was the mastermind of the Republican attack against the story, and I think he was, as always, brilliant. While White House officials scrupulously avoided saying they thought the Killian memos were forged in case they were later proved to be true, Rove's minions attacked every element of the documents in an attempt to knock the story down. They came after us under cover of darkness, swarming us like a computer-age re-creation of Custer's last stand. And it worked, long enough to get through the election, long enough to cost me my reputation, Dan Rather his position, and the entire CBS News division its pride. Once again, the technique was deceptively simple, a technique straight out of the school yard.

It is called "the whopper" and Rove, like a brainy school-yard bully, knows that if you tell a lie loud enough and long enough, no matter how ridiculous or unlikely, you will fool enough people enough of the time to shout down arguments and ward off adversaries. This tried-and-true strategy has worked in propaganda, advertising, and elections.

You've seen those weight-loss ads in magazines that you don't want anyone to catch you reading. Those wild promises that you'll drop a dress size in a day, lose six inches off each thigh in a week, or fit into your bathing suit by bedtime. All you have to do is take a magic pill or munch an herbal supplement, and success will be yours.

Who believes that stuff? Well, as the companies selling it know, the truth is that enough gullible customers believe it, or want to, for these companies to pull in a profit. It certainly worked like a dream in our case, where an unrelenting current of outrageous and unfounded criticisms overwhelmed reason, where a computer parlor trick persuaded many people that they, too, could do their own document analysis, where the big lie about the memos made it around the world while truth was still lacing up its boots.

The lies against our story were so successful that the radical right tried to repeat its whopper technique in another memo case shortly after vanquishing CBS.

In March 2005, as a life-and-death political battle raged around Terri Schiavo's hospice bed, ABC News reported the discovery of a set of Republican "talking points" about the Schiavo case. The memo seemed to be a primer on the political exploitation of a family tragedy, crowing that the Schiavo case presented "an important moral issue and the pro-life base will be excited that the Senate is debating this important issue." The memo declared the Schiavo case "a great political issue because Senator Nelson [a Democrat from Florida] has already refused to become a cosponsor and this is a tough issue for Democrats."

No matter how you viewed the tragedy of Terri Schiavo's abbreviated life and prolonged death, whether you believed she should have been sustained through a feeding tube or allowed to die without one, it was horrifying to see such a cold political calculus made in her heartbreaking case.

Republicans immediately disavowed all knowledge of the memo. And bloggers on the far right, in many cases the same folks who attacked the Killian memos, latched onto a new whopper.

This memo was fake as well, the bloggers argued. What lengths wouldn't the Democrats go to? Was there no stunt too low or too obvious for the liberal media and the amoral minority party to try? The bloggers raised many of the same issues about the Schiavo memo that they raised in the Killian case.

They said the memo looked funny. There was no letterhead. There were misspellings, including Terri Schiavo's name, and an error in listing the Senate bill under consideration, the same kind of small variations that bloggers determined to have hurt the credibility of the Killian memos. The blogs blabbed for a couple of weeks about the suspect memos, until something incredible happened. The Republican aide who wrote them—misspellings, intended political exploitation, and all—was discovered. Brian Darling, a thirty-nine-year-old aide at Florida Republican senator Mel Martinez's office, resigned. Those on the radical right quit talking about it in a heartbeat, never admitting they were wrong, and moved on to the next political fistfight.

For a time, they had once again been on a roll, using the same arguments, the same kind of whopper-swapping, in an attempt to crush another true story.

Truth had an advantage in the Terri Schiavo talking-points story. The memo was a fresh creation, not a thirty-year-old artifact. The man who wrote it was alive, the political climate in which it was written was easy to discern.

One of the difficulties in interpreting the Killian memos and in determining whether they are authentic is in understanding the atmosphere in which they were written. Some newly discovered Texas National Guard memos illuminate that era and the forces of favoritism that were at play. The documents were uncovered by Steve Jones, the respected head of Lyon Research who searched through the archives at the Texas National Guard headquarters at Camp Mabry and at other Guard document stockpiles. He focused on communications to and from the Guard's adjutant general's office and came up with many glittering bits of information that help explain the atmosphere and the antics going on inside the Guard in the early 1970s.

None of the memos here is a smoking gun regarding the president's service, although they make it clear that George W. Bush leaped into the Guard at a time when there were long waiting lists and his testing scores fell far below those of at least some of the other candidates who were rejected. On the other hand, some of the memos, like parts of the official record, can be interpreted in ways that favor Bush. For instance, there are indications here that the F-102 was being phased out.

But taken as a whole, this cache of documents reveals an institution deeply divided by politics and personal infighting, struggling to cope with the Guard's surge in popularity as young men tried to insulate themselves against going to war in Vietnam.

These documents speak to the era when Bush entered the Guard, when many Texans were desperately trying to use any influence they had to move their son or a friend's son a step closer toward a safe spot in the National Guard. For the record, these documents also contain many examples of proportional spacing, right-hand signature blocks, and odd abbreviations, factors the critics of CBS used to charge that the Killian memos were forged.

The documents also reveal the overflowing supply of applicants and refute a key point that Bush backers have long claimed—that Bush was one of the few who wanted to commit to pilot training. In these papers, it is clear that there were other men who wanted to fly for the Guard but weren't able to, even though they met the qualifications. The documents show there were blatant attempts by some politicians and other powerful people to influence Guard leaders into granting special treatment to some young men. Sometimes it worked; sometimes it didn't.

These new letters, memos, and documents reveal the seemingly arbitrary choices made by Texas National Guard leaders in allowing some applicants into their units while telling others they would have to remain on waiting lists, sometimes years long. For example, a letter dated May 1969 from Texas governor Preston Smith regarding a young man who wanted to get into the Guard stated that "the Air National Guard has over 2,000 applications on file." This was written just one year after George W. Bush had been allowed to enter the Guard without any wait at all.

In a letter about the same young man, Gen. Walter "Buck" Staudt wrote that "pilot training quotas are practically nonexistent and a guess would be that it would be from one to two years minimum before this person could be sent to pilot training." That is certainly not the kind of wait that George W. Bush had to endure to join the Guard and qualify for pilot training.

The notion that Bush was a top-notch candidate for pilot training gets bruised a bit in this freshly discovered collection of memos.

According to the official records, George W. Bush scored a 25 on pilot aptitude and a 50 on the navigator's test before he was accepted. His overall score was only 65.

The new documents lay out the story of another young man who was already a civilian pilot in 1970 and was very close in age to Bush. This hopeful applicant reported that he scored an 85 and a 90 on his pilot-qualifying test. Unlike Bush, he was turned down repeatedly for entry into the Guard's pilot-training program and told in no uncertain terms that he could not be put ahead of several others on the waiting list. General Staudt wrote that "pilot training quotas are given to units in numbers of one to two per year." In other words, don't get your hopes up.

A court of civil appeals judge was turned down when he wrote to the head of the Texas Air Guard in December 1970, trying to help his son land a Guard slot. Gen. Ross Ayers, the Guard's adjutant general, responded to the judge that the Texas Guard units "have an extremely long waiting list and they have not been allowed to enlist a single man since July 1, 1970." He said the applicant's age would "make it practically impossible for him to ever be taken" into the Texas Air National Guard. General Ayers explained that the Guard "units are able to fill all vacancies with prior servicemen who have first priority."

The notion of giving those already in the service first priority jibes with one of the Killian memos, dated August 1, 1972. This memo called for Bush to be replaced by "a more seasoned pilot from the list of qualified Vietnam pilots that have rotated."

Something very close to that did happen, according to a Florida woman named Janet Linke, who was interviewed in late September 2004 by Russ Baker for *The Nation* magazine.

Linke said that her husband, Jan Peter Linke, was brought in to replace Bush in 1972. Janet Linke said that Jerry Killian told her at a squadron social gathering that Bush was "mucking up his flying very badly and he couldn't fly the plane."

"Killian told us that he was having trouble landing and that possibly there was a drinking problem involved in that," she continued.

Linke's husband, who died in 1973, was pictured in the Guard unit's yearbook in a group shot taken in December 1972. He had come to Texas from Florida, where he was an experienced air force pilot flying the F-102 for the Florida Air National Guard. His widow said he was hired away by Bush's commanders in Houston because "they were looking for someone they didn't have to spend extra money training."

Other newly revealed Texas Guard documents show accelerated acceptance for a number of young men who appear to be well educated and probably well connected.

One of them was a Yale graduate, like George W. Bush. Others graduated from Texas's moneyed Southern Methodist University and Trinity University in San Antonio. All three, in effect, were sent to the head of the waiting list with the approval of high-ranking Guard officials.

A 1969 letter from Gen. Ross Ayers laid out the requirements for acceptance to officer training in the Guard. "No one has been accepted for officer candidate school until he has had six months' basic training," Ayers wrote.

No one we know of, that is, except George W. Bush, who never went through a six-month basic training program first, but managed to land directly in officer candidate school right out of college.

Some of the letters are darkly humorous, as when the writer begged Guard leaders for special treatment at the same time they pretended to honor the military duty of others in Vietnam. One letter was from a vice president of the Atlanta Braves, who asked that two young ballplayers from Texas be excused from active duty with the Guard until after the baseball season had ended:

> Realizing that it is not the patriotic thing to do to ask that young people be excused from military duty, I still feel the necessity of appealing to you. We here at Atlanta feel that they are two of the brightest prospects we have had in many years. . . . It is my feeling that if they could play a full season of baseball this year, both of them could possibly be playing in the major leagues next year.

The two players were turned down. It seems their short stint of active duty did not destroy their baseball prospects. But neither did they live up to their glowing billing. Both went on to have unremarkable Major League careers that lasted into the mid-1970s.

The documents also lend perspective to another aspect of Bush's military career: his early release from Guard commitments. He and his supporters have said that he was allowed a premature exit to attend school in 1973 because there was no longer a need for him to serve as a pilot—despite the fact that other F-102 pilots were still showing up for duty every day.

Others seeking early discharge were not as lucky. In a 1969 letter to the head of the state Guard, a Texas state legislator requested that a young guardsman be allowed out of Air Guard service two weeks early so he could return to his seasonal work as a crop duster. He was told no, that he was needed in his unit for the final two weeks.

The inflexibility of the Guard regulations, at least on paper, is underscored in another letter written by General Ayers. "Regulations," the letter stated, "do not give the National Guard authority to discharge a person prior to the completion of his military obligations." The letter was written in June 1972, just as George W. Bush was beginning his long unexplained absence from his Guard obligations. In contradiction to what the letter said about the Guard's inability to discharge anyone early, that is precisely what was done for Bush a little more than a year after the letter was written. Like it or not—whether it looked good or not—George W. Bush was allowed to leave the Guard early while others who tried to get out were flatly turned down.

Gen. Buck Staudt, a longtime defender of the president, has always insisted that he used fair-and-square techniques to help George W. Bush get into the Guard. Staudt has downplayed any influence from former lieutenant governor Ben Barnes and has vouched for the president at every opportunity. Staudt has attacked reporters questioning Bush's service with denials issued in a barrage of bathroom language. I have been on the receiving end of his language and anger more than once.

One of the memos that Steve Jones found in Camp Mabry's archives indicated that General Staudt had his own troubles to contend with while in the Texas Air National Guard. The memo referenced an investigation into what is described as a civilian public affairs operation. Reading the memo today, the whole airlift sounds to me like a boondoggle of the first order. "General Staudt countermanded orders issued by higher headquarters concerning the duration of a public affairs airlift of civilians to Nellis Air Force Base in Las Vegas, Nevada, in August 1970," the memo said.

A public affairs airlift of civilians to Las Vegas? Rough duty. Apparently, the trip was originally approved to last two days, but was extended for an additional day by Gen. Ross Ayers, the memo said. The document closed with an enticing and more substantive reference. "There were two additional charges relating to Brigadier General Staudt," it said. "One charge relating to the falsifying of records and one charge related to improper solicitation of funds. Neither of these allegations were [sic] substantiated after a thorough investigation in part by the Federal Bureau of Investigation." One of President Bush's staunchest backers was investigated for falsifying records? Even though Staudt was cleared by the FBI investigation, it was one more confirmation that the Texas Air National Guard in the 1970s seemed to be in a constant state of investigation, denial, accusation, and upheaval.

Former Texas lieutenant governor Ben Barnes told me that he, too, was the focus of an FBI investigation, starting in 1970, into whether or not he had accepted money to get young men into the Guard. Barnes said that President Nixon instigated the investigation as a way of attacking a political enemy, certainly not an outlandish charge, given what we know about the Nixon White House.

The uncertainty created by FBI investigations of whether the Guard engaged in preferential treatment might explain why someone such as Lieutenant Colonel Killian decided to keep notes in his locked desk, write "CYA" memos, and stash papers on some of the men in his unit, especially when there were irregularities in a particular airman's service record. And we know indisputably that there were *many* irregularities in then-lieutenant Bush's service.

Maurice Udell was quoted repeatedly in print and appeared regularly on television to denounce the Killian memos as fakes and praise the president as a pilot whose glowing record was being unfairly questioned by CBS and *60 Minutes*. Countless newspapers, other networks, and the "independent panel" used Udell's opinion to knock down questions raised by the Killian memos.

What those other reporters didn't note was Udell's own problematic exit from the Texas Air National Guard, reported first in the *Columbia Journalism Review* by Corey Pein. "In 1985, after an Air Force investigation into contract fraud, as well as misuse of base resources, Udell was ordered to resign. The initial probe included an allegation of illegal arms shipments to Honduras, but the charge came up dry," Pein wrote.

In 1993, Udell filed a twenty-million-dollar lawsuit against the state adjutant general's office, alleging he was defamed by unjustified allegations of criminal wrongdoing. The suit claimed the investigations were designed to sabotage his military career and were launched by people within the Guard who opposed Udell for personal or political reasons.

I called Udell in early September 2005. He was clearly stunned to hear from me and when I asked whether his suit was settled, he said he would rather not discuss it. Finally, he said it had been settled. Then, in a quivering voice, he practically shouted into the phone, "I don't want to talk to you any more . . . I prefer not to talk to you, especially you." He hung up.

Oh yes, Dean Roome also sued the Texas National Guard, saying he was retaliated against and removed from his Ellington Air Field post for pointing out "fraudulent practices involving professional military examinations." It is unclear whether his suit is ongoing.

The festival of lawsuits and countersuits, the charges and countercharges, and the incessant infighting that swirled through the Texas National Guard illustrate that this was no ordinary military organization. This was a hyperpolitical, highly agitated, and extremely active group of reservists who have been defending each other, defaming each other, and keeping the courts busy for years.

More important, these men, along with others, formed what Corey

Pein rightly called a "feedback loop," a circle of people who would vouch for the president, put reporters in touch with other people who would vouch for him, and continue "promoting a version of events in which Bush's service is unquestionable, even exemplary. With such big names and old grudges in play, journalists are obliged to keep digging." But almost without exception, journalists didn't.

Like the panel, reporters lazily took at face value the word of men like Dean Roome and Maury Udell, and they treated anyone who didn't entirely accept Roome and Udell's version of events—meaning those of us at 60 Minutes—as though we were the ones who had it wrong.

Another memo that Steve Jones found was written by Polly Coffin, a secretary who worked for Gen. James Rose, the head of the Texas Air National Guard until he was ousted in a politically inspired shakeup in 1971.

Coffin wrote a scathing letter to Gen. Ross Ayers, the adjutant general, protesting what she saw as the unfair ouster of her boss, General Rose, and describing the atmosphere in the Texas National Guard as a political jungle. She quit rather than stay on in what she saw as a poisonously political organization. She wrote:

> With the knowledge that I have of the petty and personal politics that have been brought into the National Guard, which is too important and vital a force to be wrecked to this degree by politics, I cannot remain in the employ of this Department after he has been relieved in such a manner. There have been too many personal rather than professional hatchet jobs, both in the Department and in the field. It is virtually impossible at times for a person to do his job without fear of losing his job. Unnecessary jobs have been created at the expense of necessary functions and people. . . . It is a sad situation when even secretaries and clerks work in constant fear of losing their jobs for no rhyme or reason that they can see.

The Texas National Guard was not, as President Bush and his supporters insist, a crack military unit where politics and personal connections held no sway. Far from it.

Steve Jones also found letters from George W. Bush's father recommending someone for a post within the Guard and another, almost prescient letter that appears to have been written on behalf of a constituent.

In that letter from August 1970, less than a year after his son began flying at Ellington Air Force Base in Houston, then-congressman Bush asked General Ayers how a Guardsman could transfer from one unit to another. The irony of the exchange was that just twenty-one months later, Congressman Bush's own son would make use of that same advice.

The dearth of material available in the Texas Air Guard archives has long been the bane of reporters looking for insight into how Bush got into the Guard, how he performed, and how he was able to walk away without fulfilling his entire enlistment.

Bill Burkett has long maintained that he witnessed the "scrubbing" of then-governor Bush's personal Guard file in 1997. It has been hard to find confirmation of Burkett's story, in part because of the withering criticism he faced after going public. Burkett has always claimed that the scrubbing was done by a handful of workers at Camp Mabry under the direction of the Guard commander. As I continued to investigate the Bush-Guard story after leaving CBS, a Camp Mabry employee offered the first confirmation of document shredding there in 1997. This employee, who claimed to be a Bush voter, confirmed what may be part of Burkett's story—a document destruction so massive that it took several days to accomplish. The Camp Mabry worker didn't want to be identified because of possible retribution.

This employee was assigned to shred documents when the Texas National Guard was shifting from one commander to another. This person said the shredding was not that unusual, that a commander reasonably might want to destroy evidence that could be used against him or his friends later. The employee said the shredding and sorting took place in Camp Mabry's Building 8 on the second floor.

The destruction was so widespread that the worker said at one point there were three large trash bins stacked high with a mixture of air force and army Guard records that were to be shredded.

This person also recounted overhearing a conversation around the same time among Burkett and two other officers at Camp Mabry. "Bush didn't take a drug test," the worker remembered one of the officers saying in front of Burkett. "He was a no-show."

Erik Rigler, the private investigator hired by CBS News to look into the story after the journalists were pulled off of it, spent a great deal of time interviewing people in and around Camp Mabry.

"It was well known for years at Camp Mabry about Bush, his failure to serve in the Texas Air National Guard. It was so very, very common." Rigler said in a taped phone conversation with Mike Smith in late 2004. "Those people looked at him as a draft dodger. They didn't really hold him in high regard, with any high regard at all. But what I am trying to say is that the story, and I've talked to people at Camp Mabry, had floated around for years and for that reason it makes me think it likely true." Rumors about President Bush and his shortened National Guard service had also been part of the Texas political scene for years.

If people who knew negative details about Bush were reluctant to come forward before my story aired, they all but had their mouths sewn shut afterward. Anyone associated with our story joined a kind of journalistic undead, becoming walking reminders of what could happen when you tangled with the Bush administration on the subject of W.'s military services.

I had been fired, along with three others at CBS, and legendary reporter Dan Rather had lost his longtime anchor position at *CBS Evening News*. Months after the dust settled, researcher Mike Smith's name was still being bandied about on Rush Limbaugh's radio show. Limbaugh accused Mike of a range of nefarious acts, including attempting to help the hapless John Kerry campaign as well as uncovering the explosive "Downing Street memos" in London, which characterized the United States as dead set on war with Iraq, despite the lack of evidence that Iraq had weapons of mass destruction.

The discovery of the Downing Street memos was actually the work of Michael Smith, a British newspaper reporter, but then Limbaugh specializes in rushing to conclusions and has never been big on facts, at least in my experience.

Our original source for the Killian documents, Bill Burkett, has remained a favorite punching bag for the right. His participation in our story has led to vicious personal and political payback. Burkett was questioned within his ranching community, threatened at home, burned in effigy in a nearby town.

It seems terrible treatment for a man who spent more than twenty-eight years in uniform, far more than many of his critics put in serving their country.

For the record, I believe Burkett did nothing more than hand off documents he had been handed. I don't believe for an instant that he forged them or had anything to do with anyone who did. But then I don't believe they are forged. And neither do a number of other experts who have conscientiously looked at them and taken the time to come to careful conclusions.

One of those experts is David Hailey, a Ph.D. who teaches technical writing at Utah State University. One of his vocations is document examination and, while he is not a professional analyst, the former army illustrator and full-time computer whiz has come up with a number of innovative ways to look at typeface and font and determine their origins. Hailey brings extensive experience in both typewriters and computer graphics to his work.

At the beginning of the CBS memo debacle, Hailey saw the criticism of the Killian documents and was intrigued enough to take a look on his own. When he came across a number of elements that challenged the idea that the memos were forged, Hailey began working up a formal research paper on his techniques and findings. He posted his paper on the university's Web site, including the possibility that the documents had been typed, not created on a word processor. In the spirit of intellectual endeavor, he thought others might find his work interesting.

Poor Professor Hailey misjudged the ferocity and venom that the far right brings to any discussion. This had nothing to do with the free exchange of ideas, a supposed founding principle of bloggers who perpetuate the grand hoax that theirs is a democratic, self-correcting enterprise. Professor Hailey found out the hard way that this was war.

When a draft of his paper was posted on a conservative Web site called Wizbang, Hailey and his university were inundated with angry e-mails, accusing him of being a "liar, a fraud, and a charlatan." Screaming bloggers called the school, demanding Hailey's resignation. His in-box was filled with political hate mail. Bloggers wrote Hailey and his school. The examples remind me of what they said about me. "Way to go, moron. Nice forgery." "Situational ethics, relative moralism, the means justify the ends. Good little leftist, good boy, sit, heel, f— off!" "Professor, I also had an interesting phone call with the head of your department. You might give him a call."

For a professor unaccustomed to political trash talk and naked slander, the blog mob and its name-calling and irrational demands were personally devastating. After less than a week of the attacks, Hailey literally cried with relief when university officials expressed their support for him and his right to do research. Hailey continued to work on his paper and draw fire from the right. By December 2004, the unrelenting criticism had taken a heavy toll on him.

On December 14, he drank too much, went online, and went after his critics on their own Web sites. By the following evening, Hailey had posted a public apology online. "At some point, I felt the need to try to explain to your community what I think I am doing and what I think is wrong with our communication," he wrote.

"My behavior was inexcusable. My only excuse is I had (am still having) a complete emotional breakdown. I am still not in control of my emotions." Near the end of his letter, he added, "I still stand by my report, however, and my approach to writing it." Some would view Hailey's actions as unusual or indicative of a certain psychological fragility. Having gone through some of what Professor Hailey did, I wouldn't be so harsh. Being targeted by an all-out multimedia attack, including a public dissection by a cruel chorus of anonymous bloggers and undiscerning reporters and editors, is painful, dehumanizing, and hurtful. It is enough to make anyone think about having a few drinks and lashing back at those who have attacked you.

David Hailey kept at his analysis of the Killian memos. After the panel's report, Hailey examined copies of the documents that had not been faxed, something no analyst other than Marcel Matley had seen. Everyone else looked at documents that had been faxed at least once or twice. Those who tried to examine the documents that were posted online did so without the crucial benefit of microscopic details contained only in the pre-faxed versions.

Professor Hailey's scrupulous study obliterated the arguments that were so quickly manufactured by critics who shouted that the documents were faked. His new report concluded indisputably that the documents we used in our story were produced on a typewriter, debunking the right wing's computer-generated parlor trick that the memos were dashed off in a common Microsoft font style, a central claim of the forgery/conspiracy camp.

"I can, with certainty, state that the memos were not produced in Times New Roman. Furthermore, I believe this document will demonstrate the documents were typed," Hailey wrote after spending weeks enlarging and examining the *unfaxed* memos.

Hailey said he saw clear signs in the memos of the "character wear and damage" that a typewriter produces, something that would be impossible to fake in a digital creation of a document. "Differences in wear in key characters occur in a manner consistent with the memos having been produced at different times," he wrote.

Hailey also said that the memos' headings were not centered or aligned as critics had wrongly claimed in arguing that the documents were created on a computer. And he said he saw indications that the vertical spacing included "fractions of carriage returns" and that digital software does not do partial carriage returns.

Hailey's report is filled with comparisons of one letter to another, which he did after blowing up images to what he called "the size of sofa cushions." That is something most of us cannot do at home, and is certainly something none of the bloggers were able to do before spewing their hasty conclusions across the Internet. He also found that some of the characters overlapped in ways that clearly showed they interacted with one another—literally pushing against each other on the paper at a microscopic level. That's possible only in a typed document.

What Hailey's report did not and could not say is that the typography itself contains conclusive evidence that the memos are authentic. Hailey's work is not a substitute for the kind of ink test that could definitely demonstrate an original document's authenticity. There are limits to what research can do with photocopied documents and Hailey was clear about those limits.

Professor Hailey concluded that the documents represented important evidence that should have been presented to the American public and that CBS, when strongly criticized, reacted poorly:

> CBS did exactly the opposite of what it should have done. It should have carefully continued its narrative to its conclusion.

Suppose the memos are not authentic (and I have never said they were authentic). That is a conversation worth following to its end. Instead, I am convinced that when it failed to follow the evidence to its conclusion, CBS advanced the agenda of extremists who would stop all discourse on whatever topics that displease them.

Amen.

Those of us who worked on the Bush-Guard story knew that we had corroborated information that we had a duty to report. Nothing has changed our conviction. The only thing we wanted to do was tell the American people about what seems, more than ever, the clear evidence in some newly found documents.

I believed then and I believe now that we were advancing a long-running story and contributing to an honest, open discussion of the president's military service. It was a chance to shed light on an important chapter that too many people have been too intimidated to talk about for too long.

I have never come across a story that has so many people so scared for such good reasons. The Clintons used to lament the politics of personal destruction. To me, all that looks like the good old days. The fear this story creates has never been more clear than when I called Gen. Bobby Hodges this past September. This time I recorded the call, not trusting what he said to my notes, as I had done before. General Hodges remembered me and we chatted about our disagreement over what had been said. His voice was nervous. I could hear his wife in the background, urging him to hang up. Hodges told me, "You questioned me for thirty minutes . . . that night and I probably said some things that I shouldn't have said. . . . You tried to pin me down and change my wording when I talked about it and so forth."

I interrupted. "You said he [Killian] was a hardnose, an overboard hardnose."

Hodges parsed his words carefully. "I said hardnose, I didn't say overboard. I said he was a little hard-nosed when it came to some things."

Again, I read to him from my notes. "You said Jerry was miffed."

"I may have said miffed. I didn't say he was angry," General Hodges countered.

It was an absurd conversation, but it once again made me feel confident that I was right about what he had said so long ago. My notes were right. They were just taken when I was talking to a man who didn't know that his opinion would matter, didn't know that it would be made public, didn't know that it would put him in a position to be criticized by the president's overly aggressive defenders.

General Hodges's wife picked up the extension and begged him to hang up. "Mary, get off the phone. Leave us alone. Please. Please."

I felt badly for everyone who had been hurt by this story, by all the discomfort it had caused and all the denials and all the rage that have been directed at so many people because of the remaining questions about the president's long-ago service in National Guard.

We are living in an age of anger and instant communication, where political blood-feuds lead to personal attacks on both journalists and just plain folks for bringing up unpopular subjects. The past year has been humbling for me. If I ever thought I knew it all, that feeling is long gone. I know I used to feel lucky. Now I feel lucky to have survived.

I am older and wiser and I have a wish list for everyone who has participated in my latest round of life's education. I wish for all the bullying radical bloggers—the anonymous people who sit in the dark and mindlessly attack the mainstream media—a chance to live in a country without a free press. It couldn't happen to a nicer group of people.

I wish for the mainstream media a chance to get off the defensive, get off each other's back, and get on with the business of provocative reporting. I wish for them a chance to love their jobs again and a chance to win back the high regard of the public they serve.

I wish for Karl Rove to have the opportunity to someday be on the business end of his bruising and unfair techniques.

I wish for President Bush a chance to make peace with whatever it is he has worked so hard to cover up about his on-again, off-again aborted service in the Texas Air National Guard.

And I wish for the people of this country a chance to believe again in the press and its duty to ask questions on their behalf, to believe that reporters care about real-life Americans, to believe that knowledge is power, to believe that the truth really can set us free.

AFTERWORD

I felt nervous about being with my friends from CBS again. It had been months since I'd seen Dan in person, even longer since I'd seen Betsy West. I hadn't been with Jeff Fager or Patti Hassler in aeons. But they had encouraged me in a flurry of phone calls to come to New York in May 2005 to attend the Peabody Awards and be there when *60 Minutes II* was recognized for its hard work on the Abu Ghraib story. It was a prestigious occasion and despite my banishment over the Bush-Guard story, Jeff had graciously insisted that CBS fly me back to New York, buy my ticket to the ceremony, and find me a place to stay in the crowded city.

Mark and Robert went to New York with me, in part because of my nerves. It had been years since I had felt this shy. I dressed carefully and self-consciously that day. What would my friends think? Did I look older than before? Sadder? Wiser?

Robert stayed in our hotel room with an attractive young babysitter—a dream come true for him—while we went to the ceremony. While Robert was playing happily and showing off, I was still working on my attitude. Mark, as always, was a rock, telling me, "You're going to have fun. You deserve this. Relax. Let's go."

When we got to the hotel where the ceremony was being held, I looked around for anyone I knew and drew a blank. Dana couldn't be there for the worst kind of reason. Her father had died suddenly a few days before and she was in Michigan with her mother.

Finally, jumbled in the crowd, I saw Betsy. We hugged and laughed and it *almost* felt like old times. I saw Mary Alfieri, the bright and talented editor who had worked so hard putting our stories together. She told me that everyone at *60 Minutes II* was facing my fate—unemployment—in a few days. The broadcast was awaiting word on whether it would be cancelled for the following season.

Mark and I sat at a table with Dan and his wonderful wife, Jean. Once again, Dan's support, public and private, meant the world to me. As we waited to be called to the front, my heart galloped at the possibility that I might be booed, that my presence might embarrass Dan, that my pride at winning broadcasting's most coveted award could backfire in an awful public moment.

When our award was announced, Dan, Mary Alfieri, and I made the long walk to the stage. I desperately wished Dana had been there with us. I listened for boos, but heard nothing but applause and felt the beginnings of something else from the crowd. It was something like sympathy, something like empathy, something like a growing sense that people were beginning to understand the unfairness of what had happened at CBS and to realize that it could happen to them, too.

Dan acknowledged the hard work so many of us had done on the Abu Ghraib story, singling out me, Mary, Dana, Betsy, Jeff, and Patti for special mentions. "They did most of the work, bore the heaviest burdens, and took most of the criticism," he said.

I knew Dan was proud of all of us. He told the crowd, "It took guts and they had them."

From the stage, Dan shared some of his deepest beliefs about news and the bravery it often takes to do the very best stories.

He told the audience what he has always told the people lucky enough to work with him. "Never give up, never back up, never give in, while pursuing the dream of integrity-filled journalism that matters."

The crowd was warm, the applause the most sustained at the event. For the people in the audience who worked at *60 Minutes II*, or the people who had started the broadcast, this Peabody ceremony was a last hurrah. None of us knew it then, but Les Moonves and Andrew Heyward had already quietly decided to cancel the show and lay off many of its fine employees.

Within two weeks of picking up our Peabody, two *60 Minutes* senior producers were moving through the eighth and ninth floors of the CBS building on West Fifty-seventh like reluctant angels of death. Passing a doorway here, knocking on another there, they had the sad task of telling the people behind those doors—the producers, associate producers, and assistants—that their jobs had ended. CBS News had decided it no longer needed their services.

This journalistic Passover at 60 Minutes had been anticipated for days, ever since CBS News president Andrew Heyward had made a rare appearance at the 60 Minutes office to announce that the Wednesday show would be cancelled after seven seasons. Workers there knew it was a matter of time until people started hearing what plans, if any, the company had for them.

They waited and worried and, finally, word came that everyone would find out his or her fate that day before five o'clock.

A handful of my former colleagues would be relocated upstairs to the 60 Minutes Sunday show, the flagship broadcast. But those lucky few spent the hours nervously waiting for someone to show up at their door as well. At least fifty people were given the worst news. They were let go, cut loose, told to clean out their offices. Amid hugs and offerings of sympathy, those who didn't make the cut were left to hope for the best.

As the day dragged on, employees would hear a knock on the office next door and know what was happening. Another friend, another colleague was having his or her career unceremoniously ended, a victim of Viacom's decision that 60 Minutes Wednesday's ratings weren't high enough, its demographics weren't low enough—and so the corporate bureaucrats had determined it was time for the stopwatch to stop ticking.

Those who hadn't yet been told one way or another sat alone and scared in their small offices, left to hope they weren't next or that if they were fired, they could get through the summer—come up with college tuition, or scrape together enough money to extend their health insurance.

Sometimes there were tears, sometimes anger, always regret. The halls were dotted with people embracing, eyes reddened. Employees moved quietly through the building, shell-shocked and sullen.

For many who'd spent more than a quarter century at CBS News, there was a Depression-era fear about what would happen next. One friend told me, "I know what people will see when they look at me, an old fat guy with gray hair." He feared prospective employers would never be able to see the hard-charger within him, the man who would race out of the building as eager as any kid to get on a plane, chase down a story, and wrestle it onto the air, the grown-up whose long career gave context to his current work, making it better, smarter, braver.

Many of the people let go had all but walked through walls for CBS News. They had braved war zones, battled deadlines, marched through prisons to choruses of catcalls, and worked through the night again and again for the company they loved, doing work they believed was so important that it was worth the personal risk, the time away from home, the professional setbacks.

They had grown up and grown older still believing. Now, like me, they were paying dearly for their naïveté.

I heard about the layoffs in agonized phone calls as I sat alone halfway across the country. I felt like a refugee whose home village was being bulldozed. Just because I was no longer there didn't mean I didn't hurt for my close friends or that my heart didn't ache for my former colleagues. I knew how they felt.

I had spent fifteen years at CBS News, simplistically believing that CBS was the company I worked for. I found out that when the sledding got tough in September 2004, I didn't work for CBS at all. I worked for Viacom. And Viacom did not have the loyalty or the love of journalism that had permeated the old CBS.

Now the other people on the broadcast were making the same painful discovery.

It must have been particularly tough on Patti Hassler, now the senior producer of the 60 Minutes Sunday broadcast, who had the nightmarish job of telling many of the layoff victims that it was over. She and Jeff Fager had hired many of those people when the 60 Minutes Wednesday broadcast was created in 1998.

Through the years, Patti had served as the broadcast's chain-smoking den mother, a woman willing to slap, kiss, or kick in the rear end every one of her producers and correspondents in a drive to get the best stories told in the best way possible. I loved working with her.

Now she literally had to take her team apart, telling many of the people she had fought with and fought for that it was finished. When I heard that Patti spent the day crying at least as hard as the people she had to let go, I wholeheartedly believed it.

But the bottom line in network news today is that none of this matters. People don't matter. The public's right to know doesn't matter and, God knows, the news doesn't matter. What matters most—first, last, and always—is money.

The day after the mass firings at 60 *Minutes Wednesday*, Viacom held a triumphant annual investor meeting, where chairman Sumner Redstone crowed over his company's strong financial performance. Even though Viacom's stock price went down about 18 percent that year, the company leaders had been given massive paydays. Redstone saw his paycheck surge to fifty-six million dollars for 2004. Les Moonves and Tom Freston, chief operating officers, each pocketed a whopping fifty-two million for the year.

Just a few years ago, this kind of corporate executive largesse was unheard of. Now, these media Masters of the Universe have taken over the public airwaves and they have one obligation: making a profit.

When I came to CBS News in 1989, long after what old-timers considered the halcyon days of network news, it was already seen as one of the last bastions of hard-hitting commercial broadcast journalism, a safe place where 60 *Minutes* and the network's proud history ensured that good reporting would endure.

It was never a perfect place, something I learned on my very first day when I stood in the fishbowl in New York, where the *CBS Evening News* was prepared.

I had quietly watched the *Evening News* producers lay out that night's broadcast and juggle stories for most of the day when I heard someone mention, "Hewitt's going to stop by." My heart began to pound.

My God, for a young producer, this was like getting a visit from the Pope. I couldn't believe my good fortune, that Don Hewitt, 60 *Minutes* creator and television icon, was about to breathe the same air I was breathing.

I was taken aback when a tiny man in a loud plaid coat leapt into the room looking like a vaudevillian refugee and proceeded to tell a series of what he called "tit" jokes. Roaring with laughter, Hewitt went on and on. By the time he was finished, I could feel that my face was bright red. I was mortified not just about the jokes, but about my dashed beliefs that I had gone to work in some kind of journalistic temple.

Over the years, however, I learned that people like Hewitt, and the other aggressively politically incorrect big mouths and bad dressers, did worship some of the same principles I did. Nothing mattered like the story. Nothing mattered as much as getting it out. Nothing mattered as much as making news. All of us loved our jobs and loved journalism.

One friend laid off last spring told me, "That's all over. We're in the dying throes of it now. It's all over at CBS."

Money is the master. That is the bottom line to what happened at CBS that fateful fall when we aired a story that, like all stories, was imperfect, but was absolutely grounded in fact. It was well researched and well documented. But when Viacom saw that the story was not well received and that a conservative firestorm was threatening the corporation's financial well-being, their collective wallets started itching. As a result, I believe CBS News, 60 Minutes, Dan Rather, and journalism itself got badly scratched.

I am praying we can all recover, not just for ourselves, and not just for our country, but for people like the Spanish writer/director who spoke to the crowd at the Peabody Awards, begging us to do our jobs.

Carlos Bosch had won a Peabody for a documentary and, in his acceptance speech, offered the audience both great humility and great commitment. He struggled with his English and with how to communicate something he clearly thought was terribly important. Speaking to the American journalists gathered there, he delivered this message: Please don't stop reporting. Please do your jobs. We need you and we're counting on you. Don't give up even when it is hard and people don't want you to tell the truth, because what you report here in America makes a difference everywhere. What you report can change the world.

I won't give up. I promise.

APPENDIX 1:
A KILLIAN MEMO

A fundamental problem with the claim that the Killian memos were not authentic was that the critics never saw the best copies of the documents. The reproductions of the memos examined online by bloggers and "experts" around the country had been faxed—sometimes more than once—as well as photocopied, scanned, and downloaded. Each process has the potential to change the proportions of the printed material, the details of the font style, and the clarity of the image. Faxing, in particular, can radically alter a document's appearance.

The following two versions of the same document have undergone more changes to fit into this book, but make the point. The copy on the left has not been faxed. The one on the right has. As a result, they almost appear to be different documents.

Please don't make the mistake of trying to examine these images to draw conclusions about the document's authenticity. Document examiners doing formal analyses work with the physical document, not an electronic image and certainly not something reprinted in a book.

For more documents and primary material, go to www.truthand duty.com.

111th Fighter Interceptor Squadron
P. O. Box 34567
Houston, Texas 77034

01 August 1972

MEMORANDUM FOR RECORD

SUBJECT: Bush, George W. 1st Lt.3244754FG
Suspension of Flight status

1. On this date I ordered that 1st Lt. Bush be suspended from flight status due to failure to perform to USAF/TexANG standards and failure to meet annual physical examination (flight) as ordered.

2. I conveyed my verbal orders to commander, 147 th Ftr Intrcp Gp with request for orders for suspension and convening of a flight review board IAW AFM 35-13.

3. I recommended transfer of this officer to the 9921 st Air Reserve Squadron in May and forwarded his AF Form 1288 to 147 th Ftr Intrcp Gp headquarters. The transfer was not allowed. Officer has made no attempt to meet his training certification or flight physical. Officer expresses desire to transfer out of state including assignment to non-flying billets.

4. On recommendation of Harris, I also suggested that we fill this critical billet with a more seasoned pilot from the list of qualified Vietnam pilots that have rotated. Recommendations were received but not confirmed.

JERRY B. KILLIAN
Lt. Colonel

111th Fighter Interceptor Squadron
P.O. Box 34567
Houston, Texas 77034

01 August 1972

MEMORANDUM FOR RECORD

SUBJECT: Bush, George W. 1st Lt. 3244754FG
Suspension of Flight status

1. On this date I ordered that 1st Lt. Bush be suspended from flight status due to failure to perform to USAF/TexANG standards and failure to meet annual physical examination (flight) as ordered.

2. I conveyed my verbal orders to commander, 147th Ftr.Intrcp Gp with request for orders for suspension and convening of a flight review board IAW AFM 35-13.

3. I recommended transfer of this officer to the 9921st Air Reserve Squadron in May and forwarded his AF Form 1288 to 147th Ftr Intrcp Gp headquarters. The transfer was not allowed. Officer has made no attempt to meet his training certification or flight physical. Officer expresses desire to transfer out of state including assignment to non-flying billets.

4. On recommendation of Harris, I also suggested that we fill this critical billet with a more seasoned pilot from the list of qualified Vietnam pilots that have rotated. Recommendations were received but not confirmed.

JERRY B. KILLIAN
Lt. Colonel

APPENDIX 2:
MESHING DOCUMENT

This is an explanation of the techniques I used to compare the Killian memos to the official Bush records that had been made public over the years. Before we aired our story on September 8, 2004, I had essentially tried to marry the Killian documents with the official record. I was looking for anything that didn't fit: dates, names, references to rank, and a variety of other factors. I was looking for a stopper, a place where the Killian memos clashed with the official record, something that would indicate to me that the new memos weren't real.

I couldn't find it. I wanted the panel to know that far from simply taking documents and rushing them onto the air, we had done a complicated and multifaceted check on how these new documents fit with the ones we knew to be real, and used that comparison in making a judgment that the story was ready to air.

The documents referred to in the meshing document are available at www.truthandduty.com.

Dear Governor Thornburgh and Mr. Boccardi,

During our discussions, I presented a compilation labeled TAB 57 and explained why the information revealed by meshing the Killian memos with the official Guard documents was so important in establishing the reliability of the documents.

This element is so crucial that I offer herein this written guide to TAB 57.

The Killian memos, when married to the official documents, fit like a glove. There is not a date, or a name, or an action out of place. Nor does the content of the Killian memos differ in any way from the information that has come out after our story, and most of which is from the Associated Press and its lawsuit filed to force production of long-missing documents.

Add to that equation the confirmation of content stated by Gen. Bobby Hodges and Marian Carr Knox, and the result is a compelling case that the documents are real.

In order to conclude that the documents are forged or utterly unreliable, two questions must be answered: 1) how could anyone have forged such pristinely accurate information; and 2) why would anyone have taken such great pains to *forge the truth*?

CBS 001195   2 February 1972   KILLIAN TO HARRIS

This memo is addressed to Maj. William Harris, Killian's second in command, and the man responsible for writing the Officer Efficiency Training Reports (OETRs) for pilots in the unit.

The memo asks Harris to "Update me as soon as possible on flight certifications. Specifically—Bath and Bush."

When we aired this story, we knew something that had not yet been reported: that in February 1972, Lieutenant Bush had started having trouble landing his F-102. In fact, Lieutenant Bush had been bumped back to the T-33, a training plane. Then he was bumped back to the copilot position on the T-33. Then he began logging additional time in the flight simulator. This was a huge change from his previous flight logs and training pattern in 1970–1971.

The February date on this memo, coupled with what we knew about the February flight difficulties Lieutenant Bush was having, underscored the likelihood that the content of this memo was authentic.

This memo was given to Mike Smith by Bill Burkett on Sunday, September 5. I did not air this document, primarily because I felt it required too much explanation and it also raised the name of James Bath, a controversial and politically volatile figure in Bush's background.

USA Today got this same document from Burkett and chose to run it in their story on September 9.

CBS 001856–001857   ASSOCIATED PRESS REPORT ON SEPTEMBER 10, 2004

This is a copy of an Associated Press analysis of then-lieutenant Bush's downward spiral in flight performance, beginning in February 1972. There was no sharing between AP and CBS of the facts complied in this report or in our story that aired on September 8, 2004.

CBS 001196   4 May 1972   ORDER TO TAKE PHYSICAL BY MAY 1972

This is a Killian memo given to Mike Smith by Bill Burkett on Sunday, September 5.

Dated May 4, 1972, the document is a direct order for Lieutenant Bush to report for a physical on May 14. That date is very close to the May dates when his two previous annual flight physicals were completed in 1970 and 1971.

The address used for Bush is his parents' home, the official address used for much of his military documentation. The address of the 111th Fighter Interceptor Squadron is correct. The Air Force Manual regulation referred to as AFM 35-13 is the appropriate regulation for this order, according to the Air Force Manual in use in 1972.

Document and handwriting analyst Marcel Matley felt very strongly that this signature was a classic Killian signature, where the lieutenant colonel had a habit of turning the tail of the "y" at the end of Jerry to the top of the "K" on Killian.

The content of this document is also supported by Gen. Bobby Hodges and later, by Marian Carr Knox. Both said that Colonel Killian fully embraced the requirement of an annual flight physical and Ms. Knox said she remembered Colonel Killian issuing this order.

The Hodges and Knox confirmations coalesce in a most compelling fashion. In the case of Hodges, his emphatic assurance that Colonel

Killian's feelings are accurately reflected in the content of the memorandum was expressed telephonically, without the distraction, if you will, of any document. He simply states, without equivocation, that Killian ordered Lieutenant Bush to take his annual physical. Ms. Knox, not withstanding her focus on the typed documents, likewise assures that Killian ordered Lieutenant Bush to take his flight physical. In each instance, the content of their recollections dovetails with the document.

CBS 00119   19 May 1972   MEMO TO FILE

This is a Killian memo given to Mike Smith by Bill Burkett on Sunday, September 5.

This purports to be a Memo to File, so the fact the format is not official is not surprising. Ms. Knox confirmed that Colonel Killian had a separate personal file locked in this top drawer where he kept notes like this to himself.

This document is dated May 19, 1972.

The subject: Discussion with First Lieutenant Bush.

This would have been written five days after Lieutenant Bush had missed the physical he was ordered to take on May 14.

The memo says that Killian and Bush "discussed options of how Bush can get out of coming to drill from now through November." Killian suggests three months of equivalent training (ET), which was the maximum allowed in the Guard at that time, or a transfer to another unit. The rest of the first paragraph fits with what is known about Lieutenant Bush's desire to go to Alabama to work on the Blount campaign.

The second paragraph references talking about "getting his flight physical situation fixed before his date." This is completely in line with what we know about Texas Air Guard pilot procedure, wherein a pilot must have his flight physical completed before his birthday. In Lieutenant Bush's case, that would be July 6.

Later in the memo, Killian "advised him of our investment in him and his commitment." That advice has not been memorialized in any other Bush-related documents, but it is something that every pilot I have spoken to has told me is part of a commander's duty when faced with a pilot who was not performing or was underperforming: to remind the individual of the heavy financial investment that the U.S. military has made in him. The memo also says that Killian reminded him of his "commitment" . . . the amount of time Lieutenant Bush promised to fly for the USAF/Texas Air National Guard. It is mandatory for a commander to state this to a pilot who is in a situation of this sort, according to countless other officers I have spoken with.

Killian mentions that "I told him I had to have written acceptance before he would be transferred."

The last line of the memo indicates that Killian "think[s] he's also talking to someone upstairs." The next official document we have in TAB 57 speaks to this.

CBS001297   26 May 1972   ACCEPTANCE OF APPLICATION FOR ASSIGNMENT

This *official* document, which I believe I received in a FOIA in 1999, shows that *just one week* after Killian asked for "written acceptance," Lieutenant Bush appears to have gotten it. Anyone familiar with the molasses-like movement of paper in the military will tell you that this is an extraordinarily swift action on the part of the Alabama unit led by Reese Bricken. The 9921 Air Reserve Squadron was a postal unit, not a ready reserve unit.

CBS 002071   2 June and 5 June 1972   SENIOR OFFICER APPROVALS OF ASSIGNMENT

This is an *official* document that I received through a FOIA in either 1999 or 2000.

It basically marks the approval of two senior officers, one in Austin and another in Houston, for Lieutenant Bush to go to the 9921 Air Reserve Squadron and it is dated the second and fifth of June.

By this time, Lieutenant Bush had already cleared the 111th Fighter Interceptor Squadron base and was no longer performing his duties there.

CBS 002070   31 July 1972   REJECTION OF ASSIGNMENT

This is an *official* document obtained through a 1999 FOIA request.

Marked July 31, it is the Air Force's official response to Lieutenant Bush's planned move to the 9921. The Air Force turns down the request, saying that "a review of his Master Personnel Record shows he has a Military Service Obligation until 26 May 1974." It goes on to say that "an obligated Reservist can be assigned to a specific Ready Reserve position only. Therefore, he is ineligible for assignment to an Air Reserve Squadron."

So, Lieutenant Bush's transfer was turned down . . . even though he had already been gone from his unit since April or May. He had not had his physical by his birthday of July 6 and was no longer on flight status or assigned to any unit.

CBS 001192   1 August 1972   MEMORANDUM FOR RECORD

This is a Killian memo I received from Bill Burkett on Thursday, September 2.

It is dated August 1, 1972 . . . just one day after the previous official document (CBS 002070) turning down Bush's transfer to Alabama.

This Memorandum For Record includes Lieutenant Bush's correct service number, something that is regularly redacted on many official documents . . . another point that serves to underscore the reliability of the document.

The memo says that "On this date I ordered that Lt. Bush be suspended from flight status due to failure to perform to USAF/TexANG standards and failure to meet annual physical examination (flight) as ordered." The reference to "as ordered" is consistent with the order we saw earlier in Killian memo CBS 001196. So there is consistency within the Killian memos themselves.

In paragraph 2, Killian calls for a flight review board, a very important *USAF requirement* in the grounding of any pilot under any circumstances. This call for a review board has never been referenced in any other official document in President Bush's records.

In paragraph 3, Killian says that he "recommended transfer of this officer to the 9921st Air Reserve Squadron in May and forwarded his AF Form 1288 to 147th Ftr Intercp Gp headquarters. The transfer was not allowed."

Bush's attempted and aborted transfer to the 9921 has not been a highlighted or discussed or generally reported part of the president's service story. The fact that it is mentioned here is another small but key point that shows that these documents are based in fact, sometimes even obscure fact.

In his last paragraph, Killian "suggested that we fill this critical billet with a more seasoned pilot from the list of qualified Vietnam pilots that have rotated."

After our story aired, a woman named Janet Linke came forward to say that her husband, an F-102 pilot who had rotated out of active duty in Europe and joined an Air National Group in Florida, where he was recruited to take Bush's place in the 111th Fighter Interceptor Squadron, and that Killian told her that "Lieutenant Bush just had not wanted to fly anymore." That account was published in a number of newspapers, including *The Nation*, whose story was written by Russ Baker.

CBS 001141   29 September 1972   CONFIRMATION OF ORDERS

This is an *official* document I received in 1999, which states that on "Verbal orders of the Comdr on 1 Aug 72 suspending 1st LT. George W (Bush) . . . from flying status . . . Reason for Suspension: Failure to [acc]omplish annual medical examination."

The commander referred to in this document is Jerry Killian, Lieutenant Bush's commander.

The August 1, 1972, date matches the suspension order by Killian in CBS 001192.

CBS 002072   6 September and 8 September   TURNDOWN OF BUSH REQUEST FOR TRANSFER TO 9921ST IN ALABAMA

This is an *official* document I received through a FOIA request in 1999 or 2000.

The office of the Texas Air National Guard Adjutant General is pointing out in this document that Lieutenant Bush has been turned down on his request for a transfer to the 9921st in Alabama.

At the top of the document, there is a reference to the July 31, 1973 Air Force denial of Bush's transfer (CBS 002070).

Part of the document reads that "attention is invited to basic communication"; in military speak, the adjutant general is telling the commander in charge of the 147th to pay attention to the fact that Bush's transfer to the 9921st has been turned down, and as a consequence, Lieutenant Bush is still under the command of the 147th.

Dated August 3, 1972, it comes just two days after Bush's flight status has been suspended and just three days after he was formally denied transfer to the 9921st in Alabama.

CBS 001022   6 September and 8 September 1972   PERMISSION TO GRANT EQUIVALENT TRAINING WITH THE 187TH IN ALABAMA UNIT

This is an *official* document I received through a FOIA request in 1999 or 2000. It is an approval dated September 6, 1972 and September 8, 1972 from Lt. Col. Jerry Killian and then–Col. Gen. Bobby Hodges for Lieutenant Bush to be allowed to do Equivalent Training with the 187th in Alabama.

By this time, Lieutenant Bush has been gone from the 111th since April or May and has still not landed in an approved transfer or equivalent training slot.

CBS 002069   24 June 1973   KILLIAN TO "SIR"

It is unclear to whom the memo is addressed, but clearly it is intended for someone north of Killian in the chain of command.

This June 24, 1973 memo appears to be addressed to someone who had a staffer call Killian concerning the evaluation or Officer Efficiency Training Report on then-lieutenant Bush.

By this time, Lieutenant Bush had been away from his unit for nearly a year.

The reference in that "Neither Lt. Col Harris or [sic] I feel we can rate 1st Lt. Bush since he was not training with the 111th since April 1972" is significant. It was reported recently for the first time, that Bush's last flight in an F-102 was on April 16, 1972. This is a document I received from Bill Burkett on September 2. I did not use this document on the air. *USA Today*, which also received the document from Burkett, did use it on their Web site linking to their story on September 9.

The memo includes a crucial line in it, however—when Killian says "His recent activity is outside the rating period," a point that becomes important when read with the next official document.

CBS 001077   STATEMENT OF POINTS EARNED BY DATE

This is an *official* document I received through a FOIA request in 1999 or 2000.

It is a Statement of Points Earned by Lieutenant Bush . . . beginning May 29, 1973, when he returned to his unit, the 111th Fighter Interceptor Squadron in Houston.

In the previous Killian document, when Colonel Killian references the "recent activity is outside his rating period," it is clear that the May '73 activity is what he is referencing.

Officer Efficiency Training Reports or OETRs are done on a time period that runs roughly from April 30 of one year to May 1 of the next year.

Lieutenant Bush's reappearance in late May of 1973 did not fit into the rating period for which Killian was being asked to evaluate Bush.

CBS 002075   29 June 1973

This is an *official* Air Force document demanding that ratings (an OETR) be entered on Lieutenant Bush during his rating period from 1 May 1972 to 30 April 1973.

The document asks that an "AF FM 77a [an OETR] should be requested from the training unit so that this officer can be rated in the position he held. This officer should have been reassigned in May since he is no longer training with his unit of assignment."

CBS 001194   18 August 1973   MEMO TO FILE

This is a memo that Mike Smith got from Bill Burkett on September 5.

It is a memo to file, marked "CYA" . . . and the format is quite informal. The date is August 18, 1973, long after the May date when Lieutenant Bush's evaluation report was due and more than a month since the Air Force document CBS00275 had arrived at Ellington Air Base.

In this informal memorandum, Killian says that "Staudt has obviously pressured Hodges" about Bush. And Killian says "Harris gave me a message today from Grp regarding Bush's OETR." He writes that "Staudt is pushing to sugarcoat it." It goes on: "Bush wasn't here during rating period and I don't have any feedback from the 187th. I will not rate. Austin is not happy today, either."

By August 1973, Buck Staudt had formally left the Guard, but was working as an executive pilot for Conoco Oil Company, in a position based at Ellington Field. He was also on the Houston Chamber of Commerce Aviation Committee, a group he would eventually chair. Because the city of Houston owns the land on which Ellington

Field sits, city politics and business interactions were crucial to the way the decisions were made about how the Texas Air National Guard and Ellington Field were operated logistically.

Staudt was on base regularly and wielding as much or more clout than he had in his days in the Guard.

Robert Strong told me that even after Staudt's retirement, "Bobby Hodges wouldn't go to the bathroom without Staudt's permission." Others backed up this assessment of Staudt's influence after he left the Guard.

And the memo itself mentions that "Austin is not happy today, either," a reference to the Texas Air Guard adjutant general position Staudt held previously in Austin. So there is no conflict within this memo, either to Staudt being out of Austin and into retirement or still wielding great influence.

At the end of the memo, Killian says, "I'll backdate, but won't rate." That is borne out in the next official document.

CBS 001305   2 May 1973   RATING FORM

This odd *official* document has always been a source of interest for reporters. Why was there not a rating? Without a rating, why was any paperwork filled out at all? Why would the 111th even be doing an evaluation if Lieutenant Bush had been in Alabama?

The rating says simply "Lt. Bush has not been observed at this unit for the period of report. . . .

"He cleared this base on 15 May 1972 and has been performing equivalent duty with the 187 Tac Recon Gp, Dannelly ANG Base, Alabama."

By the way, the abbreviation Killian uses for Group in this memo, "Gp," was one of the many minor criticisms leveled at the Killian memos for being wrong in terms of form. Clearly, if Killian used the same abbreviation in this official document, it would appear that this was a normal form for him.

Also, at the bottom of the page, you can see that the evaluation is dated May 2, 1973 . . . backdated, just as the Killian memo said it would be. Not rated, just as the Killian memo said it would be.

CBS 001143   Explanation of Non-Rating for 1 May 1972 Through 30 April 1973

This is an *official* document I got in 1999 or 2000. This appears to be a response of some kind of a rejection or request for further information of the Killian nonrating for Lieutenant Bush dated May 2, 1973—a document that, according to the Killian memos, was actually written in August 1973.

Major Rufus Martin, who served under General Bobby Hodges in the 147th, filed this new document and sent it to the Air Force. This one claims that Bush was "not rated for the period 1 May 1972 through 30 April 1973." Then he goes on to say, "Report for this period not available for administrative reasons."

Most interesting is the date on which Rufus Martin signed this. It is not back in July or August. It is on November 12, 1973, a date which falls in line with the August memo Killian wrote saying he would not rate, but would backdate.

This November date is particularly telling in revealing the months-long back and forth between the Texas Air National Guard and the Air Force on trying to paper over the problems with then-lieutenant Bush's service between 1972 and 1973.

CBS 002073   ASSOCIATED PRESS STORY: FULLER PICTURE
OF GUARD YEARS EMERGES

This is an Associated Press story that underscores the special treatment that Lieutenant Bush received in Texas Air National Guard. There is nothing in this story that varies in any way from the information contained in either the official documents or the Killian memos.

CBS and AP did not collaborate on their respective Guard stories.

ACKNOWLEDGMENTS

There are many people to thank for the book you now hold in your hands. First and foremost, my husband, Mark Wrolstad, who proved to be a talented and demanding first editor. He made everything I wrote better. And there was never a cross word spoken between us. Seriously. No, really.

Many days as I wrote, my son, Robert, sat beside me in my office, listening to music or watching movies, wearing a headset, so we could be close even if we couldn't converse. Every now and then we would hold hands. He may not be a mama's boy, but I am hopelessly a boy's mama.

My editor at St. Martin's Press, Elizabeth Beier, cracked the whip in as friendly a fashion as possible, making sure we met our deadlines without killing each other or the project. I don't know what I expected from a print editor, but I certainly didn't expect to find a friend. Luckily, I did. We probably had far too much fun working on this than we should ever admit. My lips are sealed.

The people at St. Martin's Press treated me like family from the first. I think the world of them, anyway. Sally Richardson, George Witte, Paul Sleven, John Murphy—all of them brought such skill and exuberance to this book. Amelie Littell, Bill Rees, and Julie Gutin worked brilliantly as managing editors on this unmanageable project. Steve Snider's work as art director was smart and savvy. James Sinclair's handling of the interior design gave my words gravitas. And Karen Gillis, the overworked production director, is the real reason this book made it to print. Her perseverance was more than I could have hoped for.

Mike Smith, the Texas-based researcher who worked with me on the original Bush-Guard story, luckily came back to help me with this book, bringing with him his *savant* sensibilities for digging up information. He has been true blue to this story and to me far longer than I deserve.

Speaking of true blue, friends don't come any truer than Dan Rather. He has my respect and affection always. Working with him made me a better journalist. Knowing him has made me a better person.

My friend and colleague Roger Charles has always been available to answer any question, whether it is about the military, the best way to raise kids, or how to keep your marriage on the right path. He's a great friend.

My agent, Wes Neff at Leigh Bureau, convinced me I could do a book and then convinced me someone outside my family would be interested in buying it. The fact that you are reading this proves he was right.

Ellis Levine, the attorney for St. Martin's Press who went through this manuscript with me, line by line, deserves some kind of special reward for his hard work. I'm thinking of a trip to Atlantic City.

Dick Hibey, who represented me in front of the CBS/Viacom panel, was kind to me when that was what I needed and willing to give me a swift kick when that was called for.

Wahid Manawi, our Afghan surrogate son, helped me more than he will ever know. His very presence reminds me of how lucky we are that fate is in control of our futures. Who would have thought we'd be together from Kabul to college graduation?

Angie Hudson, our wonderful friend, kept our house running smoothly when I disappeared into my office for weeks at a time. She deserves a medal and some less demanding friends.

My buddies Lisa Cohen, Micki Flowers, Margaret Larson, along with former colleague and forever friend, Dana Robertson, kept me laughing and sitting upright through most of the past year. I would have been lost without them, their phone calls, their funny stories, and our all-girl getaways.

Veteran CBS correspondent Bob McNamara was a great friend throughout this whole mess. He kept me looking on the bright side. The fact that Bob's nickname at CBS was Black Mac, in honor of his well-deserved reputation as a grump, tells you all you need to know about how blue I was and how bad this experience was. Bob and his wife, Jane, made this past year better.

A hundred friends, colleagues, neighbors, and family members supported and helped me in a hundred ways. Extra special thanks to Sue and Patty. I will never forget your kindnesses.

My four sisters are in the pages of this book, whether the reader can see them or not. Gloria, Diane, Frances, and Peggy talked with me during this process, encouraging me, editing me, pushing me to create something that would make my mother proud. I hope Mom *is* proud. I hope I made my sisters proud, too.

Finally, no acknowledgment would be complete without a wag of the tail to my four-legged friends who were with me nonstop as I went through a tough year, and then painstakingly recreated it, pecking at the keyboard and replaying in my head some of the worst months of my life. Honey, my mother's old golden lab; Scout, our wild Westie terrier; and Mattie, our dark-eyed little Scottie, were at my feet every day. Forever patient, always friendly, ever forgiving—I couldn't have done it without them.

INDEX

ABC News, 15
Abdullah, Abdullah, 96–97
Abu Ghraib, 4, 139, 163, 258, 273–74
    See also specific individuals
    CBS and, 26, 102, 125, 128, 129,
      293–94
Adger, Sid, 57, 59, 181
Afghanistan, 92–102
    CBS in, 95–96, 102
    lives lost in, 40
    war in, 135
Air Force Personnel Records Center,
    Denver, 61
Alfieri, Mary, 334
Allison, Linda and Jimmy, 314
American Idol, 37
Andrews, Wyatt, 272–74
anthrax assaults, 91–92
Arbusto, 84, 134
Ashcroft, John, 25
Associated Press (A.P.), 264, 282, 345,
    353
Ayers, Gen. Ross, 320–22, 326

Baer, Bob, 124
Baghram Air Base, 92–93, 102
Baker, Russ, 321, 348

Barnes, Ben
    Bush-Guard story and, 1–2, 9–10,
      42, 56–57, 134, 152, 154–55,
      164, 172, 176, 180–82, 185, 188,
      278
    FBI and, 323
    Kerry, John, and, 10, 185
    as lobbyist, 10
    politics and, 2, 9–11, 155
    Rather, Dan, and, 1–2, 172, 180–82,
      292, 304
Bartlett, Dan
    Heyward, Andrew, and, 309
    on Killian memos, 6, 184–87
Bass, Jack, 104
Bath, James Reynolds, 84–86, 138, 159,
    344–45
Bentsen, Lloyd, 59, 160, 279
Berry, Shawn, 73–78, 80–82
Big Brother, 35–36
Bin Laden family, 84, 135, 138
Bishop, Gen. Thomas, 309
Blair, Jayson, 6, 199, 290, 295
Bloom, David, 180
Blount, Winton, 2, 62, 158, 314, 346
blue-chippers, 68–69, 162
Boccardi, Lou, 344

Boccardi, Lou (*continued*)
  Blair, Jayson, and, 295
  investigation and, 25, 250, 252, 256,
    257–60, 264, 272, 275, 277–78,
    282, 290, 293, 294, 301
Brewer, Lawrence Russell, 72, 75–76
Bricken, Reese, 347
Broadcasting & Cable, 309
Brokaw, Tom, 92
Brooks, Foster, 267
Brown, Dana, 45–46
Bryce, Christina, 139
Buckhead, 7, 197–199, 200–2, 204
Bullock, Bob, 43
burkas, 93, 95, 98, 101
Burkett, Bill, 140–47, 148, 176, 189, 196,
  256
  acquiring memos, 212–15, 216,
    218–19, 226–27, 227–29, 234, 258
  conference call with, 211–15, 216, 226
  document shredding and, 140, 212, 326
  handing over memos, 144–47,
    148–51, 154, 156, 218–19, 226–27,
    228, 239–40, 242, 258, 328
  Heyward, Andrew, and, 211–16,
    219–21, 228, 236
  Howard, Josh, and, 211, 237–43, 244
  interview with, 216–30
  investigation and, 300
  Rather, Dan, and, 211–14, 219–23,
    225–29
  Scott, Lucy, and, 221, 223, 227, 229
  Smith, Mike, and, 142–48, 156, 161,
    176, 218, 221, 229, 241, 299,
    345–46, 351
  West, Betsy, and, 211–13, 214, 216,
    221–23, 225–29, 237–40, 244
Burkett, Nicki, 144–47, 214
  background of, 225–26
  Bill's interview and, 222, 225–30
Burns, John, 274
Bush backers, 18–19, 66–69, 173. *See
  also specific individuals*
Bush, Barbara, 39, 90

Bush, George H. W.
  autobiography, 137
  Barnes, Ben, and, 57
  Bentsen, Lloyd, v., 160
  CIA, Bath, and, 85
  letter from, 326
  military service of, 40, 315–16
  as politician, 64
Bush, George W. *See also* Bush-Guard
    story; Killian memos
  aircraft carrier landing by, 138, 178
  as baseball team owner/president, 21
  Bin Laden link to, 84, 134–34, 138
  birth date of, 136–37
  Blount, Winton, and, 2, 62, 158, 314,
    346
  books about, 69, 83, 137–38, 142–43,
    209–9
  criticisms/questions about, 9, 13,
    39–40, 55, 69, 90, 135, 138, 178, 186
  on death penalty, 43–44, 47–50,
    52–53
  documentaries about, 135, 255–56
  drugs and, 208, 326
  family's status, 2
  Friends of, 307
  as governor, 42–44, 47–50, 52–54,
    141, 181
  on Iraq, 33, 40
  King, Larry, interviews with, 39, 52
  Nixon, Tricia, and, 64–65, 137
  on physical discipline/working out, 43
  policies/bipartisanship of, 43, 137
  presidential campaigns, 19, 42, 48, 55,
    134, 135, 137, 138, 181, 185
  public perception of, 40, 135, 171,
    209, 313, 315
  religion and, 49, 90
  reporters' nicknames and, 53
  Republicans on, 66, 90, 141
  run for Congress, 137
  Sheehan, Cindy, and, 19
  Tucker, Karla Faye, and, 44, 47–50,
    52–53

during Vietnam War, 2, 22, 42, 63–66, 135
Bush Leaguers, 19
Bush-code, 49
Bush-Guard story, 1–9, 11–14. *See also* Killian memos; meshing document; *specific individuals*
  admission to Guard, 60
  Alabama transfer and, 62, 138, 145, 149, 157–58, 160, 167, 170, 173, 186, 314, 345–50
  attacks on, 6–16, 18, 192–209
  Bush as pilot and, 2, 42, 56–57, 60–65, 83–84, 87, 136–38, 145, 157–60, 168, 173–74, 186–87, 210–11, 308, 313–15, 320–22, 324
  departure from Guard, 2, 3, 6, 62–63, 68, 69, 85–87, 90, 136, 149, 158, 322–23
  e-mails on, 249, 259, 261–62, 280, 282, 296–99
  end to work on, 89, 254, 264
  errors/mistakes in, 30, 39, 150
  fulfillment of Guard duties, 2, 42, 186, 314
  gap in service, 68, 148, 156–58, 160, 169–70, 171, 187, 314
  honorable discharge and, 85, 158, 186
  impacts of, 234–36
  investigation and, 23, 24–25, 27–28, 31, 233–34, 241, 244–45, 248, 249–66, 271–95, 299–309, 312, 313
  media and, 28–29, 193, 195–96, 198–99, 247–48, 263, 272, 273, 284, 288–89, 310–11
  military service records and, 39–40, 55, 61–63, 85–86, 134–47
  notes on, 70–71, 249, 252–54, 259, 272, 275, 280, 282
  physical exams and, 2, 61–62, 145, 149, 159, 172–73, 185–86, 210–11, 305–6, 340–1, 348–49
  promotion and, 62
  ratings and, 156–57, 160, 350–53

script for, 175–77, 184, 187–90
  suspension from flying and, 83–84, 145, 149, 159, 160, 173, 185, 348
  verifying information for, 42, 143, 146–51
  White House response to, 6, 177, 180, 184–86
Bush's Brain (Moore, Jim), 142
Bush's War for Reelection (Moore, Jim), 142–3
Byrd, James, 72–76, 82

Camp Mabry, 304, 319, 323, 326–27
Carlisle, Kitty, 3–4
Carlson, Tucker, 52
Carter, Jimmy, 315
Casey, Thomas Michael, Jr., 137
Cash, Johnny, 269, 275
CBS Early Show, 33, 287
CBS Evening News. *See also specific individuals/stories*
  changes at, 234–36, 283–84
  Jonesboro shootings and, 112–13
  King conviction on, 79
  Tucker on, 50–52
CBS News. *See specific individuals/programs/stories*
  in Afghanistan, 95–96, 102
  apology by, 23, 231, 233–34, 255, 304, 310, 311–12
  attacks on, 6, 9, 13, 18–19, 29, 192–93, 199, 200–6, 220, 263, 307, 311–12
  Black Rock of, 249–51
  equipment at, 179–80
  "full," 220–21
  internal politics at, 182–83, 225, 338
  investigation and, 23, 24–25, 27–28, 31, 233–34, 241, 244–45, 260–61, 264–65, 277, 280, 283–93
  public relations at, 202–5
  security and, 223–24, 251
  September 11 and, 91–92
  trust at, 284
  Web sites criticizing, 6, 9

celebrities, 38, 108, 114, 203, 252, 266, 267. *See also specific individuals*
A Charge to Keep (Bush, George W.), 137–38
Charles, Roger
  Abu Ghraib and, 116–18, 124, 127–28, 129
  Burkett, Bill, and, 221, 228–29
  Bush-Guard story and, 13, 134, 138, 148–49, 154, 163–64, 172–74, 176, 259
Chateaux Dijon, 137
Chen, Julie, 33–36, 281
Christian Broadcasting Network, 47–48
CIA
  Abu Ghraib and, 119, 120, 124
  Bush, George H.W., Bath and, 85
Clanton, Chad, 240–41
Cleland, Max, 40, 237
Clements, Bill, 58
Clinton, Bill, 177, 331
  Jones and, 200
  scandals, 24
  women and, 315
Clinton, Hillary
  interviews of, 107
  on right-wing conspiracy, 28
Clooney, George, 139
CNN, 30
Cold War, 64
Colombia, American hostages in, 104
Columbia Journalism Review, 307, 324
communism, 9, 27, 278, 280
computers, 129, 197, 202, 317, 329–30
Condit, Gary, 107
Conn, George, 213
Connally, John, 11, 59, 84, 279
Connally, John, Jr., 59, 279
Conoco, 208, 209, 351
conservatives. *See also* Internet
  attacks by, 9–10, 18–20, 22, 27–28, 30, 38, 193–94, 196–201, 272, 313, 328
  Christian, 47–49
  on communism, 9, 27

  liberals v., 9–10, 18–20, 22, 198, 248
  radio, 28, 200, 245–47
Cooke, Janice, 288
Cowan, Lt. Col. Bill, 124
crashing stories, 5, 175, 179, 189, 265
Crescent Court, Hotel, 222–30
Cronkite, Walter, 198
Cuba, 64
  Guantánamo Bay, 115–16

Dallas Morning News, 58–59, 207, 209
Dannelly Air National Guard Base, Alabama, 62, 157
Darby, Joseph, 122
Darling, Brian, 318
David Letterman, 203
Dean, Howard, 237
death penalty
  Bush, George W., on, 43–44, 47–50, 52–53
  in Georgia, 83
  King, Brewer and, 72
  in Texas, 42–54
Defense Intelligence Agency, 120
Delay, Tom, 234
Democrats, 10–11, 219
Dionne, E. J., 53
documentaries
  about Bush, George W., 135, 255–56
  in journalism, 38
Dole, Bob, 40
Dowd, Maureen, 274
Downing Street memos, 327
Drudge, Matt, 307
Drudge Report, 11–12
drugs
  Bush, George W., and, 208, 326
  Tucker, Karla Faye, and, 46–47

Ellington Air Force Base, Houston, 85, 137, 157, 160, 306
  Knox at, 219–20

Roome and, 308, 324–5
Staudt and, 66, 208, 351

Fager, Jeff, 111, 152
   Abu Ghraib and, 123, 126, 127–29,
      131, 333–34
   Bush-Guard story and, 6, 69, 164–66,
      175, 182–83, 243–44
   relationship with, 103
   60 Minutes II and, 114, 166, 336
   on stories, 72
   on Thurmond/Washington-Williams
      story, 110
   on Tucker story, 52
Fallujah, 126–27
FBI
   Abu Ghraib and, 120
   National Guard and, 323–24
Felt, Mark, 258
*First Son: George Bush and the Bush
   Family Dynasty* (Minutaglio), 69,
   83, 309–10
Fletcher, Claire, 92
Flores, Gen. Belasario, 63, 85–86, 176
Fortunate Son (Hatfield), 208–209
FOX News, 9, 12, 19, 28, 48, 309
   Burkett, Bill, and, 222–23
Frederick, Chip, 117–22, 127–8
Frederick, Martha, 119, 120
Free Republic, 6, 7, 197, 200, 206
Freedom of Information Act, 61, 84, 157
freedom of press, 20, 32–33, 316, 332
   Jasper, Texas and, 70–71, 79–80
Freepers, 200–201
Freston, Tom, 337

Gannon, Jeff, 19, 248
Gatesville, Texas, 44–46
Gelber, David, 12
Geneva Convention, 120
ghost soldiers, 58, 141, 145, 237
Gibbons, Clarence, 133
Gibson, John, 28
Glass, Stephen, 199, 290

Glauber, Steve, 5, 12
Golden, Andrew, 112–13
Golden, Joe Bob, 70, 71, 79
Gonzales, Alberto, 43
Good Morning America, 106
Goodale, James C., 303–4
Graham, Billy, 151
Gray, District Attorney Guy James, 78
Green River Killer, 115
Gulf War, first, 93, 100

Hackworth, Col. David, 117, 168–70,
   189
Hagel, Chuck, 40
Hailey, David, 328–31
Hannity, Sean, 28, 206
Harris, Lt. Col. William, 157, 160,
   171
   meshing document and, 344,
      350–51
Harvard Business School, 68, 314
Hassler, Patti, 152
   Abu Ghraib and, 123, 127, 131,
      333–34
   Bush-Guard story and, 6, 69, 164–66,
      175
   relationship with, 103
   60 Minutes II and, 114, 336
hate crimes, 82
Hatfield, Jim, 208–9
Hawthorne, Lum, 73
Hersh, Seymour, 124, 129, 130, 267,
   274
Hewitt, Don, 131, 165–66, 337–38
Heyward, Andrew, 167
   Abu Ghraib and, 126, 292–93
   Bartlett, Dan, and, 309
   Burkett, Bill, and, 211–16, 219–21,
      228, 236
   Bush-Guard story and, 15, 37, 150,
      191, 198, 205, 231, 292–93, 311
   firing of Mapes, Mary, 285–86
   investigation and, 233, 234, 244–45,
      260–61

Heyward, Andrew (*continued*)
  Moonves, Redstone and, 296–97
  relationship with, 239
  60 Minutes II and, 334–35
  Viacom and, 293
Hibey, Dick, 24–28, 30–32
  investigation and, 249–52, 260–61,
    271, 275–78, 281–82, 286
Hinton, Karen, 180
Hodges, Gen. Bobby
  Bush-Guard story and, 3, 13–14, 67,
    171–74, 177–78, 188–89, 196, 283,
    305
  Killian, Jerry B., and, 171–73, 188–89,
    196, 305–6
  meshing document and, 344, 350,
    351
Hollowell, Bill, 69
Honeycutt, Tom, 67
Howard, Josh, 4
  Burkett, Bill, and, 211, 237–43,
    244
  Bush-Guard story and, 11, 12, 15, 141,
    143–44, 148–49, 151–52, 164, 165,
    175, 180, 182–84, 187–91, 205,
    219, 265
  resignation of, 286–87, 289
  60 Minutes II and, 131, 133
Hughes, Karen, 138
Hunt, H. L., 59, 279
Huntsville, Texas, 51
hurricanes, 131–33, 150, 153,
  155–56
Hussein, Saddam, 100, 101, 111, 124

Intercontinental Hotel, 95–96
Internet. *See also* Web sites
  bloggers, 7–9, 12–14, 20, 24, 27–30,
    32, 192–207, 221, 226, 234, 245,
    247, 248, 254, 262, 265, 273, 283,
    284, 288, 295, 307–8, 310, 312–13,
    318, 328–32
  impacts of, 130–31, 205–6
  video on, 154, 155

Iraq. *See also* Abu Ghraib; Hussein,
  Saddam
  Apache helicopter pilots in, 5–6,
    103–4, 107
  Bush, George W., on, 33, 40
  Fallujah, 126–27
  journalism and, 30, 39
  lives lost in, 30, 40
  poverty in, 100–1
  religious extremism in, 100
  war in, 88, 134, 135, 138, 327
Isikoff, Michael, 218, 274
Ivins, Molly, 256

Jackson, Janet, 296, 312
jail, 69, 79, 80, 81, 206, 257
James, Linda, 153, 168, 189
James, Raymon, Jr., 137
Japanese, during World War II,
  270–71
Jasper, Texas, 71–76, 79, 81–82, 206
Jensen, Bruce, 184
Jensen, Tom, 115
Johnson, Jake, 65–66
Johnson, Lyndon, 315
Johnson, Mitchell, 112–14
Johnson, Sam, 40
Johnson, Scott, 113–14
Jones, Paula, 200
Jones, Steve, 319, 323, 325–26
Jonesboro shootings, 112–14
Jordan, Eason, 30
journalism. *See also* reporters
  credibility in, 35–36, 188–89, 196–97,
    199–200
  document copies in, 150–51
  documentaries in, 38
  ethics/principles in, 30–33, 199–200,
    257, 282, 288–90
  foreign coverage in, 38
  humor in, 242, 256
  investigative, 29, 32–33, 36, 38,
    236–37, 267, 287, 293, 297
  Iraq and, 30, 39

job loss/criticism and, 1, 22, 23, 38–39
oversight and, 31–32
as patriotism, 39, 41
roles of, 30–33, 40–41, 315–17, 338
rules of, 31–32, 37–39, 40–41
sources/notes in, 70–71, 77–78, 81,
    82, 147, 258–59, 299–300
superficial nature of, 29
in U.S. Constitution, 33
Justice Department, statues at, 25

Karpinski, Brig. Gen. Janet, 120, 122
Karzai, Hamid, 98
Kelley, Jack, 198, 199, 290, 295
Kelly, Matt, 159
Kennedy, President, 53
Kerrey, Bob, 40
Kerry, John
    Barnes, Ben, and, 10, 185
    campaign of, 19, 134, 196, 237–43,
        254, 287, 327
    military service record of, 40
    during Vietnam War, 19, 134
Killian, Gary, 176, 305
Killian, Lt. Col. Jerry B.
    death of, 2, 171
    family of, 146, 176, 196, 306
    Hodges and, 171–73, 188–89, 196,
        305–6
    Knox and, 209–11, 305–6
    Strong and, 153, 162
Killian memos, 340, 341. *See also*
    Burkett, Bill; meshing document;
    specific individuals
    abbreviations on, 276–77, 310–11
    analysis/authentication of, 2–3, 6–9,
        11–15, 146–54, 157–62, 164,
        167–74, 176, 183–84, 187–89,
        193–205, 231, 233, 265, 272–73,
        291, 300–6, 310–11, 316–17,
        319–21, 328–31
    August 1, 1972, 149, 321
    August 18, 1973, 156–57
    on Bush's civilian job, 62

faxing of, 8, 148, 150, 156, 167, 169,
    193, 194, 218, 219, 259, 329–30
February 1972, 159
feelings about, 209
as forgeries, 6–9, 12–15, 159–60, 167,
    173, 178, 185, 186, 194–198,
    201–2, 210, 222, 226, 259, 273,
    276, 287, 305–7, 310–11, 316–17,
    324, 329–30
June 24, 1973, 160, 171–72
May 2, 1973, 157
May 4, 1972, 149, 185–86
May 19, 1972, 160
official documents v., 2–3, 6–7, 15,
    148, 149, 151, 157–59, 161,
    167–68, 169, 174, 183–85, 187,
    194, 196, 204, 249, 273, 276–77,
    304, 310–11
source of, 217–19, 233–34, 288,
    327–28
spacing/signatures of, 6, 9, 12, 149,
    153–54, 167–71, 174, 183–84,
    193–200, 202–5, 274, 276, 310–11
typeface/fonts of, 6–9, 12, 149, 153,
    167, 168–71, 271–73, 276, 300–2,
    329–31
typewriters and, 7, 171, 183–84,
    193–97, 274, 306, 310–11, 329–30
Web sites criticizing, 6–10, 12–15
Kimmit, Brig. Gen. Mark, 131
King, John William, 72–73, 75–76, 79
King, Larry, 289
    Bush, George W., interviews with, 39,
        52
Kirkpatrick & Lockhart Nicholson
    Graham, 250, 253, 256, 275
Knox, Marian Carr, 209–11, 306
    meshing document and, 344, 345–46
Kurtz, Howard, 310–11
Kuwaiti pilots, 60–61

Lanpher, Larry, 253, 256, 257, 260,
    275–77
Lawson, Bill, 117–20, 127–28

Leissner, Janet, 180
Lewis, Dan
  investigation and, 249, 251–52, 257,
    281–82, 284–85
  meshing document and, 271, 276
liberals
  conservatives v., 9–10, 18–20, 22, 198,
    248
  elitist, 20–22, 198
  Mapes, Mary, as, 20–22, 247–48, 250,
    278, 280
Limbaugh, Rush, 24, 28, 248, 307, 327
Linke, Janet, 321, 348
Little Green Footballs, 6, 12, 198
Lively, Earl, 66–67, 208, 209
Lloyd, Albert, 67
lobbying
  Barnes, Ben, and, 10
  Viacom and, 25–26, 295–98
Lockhart, Joe, 240–41
Los Angeles Times, 16, 202

MacDougald, Harry W. *See* Buckhead
magazines, 108. *See also specific*
  magazines
Mahfouz, Khalid bin, 84
Mansion on Turtle Creek, 230
Mapes, Diane (sister), 246
Mapes, Don (father), 245–48
Mapes, James (grandfather), 270
Mapes, Mary
  background of, 20–21, 253, 337
  CBS departure of, 238–39
  childhood of, 20–21
  clearing name of, 264
  coffee mug w/ photo, 81–82
  firing, 39, 257, 265, 281, 285–87,
    290–92, 327
  friends/colleagues of, 267–68, 286–87,
    333–36
  husband (Mark), 3, 16–17, 21, 27, 37,
    53, 81, 86, 89, 90, 99–100, 101,
    120, 126, 153, 233, 245–48, 263,
    266, 268, 283–84, 286, 333

  in jail, 69, 79, 80, 81, 206, 257
  job loss, 1, 21, 22, 23, 38–39, 41, 144,
    212, 220, 250, 257, 259, 263–65,
    267, 275, 281, 285–87, 290–92,
    327, 334
  knitting by, 267–68
  as liberal, 20–22, 248, 250, 270, 280
  as mother, 230–31, 278
  mother of, 86, 87–91, 246–48
  photos of, 23, 80–82, 206–7
  politics of, 277–78
  rebuke of, 243–44
  sisters of, 81, 88–89, 90, 245–48, 271,
    286
  son (Robert), 3, 16–17, 21, 27, 39, 75,
    81–82, 89, 90, 99, 101, 120, 132,
    153, 233, 235, 245–46, 263,
    268–69, 286, 333
Mapes, Nora/Nunna (great-
  grandmother), 269–71
Mapes, Oscar (great-grandfather), 270
Mapes, Peggy (sister), 89, 246
Martin, Rufus, 352
Martinez, Mel, 318
Mason, Linda, 297–399
Matley, Marcel
  Killian memos and, 3, 8, 12, 153,
    167–71, 183–84, 188, 329, 345
  in meshing document, 345
McCain, John, 19, 40
  Abu Ghraib and, 123–24
  during Vietnam War, 19
McCarthy, Joseph, 9, 27, 198, 278, 280
McElroy, Robert, 68
McNamara, Bob, 46, 51
McVeigh, Tim, 209
media. *See also specific media*
  on Burkett, 217–19
  Bush-Guard story and, 28–29, 193,
    195–96, 198–99, 247–48, 263, 272,
    273, 284, 288–89, 310–11
  mainstream, 9, 13, 28–29, 193, 195–96,
    198–99, 247–48, 263, 272, 273,
    283–84, 288–89, 310, 312, 331–32

oversight of, 29–30
print, 108
as referees, 22
saturation, 112–14
self-criticism and, 107–8, 289–90
in Texas, 42
meshing document, 188–89, 194,
    344–53. *See also specific*
    individuals
investigation and, 249, 271–77, 283
Miller, Yvonne, 150, 163–64, 176, 186,
    239
Minutaglio, Bill, 69, 309–10
Missal, Mike, 251–53, 255–57
Moniz, Dave, 237
Moody Air Force Base, Georgia, 64–65,
    135–37, 157
Moonves, Les, 33–37, 203, 235, 337
    after investigation, 287, 290–92
    Chen and, 33–35, 281
    Redstone, Heyward and, 296–97
    60 Minutes II and, 334
Moore, Jim, 142–43
Moore, Michael, 134
Mueller, Greg, 307
Murphy, Jim, 92
Murphy, Mary, 131–32, 134, 164, 165,
    205
    resignation of, 286–87, 289
Murrow, Edward R., 9, 179, 192, 198,
    282.
My American Journey (Powell), 59
Myers, Gen. Richard, 126–27

National Guard. *See also* Bush-Guard
    story; *specific individuals/units*
    document shredding and, 140, 212, 326
    early release from, 321–22
    FBI and, 323–24
    Florida, 321
    ghost soldiers and, 57–58, 141, 145,
        237
    politics and, 2, 55–59, 64–67, 162–63,
        181–82, 325–26

Powell on, 59–60, 66
    problems/scandals in, 57–61, 67,
        140–43, 145, 153, 212, 323–26
    racism/discrimination in, 66–67, 85,
        143
    transfers in, 325–26
    during Vietnam War, 2, 56, 59–60,
        62–66, 68–69, 159, 163, 170,
        180–82, 278–79, 314–15, 319–22
The Nation, 321, 348
NBC. *See Today*
Neiman Marcus, 269
Nellis Air Force Base, Las Vegas, 323
Neufeld, Victor, 111
The New Republic, 199
The New York Post, 12
The New York Review of Books, 303
The New York Times, 108
    Abu Ghraib and, 128
    Blair, Jayson, and, 6, 199, 295
    Bush-Guard story and, 1, 12, 16, 28,
        140, 182, 217, 218, 243–44, 288,
        305
The New Yorker, 124
"news Ebola," 263
newspapers, 29, 243. *See also specific*
    newspapers
Newsweek, 108, 217, 218
    on conventional wisdom, 273
Nixon, Richard, 64, 258, 282, 315
Nixon, Tricia, 64–65, 137
Noonan, Peggy, 28
Northern Alliance, 94, 96
Nunnellee, David, 46

187th Tactical Recon Unit, 62, 157–58
111th Fighter Interceptor Squadron, 64,
    145, 160, 183, 349–52
147th Fighter Group, 64, 171, 349
    Flores and, 85
    roster of, 59
    Staudt and, 279
O'Reilly, Bill, 118
O'Rourke, P. J., 274

Pakistan, 92, 100
Paley, Bill, 192
Paramount, 25
patriotism
    after September 11, 38
    journalism as, 38, 41
Peabody Awards, 26, 333–34, 338
Pein, Corey, 307, 324–25
Penny, Bill, 68
the Pentagon
    Abu Ghraib and, 116–17, 118–19,
        124–30
    Papers, 150, 303
Perry, Rick, 308
Pierce, Jim
    investigation and, 300–3
    Killian memo analysis by, 3, 167–68,
        189
    Rather, Dan, and, 301–3
The Pierre, 3–4, 15, 163
pilots. See also Bush-Guard story
    Apache helicopter, 5–6, 103–4, 107
    Kuwaiti, 60–61
    Staudt on, 320
politics. See also Democrats; Internet;
        Republicans
    attack, 8–13, 18–20, 27, 38, 206
    Barnes, Ben, and, 2, 9–11, 155
    at CBS, 182–83, 225, 339
    Guard and, 2, 55–59, 64–67, 162–63,
        181–82, 325–26
    of Mapes, Mary, 277–78
    in Texas, 2, 9–11, 47, 56–59, 83,
        216–17
Pollard, Jonathan, 24
Pomeroy, Marilyn, 53
Powell, Colin, 59–60, 66
Powerline, 6, 12, 198, 201

Al Qaeda training camps, 98

racism. See also Thurmond, Strom
    murder trial and, 69–77
    in National Guard, 66, 85, 143

radio
    conservative, 28, 198, 245–48
    hate talk, 32
Rafi, 96, 97
Ramirez, Lucy, 213–14
Raspberry, Lawrence, 137
Rather, Dan, 16
    Abu Ghraib and, 4, 102, 114–15, 118,
        119–23, 125–28, 129–30, 333–34
    in Afghanistan, 92–102
    apology/stepping down by, 231–36,
        289, 304, 306–7, 312–13, 317,
        327
    attacks on, 6, 19–20, 29, 192, 206,
        210, 222–24
    Barnes and, 1–2, 172, 180–82, 292,
        304
    Berry interview and, 70, 76
    Burkett, Bill, and, 211–14, 219–23,
        225–29
    Bush-Guard story and, 1–2, 11–12,
        13–15, 23, 69, 149–50, 153,
        155–56, 161–64, 170–72, 174,
        180–85, 190–91, 289, 292, 309–10,
        313, 338
    as celebrity, 223–25
    Clooney, George, and, 139
    Drudge Report and, 11–12
    e-mails and, 298
    on getting interviews, 106
    Hodges and, 14–15, 172
    hurricanes and, 150, 153, 155–56
    investigation and, 276–77
    on Killian memos, 23
    King, John William, and, 73
    Knox on, 210
    Moonves, Chen and, 34–35
    in New York, 78, 91
    Pierce, Jim, and, 301–3
    relationship with, 103, 232, 238, 256,
        266–67
    Strong, Robert, and, 68–69, 153,
        161–63
    subpoena of, 78–79

Thurmond, Washington-Williams and, 104, 110–12
  Watergate and, 198
Rather, Jean, 111, 120
Rather, Robin, 229, 232–33
Reagan, Ronald, 315–16
Redstone, Sumner, 284, 296–97, 337
religion
  Bush, George W., and, 49, 90
  extremism in Middle East, 100
  television and, 46, 48–49
  Tucker, Karla Faye, and, 45–51
reporters. *See also specific individuals*
  Bush's nicknames for, 53–54
  conventional wisdom and, 273–74
  debunkers, 218
  hiding questions and, 218
  memory for details and, 53
  "perp walk" and, 80
  shield laws for, 77–78, 82
  talking to, 243–44, 253–55, 286, 311
Republicans. *See also specific individuals*
  on Barnes, Ben, 10–11
  Burkett, Bill, and, 219, 225
  on Bush, George W., 66–67, 90, 141
  Bush-Guard story and, 317
  Democrats v., 10–11, 219
Rich, Frank, 19
Ridgway, Gary, 115
Rigler, Erik, 244–45, 260–61, 327
Ritacco, Krista, 308
Roberson, Dana, 5, 98, 156
  Abu Ghraib and, 114–16, 123, 127, 333–34
  on maternity leave, 134, 150, 163
  Moonves, Chen and, 34–36
  office of, 163, 178–79, 184, 190, 211, 236–37, 238
  relationship with, 103, 163
  September 11 and, 90–91
  Thurmond, Washington-Williams and, 104–12
Roberts, John, 185–86

Robertson, Pat, 48–49
Roome, Dean, 67, 176, 307–8, 324–25
Rooney, Andy, 12
Rose, Gen. James, 57, 65–66, 180, 325
Rose, Mark, 57
Rove, Karl, 18, 142–43, 185, 316–17, 332
Rowles, Sheriff Billy, 74, 77
Rubin, David, 6
Rumsfeld, Donald, 301
Rutenberg, Jim, 243

Safire, William, 28
Sakuma family, 270–71
Saudi Arabia, 93, 138
sausage making, 5, 190
Schiavo, Terri, 317–18
Schwartz, Gil, 203–5
Schwarzenegger, Arnold, 285
Scott, Lucy, 134, 163–64
  Burkett, Bill, and, 221, 223, 227, 229
  Knox and, 211
  Staudt and, 176–77
Seattle, Washington, 90, 115, 246
September 11, 2001, 38, 90–92, 94, 135, 138
The 700 Club, 46, 48–49
Sharpstown, Texas, 10–11
Sheehan, Cindy, 19
shield laws, 77–78, 82
Simon & Schuster, 25
Simpson, Jessica, 287
60 Minutes, 106. *See also specific individuals/stories*
  Christmas party, 111–12
  internal politics and, 182–83
  mirror at, 239–40
  screening room for, 165–66
60 Minutes II, 55, 69, 103, 106. *See also specific individuals/stories*
  name change, 131
  screening room for, 165–66
60 Minutes Wednesday, 4, 131
  cancellation of, 334–37

Slater, Wayne, 142
Slover, Pete, 207–9
Smith, Michael (British reporter), 327
Smith, Mike
    Burkett, Bill, and, 142–48, 156, 161,
        176, 218, 221, 229, 241, 299,
        345–46, 351
    Bush, George W., documentary and,
        135, 255–56
    Bush-Guard story and, 13, 69, 83, 85,
        135, 156, 161, 163–64, 327
    Limbaugh and, 327
    on Mapes, Don, 245–47
Smith, Preston, 320, 322
Social Security, 21
Soldiers for the Truth, 117
Southeastern Legal Foundation, 200
Southern Methodist University (SMU),
    98–99, 134, 321
Stahl, Lesley, 46–47, 48, 49, 51
Star Chamber hearings, 27
Starr, Linda, 140
Staudt, Gen. Walter "Buck," 56, 57, 69,
    136–37, 322–3
    Ellington and, 66, 208, 351–52
    147th Fighter Group and, 279
    on pilots, 320
    Scott and, 176–77
    Slover on, 207–9
Strong, Robert, 68–69, 152–54, 161–63,
    209, 352
subpoenas, 77–79
Survivor, 28, 36, 203, 212
Swift Boats, 19, 134, 237, 241–42, 307

Taguba, Maj. Gen. Antonio, 126
Taliban, 93, 95, 97
Talon News, 19, 248
television. See also specific shows/stations
    bookers, 105
    categories within, 108
    celebrity culture and, 114
    getting interviews/stories for, 106–8

as journalism, 29, 32, 33
producers, 242–43
religion and, 46, 47–49
victim stories on, 236–37
Texas, 21–22. See also National Guard;
    specific cities
    as Capital of the World, 216
    death penalty in, 42–54
    hate crimes in, 82
    media in, 42
    politics in, 2, 9–11, 47–48, 56–59, 83,
        217–18
    stories in, 214–15
    subpoenas in, 77–79
Thomas, Helen, 274
Thompson, Marilyn, 104–5, 110
Thornburgh, Dick, 351
    investigation and, 25, 231, 250, 252,
        256, 257–58, 261–62, 272, 275,
        277–80, 282, 283, 287, 290, 293,
        294, 301
    as politician, 282
Thurmond, Strom, 104–5, 109–12, 274
Time, 85, 108
Tisch, Larry, 284
Today, 106, 113
Trinity University, 321
Tucker, Karla Faye, 44–53, 55, 166
typewriters. See Killian memos

Udell, Maurice, 65, 67, 175, 307–8,
    324–25
U.S. Constitution, 33
USA Today, 108
    Bush-Guard story and, 1, 140, 217,
        237, 239–40, 308–09, 345, 350
    Kelley and, 199, 295
Utah State University, 328

Van Os, David, 221, 222, 226–27,
    230
Vanity Fair, 108, 134, 140
Via, Richard, 306

Viacom
  Bush-Guard story and, 23, 25–27,
    234–36, 264, 280, 283, 287,
    295–99, 304, 309, 312, 338
  Heyward and, 293
  lobbying and, 25–26, 295–98
  60 Minutes Wednesday and, 335,
    337
Vietnam War. *See also* Bush-Guard story
  Barnes and, 154–55
  Bush, George W., during, 2, 18–19,
    22, 42, 63–66, 135
  Canada and, 182
  Cronkite on, 198
  deaths during, 136–37
  deferments during, 63, 137, 279
  draft during, 90, 181, 280, 329
  Guard during, 2, 56, 59–60, 63–66,
    68–69, 159, 163, 170, 180–82,
    278–79, 314–15, 319–22
  Kerry during, 19, 133–34
  McCain during, 19
  military service records and, 40
  video from, 178
Vietnam War Memorial, 40, 136, 154
Viguerie, Richard, 307
virtue and vice police, 93
vote, right to, 22

Wahid, 96–100, 101, 123
Wallace, Mike, 203
The Washington Post, 12, 30–31, 108.
  See also Thompson, Marilyn
  attacks by, 28–29
  Bush-Guard story and, 1, 14, 16, 217,
    219, 310–11
Washington-Williams, Mrs. Essie Mae,
  104–12, 274
Watergate, 30, 198, 274
  Deep Throat and, 258

Web sites. *See also specific sites*
  anti-Bush, 140, 201
  Killian memos criticized by, 6–10,
    12–15
  Soldiers for the Truth, 117
  Utah State University, 328
  White House/CBS, 195
The Weekly Standard, 28
West, Betsy, 5
  background of, 225–26
  Burkett, Bill, and, 211–13, 214, 216,
    221–23, 227–29, 234–40, 244
  Bush-Guard story and, 5, 15, 165,
    166–67, 174, 184, 189–90, 205
  resignation of, 286–87, 289
  traveling with, 230–31
  on Web site criticisms, 11, 12, 201–2,
    262
Westinghouse, 284
whistle-blowers, 256–57. *See also*
  Burkett, Bill
White, Bill, 84, 134, 138–39
Whitney, Mike, 166
Will, Emily, 167–68, 183, 189
Williams, David, 5
Williams, Justin, 108–9
Williams, Mrs. *See* Washington-
  Williams, Mrs. Essie Mae
Williams, Wanda, 109
Winfrey, Oprah, 235
Wizbang, 328
Woodman, Advil, 101
Woodward and Bernstein, 274
World Trade Center, 90–91
World War II, 90, 135, 316
  Japanese during, 270–71

Yale, 181, 321
Young, Ron, 5
Yusuf, 97–98